TO CATCH A SPY

TO CATCH A SPY

How the Spycatcher Affair Brought
MI5 in from the Cold

TIM TATE

ICON

Published in the UK in 2024 by
Icon Books Ltd, Omnibus Business Centre,
39–41 North Road, London N7 9DP
email: info@iconbooks.com
www.iconbooks.com

ISBN: 978-183773-117-6
eBook: 978-183773-118-3

Text copyright © 2024 Tim Tate
The author has asserted his moral rights.

Every effort has been made to contact the copyright holders of the material reproduced in this book. If any have been inadvertently overlooked, the publisher will be pleased to make acknowledgement on future editions if notified.

No part of this book may be reproduced in any form, or by any means, without prior permission in writing from the publisher.

Typeset by SJmagic DESIGN SERVICES, India

Printed and bound in the UK

DEDICATION

To Howard and Annie Barlow, for six decades of friendship

'Old wood is best to burn, old wine to drink, old friends to trust, and old authors to read.'
(Francis Bacon, philosopher and statesman; 1561-1626)

'If your Snark be a Snark …
You may seek it with thimbles—and seek it with care;
You may hunt it with forks and hope
You may threaten its life with a railway share
You may charm it with smiles and soap …

'But oh, beamish nephew, beware of the day,
If your Snark be a Boojum! For then
You will softly and suddenly vanish away
And never be met with again.'

Lewis Carroll: *The Hunting of the Snark: An Agony in Eight Fits*, 1876

CONTENTS

Prelude xi

Introduction 1
1. Sui Generis 5
2. Special Facilities 17
3. Penetration 25
4. 1963 35
5. Confessions 45
6. Blunt 57
7. DRAT 73
8. 'Norman John Worthington' 85
9. Rothschild 101
10. Exposed 113
11. Plots 123
12. Pincher 133
13. Who Is Talking? 143
14. Out in the Open 157
15. Dirty Tricks 167
16. Hubris 179
17. Turnbull 191
18. Charades 203

19. Economical with the Truth	213
20. The Havers Conundrum	227
21. Smears	241
22. The Spycatcher	257
23. Judgments	273
24. Contempt	285
25. Farce	297
26. Losses	311
Epilogue: Forty Years Later	321
Author's Note	327
Acknowledgements	329
Selected Bibliography	331
Endnotes	333
Index	379

PRELUDE

Tuesday, 18 November 1986
Supreme Court of New South Wales, Sydney

....

'What is the difference between a misleading impression and a lie?
'A lie is a straight untruth. A misleading impression is
being economical with the truth.'
SIR ROBERT ARMSTRONG, BRITISH GOVERNMENT
CABINET SECRETARY
UNITED KINGDOM VS. PETER WRIGHT.
CROSS EXAMINATION DAY I

....

Sir Robert Temple Armstrong was an accomplished liar.
Over the course of a gilded career in Whitehall he had trekked through the foothills of fudge and ambiguity, climbed beyond the base camps of prevarication and obfuscation, before conquering the chilly peaks of circumlocution and periphrasis. He had ascended, seemingly effortlessly, through the senior ranks of Britain's politely cut-throat Civil Service and garnered its most coveted honours. With a knighthood and the insignias of the Royal Order of the Bath and the Royal Victorian Order burnishing his entry in *Who's Who*, Armstrong had been *consigliere* to four prime ministers and their conduit to the officially non-existent spy services MI5 and MI6. Now, aged 59 and with promised sinecures and a handsomely remunerated retirement in prospect, he served as both Cabinet Secretary to Margaret Thatcher and her chief advisor on intelligence matters; for good measure he combined these roles with the responsibilities of head of the Civil Service.

To Catch a Spy

Sir Robert enjoyed the exercise of power, and took for granted that his integrity was, by virtue of his position, unimpeachable; his words, when whispered in the ears of ministers and fellow mandarins, or delivered on paper in the stately Victorian surroundings of England's courts, were received with the respect traditionally accorded to tablets of stone.

And yet here he was, in the drab surroundings of a drearily modern courtroom in an unpleasantly hot city halfway across the world, facing an impertinent young Australian lawyer – a fellow who didn't even have the decency to wear the traditional horsehair wig – ruthlessly questioning him into a corner, and a judge who seemed to view him as an unwelcome reincarnation of bygone colonial governance. Sir Robert Armstrong shifted uncomfortably in the witness chair and wondered how it had all come to this.

His week had not begun well. When he arrived at Heathrow Airport for the long flight to Sydney, a press photographer had approached him outside the terminal's VIP suite, and asked permission to capture the historic moment. Unaccustomed to such impudence, the Cabinet Secretary to Her Majesty's Government promptly lashed out with his briefcase, knocking the unfortunate snapper to the floor and smashing his camera. Now, six days later, an unruly phalanx of reporters occupied the court press benches and had the bad form to snigger as he gave his carefully circuitous evidence.

Sir Robert hadn't wanted to come to Australia in the first place. Indeed, he had been shocked to discover that, as the British government's chosen representative, the court would insist on him testifying in person. He had also been warned by the Attorney General, in whose name the attempt to suppress Peter Wright's memoirs was officially launched, that the entire case rested on distinctly shaky legal foundations.

The cross-examination was fierce and unforgiving. Question followed relentless question. And this was only day one: an indefinite succession of further days of torment in the witness box stretched ahead. Embarrassment would be heaped upon discomfort, and each afternoon when the court adjourned, the Cabinet Secretary faced the lengthy trudge back to his temporary office; here he would face a difficult debriefing from his mistress and her staff in Downing Street – all of whom were just starting their days, but who would already have pored over the morning's press coverage.

Newspaper and television reports of that afternoon's proceedings would, Armstrong knew, be universally hostile. The representative of Her Majesty's Government – the most senior official in London – had been accused of dishonesty. His deliciously clever *bon mot* about 'being economical with the truth' – a witticism that would have earned patrician praise inside Whitehall – had been greeted here with naked hostility. He wondered what story he could conjure up to explain the unfolding disaster.

If Sir Robert Armstrong had been more honest – not least with himself – he would have reflected that the argument he was making in support of the plea for an injunction – that intelligence officers owed a lifelong and never-broken duty of silence to the Crown – had been flouted whenever it suited the government's interests. Both MI5 and MI6 routinely fed unattributable stories to newspapers, and he, himself, had been the instigator of an earlier scheme to leak top-secret information to a 'tame' journalist – who had then written a book with Peter Wright.

The files on that conspiracy – a tawdry plot involving the Prime Minister, MI5 and a former Attorney General – were, of course, safely under lock and key inside the Cabinet Office; yet somehow Wright's lawyer had discovered enough of their import to challenge him. Armstrong decided there was only one course of action open to him: he would deny everything and lie, repeatedly and on oath, to the court for as long as it took to bury the story.

It was a strategy doomed to failure and, had he troubled to search his memory, Sir Robert would have known it. Peter Wright was no ordinary intelligence officer: for twenty years he had been MI5's most senior 'molehunter', a man whose life was entirely devoted to sniffing out traitors – real or imagined – working on behalf of the Soviet Union. And if anyone in the British government should have realised the man's unquenchable obsessions, it was Sir Robert Armstrong. A decade earlier Wright had delivered a lengthy report on Russian penetration to Number 10; Armstrong – then the Prime Minister's Principal Private Secretary – had praised its relentless thoroughness.

Now he faced the same grim-faced old man glaring at him across the court. There had never been any real doubt about the lengths to which Peter Wright would go to catch a spy; the only question remaining was how far Her Majesty's Government would go to silence him.

INTRODUCTION

Between 1985 and 1991, the British government fought a succession of vastly expensive, hugely damaging and ultimately unsuccessful battles in courts across the world to prevent a retired spy from publishing his memoirs.

Peter Wright, a senior Security Service officer for more than twenty years, had been at the centre of many of the most damaging intelligence scandals of the 1950s and 1960s. He had been MI5's chief counter-espionage officer, leading its efforts to catch Kim Philby, to uncover Soviet penetration of Britain's twin intelligence agencies, MI5 and MI6, and to root out the long tentacles of Moscow's infamous 'Ring of Five' spies, embedded in the heart of the British Establishment.

Wright's book, *Spycatcher*, was a very personal account of his own obsessive and relentless hunt for suspected Russian 'moles' inside his own Service, including a decade-long secret investigation into the former head of MI5, Sir Roger Hollis. But it was also a form of confessional: a platform for him to acknowledge his own role in MI5's widespread criminality on behalf of the Crown.

Because the Security Service did not officially exist, and operated outside any legal framework, Wright and his colleagues were free to indulge in wholesale law-breaking, 'bugging and burgling' offices, homes and foreign embassies across London.

Peter Wright was an unlikely whistleblower. Virulently right-wing and rabidly anti-communist, he believed – on scant evidence – that British trade union leaders and Labour politicians were either paid Soviet spies or, at the very least, agents of influence for Moscow. Encouraged by elements of the CIA, he had fed top-secret MI5 monitoring of these supposed traitors to leading industrialists and Britain's conservative press. He had also led an extraordinary – and entirely illegal – plot by a cabal of rogue intelligence officers to blackmail Labour Prime Minister Harold Wilson and force him into resigning.

Wright's realisation that MI5 was out of control and needed to be reined in had been reluctant and belated, but by the time he retired to run a horse stud farm in Australia in 1976, he was ultimately convinced that writing an account of his experiences was his patriotic duty. From the outset, *Spycatcher* was intended to drag Britain's shady and unaccountable intelligence services into the light of a modern democracy.

The attempts by Margaret Thatcher's government to block the book in London, Australia, New Zealand, Hong Kong, Brussels and Strasbourg captured unprecedented global attention; day after day, month after month, newspapers across the world splashed the story on their front pages.

The trials were all in civil, not criminal, courts. Because Wright lived in Tasmania, he was beyond the reach of Britain's punitive Official Secrets Act. Instead, Her Majesty's Government applied for injunctions to prevent publication of *Spycatcher*, first in the Supreme Court of New South Wales, then in country after country across the globe. Parallel proceedings in London courts yielded draconian injunctions against national newspapers and individual journalists as the international cases unfolded.

In Britain, and throughout the world, the affair was viewed as both a chilling attempt to hide from the British public the truth about its intelligence services and political elites, and an absurd farce. The government argued that former spies had a lifelong and unbreakable duty to keep silent, yet it had regularly sanctioned semi-official press briefings by the Security Service. It had also allowed retired MI5 Director General Sir Percy Sillitoe and its in-house traitor Anthony Blunt to write their own memoirs, and had taken no action against Wright himself when he gave a lengthy television interview in 1984.

To justify this double-standard, the British government twisted itself into legal and political knots. Wright's allegations of Soviet penetration of MI5, and of MI5's habitual law-breaking, were simultaneously admitted as true for the purposes of the Australian trial but pronounced false in the House of Commons. When, at the start of the hearings in Sydney, Sir Robert Armstrong was cornered in the witness box and forced to confess that he had been 'economical with the truth' while giving evidence on oath, the government's global reputation was shredded.

The international press and media covered the trials with a mixture of condemnation and incredulity. Downing Street's increasingly desperate

Introduction

contortions seemed to combine a disturbing assault on the public's right to know what its intelligence services had been doing, with an absurdist charade that could have stepped from the libretto of a Gilbert and Sullivan comic opera or the pages of *Alice in Wonderland*.

When an American edition of *Spycatcher* was released in the middle of the trials – US courts were beyond the reach of British government lawyers – more than a million copies were sold within a few weeks; many of them were exported to London. Yet although the book was banned in Britain, and public libraries were forced to remove imported copies from their shelves, there was no action taken against anyone selling them here.

Simultaneously, while choleric English judges granted injunctions prohibiting the domestic media from publishing any reference to the book's contents – even banning newspaper reports of proceedings in open court in Australia – the British government was contractually obliged to distribute official journals containing extracts of *Spycatcher* that had been read out in the European Parliament.

And across Britain, while police forces made no attempt to interfere with numerous public recitals of extracts from Wright's memoirs, former Prime Minister Edward Heath was warned he faced prosecution if he read *Spycatcher* for himself – though he would be safe from arrest should he instruct his housekeeper to read it to him. Not since the equally doomed bid to ban publication of *Lady Chatterley's Lover* more than two decades earlier had the attempted suppression of a book generated such ridicule and denunciation.

The *Spycatcher* trials cost taxpayers at least £3 million – equivalent to £8 million today – all of which ended in defeat for the British government. Wright's book became an international blockbuster, selling almost four million copies worldwide; his publishers, and later gagged newspapers, were awarded substantial damages and costs. The affair severely damaged Britain's international reputation and had a devastating effect on morale inside the Security Service. Ultimately, far from protecting MI5 from scrutiny, the doomed litigation helped bring the intelligence services under parliamentary oversight for the first time.

But the secret history of *Spycatcher*, Peter Wright and the British government's quixotic crusade to silence him is more sinister than this story of low farce and high treason. Previously unpublished evidence from the Australian trials, together with official files suppressed for more than 35 years, have revealed an extraordinary plot by MI5 and the Thatcher administration to conceal Britain's most damaging espionage failures and scandals.

The Security Service was determined to cover up the truth about Soviet moles in its ranks, to conceal its habitual domestic law breaking and to prevent any democratic supervision of its actions. It persuaded Margaret Thatcher to lie on its behalf to Parliament; and at its behest, the Prime Minister and the Cabinet Secretary conspired to defuse the ticking time bomb of the investigation into Sir Roger Hollis by leaking top-secret information to a tame journalist and intelligence service asset, Chapman Pincher.

He, with official approval and the backing of Lord Victor Rothschild, himself a former spy, used this material to publish a book about the case in 1981. And Pincher's secret co-author – as the British government knew – was Peter Wright.

It was to protect this tawdry scheme and to cover up MI5's scandals that Sir Robert Armstrong, Cabinet Secretary and Britain's most senior civil servant, was sent to lie, on oath, in the *Spycatcher* trials around the world.

It was a cynical conspiracy to deceive courts, judges and Parliament, and one that revealed the lengths to which the British government would go to silence a troublesome former spy. All that stood in its way was an elderly, difficult and obsessive man and his determination finally to expose the truth.

1. SUI GENERIS

'Security Service ... work very often involves transgressing propriety or the law'
JOHN CUCKNEY, MI5 TRAINING OFFICER, 1955

On a cool, dull day in June 1955 a tall and intense figure strode through the warren of streets between Park Lane and Piccadilly in the heart of London's West End. His purposeful gait, as he marched through Mayfair, was the result of a long-awaited summons.

Peter Maurice Wright was 39. A self-taught but often innovative scientist, he was impatient, unruly and unashamedly ambitious. He had toiled for years in the sluggish backwaters of the Admiralty's research divisions, developing anti-submarine equipment. To his mind, at least, his talents were disappointingly underappreciated. True, he had earned some kudos from both British and American intelligence services for unravelling the mysteries of Soviet wireless surveillance technology, but thus far his career had been a frustrating struggle for recognition.

Now, at last, his abilities were finally being acknowledged. Peter Wright was about to join the most famous spy service that didn't – officially – exist.

Halfway down Curzon Street was an anonymous six-storey building. There was no brass nameplate on the red-brick walls to identify who, or what, occupied the premises, but the address and its purpose was an open secret.

For eight years Leconfield House had been the headquarters of the Security Service, and bus conductors habitually announced to passengers on London's red double-deckers rumbling along Park Lane that the next stop was 'Curzon Street and MI5'.[1]

Peter Wright was ushered through the notional security of a wood- and glass-panelled alcove by a uniformed guard, before being escorted into an old-fashioned lift, operated by an equally archaic brass lever. The contraption slowly wheezed him to the fifth floor, where he was guided through a maze of shabby corridors and into MI5's inner sanctum: the office of the Director General, Sir Dick Goldsmith White.

For the next twenty minutes, White grilled Wright about the newly created role for which he was being proposed. MI5 had never employed an in-house scientist, and Britain's chief spymaster remained sceptical of the need for one, let alone what benefits this unconventional candidate might offer for the defence of the realm. 'I'm not sure we need an animal like you in the Service,' he mused. 'But if you are prepared to give it a try, so are we.'[2]

Before dismissing Wright to the bowels of the building for the initial induction process, White stressed the unique and ambiguous position of the Security Service: it was not, he emphasised, like any other department of state.

MI5 was 'unacknowledged' by the government: its name would never be spoken in Parliament or by ministers, its efforts to defend the country would go unacknowledged in public, and its officers held no official rank. If there was one unshakable article of faith, it was that what transpired within the walls of Leconfield House was never to be revealed outside them.

Yet this fundamental principle of lifelong *omertà* was – at that very moment – being tested. Within the dusty corridors of Whitehall, a bad-tempered and bitterly fought dispute had been rumbling for a year, and its cause was Dick White's immediate predecessor as Britain's chief domestic spy. Sir Percy Sillitoe, the recently retired Director General, intended to publish his memoirs.

The organisation that Peter Wright was set to join was antiquated and barely fit for purpose. By the summer of 1955, MI5 was stranded between the warm glow of fading glories earned during the Second World War and the first harbingers of a much less winnable conflict in the new Cold War with the Soviet Union. That several of these unwelcome heralds turned out to be skeletons emerging from within its own dusty closets rather highlighted the problem.

After a shaky start in 1939, MI5 had enjoyed a good war. During the 1930s it had been allowed to wither on the vine of governmental indifference, budgetary reductions and staff cuts. When war with Germany became inevitable, MI5 was short of funding and personnel, and staff adopted an unconventional approach to solve the urgent need for recruitment. As the newly installed Director General, Sir David Petrie, recorded in an internal report in 1941:

> When the war broke out, each officer 'tore round' to rope in likely people; when they knew of none themselves, they asked their acquaintances. Occasionally recruits were brought in who knew other 'possibles' ... If I am correctly informed, there have been cases in which recruits have been taken on by divisions (or sections) without so much as informing Administration.[3]

Many of these new – and entirely unvetted – spies were drawn from the traditional intelligence hunting ground of Cambridge University. None had any prior association with espionage or defence, but were appointed on the assumption that they were the intellectual, and often aristocratic, elite of their generation. Two, in particular, would encapsulate the simultaneous strength and weakness of this scattergun policy: Victor Rothschild, glamorous playboy scion of the eponymous international banking family, and his friend Anthony Blunt, an effete expert in art history whom Rothschild recommended to MI5 shortly after he joined the Service.[4]

Both men spent the next five years inside MI5, only departing, along with Petrie, in the wholesale exodus of its wartime recruits in 1945. But each – for very different reasons – was to become a dominant figure throughout Peter Wright's career.

Petrie's replacement was an unpopular choice inside the Security Service. Sir Percy Sillitoe was a career policeman; now 58, he had been chief constable of a succession of forces where he had earned plaudits for introducing the use of radio communication between squad cars and their headquarters, and for breaking the power of Glasgow's notorious razor gangs in the interwar period. But to the rarified minds of MI5's senior management – several of whom had unsuccessfully applied for the top job – Sillitoe was a plodding flatfoot whose appointment 'puts the stamp of the Gestapo on the [Security Service]' and 'generally downgrades the office';[5] he had also committed the unpardonable sin of having a very public profile.

Sillitoe had, however, a very powerful backer: Clement Attlee. The Prime Minister, like many in the new post-war Labour government, harboured a lingering distrust of MI5 – a misgiving dating back to the Zinoviev letter scandal two decades earlier.[6] Attlee led the charge for his man, and Sillitoe entered the DG's office on 1 May 1946.

He arrived with little knowledge of the organisation's structure and, aside from a firm conviction that Soviet communism had infected the gilded generation who had studied at Cambridge and Oxford universities in the 1930s – 'long haired intellectuals' as he habitually scorned them[7] – even less understanding of what the Security Service should actually do. Additionally, as he admitted on his retirement, from the very beginning he had held an outsider's distrust of the cloak of secrecy under which the Service sheltered.

> In common with the vast majority of the public, I knew very little of the work of MI5 ... Since its earliest beginnings MI5 has alternately intrigued and infuriated the public by the aura of 'hush-hush' with which it has seemed to be surrounded, and when I joined I found it ... extremely difficult to find out precisely what everyone was doing ...[8]

Sillitoe's bemusement was understandable. Although the Security Service had been at work for more than 30 years, he discovered that there appeared to be no legal basis for its existence and precious little in the way of control over how it operated.

The first – indeed only – official document setting out its purpose and functions had been written six months earlier and, in keeping with Britain's habitual addiction to secrecy, had never been distributed outside a very narrow circle.[9] It was also remarkably short on formal guidance.

> The purpose of the Security Service is the Defence of the Realm and nothing else ... There is no alternative to giving [the Director General] the widest discretion in the means he uses and the direction in which he applies them – always provided he does not step outside the law.[10]

The Service's democratic parentage and its operating budget were equally opaque. Notionally, it was the responsibility of the Home Secretary, while its funds were allocated by the Treasury on the recommendation of a mysterious body known as 'The Secret Vote Committee'. In practice, the former had little, if any, control over what MI5 got up to, while the latter never actually met.[11] Instead, the Director General was expected to calculate the cost of defending the realm and pass his estimate to the Prime Minister, who would – without consulting Parliament – ensure that the requested quantity of taxpayers' money quietly landed in the Security Service's bank.

'I realised,' Sillitoe recalled, 'that I had a big job and heavy responsibilities, but I thought I could tackle them adequately with common sense and energy, a fresh outlook on old obstacles and an enterprising approach to new problems.'[12]

To Sillitoe's numerous critics, throughout his term as Director General he remained an old-school policeman: 'vapid and shallow' was the uncharitable assessment of his deputy and successor, Dick White.[13] Yet he brought about the first stirrings of modernisation, establishing a committee to provide scientific advice to the Service; and during his tenure, MI5's efforts led to the prosecution of three Soviet spies inside the nuclear establishment, the diplomatic service and the army.

If William Marshall and Tony Dewick were small fish, Klaus Fuchs was a sizeable catch. He had worked on both Britain and America's top-secret wartime projects to develop the atom bomb, passing key documents to his Soviet controller throughout; by any metric, his apprehension was a feather in MI5's cap. But Sillitoe committed the unforgivable sin of being photographed outside Fuchs's Old Bailey trial in 1950 and publicly identified as the Director General – a transgression he repeated at London Airport a year later. Once again, the head of Britain's Security Service allowed himself to be snapped by the press, this time en route to brief the FBI in Washington DC in the wake of the defections of two Foreign Office officials (and Soviet agents), Guy Burgess and Donald Maclean.

In April 1952, as he contemplated his approaching retirement, Sillitoe decided to write and publish his memoirs. These, he explained to a senior Cabinet Office official, would largely cover his years as a policeman but would also feature 'some concluding chapters about his time in MI5'.[14] In doing so, he fired the first shot in a war that would culminate in court in Sydney three decades later.

Sillitoe's proposal horrified much of Whitehall's upper echelons. 'The more I think about this project the more doubtful I feel about it,' Sir Edward Bridges, head of the Civil Service and a former Cabinet Secretary, wrote to his successor in Downing Street. 'My doubts are in part instinctive and are a good deal stronger than perhaps I can justify by a process of logical reasoning … [but] to take first of all the question of principle whether a former head of MI5 should be encouraged to write for publication on these sorts of lines at all, I am apprehensive both about the direct effects and about the precedent which will be created … I cannot but think that officers in this or comparable posts should be anonymous; and certainly that they should be entirely silent in public.'[15]

For the next two years, Sillitoe fought a running battle to prevent the government and MI5 from censoring his book. He was determined to lift the cloak of secrecy under which MI5 shrouded its existence and activities. 'My position as head [of the Security Service] is fairly well-known and it would create an anticlimax if I were to say nothing about it,' he complained to Bridges,[16] and his manuscript set out details of the Fuchs, Marshall and Dewick cases,[17] as well as the hidebound attitudes he encountered inside Leconfield House and Whitehall.

None of this was palatable to the mandarin. Bridges summed up the problem in a last-ditch attempt to block the book. In a memo to Sir Frank Newsham, Permanent Under-Secretary at the Home Office, he foresaw the troubles that would come to plague the British government in the *Spycatcher* trials: 'publication will make it infinitely harder to deal with others in the ... Service who may wish to embark on undesirable publicity'.[18]

Four words are missing from the record of this storm in a Whitehall teacup: 'lifelong duty of confidentiality'. The phrase upon which the government would base its entire case against Peter Wright does not appear at any point in the pages of this voluminous correspondence.

There was a reason for this. Not only did MI5 not officially exist, but even in its spectral form it was not a government department; instead it operated under the archaic and unwritten royal prerogative. Officers who served in it – from the Director General down – owed a duty to the Crown, not to the political administration of the day. As a later Cabinet Secretary would ruefully observe, 'the Service is in many ways *sui generis*'[19].

That same description matched exactly the man who, in the summer of 1955, was about to become MI5's first-ever scientific officer.

Peter Wright was a second-generation boffin. He was born in 1916, the son of an engineer theoretically employed by the Marconi Wireless Telegraph Company in Chelmsford, Essex. Maurice Wright had joined Marconi four years earlier; fresh from university, he was set to work on improving the techniques of detecting long-range radio signals. But two days before the outbreak of the First World War, while testing an experimental vacuum receiver, Wright Senior found himself listening in to signals from German ships.

Since the focus of the looming conflict was widely anticipated to be a struggle for supremacy between the Royal Navy and the Kaiser's Imperial fleet, the discovery had urgent potential: Maurice Wright was summoned to meet the head of Naval Intelligence, and in short order Marconi was ordered to release the young engineer to develop his direction-finding device under military supervision.

In 1915 Maurice was dispatched to Norway to test the latest iteration. Norway was then a neutral country, but one which occupied a strategic location in the battle for the seas. British and German spies closely monitored each other's activities on the coast – which made it impossible for Wright to be given official accreditation; instead he was co-opted into the Secret Intelligence Service – MI6 – and, posing as a commercial traveller dealing in agricultural medicine, for six months operated a clandestine wireless detection station in the attic of a hotel.

While he was there, his son was born, prematurely, at his grandmother's house in Chesterfield. A Zeppelin bombing raid coincided with Peter Wright's arrival, preventing him from being taken to hospital for neonatal care; for much of his early childhood the boy had a severe stammer and suffered from rickets, requiring him to wear cumbersome leg irons.

According to Wright family lore, MI6 spirited Maurice out of Norway after German intelligence identified him as a British spy; the escape story he told his son involved a desperate ten-mile hike to the coast, then a hazardous journey across the North Sea on a Royal Navy destroyer.

True or not, it planted a seed in Peter's youthful imagination, sparking a determination to follow his father into both science and the intelligence services.

After the war, two siblings arrived to join Peter in the Wright household, and Maurice returned to Marconi. At the same time, and with the company's blessing, Wright Senior continued to work for MI6. The service's legendary chief, Captain Mansfield Cumming, and Admiral Reggie 'Blinker' Hall, the equally celebrated head of Naval Intelligence, were frequent visitors to the family home, further exciting Peter's youthful espionage ambitions. But it was the lessons learned from his father's approach to science that resonated most strongly, and which would shape Peter Wright's character.

> My father was an intense, emotional, rather quick-tempered man – more of an artist than an engineer. As early as I can remember he used to take me ... onto the open fields above the Essex beaches to teach me the mysteries of wireless. He spent hours explaining valves and crystals and showed me how to delicately turn the dials of a set so that the random static suddenly became a clear signal. He taught me how to make my own experiments.[20]

In the summer of 1931 Peter passed his school certificate – the then standard educational qualification – and was expected to win a scholarship to Oxford or Cambridge University. But within days his father was made redundant from Marconi and the family finances collapsed; shorn of income and status, Maurice quickly spiralled down into alcoholism. At the age of fifteen, Peter was removed from his private school and told to find a job. For the next three years he worked as a farmhand in Scotland and Cornwall, before scraping together enough money to fund a place at the School of Rural Economy in Oxford, studying the science of food production.

But war was again looming, and in September 1939 the college closed down. Maurice had managed to bring his drinking under control and joined the Royal Naval Scientific Service, analysing intercepted German communications. The head of RNSS, Sir Frederick Brundrett, was an old family friend, and in late 1939 he arranged for Peter Wright to come aboard, working on the urgent problem of 'degaussing' British ships to disguise their magnetic field and thus protect them against mines.

There was no manual for this, so Wright and his colleagues invented one. Giant coils of wire were wound round the ships' hulls, and the makeshift infrastructure was connected to an electrical current. The technique worked; the vessels' polarity was neutralised, and throughout the war the team 'degaussed' everything from battleships to submarines. The experience reinforced the lesson Peter had learned from his father.

> The war taught me the value of improvisation, and showed me, too, just how effective operations can be when the men of action listen to young men with a belief in practical inventive science.[21]

When the war ended Peter Wright took the Scientific Civil Service exams, passing out joint first with a score of 290 from the maximum total of 300. In 1946 he was given a full-time appointment at RNSS, with the rank of principal scientific officer. It was a permanent and well-paid position and, just as importantly for a young man who remembered his family's financial struggles during the 1930s, it had the benefit of a generous pension scheme.

Wright arrived at RNSS with a sizeable chip on his shoulder; unlike many of the service's more traditional staff, he had no relevant academic qualifications and bore an ill-concealed contempt for the scientific conservatism of those who did. This, and the lessons taught by his father on the Essex coast, had convinced him that 'on the big issues the experts are very rarely right'.[22]

His impatient self-confidence infuriated at least some of his new colleagues. Neville Robinson, a Cambridge graduate who served under Wright from 1947 to 1950, later denounced his boss as 'an ignorant shit' and complained that: 'Nothing Wright touched ever came to anything ... He was more of a radio repair man, a kind of ham radio enthusiast, than a physicist with a good grounding in the subject.'[23]

The head of RNSS was, however, rather more supportive. In 1949, on the orders of Sir Percy Sillitoe, Frederick Brundrett set up an ad-hoc committee to provide MI5 with scientific advice; he chose Peter Wright to be its leading member, deliberately bypassing, according to Wright's subsequent Australian affidavit, other more qualified scientists.

> Brundrett ... told Sillitoe he did not need an eminent scientist with an FRS [Fellowship of the Royal Society] to assist the Service with scientific matters. He said 'you need a young man with a good war who is a problem solver, as opposed to an analytical theorist'.[24]

The first issue confronting Wright was the antediluvian state of MI5's technical capabilities. The Security Service had previously been at the forefront of espionage technology; during the Second World War it had become adept at installing then state-of-the-art covert microphones to record discussions between pro-Nazi sympathisers in London,[25] as well as bugging the cells of captured German personnel in PoW facilities across the South East.[26] But since then it had fallen back into the torpor of the 1930s, just as its Cold War enemies in Moscow were making rapid advances in the new primary battleground of electronic espionage.

Wright was alarmed to find that 'there was no application or understanding of science'; the sum total of technical services available to British intelligence officers were the Post Office's Special Investigations Unit and 'a pretty elementary chemical laboratory for detecting secret writing and developing secret inks. It was almost a schoolboy operation.'[27]

The most urgent challenge was to upgrade the antiquated surveillance technology. MI5 realised that legions of Soviet spies operated under diplomatic cover inside the Embassy, and their subagents were scattered across London in trade missions and client organisations – to fight the new intelligence war it was vital to eavesdrop on their discussions.

Unfortunately, MI5's existing microphones were not equal to the task, since they had to be permanently connected to a power source, and once activated could not be switched off. This generated a clear electronic signal – 'howl round' – which made the bugs easy to detect in routine sweeps by Russian security staff.

For the next two years, Peter Wright worked for Brundrett, unpaid and in his spare time, to develop a new generation of microphones that required no electrical hardwiring, and which could be activated at will by a radio signal. Then, in March 1951, British and American intelligence discovered that Russia's scientists had beaten them to the punch.

The British air attaché in Moscow was monitoring a Soviet Air Force radio channel when he overheard conversations between American diplomatic personnel inside the American Embassy coming through the ether. US State Department investigators swept the building and eventually located a telltale signal emanating from the Ambassador's office; further searching revealed the presence of an entirely new type of microphone, hidden inside the Great Seal of the United States – a substantial wooden carving of the national emblem, gifted to the Embassy by the Kremlin in 1945 – which had been mounted proudly on the wall.

'The Thing', as the FBI termed the device, was removed and taken back to Washington DC. For several months US scientists probed and prodded at the microphone, trying without success to discover how it worked.

Finally, they conceded defeat; the Seal and the microphone were shipped to Britain and handed to Peter Wright for analysis. For three months, using homemade detection equipment, he experimented with a wide variety of frequencies; early in 1952, after painstakingly winding his dials up and down the wireless spectrum, just as his father had once shown him, he found the magic number of megahertz. The microphone suddenly 'illuminated' and emitted a clearly detectable signal.

MI5 was delighted. Using 'The Thing' as a prototype, British intelligence would now be able develop its own radio-controlled microphones; Wright was duly tasked with producing a prototype. There was, however, a problem. MI5 could provide none of the necessary funding: the budgetary inflexibility of the Secret Vote – and the impossibility of asking Parliament to authorise extra funds in an 'open' vote for an organisation which didn't officially exist – meant that there was no money to pay for the unanticipated work.

Instead, Wright was instructed to go, cap in hand, to his employers and plead with the Admiralty to stump up the cash. 'This,' he later recalled, 'was my initiation into the bizarre method of handling Intelligence Services finance ... Instead of having resources adequate for their technical requirements, [they] were forced to spend most of the post-war period begging from the increasingly reluctant Armed Services.'[28]

Happily, the Admiralty proved supportive, paying for a purpose-built workshop inside Marconi's laboratory building and seconding six Navy scientists to work under Wright's direction. The project was assigned a codename – SATYR – and over the next eighteen months the team assembled a functioning prototype; by the autumn of 1953 it was ready.

SATYR Mark 1 fitted inside a small suitcase. In addition to the main set's collection of valves and dials, two aerials disguised as ordinary umbrellas housed the transmitter and receiver. Wright brought the apparatus to Leconfield House and positioned the umbrellas in the Director General's office, then took the suitcase to a safe house nearby and flicked the switch. Seconds later, conversation from inside MI5 came through loud and clear.

The success of SATYR – and the lack of any in-house scientist – prompted the Security Service to call repeatedly on Wright's services over the next six months; by the spring of 1954 he was spending two days a week inside Leconfield House, and MI5's senior management realised they needed a full-time advisor on technical surveillance problems.

Characteristically, the approach to Wright was made over a generous lunch of quail eggs in the dining room of an exclusive Pall Mall club – and, equally typically, it came with a significant catch.

Custom and precedent precluded Whitehall departments from poaching each other's staff: even though MI5 did not officially exist, the time-honoured rule apparently applied, and Wright was warned that to join the Service as its first-ever scientific advisor he would need to resign from RNSS and spend a six-month 'rustication' period in private industry. That, in itself, was no great problem, since Marconi offered to house him for the duration of his enforced 'purdah'. But the arrangement would have a distinct financial impact: not only was his annual salary to be much reduced, but he would also have to forgo all fourteen years of his Civil Service pension contributions. As he later recalled:

> The MI5 people were adamant that these ... could not be transferred over to MI5 where ... pensions were ... entirely discretionary. They said that I would not be disadvantaged, however, because they would make up any difference themselves.[29]

Reassured by this unwritten and entirely unenforceable promise, Peter Wright succumbed to the allure of working officially for the intelligence services, and in June 1955 he duly presented himself at Leconfield House. After the unexpectedly lukewarm discussion with Director General Sir Dick White, he was handed over to the officer tasked with his induction.

By chance, his arrival coincided with the long-delayed publication of Sir Percy Sillitoe's troublesome memoirs. The cover of *Cloak Without Dagger* boldly identified the author as the 'former Director General of MI5', and included a pointed foreword by Clement Attlee, who fired a well-aimed potshot at the 'obligations of secrecy' which had prevented Sillitoe from revealing more of his experiences at the head of the Security Service.[30] Nonetheless, the book contained many more details of his exploits than the Whitehall's guardians of official *omertà* believed they had, reluctantly, sanctioned. 'The manuscript goes beyond what you told him he could be permitted to include,' Sir Edward Bridges complained to the Home Office.[31]

Against this backdrop, it was hardly surprising that MI5's formal letter inviting Peter Wright to join the Service contained no injunction against talking about his new employers. On 11 July he was offered a 'temporary appointment as a Senior Principal Scientific Officer … at a salary of £1,700 p.a.'. This less than princely sum – equivalent to £36,000 today – was to rise by modest increments of £75 for each of the three years he was to be on probation, pending confirmation of permanent employment.[32] Wright accepted the offer three days later, and on 1 September 1955 reported for duty at Leconfield House.

One of his first tasks was to sign a single-page document confirming that he had read, and agreed to be bound by, the Official Secrets Acts of 1911 and 1920.[33] However, both Acts were hopelessly outdated and so broadly drawn as to be meaningless. The 1911 version, passed amid a pre-First World War public panic over alleged German spies, focused primarily on impeding international espionage, but included a second 'catch-all' section which made it an offence to disclose any official information – no matter how trivial – without government authority.[34] Wright understood that this solitary document was routine bureaucratic boilerplate, to be ignored as needed. 'I was never referred to any … confidentiality obligation other than the OSA [Official Secrets Act],' he would later testify. 'Often I discussed classified matters with non-vetted people in the course of my work.'[35]

Later that first day, his training officer bluntly laid out the realities of working for the Security Service. John Cuckney[36] warned Wright that his position rested on remarkably shaky foundations. He, as an individual officer, had no rights – 'I was told, "You can be instantly sacked without any reasons"'[37] – nor did MI5 as an organisation have any legal standing: 'the Security Service cannot have the normal status of a Whitehall Department because its work very often involves transgressing propriety or the law'.[38]

Ultimately, there was one – and only one – immutable rule. MI5 operated on the premise of the Eleventh Commandment: 'Thou shalt not get caught'.[39]

2. SPECIAL FACILITIES

'We knew we were breaking the law and we were told that if we were caught "You're on your own".'
PETER WRIGHT AFFIDAVIT: CONFIDENTIAL MATERIAL,
NOVEMBER 1986

Leslie Jagger was 'a burglar of genius'.
More specifically, he was MI5's resident master of the dark arts of housebreaking, lock picking and covert microphone installation. After a career in the Army, during which he rose to the rank of sergeant major in the Rifle Brigade, Jagger was recruited to provide the Security Service with the means and equipment for wholesale law-breaking.

At some point during the Second World War, he set up shop in the basement of Leconfield House.[1] His presence there was entirely secret: there is no public record of his appointment and his activities were controlled by nothing more tangible than whatever MI5's senior officers deemed expedient.

As the end of the war approached, Anthony Eden, then Foreign Secretary, tasked veteran civil servant Sir Samuel Findlater Stewart[2] to 'enquire into the future constitution and scope of the Security Service'.

Since his report, delivered in November 1945, would provide the new Labour government with the first formal peacetime inquiry into MI5's existence and activities, it might have offered an opportunity to put the work of Britain's domestic spies on some form of legitimate basis. It failed to do so.

Although the report noted that the wartime use of covert microphones, telephone taps and mail interception – 'special powers' as it coyly described the tactics – was 'essential if the Security Service is to carry out its responsibilities effectively', other than recommending ministerial authorisation for microphone installation and a brisk injunction that the Director General should ensure Security Service staff did not 'step outside the law', Findlater Stewart found no space in his closely typed 33 pages to consider how these conflicting obligations could be met.[3]

Unsurprisingly, therefore, when Prime Minister Clement Attlee sent a written 'directive' to his hand-picked new Director General, it gave Sillitoe no instruction on the need to operate legally. Instead, it stated only that he was to 'take special care that the work of the Security Service is strictly limited to what is necessary' for the defence of the realm, and to ensure that he kept his organisation 'absolutely free from any political bias or influence ... you will impress on your staff that they have no connection whatever with any matters of a Party political character and that they must be scrupulous to avoid any action which could be so misconstrued'.[4]

Six years later, when Conservative Home Secretary Sir David Maxwell Fife issued a marginally updated version, it too made no mention of acting within the law of the land.[5]

The legality – or otherwise – of what MI5 got up to was thus discreetly swept under a tasteful Whitehall rug, where it stayed until the 1950s drew towards a close. Even when a Committee of Privy Counsellors considered the issue in 1957, ruefully reporting that there was no legal basis for much of MI5's 'special powers' and that the only fig leaf of justification was 'long usage', nothing was done to resolve MI5's precarious legal position. The result, as a leading legal scholar warned, was 'that the Security Service, itself a body unrecognized by law, continues to rely on a practice which is also not recognised by law'.[6]

If mail interception and remote telephone taps were – notionally at least – authorised once a month by the Home Secretary, by the time Peter Wright was fully inculcated into MI5's secretive brotherhood, no prime minister or Whitehall mandarin had given any thought to the mechanics of how Britain's domestic spies were carrying out other clandestine missions which required physical access to a target's premises.

For the Security Service, Leslie Jagger was – quite literally – the key. A large, broad-shouldered man, habitually clothed in a drab black suit which matched his often-dark sense of humour, Jagger's basement workshop was an Aladdin's cave of housebreaking equipment. Thousands of keys to homes and offices lined the four walls: each had been acquired by MI5 staff, copied and then painstakingly indexed, providing what Jagger proudly proclaimed to be 'access ... to premises all over Britain'.[7]

The source of these duplicate keys was distinctly questionable. Some had been obtained during operations against legitimate Soviet Bloc intelligence targets: in one typical case, an agent recruited inside the Czechoslovakian Embassy covertly took a plasticine copy of the key to the safe holding cipher pads and passed it to Jagger, who made a working version. Looting the safe ensured that Britain's spies gained access to top-secret coded Czech messages for a full six months. Others, however, had been pilfered in less excusable circumstances – during burglaries on 'offices, hotels and private houses'.[8]

But this illicit key collection was merely the first, and easiest, line of attack. Should the Security Service be confronted with a door to which it didn't possess a key, or a safe which had to be opened, Jagger trained its officers in the delicate art of lock-picking: using pieces of fine wire with a tiny hook at the end, he taught Wright and his colleagues how to 'stroke' the inside of locks to release the pins which held them shut.

Mere possession of this equipment – let alone using it – would have been enough to guarantee a prison sentence for anyone outside MI5's ranks. But Jagger's concern was less for legality than the risk of alerting his targets. 'It's virtually impossible to pick a lock without scratching it,' he warned Wright. 'That'll almost certainly give the game away to a trained intelligence officer. He'll know the premises have been entered ... Only pick the lock as a last resort.'[9]

MI5's unlawful activities reached an early apogee in June 1955, when Operation PARTY PIECE encapsulated both the technical ingenuity and the moral ambiguity of its methods. The Communist Party of Great Britain had long been the subject of Security Service attention; since the 1930s, MI5 officers and agents had infiltrated CPGB branches to monitor what the membership was up to on behalf of the Soviet Union. This interest was unquestionably justified: for decades, Moscow had funded and largely directed the policies and actions of Britain's communist leaders.

But although CPGB had, in the words of Findlater Stewart's report, been 'linked ... with Russian espionage', it was not banned and remained a legal political party; while most of its members were open about the fact and were 'reputable people who have not pledged themselves to extremist doctrines',[10] MI5's moles inside the Party reported that beneath them were thousands of secret members, whose existence was too sensitive to be acknowledged publicly.

In spring 1955 the Service acquired a tantalising piece of intelligence: all the secret membership rolls were stored in the north London home of a wealthy communist couple, Ronald and Nancy Berger. Phone taps, mail intercepts and visual surveillance of the address, in Grove Terrace, Highgate, soon threw up another stroke of good fortune. Nancy Berger phoned her husband at work, saying she was leaving the house and would be out for an hour; she told Ronald she would leave the key for him under the front doormat. Within minutes of her departure, MI5 officers arrived and copied it.

Further phone taps revealed that the Bergers were planning a weekend in the Lake District. While 'watchers' from MI5's A Branch shadowed the couple on their brief holiday, a second team used the stolen key to burgle the house. They then employed Jagger's lockpicks to open filing cabinets holding the membership records and photographed a haul of 6,000 documents.

Three months later the burglars returned for a second, late-night raid. They rushed 48,000 additional records to Leconfield House where banks of pedal-operated microfilm machines were waiting to copy them; by dawn the next day, all the original files were safely back in place in the Bergers' house.

Peter Wright – now one of Jagger's most frequent customers – was jubilant. PARTY PIECE gave the Security Service 'total access' to CPGB's membership; the purloined documents recorded not just the names and personal details of all its known members, along with their reasons for joining the organisation, but many of the files belonged to the Party's covert members. Their identities and occupations sparked the ready kindling of Wright's nascent belief in a dangerous communist fifth column, which he believed had burrowed into politics, industry and Whitehall itself: 'These were people in the Labour Party, the trade union movement or the Civil Service ... who had gone underground.'[11] Over time, Wright would fan these smouldering embers of suspicion into an overarching obsession with rooting out Moscow's agents in government, labour and civil rights organisations – and within MI5 itself.

By MI5's metrics at least, PARTY PIECE was an operational triumph: at the end of the Second World War, the Security Service's card index had recorded the identities of just 413 men and women subject to monitoring on the basis of their 'left wing' views – a tiny fraction of the total of 1.2 million names stored in its central database, the Registry.[12]

The raid on the Bergers' files added tens of thousands of names to the roll call of those suspected of some form of disloyalty or subversive activity on behalf of the Soviet Union. Better still, until Wright revealed the story, CPBG remained blissfully unaware that its secrets had been stolen and its clandestine members uncovered.[13]

Operation PARTY PIECE was followed by a succession of break-ins at the London headquarters of Soviet Bloc countries. Two of these highlighted the personal risks MI5 expected its officers to take in the line of duty.

In a late-night operation to install microphones inside the Polish Embassy in Portland Street, a team from A Branch broke into the adjoining empty house next door. As they threaded cables under the second-storey floorboards, carefully pushing them beneath the shared wall, Wright lost his footing and fell through the ceiling of the room below. Jagger was summoned to effect emergency repairs to the plaster and paint, and the burglars counted themselves lucky that the racket went unnoticed by neighbours or Embassy guards. They were not always so fortunate.

In a mission to mount eavesdropping equipment inside the Hungarian Embassy, Wright clambered on to the roof of an adjacent house. His ascent was spotted by a neighbour, who phoned the police to report a burglary in process. Within minutes uniformed officers hammered on the front door, ordering whoever was inside to open up, come out and explain themselves. When this produced no response, they started to force entry. MI5's scientific officer hurriedly stuffed cables, microphones and receivers under the attic floorboards, then rushed sheepishly downstairs to talk his way out of trouble, implausibly claiming the house owner had contracted him to carry out 'late night renovations'.[14]

Wright viewed these adventures and close calls as 'fun': they were precisely the sort of spy capers that had characterised his father's early career and had sparked his own determination to join British intelligence. But his masters in Leconfield House left him in no doubt that should a mission go badly wrong, they would deny all knowledge of his illegal activities. 'When we were instructed to burgle an embassy or something of that kind, we knew we were breaking the law,' he would later testify in a secret court session in Australia. 'We were given Special Branch[15] passes which usually enabled us to escape from any serious problems, but ... we were told that if we were caught, "You're on your own".'[16]

If illegal break-ins at the premises of the Soviet Union, its Warsaw Pact allies and its British satraps could be justified by the *realpolitik* of fighting the new Cold War, other operations were rather more dubious. As the British government struggled to come to terms with the winds of change buffeting the Empire, MI5 was tasked with mounting covert surveillance operations against the leaders of independence movements in its colonial outposts and the Middle East.

In 1956, when Prime Minister Anthony Eden launched an ill-fated military adventure to oust Egyptian President Gamal Nasser and seize back control of the Suez Canal, Wright installed microphones in the walls of the Egyptian Embassy to record and then unpick coded cypher messages sent from London to Cairo. Although the operation was a technical success, providing Eden with advance notice of Nasser's plans, it failed to save either the British mission or Eden's premiership.

The Egyptian bugging was swiftly followed by the wholesale installation of covert microphones inside the Lancaster House conferences, at which several of Britain's Imperial colonies negotiated their independence. Every word of the private conversations of representatives from Kenya, Malaya, Nigeria and Cyprus was recorded, transcribed and passed back to Downing Street.

All of this stretched MI5's conveniently elastic remit – that its operations were 'strictly limited to what is necessary' for the defence of the realm. A subsequent operation against the French Embassy unambiguously shattered that still-secret instruction.

In 1961 the British government applied to join the European Economic Community – the forerunner of the European Union – and Downing Street was consumed by the desire to discover the views of its most resolute opponent, President Charles de Gaulle. Wright had the Embassy cipher cables tapped, and for the next three years all messages between London and De Gaulle's private office were delivered to the Foreign Secretary and Prime Minister. Wright was duly thanked for the 'priceless intelligence' provided.[17]

Eavesdropping on the private conversations of the remnants of Empire at the same time as negotiating their independence – let alone intercepting the diplomatic traffic of a friendly ally in peacetime for political advantage – amounted to major international offences. But Wright and his colleagues in A Branch – 'a place of infectious laughter' – were cheerfully untroubled. He later recalled that, free from any oversight or legal constraints, 'for five years we bugged and burgled our way across London at the State's behest, while pompous bowler-hatted civil servants in Whitehall pretended to look the other way.'[18]

He was, in truth, rather more exercised by the antediluvian state of the technology at his disposal. His earliest impression of the Security Service was of a complacent and insular department, living on its wartime successes and still 'covered with a thick film of dust'.[19]

True, the 1940s had seen some genuine progress: MI5's chief weapon – referred to internally as 'Special Facilities' – was the ability to tweak the wiring of almost any telephone system and turn the handsets into surveillance devices. But when Wright joined, recordings from all covert microphones were still captured on antiquated Dictaphone cylinders or ten-inch acetate discs: all of this equipment was bulky and clumsy, and both the cylinders and discs had very limited capacity.[20]

Special Facilities

Magnetic open-reel tape recorders had been on the market for more than two decades, and near the end of the Second World War, Allied armies had captured several German machines in their progress across the ruins of the Third Reich. But by the middle of the 1950s, this new technology had yet to find its way into MI5's armoury. Wright begged enough funds from the Security Service's threadbare budget to replace the old-fashioned machinery with what amounted to state-of-the-art reel-to-reel recorders: if these, too, were heavy and cumbersome, their tapes at least made extended recording possible.

But Wright also realised that MI5's primary problem was the microphones at the front end of its surveillance equipment. Installing them generally required physical access to the target premises – which meant burglary and the risk of being caught in the act – but they also had to be hardwired to both a receiver and the local electricity supply: unsurprisingly, the cables were frequently detected by routine counter-surveillance sweeps.

Simultaneously, however, he and the Post Office Special Investigations Unit were hard at work on an upgrade to the long-standing Special Facilities. Codenamed CABMAN, this combined the ingenuity of Wright's radiation concept with the anonymity of commonplace existing equipment already in place: the humble telephone.

Using a narrowly directed radio 'beam', MI5 was able to remotely activate the microphone inside the handset. Parallel experiments produced a transmitter which did not require an external power source and its telltale rats' nest of cabling: codenamed MOP, it promised to revolutionise British intelligence surveillance technology.

'Peter Wright was, above all, a boffin,' recalled Paul Greengrass, who worked closely with the old spycatcher as co-author of his book. 'Inventions and innovations were where he was at his best, and he should really have stuck to that rather than wandering into the wilderness of counterintelligence mirrors.'[21]

Yet the two were inextricably linked. Wright's restless toying with radio frequencies – the chief lesson he had learned from experiments with his father on the Essex beaches – led him to the revelation that counter-espionage engineers inside the Soviet Embassy were listening in to the communications channel used by MI5's team of 'watchers' as they tailed suspected Russian agents through the streets of London.

He targeted the oscillator inside the Embassy's receiver, and by overloading it with his own signal was able to prove conclusively that the Security Service's supposedly secure frequency had been compromised.

RAFTER, as this new technique was named, was a counter-espionage coup; but it also offered the prospect of turning the tables on Moscow.

By blasting the Embassy with radio waves, Wright and his colleagues could discover which frequencies the Kremlin used to send instructions to its army of 'illegals' – otherwise unidentified spies operating in London under false names and deep cover. It was, Wright later boasted, 'a shattering breakthrough into the hitherto secret world of Soviet illegal communications'.[22]

But despite all these technical advances, after initial success almost all of MI5's SATYR, CABMAN and RAFTER operations against Soviet Bloc buildings failed. As he later testified in a secret session to the court in Sydney, 'the fact is that from 1951 to 1958 MI5 had no success against the Russians'.[23]

Then, as the 1950s drew to a close, Wright was handed the most plausible explanation: Moscow had a long-standing mole inside British intelligence.

3. PENETRATION

'The evidence that there had been a mole inside MI5 was overwhelming and was made up of the enormous number of operations that went wrong'.
PETER WRIGHT AFFIDAVIT: CONFIDENTIAL
MATERIAL, NOVEMBER 1986

The 36-year-old communist spy raised his right hand, swore to tell the truth and took a breath. 'I am Frantisek Tisler ... I was the Chief of the Czechoslovak Military Intelligence Residentura ... in Washington DC'.

The session of the US House of Representatives Committee on Un-American Activities was held in May 1960 behind closed doors. Tisler's appearance was unannounced, and both its exact date and location were redacted from the official record.[1] For good reason.

Frantisek Tisler rarely merits more than a footnote in histories of Cold War intelligence. The few brief mentions of his name generally refer to him as a mere 'cipher clerk'. The reality was very different: from his arrival in the United States in August 1955 until his defection in September 1959, Lieutenant Colonel Tisler was Czechoslovakia's most senior intelligence officer in the United States. More importantly, for two of those years he had also been an informant for the FBI, regularly feeding the Bureau many of Prague's most vital espionage secrets.

In spring 1958, a letter from FBI Director J. Edgar Hoover was hand-delivered to MI5's latest Director General, Roger Hollis. It contained a snippet of profoundly disturbing information, which Tisler – then still operating undercover inside the Czech Embassy – had recently provided: Russian intelligence had an active spy inside MI5, who was betraying its technical operations against Soviet Bloc targets.

Tisler's material was second-hand: over the course of a lengthy drink-fuelled conversation the previous year, the Czech Military Attaché in London, Colonel Oldrich Prybil, had let slip that he knew about the existence – but not the name – of Moscow's mole inside the Security Service. Raw intelligence of this nature was not uncommon: Britain's spies were constantly on the alert for drunken gossip or hearsay, and in other circumstances Hoover's tip might have been filed away until another fragment of evidence offered corroboration. But according to Tisler, Prybil had also identified another agent he was personally running in an aerospace company in Sussex – a revelation that turned out to be depressingly accurate and led to a successful prosecution for espionage.[2]

With these *bona fides* established, Hollis could not ignore the accompanying claims of a spy inside Leconfield House: he summoned Peter Wright to the Director General's inner sanctum on the fifth floor and asked him to investigate. It was the start of an obsessive quest that would dominate Wright's life for almost 30 years.

He began with an analysis of Prybil's disclosure that he had been alerted to a recent alteration of tactics by MI5's 'watchers': since only a small number of senior officers knew about the change, it suggested the Kremlin's man was highly placed – either within the watchers themselves or in the upper reaches of Security Service management. Wright decided to flush out the mole with a 'barium meal' – a succulent morsel of bait so tempting that the alleged traitor would be certain to relay it to his masters in Moscow.

MI5 was then running a double agent who had allowed himself to be recruited by the Russian Naval Attaché, and Wright let it be known within MI5 that Special Branch planned to arrest both men at their next scheduled meeting: if there was a Soviet agent inside Leconfield House, the Attaché would, Wright assumed, simply not show up. But the operation fell flat. The Russian arrived at the rendezvous and met the double agent exactly on schedule: he was promptly arrested and subsequently sent back to Moscow. The Security Service breathed more easily. Prybil's information about a spy in its ranks appeared to be false.

But within two years, evidence from another Soviet Bloc intelligence defector offered a troubling explanation – and provided additional leads about a mole inside MI5.

Like Tisler, Lieutenant Colonel Michał Goleniewski had proved his value: as a senior officer in Poland's espionage service, simultaneously employed by the KGB, he had worked undercover for the United States, handing over information which led to the breaking of the British Portland spy ring and the arrest and imprisonment of George Blake, Moscow's man inside the Secret Intelligence Service, MI6.

After he fled to the West in January 1961, Goleniewski told the CIA that it was Kremlin policy to protect its most vital assets by allowing the capture of less important spies. According to the Agency's most experienced analyst, Richards J. Heuer:

> He stated that one of the many objectives of KGB disinformation was the protection of Soviet agents by means of actions designed to mislead Western special services. … in extreme cases, the KGB would be willing to sacrifice some of its own agent assets to enhance the reputation of an agent penetration of a Western intelligence service.[3]

Then, in subsequent debriefings, Goleniewski put additional flesh on the bones of the supposed Russian skeleton in MI5's closet: he said the traitor was of 'middling-grade', who had previously served in the British Army, and still held the rank of a British officer when he was recruited by the KGB's Third Directorate. At some point in his career the mole had 'probably' worked in the Security Service's Polish section, because he 'had provided the Russians with valuable Polish counterintelligence'.[4]

To Peter Wright, the claims rang true. He was already nursing concerns about the remarkable ease with which Gordon Lonsdale (*aka* Konon Molody), the Portland spy ring's KGB controller, had been apprehended.[5] Goleniewski's revelation that Moscow was willing to give up its pawns to protect a more important piece on the espionage chessboard seemed to offer an explanation for both this and the red-handed capture of the Russian Naval Attaché.

Deeply troubled, throughout 1962 Wright began re-examining old files on previous claims of Soviet penetration. What he unearthed added fuel to the growing flames of his suspicion – not least because the evidence documented in the files stretched back over almost twenty years.

The first lead had emerged on 4 September 1945. Konstantin Dimitrievich Volkov, an NKGB officer[6] based in Turkey, walked into the British Consulate in Istanbul and, in return for political asylum as well as the sizeable sum of £50,000 – equivalent to £1.7 million today – volunteered to defect.

To sweeten the proposed deal, he offered to provide evidence that the Kremlin had 'two moles inside the Foreign Office and seven inside the British Intelligence Service'; one of those seven was the 'head of a section of the British counter-espionage service'.⁷ Volkov and his dossier of traitors' names never made it to the West. MI6 tasked Kim Philby, one of its most experienced officers, with bringing the defector back to London; but Philby delayed his departure for Istanbul, and within 72 hours Volkov was snatched by Russian agents. He was summarily executed.

The speed with which Soviet intelligence discovered Volkov's proposed defection suggested that the operation had been betrayed. But Philby was able to deflect suspicion by showing that Moscow had tapped phones inside the British Embassy in Ankara: since the operation had been discussed by officials on these compromised phone lines, the Secret Intelligence Service (SIS) decided its failure had been inadvertent.

Two days after Volkov walked into the Istanbul Consulate, another Soviet spy had better luck. On 6 September, Igor Gouzenko, a 26-year-old cipher clerk employed by the Russian Military Intelligence Service, the GRU, successfully defected in Canada.

Gouzenko had worked inside the Soviet Embassy in Ottawa for more than two years: 'extremely alert and intelligent', his time in the West 'completely converted' him from his communist upbringing. He had, as MI5's counter-espionage chief, Guy Liddell, recorded in his diary, 'realised that from his youth up, he had been deceived' by the Soviet system.⁸

At the end of his final shift in the Embassy's second-floor cipher room, Gouzenko smuggled out 109 top-secret documents and, after a nail-biting night hiding in a safe house while Russian security officers ransacked his apartment,⁹ handed them over to the Canadian police in return for political asylum. The cache was a remarkable haul of enciphered telegrams between Moscow and the GRU chief in Ottawa, including the names, cover names and personal details of a sizeable network of Russian spies, among them a Canadian MP and Alan Nunn May, a British physicist who had worked on the joint Anglo-American team to develop the atom bomb and was then assigned to its offshoot in Montreal.¹⁰

Gouzenko's initial debriefing was handled by the Royal Canadian Mounted Police (RCMP). He told the detectives that he also knew of two Soviet agents working for the British government who shared the same GRU codename – ELLI.

The first – re-christened ELLIE to avoid confusion – was quickly identified as Kay Willsher, Deputy Registrar in the High Commission at Ottawa. The second ELLI, however, would prove more problematic.

According to Gouzenko, this other ELLI was 'an unidentified agent in England',¹¹ and the RCMP immediately sent the lead to London. Under other circumstances, the ensuing investigation might have been undertaken by SIS, but under an informal and uneasy pact between the two often rivalrous British intelligence services, cases originating in Dominion countries were the bailiwick of the Security Service. When the report landed on the desk of Kim Philby at MI6 he was barred from dealing with it himself; instead he recommended it should be handled by Roger Hollis at MI5.[12]

This suggestion was, in itself, slightly unusual. Counter-espionage was notionally the responsibility of B Division, under Guy Liddell – a highly experienced case officer who had managed many of MI5's wartime successes and held the rank of Director; Hollis, by contrast, was then head of F Division, which monitored domestic 'political extremism' – subversive groups and individuals on both the political right and left – and, as an Assistant Director, was one grade lower in the Service's hierarchy.

But as Peter Wright pored over the old files, it was the Philby connection that most alarmed him. At the time of the Volkov and Gouzenko affairs Philby had been one of SIS's most senior and respected officers, who had gone on to run MI6 operations in Washington DC and to act as liaison with the newly created Central Intelligence Agency. In May 1951 two Soviet spies inside the British Foreign Office – Guy Burgess (who had also worked for both British intelligence services) and Donald Maclean – defected to Moscow;[13] MI5's counterintelligence branch suspected they had been tipped off by Philby, and that he was the 'Third Man' in their espionage ring.

Philby was recalled from the United States and summoned for interrogation inside Leconfield House; after the second four-hour interview, his inquisitor reached an uncomfortable verdict: 'I find myself unable to avoid the conclusion that Philby is, and has been for many years, a Soviet agent.'[14]

Sir Stewart Menzies, MI6's long-serving head, was less convinced. 'C', as he was known by SIS tradition, mounted a passionate rearguard action to defend his man,[15] and ensured that although Philby had to go, he was allowed to retire quietly with his pension, and his former colleagues found him a job outside the Service; they also discreetly continued to share intelligence with their tarnished star.

Four years later, after pressure from US intelligence, Philby was summoned for a further formal interview, this time in an MI6 safe house in Sloane Square in London's Belgravia district.

MI5 ordered Wright to wire the interview room with microphones and recording equipment. He listened in to the session on a remote relay, and was appalled to hear the SIS investigator actively helping the suspected spy. 'To call it an interrogation,' he later recalled, 'would be a travesty. It was an in-house interview [and] whenever Philby floundered ... his questioners guided him to an acceptable answer.'[16]

Once again MI6 pronounced that its man had passed the test and Prime Minister Harold Macmillan publicly proclaimed him innocent in the House of Commons.[17] But Wright and many of his colleagues in Leconfield House remained convinced that Philby was a very senior Russian spy. And, as he reread the old files, that raised a troubling question: given the potential damage to Soviet intelligence of Gouzenko's ELLI revelation, would its most senior mole in London have recommended Roger Hollis as case investigator unless he, too, was a traitor?

What Wright discovered next reinforced that concern. Ten days after Gouzenko's defection, a telegram – marked 'Most Immediate' – had arrived at Leconfield House from British intelligence's New York office: it specifically advised that Gouzenko's information 'may give us [a] clue to an agent in the United Kingdom'.[18]

Given the breadth and strength of Gouzenko's intelligence on the Soviet spy network in Canada – the RCMP called it 'amazingly accurate'[19] – his information about a British-based spy should have resulted in an urgent, prolonged and forensic examination. Yet two months had passed before Hollis arrived in Ottawa to investigate the ELLI allegation,[20] and when he finally met the defector in the presence of the RCMP on 21 November,[21] the interview seemed to have been surprisingly perfunctory.

According to Wright, Hollis drafted a three-page statement and had Gouzenko sign it. He then wrote up a 'somewhat disparaging' report on the man for MI5's files.[22] This hostile verdict was distinctly strange: the Canadian Royal Commission examining the case found Gouzenko to be an impressive and sincere witness and had 'no hesitation in accepting' his evidence.[23]

That evidence also formed the basis for the arrests of Kay Willsher and Alan Nunn May. Willsher confessed and, in March 1946, was jailed for three years; two months later May was convicted of passing the West's nuclear secrets to the Soviet Union and sentenced to ten years' hard labour.

Yet neither this, nor a note entered in MI5's files three years later which described ELLI as 'an agent, possibly in British counterintelligence, who provided information about the UK ... known to Gouzenko prior to his arrival in Canada, ie: in 1942 and early 1943'[24] had led to any inquiries by the Security Service. For the next three years this tip, from a source of proven accuracy, was left to gather dust in the Registry.

Nor was any effort made to investigate additional leads which Gouzenko offered up seven years later. When the RCMP interviewed him again in 1952, he denounced MI5's lack of action and provided additional details about the Soviet spy inside British intelligence. He told the Canadian detectives that he had learned about ELLI's existence from a fellow cipher clerk, a Lieutenant Lubimov in the GRU's Moscow headquarters. Lubimov said ELLI had 'something Russian in his background' and had shown Gouzenko a telegram from the agent; he had also been very specific about the organisation into which Moscow's mole had burrowed: MI5.[25]

Wright was even more troubled by the further claim that during the Second World War, ELLI had been able to remove files on Soviet intelligence officers from the Security Service Registry and pass them to his GRU controller, who immediately delivered them to Stalin – an indication of the high-level secrets they contained.

The location of those pilfered files should have offered a potential clue as to the mole who took them. In September 1940 the Registry was moved out of London to Blenheim Palace, near Woodstock, in Oxfordshire. Only those MI5 officers who also left the capital for the countryside would have had sufficiently easy access to the dossiers to borrow and then leak them to Moscow – while the majority of Security Service staff were billeted near Oxford, most of the senior men remained in London. To Peter Wright, Gouzenko's information helpfully narrowed down the roster of suspects, yet he could find no record that the lead had been followed up. He added a note on this to his growing catalogue of unexplained failures.

A further file added more fuel to Wright's growing unease. In April 1954, Vladimir Petrov, Chief Resident of the MVD[26] at the Soviet Embassy in Australia, defected in Canberra. He brought with him sheaves of Russian intelligence documents disclosing the recruitment of journalists, civil servants and a handful of federal MPs who had duly passed military, diplomatic and scientific secrets to the Kremlin.

In debriefings by the Australian Security and Intelligence Organisation (ASIO), Petrov also provided details of the route by which Burgess and Maclean had escaped, and disclosed their current locations.

But according to evidence presented at the Australian Royal Commission on Espionage in 1954, Petrov had also been tasked by his masters in Moscow with enlisting agents in the United Kingdom and 'improving the [number of] valuable agents who had access to the intelligence and counter-intelligence organisations of Britain and America'.[27]

Given this background and detail, his further warning about a Soviet spy in MI5's ranks should have carried some weight. Like Frantisek Tisler before him, Petrov's information was second-hand, but originated from a known source: Lieutenant Colonel Nikolai Razin, a senior NKVD officer with whom Petrov had served in Stockholm.

Quoting his former colleague, Petrov told ASIO that 'in 1943 ... there was operating in London a penetration agent who was a career officer and who had access to files for Russian officers'.[28]

The importance of this lead was not lost on the upper floors of Leconfield House: within days, Graham Mitchell, then head of D1 Branch (counter-espionage), sent an urgent cable to the Service's Security Liaison Office in Canberra. But his concern was less about pressing this latest defector for information about the mole than in ensuring that no hint of it was disclosed to the forthcoming Royal Commission of Inquiry. And he specifically cited the Gouzenko case as a warning.

> Information likely to emerge [from Petrov] which will form basis of subsequent investigations in and outside Australia. Most desirable keep these investigations secret. Gouzenko's 'ELLI' is an example.[29]

Yet despite Mitchell's promise of 'investigations', none had apparently materialised. Nor, it seemed, had there been any real attempt to investigate the friends and acquaintances who had been at Cambridge University with Burgess, Maclean and Philby in the 1930s, and who had been part of avowedly Marxist–Leninist groups there; many of them had been given wartime jobs in British intelligence and had then progressed to senior positions in the Civil Service.

Arthur Martin, head of the Soviet desk in MI5's counter-espionage branch (D1 Branch), 'a skilful and persistent investigator'[30] and one of the Security Service's most talented counter-espionage sleuths, requested permission to interview these former communists, but his pleas were – for the most part – refused. As Wright later recalled, the Burgess and Maclean defections had 'traumatised MI5' and it was terrified at the potential for 'political embarrassment ... [or] the ghastly possibility that vigorous further investigations might provoke further departures to Moscow ... No one was prepared to grasp the nettle.'[31]

In April 1962, the need to grasp that painful nettle became more urgent, and once again the impetus came from across the Atlantic. Four months earlier, another KGB officer, Major Anatoliy Golitsyn, had defected to the United States. He arrived clutching a somewhat meagre haul of just 23 Soviet documents – none of any great value – and was demanding and divisive from the outset.[32] He would, in time, cause substantial turmoil throughout much of Western intelligence, but by that spring his new hosts in the CIA were cautiously ready to share him with their 'cousins' in MI5; Arthur Martin was put on a plane to Washington DC.

He returned some weeks later, notably excited and bearing 153 new leads – 'serials', as they were termed in intelligence jargon – all of them reporting second-hand information about Golitsyn's conversations with his former colleagues or unverifiable accounts of what he claimed to have witnessed during his service with the KGB.

These were, to Peter Wright's forensic mind, 'tantalizingly imprecise', but ten contained specific – and incendiary – allegations.[33] The first concerned 'a group of important [British] spies who had known each other before the war at Cambridge University and had in wartime obtained posts in the Foreign Office or Secret Services'.[34] Golitsyn did not know their identities, though Wright and Martin presumed that two of them were Burgess and Maclean, while a third, who Golitsyn said was involved with Moscow's espionage efforts in the Middle East, was a close match for Kim Philby, then working as a journalist for the *Observer* in Beirut.

But Golitsyn's chief allegation was of a mole inside MI5. He claimed that KGB headquarters had a dedicated safe that held documents provided by its man inside the Security Service, and that he had personally seen the index to these papers, which included very recent material, including a list of technical equipment – some of Wright's 'Special Facilities' – used by MI5. This indicated that the penetration of British intelligence was active and ongoing.

Golitsyn's 'serials' reinforced Wright's growing conviction that there was a Soviet spy inside Leconfield House, and it quickened his anger that so many opportunities to flush the man out had been squandered. As he would testify in a secret court session in Australia, 'the evidence that there had been a mole inside MI5 during the 50s and early 60s was overwhelming … [yet] investigations were at best half-hearted'.[35]

As he finished reviewing the old files, Wright totted up the list of leads suggesting Soviet penetration. Volkov, Gouzenko, Petrov, Tisler, Goleniewski and Golitsyn: all had warned of a traitor – or traitors – betraying the Security Service from within. Yet none of their revelations, nor the defections of Burgess and Maclean, had led to a thorough investigation.

This was, he concluded, the prime reason for 'the enormous number of operations that went wrong [because] the fact is that from 1951 to 1958 MI5 had no success against the Russians'.[36]

But, as 1962 drew to a close, if Peter Wright was convinced that Soviet spies had penetrated the upper reaches of British intelligence, the Security Service's officer-class management viewed both him and Martin as 'mere NCOs' in its hierarchy[37] – lesser mortals whose opinions were of limited importance; and he remained no closer to discovering who the mole, or moles, might be.

Within a month the masters of Leconfield House would finally be dragged from their torpor and forced to acknowledge they had a problem – and Peter Wright would alight on his first prime suspect.

4. 1963

'Following Philby's defection, effort was stepped up, but senior management were always determined to limit the scope of any inquiries.'
PETER WRIGHT AFFIDAVIT: CONFIDENTIAL
MATERIAL, NOVEMBER 1986

For Britain, the winter at the beginning of 1963 would be the worst in living memory. For MI5, it was the year that 'the roof fell in'.[1]

In the dying days of December 1962 an Arctic blizzard swept across Britain, dumping twenty feet of snow across swathes of southern England; on New Year's Day temperatures dropped to minus two degrees Celsius, seas froze and the upper reaches of the Thames turned to thick ice. For weeks, power cuts plagued the electricity grid, and with underground pipes solidifying or bursting, for the first time since the Blitz families were forced to queue for water from bowsers in the streets.

The deepening Cold War matched the meteorological gloom. Three months earlier, the Cuban Missile Crisis had threatened to bring about nuclear war between America and the Soviet Union; for thirteen days the world held its breath, before both sides backed off. But within Leconfield House, senior MI5 officers knew a new bomb was about to devastate British intelligence.

In August 1962 an old friend of Kim Philby approached Victor Rothschild, one of the Security Service's most celebrated wartime alumni, to report – somewhat belatedly – her knowledge of Philby's treachery. Flora Solomon, a Russian-born Zionist and social welfare pioneer, confided that she had known for 25 years that Philby was a Soviet agent.

Rothschild persuaded her to tell her story to Arthur Martin and offered the use of his London flat for the meeting; Peter Wright was instructed to install covert recording equipment, and he listened in to Solomon's tale. She told Martin, with some reluctance, that before the Second World War, Philby told her he was working for the Comintern – the Soviet-controlled international organisation which promoted world communism and acted as an intelligence conduit for Moscow – and had asked her 'to join the cause'. She had refused.

Although Solomon insisted she would never testify publicly, and Wright thought her 'a strange, rather untrustworthy woman',[2] the information convinced MI5 that Philby should face a new interrogation; for the rest of the year Wright, Martin and a small team of specialists pored over the transcripts of her interview and planned the proposed confrontation. Martin was chosen to lead the questioning and prepared to fly to Beirut, but at the beginning of January, MI6 insisted that one of its officers – Nicholas Elliott, an old and close friend of the suspected Soviet spy – should take his place.

Armed with an offer of immunity and the hope of securing a confession, Elliott arrived in Lebanon to find his man falling-down drunk. At the end of a lengthy and sometimes heated conversation, Philby finally offered up a partial admission: he had, he confessed, worked for Russian intelligence from 1934 to 1946 – but he had then seen the error of his ways and, aside from helping Donald Maclean to defect, had not had any contact with Moscow's spymasters since shortly after the end of the Second World War.

Elliott returned to London in triumph and told both British intelligence services that Philby was ready to come in out of the cold. A final interrogation was tentatively set for the end of the month, at which MI5 believed the case would finally be closed. On 18 January, Director General Roger Hollis wrote a reassuring letter to his opposite number in Washington DC. 'In our judgment,' he told FBI Director J. Edgar Hoover, '[Philby's] statement of the association with the RIS [Russian Intelligence Service] is substantially true. It accords with all the available evidence in our possession and we have no evidence pointing to a continuation of his activities on behalf of the RIS after 1946, save in the isolated instance of Maclean. If this is so, it follows that damage to the United States interests will have been confined to the period of the Second World War.'[3]

Five days later, Kim Philby vanished from Beirut; by early spring British intelligence confirmed he was in Moscow. The 'Third Man' had made fools of his old friend in MI6 and the head of MI5, and a liar of the Prime Minister, who had exonerated him in Parliament eight years earlier.

1963

By then, Harold Macmillan's Conservative government was entering its fag-end days, with the Labour Party widely expected to win the general election the following year. The prospect of new 'socialist' masters was not viewed with enthusiasm in Leconfield House, an unease made worse when Labour's right-leaning leader, Hugh Gaitskell, died suddenly after returning from talks inside the Kremlin. MI5 was immediately suspicious, and when Harold Wilson, a self-proclaimed 'man of the people' perceived to be on the party's left flank, succeeded Gaitskell, those qualms solidified into fears of a Russian plot aimed at British democracy.

In truth, the Conservative government was managing to undermine the country and its security without much international help. As news of the Philby fiasco broke, both Downing Street and Roger Hollis knew yet another intelligence scandal was about to emerge. For almost two years John Profumo, Secretary of State for War, had been involved in an extramarital affair with a nineteen-year-old 'model' and 'showgirl' named Christine Keeler. Among her other, and simultaneous, conquests was Captain Yevgeny Ivanov; he held the official diplomatic post of Naval Attaché at the Soviet Embassy, but MI5 knew his real job was as the GRU's senior man in London, making Profumo a party – witting or otherwise – to a sex-and-spying love triangle.

Worse, once alerted, the Security Service managed to entangle itself in an ill-considered plan to persuade Ivanov to defect. The scheme failed in spectacular fashion: Ivanov was recalled to Moscow and Profumo's sordid involvement with a 'good time girl' and a known spy emerged in sensational court cases involving two of her other lovers. As the saga dominated newspaper headlines – and further strained the fraying trust of US intelligence agencies – the last thing either Macmillan or Hollis needed was further espionage scandal. Unhappily for both, they were about to be confronted by the most serious and damaging evidence yet of Soviet penetration.

In the wake of Philby's unmasking, Peter Wright returned to the old files, in search of evidence to support Golitsyn's belief in a Fourth – and possibly Fifth – Man. But he encountered an unexpected and unwavering resistance to his investigations from inside Leconfield House.

'Following Philby's defection,' Wright later testified in a secret court session, 'effort was stepped up, but senior management were always determined to limit the scope of any inquiries ... There were specific instructions from the DG of the day that we were not to take any action that might make the person being investigated defect or cause any other form of political scandal. I had to get the DG's permission before taking any such action and in Hollis' day such permission was nearly always refused.'4

Nonetheless, when Philby's wife, Eleanor, returned to Britain she was extensively debriefed about their life in Beirut. During the interviews she revealed a small detail which pointed, once again, to the existence of mole inside MI5: Philby had become very nervous in mid-1962 and had begun drinking very heavily.

The timing seemed very specific, and Wright asked his contacts in the CIA to comb their databases for records of unusual movements, anywhere in the world, by any known Soviet intelligence officers in that period. Very quickly, the analysts at Langley threw up a name – Yuri Modin, a KGB officer who had previously been suspected as the fixer for the Burgess and Maclean escapes. Modin had not travelled outside the USSR for almost a year when, in September 1962, he unexpectedly arrived in the Middle East; at the same time, Philby cut short a family holiday in Jordan and rushed back to Lebanon.

His suspicions now thoroughly heightened, Wright compared this with the date of Flora Solomon's crucial revelations and reached a firm conclusion: 'it seemed obvious ... that Modin had gone to Beirut to alert Philby to the re-opening of his case'.5

This posed an uncomfortable question: how could a senior KGB handler in Moscow have known about MI5's plans? The apparent answer, as a later Security Service report dolefully recorded, was treachery.

> It was inferred therefore that he had received warning from someone in the Security Service that [Philby] was again under investigation and that he would probably be interviewed. At the relevant time this proposal was known to only five senior officers in the Security Service.
>
> Only two of these had long enough service and good enough access to information to fit the earlier indications of penetration. They were the Director General (Sir Roger Hollis) and his Deputy (Mr. G.R. Mitchell).6

It was an incendiary and unprecedented conclusion: never before had the two most senior officers in MI5 – men who had been in the Service for decades and who were privy to all major British and American intelligence secrets – been suspected as Russian spies. If true, it meant that the Kremlin had enjoyed uninterrupted access to almost every espionage and counter-espionage operation mounted against the

Soviet Union by London and Washington before, during and since the Second World War.

But to Wright and to Arthur Martin it made sense; it explained the miserable succession of intelligence failures over several decades. The only question in their minds was which of their bosses was the mole.

From the outset, both men favoured Graham Mitchell. In Wright's view, he had 'a secretiveness about him ... a clever man, clever enough to spy'.[7] Martin felt largely the same, but based on his experience of Hollis' previous, hostile reactions to reports of suspected Soviet penetration, was willing to believe the Director General himself might be the traitor. 'I found his complacency towards the threat of Russian espionage ... inexplicable to me and to many of my colleagues,' he later told a supportive espionage writer.[8]

But the biggest problem was how to investigate – let alone prove – their thesis. Any in-depth inquiry into such senior Security Service officers would have to be signed off at the very top – impossible, since both the DG and his deputy would themselves be the targets of the investigation.

Martin found a workaround solution to this dilemma. In spring 1963 he turned to Hollis' predecessor as MI5 Director General. Sir Dick White was universally respected as 'a brilliant, intuitive intelligence officer'[9] who had joined the Security Service in 1936, had helped create the Double Cross system of turning German agents during the war, and after three years as head of the Service had been lured away to take charge of MI6. Martin laid out the evidence and asked for White's guidance.

It arrived 24 hours later. The head of MI6 authorised the section head of MI5's counterintelligence branch to open a formal investigation into the Service's two most senior leaders. The only caveats were that Mitchell was not to be told he was under suspicion, and that while Hollis was to be advised of the need to place his deputy under surveillance, he was to be kept completely in the dark about his own position in the crosshairs.

Other than Hollis' superior rank, there was some, albeit scanty, reason to start with Mitchell: as MI5's subsequent internal – and top-secret – report noted, the Deputy Director General had once held 'socialist views'.[10] In what Wright called 'the tense and hysterical months of 1963, as the scent of treachery lingered in every corridor',[11] any hint of old left-wing sympathies was enough to justify suspicion.

At the close of business on 7 March, Martin made his way up to the Director General's office and for half an hour laid out the evidence, such as it was. Hollis' reaction was, under the circumstances, unexpectedly calm. According to Martin's own account, filed away in the Service's archives:

> Throughout the telling, the DG interrupted hardly at all. He sat hunched up at his desk, his face drained of colour and with a strange half-smile playing on his lips …
>
> I had expected that my theory would at least be challenged but it received no comment other than that I had been right to voice it and that he would think it over. With that he invited me to dinner at his club.[12]

Supper, at the exclusive Travellers Club in Pall Mall, proved to be equally frustrating. The DG resolutely avoided discussion of the problem and Martin realised that his boss wanted to 'get rid of me as quickly as possible'. Only as they stood in the street while an official car was summoned was the subject finally raised; Hollis promised to respond within a few days, and dismissed his head of Soviet counter-espionage with the strict admonition not to speak to anyone else.

Five days later Martin was summoned to Hollis' home and authorised to delve discreetly into Mitchell's background; he was to report his findings to his immediate line manager, Director of D Branch Martin Furnival Jones. A new case file was opened in the most restricted section of MI5's registry, bearing the codename now assigned to the Deputy Director General: PETERS.

In little more than a month Martin assembled enough prima facie evidence to justify expanding the investigation. In mid-May a second officer was 'indoctrinated' into the secret inquiry: Peter Wright became, for the first time, an authorised spycatcher.

As the pair worked and reworked the troublesome 'serials', Wright took a private, personal pledge: for too long the leads pointing at Soviet penetration had been ignored or brushed under the Leconfield House carpets. 'This time,' he vowed, 'there will be no tip-offs, no defections. This one will not slip away.'[13]

It was a fine hope, but one that was almost strangled at birth. He knew that to stand any chance of proving Mitchell's guilt, all of MI5's Special Facilities and surveillance expertise would have to be brought to bear; but although Mitchell's office was searched and he was covertly followed for a small part of his journey from the office to his house, Hollis resolutely refused all requests to sanction a tap on his home phone or to permit full surveillance by A1's team of dedicated 'watchers'. Martin became increasingly frustrated, and in an angry confrontation threatened to take his complaints about this half-hearted approach directly to the Prime Minister.

Remarkably, Hollis had taken the decision to keep Macmillan – a man who loathed espionage and its incessant scandals – in the dark about the most serious suspected penetration in the history of the Security Service. Martin's impassioned threat was thus both a direct challenge to his authority and the chain of command, and would inevitably plunge the already-tottering government into further crisis.

For the second time in two months Dick White was called in to defuse the escalating row. He summoned Martin, Wright and Furnival Jones – now fully signed up to the case against Mitchell – to afternoon tea in his flat behind MI6 headquarters on Broadway. On the study floor Wright laid out charts and tables highlighting all the operations which had failed, and the evidence pointing at betrayal from within. By early evening the SIS chief had seen enough: he promised to provide a discreet MI6 operational apartment in Chelsea, inserting much-needed distance between the investigators and Leconfield House, and to put pressure on Hollis to end the obstruction.

At the start of June the investigative team doubled in size and Hollis finally sought Home Office warrants to tap Mitchell's home and office phones. He also made the trek to Downing Street to brief the Prime Minister about the PETERS investigation: it did not go well. Macmillan, who already held a poor opinion of the Director General, was appalled.

But with the internal logjam broken, Wright and Martin were given a free hand to operate. Wright installed a closed-circuit television system behind the mirror in Mitchell's MI5 office and, with Hollis' agreement, fed barium meals of intelligence to his target. These excerpts from British intelligence analyses of Soviet radio communications were calculated to be too tempting for a paid-up traitor to overlook. If Mitchell was the mole, he would be sure to alert Moscow.

But the Deputy Director General showed scant interest in the material, and the covert monitoring of his office initially revealed very little that could be construed as incriminating. True, the man had an odd habit of mumbling to himself when alone at his desk, but the still-limited technical capabilities of MI5's hidden microphones meant that it was impossible to be sure what, exactly, he was saying. In late August the recordings of his musings following his digestion of a new barium meal about a projected operation against GRU officers highlighted the problem: one transcriber came up with a version in which Mitchell had mumbled 'I must tell Yuri that they are …', while a second produced a version in which he had said merely 'I am most terribly curious if they are …'.[14] It was a very long way from damning evidence.

To Peter Wright, the investigation was proving to be a wretched business: sitting in the dark, watching the screen like a Peeping Tom and waiting in vain for the suspect to betray himself. Only once did Operation PETERS seem to bear fruit. One Friday evening Mitchell spent fully twenty minutes referring to a page of notes and drawing on a scrap of paper. He then abruptly ripped the sheet into small pieces and threw them into the waste bin beside his desk, before heading home for the night. Wright slipped into the DDG's office, retrieved and reassembled the fragments: they clearly formed a hand-drawn map of Chobham Common – close to Mitchell's house – with a series of arrows pointing to and from a central point marked 'RV', and with symbols representing two cars at either end of the path leading towards it.

For almost a week, teams of watchers kept the Common under observation, but neither Mitchell nor anyone else ever approached the presumed rendezvous point. The surveillance was abandoned.

Time was now a major issue. For reasons never explained, Mitchell had requested early retirement from the Security Service; Hollis acquiesced and the date for the DDG's departure was set for September. Faced with this looming deadline, the investigators became less focused on keeping their operation secret and, inevitably, Mitchell realised he was under suspicion. He began to take evasive action to lose his A Branch shadows, and the CCTV monitoring showed clearly that he was under extreme stress. Wright's recorders captured him alone in his office, groaning miserably and mumbling: 'Why are they doing this to me ?'[15]

On these shaky foundations the PETERS team concluded that Mitchell was probably guilty. But, as Martin noted in an internal report, 'we would not be able to produce evidence sufficient for a prosecution except by successful interrogation'. Since the Security Service would have no legal means to compel their target's attendance once he had left office, Martin demanded that Hollis sanction a hostile interview before the imminent retirement. For good measure, he insisted that both the FBI and the CIA should immediately be warned about the crisis.

Hollis flatly refused both pleas. He told Wright that he had sought prime-ministerial permission to haul Mitchell in for interrogation, but that – with the possibility of yet another defection uppermost in governmental minds – Macmillan had refused. In mid-September Mitchell quietly left his office for the final time, and retired to Surrey on a generous and untouchable pension.

The PETERS team was furious. Throughout that summer it had produced two reports on its investigation: both had reached the same uncomfortable verdict. As a subsequent top-secret briefing for Downing Street ruefully noted: 'Each report concluded, the second perhaps rather less confidently than the first, that he [Mitchell] might be a spy.'[16]

Wright was convinced that the investigation had been deliberately hobbled by Hollis. 'He obstructed it where he could,' he later recalled in a televised interview. 'We could not put phone taps on Mitchell at home, we could not follow Mitchell beyond the London railway station and at the end, he [Hollis] would not allow us to interrogate him [Mitchell].' And yet, as Wright saw it, had the PETERS team been given its head, the investigation might well have concluded that the Deputy Director General was not the long-sought mole – which made Hollis' behaviour even less explicable.

The game of counterintelligence is, essentially, an endless Rorschach test. Faced with the inkblot patterns of fragmentary information, interpretation is entirely subjective: what may appear as a clear picture of betrayal and penetration to one officer can – and frequently does – strike another as no more than a snapshot of random coincidences. Personal experience, prejudice and political leanings are the primary determinants of which image is seen.

Peter Wright, self-taught, self-confident and with an understandable distrust of the intelligence hierarchy, looked at the failure of the PETERS investigation and saw a conspiracy at work – one with Roger Hollis at its heart. He concluded that the DG 'was anxious that Mitchell should not be found innocent because he was the next suspect'.[17]

With the molehunt in apparent limbo, the turmoil inside Leconfield House swiftly tipped over into outright mutiny. Wright, Martin and the two other members of the team confronted Hollis at a heated Saturday morning summit; each threatened to resign unless both American intelligence agencies were told of the crisis. It was, after all, just eight months since the Director General had blithely assured J. Edgar Hoover that the breach of British and American security had been 'confined to the period of the Second World War'. Plainly, that could no longer be true.

Backed into a corner, Hollis relented. At the end of September he and Arthur Martin flew to Washington to brief the CIA and the FBI about the 'implications for certain American intelligence sources who, if Mitchell was a spy, must be considered either compromised or provocateurs'.[18]

The admission was met with anger and incredulity. 'The Americans,' Peter Wright recalled, 'simply failed to understand how a case could be left in such an inconclusive state.'[19] With the Burgess, Maclean and Philby defections still open wounds in the transatlantic relationship, both the Agency and the Bureau viewed the PETERS debacle as further evidence of British incompetence – or worse. Martin did his best to limit the damage, promising that – retirement notwithstanding – Mitchell would be summoned for an imminent and thorough interrogation.

No such interview was convened. Instead, Hollis ordered the drafting of a new report on the case – the third in less than six months; the officer handed this unwelcome task was given strict orders not to speak, much less consult with either Martin or Wright, and another cog in the wheel of the suspected conspiracy clicked into place inside the investigators' minds.

But as MI5's *annus horribilis* drew to a close, the agonising and unresolved PETERS investigation was about to be eclipsed by a new and even greater scandal – one that revealed Soviet penetration of not just the Security Service, but the very foundations of the British Establishment: industry, science, the Civil Service, the British government and the Royal Family.

5. CONFESSIONS

'The whole principle of the Russian attack is to get people when they are very young and build them up.'
PETER WRIGHT AFFIDAVIT, NOVEMBER 1986

Michael Whitney Straight was a poster boy for America's gilded generation. Born in 1916 into a wealthy and powerful Long Island family – his mother was a millionaire and his grandparents included a former Secretary of the Navy and the daughter of a US Senator – Straight was educated at the elite English public school Dartington Hall in Devon, and as a young man enjoyed all the privileges his wealth bestowed.

When he left school in the summer of 1934 he travelled to South Africa to take part as an amateur racing driver in the country's grand prix; he finished a respectable third. That autumn he 'went up' – in the contemporary argot of the upper classes – to Trinity College, Cambridge, to study economics, and became the first American to be elected president of the university's celebrated Union. He graduated three years later and returned to the United States where, with the assistance of First Lady Eleanor Roosevelt, he secured a position with the Department of State as a speechwriter for President Franklin D. Roosevelt. Other more senior federal government jobs followed until, in 1941, he resigned to work as a journalist for *The New Republic*, a liberal magazine owned by the Straight family.

Two years later he joined the US Army Air Corps (Reserve); he never served overseas or saw any combat during the war, but left the military in 1945 with a spotless record and the rank of second lieutenant. He returned to the magazine as its publisher and earned himself a sizeable reputation as an author, patron of the arts and philanthropist.

Urbane, talented – he was fluent in French, German and Russian – wealthy and a respected pillar of American society, there was only one small blemish on Michael Straight's illustrious escutcheon: he was – or at least had been – a Soviet spy. And in June 1963 he confessed.[1]

He did not do so with any great enthusiasm. The White House was considering him for a new government appointment, and Attorney General Robert F. Kennedy sent his file over to the FBI for background checks. Realising that these would almost certainly reveal his association with Moscow's spymasters during the 1930s and 1940s, Straight belatedly came clean – and for the first time exposed the depth of Soviet penetration of Cambridge University in the years before the Second World War.

The Bureau's report of his confession recorded that in his second year at Trinity College, Straight had joined a student communist group; its 25 members 'did not carry Communist Party cards, or pay regular Party dues, and were not formally associated with the British Communist Party ... they did contribute to the Party and its front organizations, and participated in its demonstrations'.

But this was merely the nursery slope for more serious pro-Soviet activity. The next level was admission to the 'secret "Conversazione Society" (The Apostles) ... similar in character to a secret fraternity in the United States'.[2]

The cloisters of Cambridge had fascinated and worried MI5 in equal measure since the Burgess, Maclean and Philby scandals. The Apostles Society was – and remains – a genuine organisation for intellectual discussion, founded in 1820 and which boasted a starry register of eminent nineteenth- and twentieth-century thinkers, including Alfred Tennyson, the future Conservative Prime Minister Stanley Baldwin and John Maynard Keynes, architect of much of Britain's post-war economic direction. None were notably left-wing, but Guy Burgess had also been inducted to its ranks and both Arthur Martin and Peter Wright suspected he had been part of an inner core of covert communist agents within it.

The defector Anatoliy Golitsyn had prompted much of that concern. For more than a year he had warned British intelligence that the three seismic defections of the past decade were the tip of a larger espionage iceberg at Cambridge. As an internal Security Service report prepared – reluctantly – for the Home Secretary later noted:

[He] stated that in the 1930s there was a very important spy network in the United Kingdom called the Ring of Five because it originally had five members all of whom knew each other and had been at University together. He knew that Burgess and Maclean were members of the ring. He thought that the network had expanded beyond the original five.[3]

Philby was clearly the Third Man, but until that summer the identities of the rest of the Ring – and what they had been doing for the Kremlin – had remained frustratingly hard to discover. Now Michael Straight's confession began to lift the veil and to name names.

The list he gave the FBI of members in the first, pre-Apostles crowd was shocking enough. 'Straight said the group was headed by ... James Klugmann, a brilliant student and dedicated Communist, who later served the British Government during World War II ... and Brian Simon ... son of Sir Ernest Simon, Governor of the British Broadcasting Company [sic].'[4]

The Bureau's description hardly did justice to the sensitivity of Klugmann's wartime role. Despite making no secret of his political loyalties, he had slipped past security vetting checks and in 1942 had joined SOE – Winston Churchill's 'secret army' of espionage and sabotage agents working in German-occupied territory. On the basis 'very largely of his Colonel's opinion of him, he was immediately cleared for Intelligence duties ... doing most secret work'.[5]

The fact that this fiasco had been noted in his Security Service file without any substantial action being taken – at the end of the war Klugmann was seconded to the United Nations – reinforced the growing doubts about MI5's willingness to root out communists with access to top-secret intelligence.

Nor did the post-university career of Brian Simon – the son of a peer of the realm – make for comfortable reading. After Cambridge, he had moved into education and been appointed to a Labour Party advisory committee, before joining the Royal Corps of Signals at the outbreak of war; he was duly attached to the GHQ Liaison Regiment, then tasked with signals deception operations against German forces.

But it was the identities of the more covert Cambridge communists – and their membership of the Apostles – which was most alarming. The FBI's primary interest was in the handful of American nationals who had passed through the Soviet intelligence grooming network, but Michael Straight made clear he had a substantial list of young, privileged English students seduced by Moscow's spymasters who had then effortlessly made their way into MI5, the scientific and defence industries, and the very heart of the British Establishment itself.

Guy Burgess – 'a drunkard [and] a notorious and promiscuous homosexual' – had been a flamboyant fixture, but the recruiter of these youthful converts was a more cautious figure: an outwardly respectable academic and fine art expert, whose subsequent career encompassed the Security Service, the rarified world of Old Masters – and the British Royal Family. His name was Anthony Frederick Blunt, and his role as the spider at the heart of the Cambridge Ring would haunt MI5 for decades to come.

According to Straight, in summer 1937 Blunt – then a professor of modern languages – instructed him to abandon his overt activities on behalf of communism in Britain and return home, where he was to infiltrate one of New York's financial titans.

'Blunt said the Third International [the Comintern] wanted a man in Morgan and Company [sic][6] to obtain economic reports and requested Straight to proceed to the United States on this mission.' When Straight objected, on the grounds of preference, not principle – 'he was not cut out to be a banker and was not interested' – Blunt referred the dispute to his own Soviet handler, who promptly overruled the protest; just before he sailed for America, the young spy was given a brisk lesson in espionage tradecraft.

> Blunt indicated he [Straight] would be contacted and requested some token from him for the purpose of identification. He … gave Blunt a small blue ink drawing of his sweetheart … which Blunt tore in half, returning one half to him and retaining the other half.[7]

For the next five years, as he progressed through the White House, Department of State and War Department, Straight had a succession of meetings with his US-based Soviet controller, passing on – by his account, at least – relatively low-level reports and intelligence until he enlisted in the Air Force Reserve.

A less well-connected leaker might have found himself facing prosecution, yet for reasons it never explained – British government documents noted only that 'for internal reasons, this confession was not used to charge Straight'[8] – the FBI gave him a free pass. But his revelations about a large number of hitherto undetected Soviet spies at Cambridge – and especially about Blunt's role in recruiting them – could not so easily be brushed under a Washington rug. After a pause of several months, the Bureau alerted its opposite numbers in Leconfield House, and in January 1964 Arthur Martin once more boarded a plane bound for Washington.

If the emergence of Blunt's name was deeply troubling, it was not exactly a surprise to Martin or his colleagues. Blunt had joined MI5 in 1940 and served throughout the war in the upper reaches of the counter-espionage branch, where he had almost untrammelled access to British

Confessions

intelligence secrets. As an internal Downing Street report later noted, 'he handled reports from agents, from deciphered diplomatic cables and from telephone intercepts ... was engaged in operations against neutrals' diplomatic bags ... had close liaison with the SIS ... was involved in double-agent operations ... handled files on some Russians living in or visiting the United Kingdom ... selected targets for surveillance operations [and] drafted fortnightly reports on the work of all sections in the Service for submission to the Prime Minister'.[9]

Blunt officially left the Security Service in April 1945, returning to the art world as director of the prestigious Courtauld Institute. Despite this ostensible retirement, over the next eighteen months MI5 sent him on at least two subsequent missions to 'resettle' one of its agents in post-war Germany, adventures he combined with assignments on behalf of Buckingham Palace to recover captured 'Royal treasures and documents' from Nazi storage.[10] Whether as reward or by happy coincidence, these operations were swiftly followed by his appointment as Surveyor of the King's Pictures and, a decade later, by a knighthood bestowed by the new Queen.

Yet British intelligence had long possessed evidence that Blunt was a Soviet spy. In 1951, in the wake of the Burgess and Maclean defections, the writer and academic Goronwy Rees – a long-term Marxist and friend of Burgess – told MI5 that in the immediate pre-war years he had discovered Blunt was working for the Comintern. Between then and 1964 the Security Service interrogated its former officer on eleven separate occasions – all of them fruitless. 'He made no admissions of performing any services for the Russians,' its internal report lamented, 'and efforts to obtain, by other means, information which would establish whether [he] ... had acted as a Soviet agent were unsuccessful.'[11]

Michael Straight's confession put paid to this lingering uncertainty and, for the first time, offered the hope of bringing Blunt to justice. When Straight met Martin in the dignified surroundings of Washington's Mayflower Hotel, he made crystal clear that he 'had been recruited by Blunt at Cambridge ... He said he wanted to make amends and that he would be willing to come to England to confront Blunt.'[12]

According to his own later and much longer account, Straight was itching to 'face Blunt ... in a British court'. For good measure, he had, he said, much more to reveal about the youthful spies recruited at Cambridge who had evaded detection ever since.

'I went to MI5 and ... gave them the names of at least 150 people,' he told a Canadian television interviewer in January 1983. 'Of those 150 I would guess that 30 or 40 had been leading the lives of "moles" in

England. That is to say as members of the Labour Party in Parliament, as barristers, as judges, various other people in public life, one or two in the Foreign Office, the Home Office, the Treasury, who've been allowed to retire … I don't know what happened to them. I simply went over with British intelligence the names I could identify and they went on from there …'[13]

Arthur Martin filled his notebook with the damning testimony and a list of potential targets, all of whom he intended to interview about their time – and possible treachery – amid the dreaming spires of Cambridge University. If Straight's account was honest, the implications were grave: just how many youthful students had Blunt recruited – and how had they been able to slip past security checks into the heart of government, politics, the law and British intelligence itself?

The first name on the list of Blunt's recruits exemplified the seriousness of the problem. Between 1934 and 1936, John Cairncross had been an associate of Blunt and Guy Burgess at Trinity College. An undoubtedly brilliant student, after graduating he sat the Civil Service entrance exams, came first in that year's intake and was speedily ushered into the Foreign Office; two years later he was transferred to the Treasury, where he became Private Secretary to Sir Maurice Hankey, the minister with special responsibility for intelligence, who was conducting an urgent inquiry into the organisation and methods of both MI5 and MI6.[14] That led, in 1942, to posts at Bletchley Park code-breaking centre and a year later to the Secret Intelligence Service, where he handled top-secret intelligence reports for the duration of the war.

Peacetime progressed in a similarly smooth fashion. He returned to the Treasury and a position within its defence matériel division, with a side role as Britain's representative on NATO and Western Union finances. In short, for thirteen years John Cairncross had access to some of the country's most sensitive intelligence and military secrets.

The twin defections of 1951 brought his career to an abrupt close. Cairncross's name, address and phone number were discovered in Donald Maclean's office diary, and a search of Guy Burgess's flat unearthed a classified intelligence document; it had been written by Cairncross.

In March 1951 he was interviewed by MI5. He denied knowing that Burgess was a Soviet agent, describing him as no more than 'a casual acquaintance', and offered the somewhat improbable claim that he had casually lent the document to Burgess, who claimed to have accidentally destroyed it.[15] It was hardly a convincing performance, and after an MI6 officer, who had been a fellow communist at Cambridge in the 1930s, identified him as a party member, the Security Service put Cairncross under surveillance. In April 1952 this established that he had scheduled a rendezvous with a known Soviet spy handler; MI5's watchers followed him to the location in London's Gunnersbury Park, but the Russian mysteriously failed to appear.

At a further interrogation, Cairncross gave yet another wildly unconvincing explanation: he said he had gone to the park for a romantic assignation with a secret lover, whose true name and address he, unfortunately, did not know.[16]

The failure of the surveillance operation should have sounded an alarm, since it suggested that the Soviet handler could have been tipped off. Yet somehow, despite Cairncross's catalogue of highly suspicious behaviour, the Director of Public Prosecutions decided no prosecution was 'justified'. The investigation was abandoned and Cairncross was quietly suspended, then allowed to resign the following year.[17] He spent much of the next decade out of the country.

In February 1964, MI5 discovered that Cairncross was about to take up a teaching post at a university in Cleveland, Ohio. It discreetly alerted the FBI and disclosed the sorry saga set out in his personal security files. But it persuaded the Bureau not to block the requisite visa with a promise that the moment Cairncross arrived, Arthur Martin would interrogate him.

On 16 February the spycatcher confronted the spy with Straight's disclosure. What ensued would set the tone for all subsequent investigations into the Cambridge spy rings.

Martin was a wily and careful investigator; he knew Cairncross was a shameless liar who had evaded justice for more than a decade, but he also realised that the man had very little reason to confess. A promise of immunity from prosecution might loosen Cairncross's tongue, but only the Attorney General could authorise it, and Leconfield House had not sought his views on the matter. Instead, as an internal Security Service account recorded, Martin was ordered to dangle a less tangible inducement.

> It was agreed that the officer [Martin] could offer to intercede with the United States authorities if Cairncross was frank, but it was stipulated that he should make no promises to him that he would be allowed to stay in the United States.[18]

The gambit succeeded – at least in part, and for the moment. Reassured that MI5 would plead his case with the FBI, Cairncross admitted spying for Moscow from 1936 to 1951. He was not, as the Security Service sheepishly noted, 'entirely frank' about his espionage activities, leaving it to make the depressing – if vague – assumption 'that Cairncross passed to the Russians everything that came his way'.[19]

In truth, the Security Service never had any intention of keeping its side of the bargain. It knew that under American law Cairncross could not be extradited back to Britain, and hoped that he could be persuaded to return home voluntarily so that his confession could be used against him in London.

It was a surprisingly naïve miscalculation. Not only was his admission unwitnessed by anyone other than Martin – an officer of an organisation which did not officially exist and who had no legal authority to operate anywhere, let alone in a foreign country – but, as subsequent and somewhat huffy post-facto advice from the Attorney General made clear, 'none of the information provided by Cairncross was admissible as evidence ... on the ground that it might be tainted by inducement'. The AG would 'only consider a prosecution if Cairncross made a statement under caution to a police officer'.

On 1 March, Martin was sent back to Cleveland to secure a written confession from his quarry and ask him to come back to Britain so that he could be arrested. Cairncross duly signed a statement in which he admitted spying for Moscow from 1936 to 1951, but unsurprisingly refused to return to London to place himself at the disposal of the Metropolitan Police. Eight days later, with the fear of a torrent of bad publicity uppermost in Whitehall's mind, Prime Minister Harold Macmillan ruled that no further action would be taken. The evidence of Cairncross's treachery was to be discreetly buried; it would remain secret for the next fifteen years.[20]

Despite this setback, Martin flew home with high hopes for the rest of Michael Straight's revelations. His return coincided with an updated report on MI5's internal molehunt, which reversed the previous assumption about Deputy DG Graham Mitchell; this third version was written by case officer Ronnie Symonds, who had been part of the earlier investigations but who – at Hollis' explicit direction – was forbidden to consult his former colleagues for the latest instalment. Symonds's verdict was that 'on present evidence PETERS is more likely to be innocent than guilty'; nonetheless, he recommended that the inquiry should continue, but that 'we should make a determined effort to look for other candidates'.[21]

The burden for both assignments would fall on Martin and the new head of research in MI5's counter-espionage D Branch,[22] Peter Wright. In January he had been promoted and initially tasked with 'the central study of hostile intelligence services' – a remit which was soon expanded to include responsibility for 'the study of the past activities of hostile intelligence services [and] ... the investigation of suspected penetration of the British Intelligence community'.[23]

But the most immediate dilemma was what to do about Sir Anthony Blunt. He had clearly worked energetically on Moscow's behalf – efforts which had evidently resulted in extensive and successful recruitment of Cambridge students. Coupled with Straight's eagerness to testify against his former mentor, it made a criminal prosecution not just desirable but a realistic option. Weighed against this was the equally likely prospect that Blunt would continue to protest his innocence and that court proceedings were, at best, guaranteed to generate an explosion of unwelcome press coverage for yet another intelligence fiasco; at worst they could end in an embarrassing acquittal. Internally, the government snatched for a fig-leaf to justify inaction, arguing that because the US Department of Justice had chosen not to prosecute Straight for his own admitted treachery, his testimony could not be used against Blunt in an English court.

There was no legal basis for this claim. 'The simple fact,' Peter Wright later testified in secret session, 'was that the law officers felt that in a conflict of testimony, a man who was a knight and Surveyor of the Queen's Pictures would be believed.'[24]

Nor did MI5's management want a trial. During meetings inside Leconfield House, the Director General made plain that he was determined at all costs to avoid a new scandal. 'Hollis,' Wright recalled, 'was acutely aware of the damage any public revelation of Blunt's activities might do to MI5, and to the incumbent Conservative Government.'[25]

There was, as it happened, a more persuasive reason to avoid court proceedings. Blunt alone knew who he had recruited, and if charged he would have every incentive to maintain his decades-long silence about their identities. In the end, as a 1979 top secret Security Service case history recorded, 'it was concluded that it was essential to try once more to establish the truth about his role and in particular [about] ... the allegations relating to penetration of British intelligence'.

The only potential key to unlocking Blunt's stubborn resistance was to promise him 'some inducement to confess'. On 15 April, the Deputy Director of Prosecutions 'authorised the [MI5] investigating officers, if they felt it necessary in order to obtain the information, to assure Blunt that there would be no criminal proceedings against him in relation to matters which had occurred 20 or more years ago'.[26]

Eight days later, on the morning of Wednesday 23 April, Arthur Martin arrived at Blunt's elegantly appointed apartment in the Courtauld Institute on Portman Square. He was ushered into a living room decorated with priceless works of art, and got straight down to business. MI5 had unequivocal evidence that Blunt had been a long-term agent and recruiter for Soviet intelligence: would he now come clean and confess?

The answer – initially – was a firm, if polite, no: Blunt insisted that it was all 'pure fantasy' and there could be no such proof since he had never been a spy. Martin then revealed Straight's testimony and, when that produced little more than a faint facial twitch, played his trump card: on behalf of Her Majesty's Government, he promised Blunt 'an absolute assurance that no action would be taken against him if he now told the truth'.[27]

According to Martin's own account in Security Service files, Blunt 'looked at me for fully a minute without speaking. I said that his silence had already told me what I wanted to know. Would he now get the whole thing off his chest? I added that only a week or two ago I had been through a similar scene with John Cairncross who had finally confessed and afterwards thanked me for making him do so.'[28]

Blunt asked for a short break; he wanted, he said, to 'wrestle with my conscience'. After five minutes, and fortified by a large glass of gin, he settled his graceful frame back in an upholstered armchair and agreed to the deal. A date for full interrogations to begin was set for early the following week.

At first Blunt seemed willing to be open and honest about his treachery. He confessed that he had been enlisted by Guy Burgess in the 1930s, that he had been 'a talent spotter' for Soviet intelligence at Cambridge, and that he'd worked for the Kremlin until shortly after he retired from MI5 in 1945. He admitted, though, that he had continued to meet his Russian handler for a further two years and that he had assisted the defection of Burgess and Maclean in 1951.

He was, however, rather less forthcoming about the identities of the spies he had recruited but who remained undetected, and Martin found himself treading a very delicate line. He was determined to prise from Blunt all the names of his fellow traitors, but MI5's management was terrified of pushing too hard. As Peter Wright later recalled, 'we had strict orders … to do nothing that might provoke Blunt to go public … If it had leaked in 1964 that Blunt was a spy and we had let him off, the consequences could well have been disastrous for the Service'.[29] The interrogations descended into a slow game of cat and mouse.

The story of Leo Long proved typical. Long, a working-class student and talented linguist, was converted to the communist cause at Trinity College in the 1930s; a contemporary of Straight and Cairncross, and a member of the Apostles, Blunt duly recruited him as an agent for the Comintern.

Confessions

In December 1940, Long joined MI14, the War Office department collecting intelligence about German military strength and actions; in the course of his work he saw reports from agents working undercover in Europe and intercepts of *Wehrmacht* communications. At a succession of fortnightly meetings in London pubs, he gave Blunt verbal reports on all the papers he had handled, for onward transmission to Moscow.

He knew that this was, by any standard, espionage. 'I was aware that what I was doing was illegal,' he recalled in a later television interview, 'but ... I perhaps had the arrogance to assume – quite wrongly – that I was a better judge of the national interest than other people.'[30]

Nor did Leo Long's top-secret career finish in 1945. At the end of the war he held the rank of major general, and until 1952 served as deputy head of intelligence for the Control Commission – the military-cum-political body which ran every aspect of life and security in the British zone of Germany. When that ended he was recommended by Blunt for a position with MI5, but narrowly failed to pass the entrance interview. He left public service for a comfortable job in private industry, hoping that his previous espionage would remain undetected.

It might well have stayed secret had Michael Straight not told the FBI that Long was one of Blunt's youthful recruits. As Blunt's post-immunity interrogations – all predicated on full and honest disclosure – continued, Arthur Martin waited for him to cough up Long's name: it was not forthcoming. Finally, at their third interview, Martin dragged it out of his reluctant interviewee. Long was duly summoned for interrogation.

Exactly what transpired at his first interview, in early summer, is remarkably unclear, since most of Long's files remain classified.[31] The official account, given to Parliament fifteen years later, records that when Long 'asked for immunity from prosecution, this was refused; but he was told that he was not likely to be prosecuted if he co-operated in the Security Service's inquiries. He then made a detailed confession.'[32] Long's own version was that immunity was never mentioned – either by him or by his MI5 interrogators, Arthur Martin and Peter Wright.

'I made a full statement of my activities – they were quite satisfied,' he told the BBC. 'I wasn't asked to sign a confession ... It was not an interview with the police or Special Branch; there was no caution or warning [about possible prosecution] given to me. It was, in the way that these things are done, "you are going to cooperate and tell us everything you know".

'I didn't leave that interview thinking that I would be prosecuted. My impression was that [they] were concerned with completing their intelligence picture, possibly following up any other leads that they could ...

It was also in my mind that Sir Anthony Blunt was very much a member of the establishment and that it seemed very unlikely they were going to bring him into the court [and] I thought if they're not going to prosecute Blunt, they're not going to prosecute Long who was a mere creature of Blunt. I suppose I was lucky ...'[33]

Leo Long owed his good fortune to the determination of Macmillan's government to avoid any further spy scandals, and to MI5's fear of public exposure – or worse. Hollis, still grappling with the implications of the abortive investigation into his deputy, was anxious to prevent news of yet another skeleton in the Security Service closets from reaching American intelligence.

But a storm was slowly brewing behind the closed doors of Leconfield House. Three golden opportunities to bring admitted Soviet spies to justice had been spurned, and Martin was becoming increasingly angry at what he perceived to be obstruction. Wright, now one of the leaders of a group of disaffected officers – 'Young Turks', as MI5's senior management dismissively termed them – saw where the problem lay.

'[Roger] Hollis' attitude was quite simple,' he later recalled. 'Blunt, Long, and Cairncross tied up some useful loose ends, the Mitchell case fell, and everything was neatly resolved. He wanted to close the case and minute the file that the question of penetration had been dismissed.'[34]

In November the simmering discontent finally erupted in a full-blown row. Hollis summoned Martin for a formal dressing down: the Director General told his most senior counter-espionage investigator he was 'at the centre of all the unrest in the office' and that MI5's management had resolved to get rid of him. The original plan had been to fire him outright but, in an attempt at some form of olive branch, Martin was instead to be transferred to MI6.

When Martin left Leconfield House in December, responsibility for leading all the inquiries into Soviet penetration was passed to Peter Wright. With the PETERS case still painfully crawling along, his most urgent task was to turn the screws on Anthony Blunt. It was an assignment that would last eight long and frustrating years, and would convince MI5's new chief molehunter that a determined cover-up was protecting traitors inside the British Establishment – and within the Security Service itself.

6. BLUNT

'Blunt only provided information against his former colleagues in espionage who were safe, i.e. out of the country or at least no longer in sensitive jobs.'
PETER WRIGHT AFFIDAVIT: CONFIDENTIAL
MATERIAL, NOVEMBER 1986

The man was everything Peter Wright despised. An effete and active homosexual – Blunt frequented public toilets and public 'cruising grounds' at a time when gay sex was illegal and less-favoured men were routinely punished by two years' hard labour – he was protected from exposure and disgrace by his intellect and his connections.

He had also enjoyed all the educational and establishment privileges that had been denied to Wright: public school years at Marlborough were followed by an easy passage into the comforts of Cambridge during the university's glamorous interwar years, and then recruitment to the inner *sancta* of the Security Service. To have betrayed the country which had gifted him such a golden ticket was incomprehensible to MI5's determined – and ultra-patriotic – spycatcher.

That Blunt had powerful friends was made emphatically clear from the outset. Before their first interview, Wright was summoned to Buckingham Palace, where the Queen's Private Secretary, Sir Michael Adeane, was pleased to convey that Her Majesty was 'content' for her appointed art expert to be interrogated, with but one proviso: should Blunt happen to mention a post-war assignment to Germany on behalf of the late King, MI5 was politely – but firmly – requested 'not to pursue this matter', which was not 'strictly ... relevant to considerations of national security'.[1] It would not be the last time Wright found guiderails erected to limit his investigations.

Although the planned interviews with Blunt were clearly vital – the man had been at the centre of the Ring of Five, and a close confidant of Guy Burgess – the Security Service viewed them as merely one part of a much wider and embarrassingly overdue inquiry. As a subsequent Downing Street briefing note emphasised, a large number of people suspected of 'Communist affiliations' had found their way into post-war government positions.

Of this sizeable – but apparently unquantified – number, twenty-seven civil servants lost appeals against their removal from sensitive material – suggesting that within the smoke of suspicion there was evidence of some kind of fire – while ten others resigned and three were summarily sacked. It was of only scant comfort that 'in the vast majority of these cases there was neither suspicion nor evidence of espionage'.

Until Blunt's confession, these skeletons had been locked firmly inside Whitehall's capacious cupboards. But his initial admissions about the extent of Soviet penetration prompted MI5 to re-examine the old case files, and led to an unwelcome realisation.

> It became apparent that our records of student Communism in the 1930s and 1940s were deficient and incomplete. It was therefore decided to mount a major retrospective investigation of ... the student Communist movement from 1929–1945 at the major Universities (primarily Oxford and Cambridge but also London, Bristol, Liverpool, Leeds, Sheffield, Manchester, Southampton, Birmingham and the Scottish Universities).[2]

This substantial undertaking landed on Wright's desk. Over the coming years, he and his staff would probe – in secret and without any reference to the Security Service's notional masters in Downing Street – the records of 8,000 individuals, and interview more than 400 – some several times.

The cloak and dagger approach was a significant hindrance to a thorough investigation, but it followed an emerging pattern within Leconfield House. Roger Hollis had allowed two months to slip by before telling Home Secretary Henry Brooke that Blunt had confessed, and a further three years would pass before MI5 belatedly briefed the Prime Minister.[3] The reason for this coyness, as Wright saw it, was 'a failure of will': terrified of the risk of 'another unsavoury Establishment scandal', MI5's management 'opted for secret enquiries, where overt ones would have been far more productive'.[4]

Blunt

The new interrogations of Blunt encapsulated the problem. If the self-confessed spy was fiercely intelligent and unquestionably charismatic – he spoke five languages fluently and Wright later described him as 'one of the most elegant, charming, and cultivated men I have met'[5] – he was also a cunning and manipulative adversary who had betrayed the Security Service's secrets and knew how to evade its operational techniques.

'Blunt confessed to passing to the Russians everything he saw,' Wright later testified in secret session. '[He] was the D-G's assistant for the first half of the war [and] he had access to almost as much information as the D-G did. One specific item he confessed to handing over was the Special Facility microphone which enabled one to turn an ordinary telephone into a microphone, thus bugging the room it was used in. He told me that he blew it the first day it was used.'[6]

Nor was Blunt embarrassed about this treachery. At the first interview he ensured that the discussion took place well away from the phone, cheerfully telling Wright that the 'SF' would not be able to record what transpired. For several weeks of the most important interrogations MI5 had ever conducted, the spycatcher relied on jotting down as much as he could in a cheap notebook, before eventually arranging for his old colleagues in A Branch to insert a tiny probe microphone through the wall of the adjacent building. Inevitably, this clandestine operation was carried out without any legal authority.[7]

Blunt had every reason to be confident. Guaranteed immunity from prosecution, and secure in the knowledge that everything he admitted would remain a closely guarded secret, he knew that MI5 had a weak hand with few, if any, trump cards to play.

In other circumstances, with other traitors, the interrogation would have been confrontational, but mindful of Hollis' warnings not to do anything which could provoke Blunt to defect – or worse, to make a public denunciation of his former employers – Wright's strategy was to play on Blunt's evident need for understanding.

For a time it worked: every few weeks the two men talked in Blunt's large and exquisitely decorated study, beside the fire and beneath a 300-year-old Poussin masterwork worth half a million pounds. Sometimes they paused for tea and finely cut sandwiches; more frequently they drank steadily throughout – whisky for Wright and gin for Blunt.

Whether or not the drink was responsible for loosening Blunt's tongue – both men had an impressive tolerance for alcohol – Wright later testified that Blunt was initially willing to speak honestly about his efforts on behalf of Soviet intelligence.

He told me that he used to take out of MI5 an attaché case of files twice a week. He told me that he used to meet a Russian in the street, hand over the attaché case and the next morning the Russian would hand back the attaché case having photographed the documents.

Later the Russians panicked and told him that he and Burgess would have to do their own photography, so he and Burgess set out a photographic studio in the Courtauld Institute. They did this for a while and complained to the Russians that they were not getting any sleep, so the Russians were persuaded to go back to the former routine.[8]

But there were limits to this apparent honesty. Blunt refused to accept that he had caused any real damage to the country he notionally served, much less to having caused harm to any British intelligence operative. Wright knew this to be a lie: during the war MI6's chief Soviet agent handler, Colonel Harold Gibson, had run a Russian spy within the heart of the Kremlin.

'This spy, known as Gibby's spy, had handed over to Gibson the minutes of the Politburo for over five years,' Wright later testified in a confidential court session. 'There had never been before or since a spy inside the Kremlin with such incredible access ... This agent was shot following Blunt's betrayal of him.'[9]

When challenged about this Blunt dropped his pose of languid charm and brought the interview to an ill-tempered end; he was not, Wright realised, prepared to acknowledge the effects of his treachery. Nor, it transpired, would he willingly betray the men and women he had recruited and who might yet face legal retribution.

Wright tried to reassure him that there was little likelihood of any of these spies ever facing justice. In a memo reporting one discussion, he wrote:

> I told Blunt ... that I had interviewed a number of people in the Blunt/Burgess circle of the last 35 years. I had not disclosed to any of them that Blunt had confessed and had no intention of doing so ...
>
> I went on to say to Blunt that nobody wanted a scandal. That so far, people identified as spies in this circle had not suffered the due consequences of the law ... speaking personally, as long as we knew who was involved and could contain the situation, I thought it was very unlikely that any action would be taken against anybody ...[10]

But Blunt remained obdurate. As he later wrote in his unpublished memoirs, 'I simply found it unthinkable that I should denounce my friends; and it certainly never occurred to me to do so.'[11]

What had occurred behind the doors of his Mayfair apartment during the Second World War was among the first of Blunt's many red lines. Number 5 Bentinck Street was owned by Victor – later Lord – Rothschild, a close friend from Cambridge University who had been recruited by MI5 during the early days of the 'Phoney War', in the autumn of 1939. The following year, Rothschild advised the Security Service to take Blunt on to its staff, and generously gave him the tenancy of the apartment.

Even by the morally elastic standards of wartime London, the coterie of residents and guests who shuttled in and out of its front door were remarkably liberated; many were also the nucleus of Blunt's 1940s espionage circle.

Rothschild himself did not live there, but his MI5 secretary, lover and subsequent wife, Tess Mayor – another Cambridge alumnus – quickly moved in with Blunt. Before long two other university chums joined the household: Patricia Rawdon-Smith, who worked (variously) in the War Office, Air Ministry and Foreign Office; and Guy Burgess, until recently a serving MI6 officer.

The flat soon became the locus for informal meetings frequently attended by a growing circle of senior civil servants and intelligence officers. Less happily, it simultaneously earned an unsavoury reputation for bed-hopping and partner-swapping.

Promiscuity was far from unusual during the war – impromptu Bacchanalian couplings in nearby St James's Park were frequent, spurred by the fear of imminent death and greatly assisted by the blackout – but the apparent intensity of the antics inside Bentinck Street was rather more ominous. According to a breathless 1956 newspaper account by Goronwy Rees, who had been the first to name Blunt as a spy, Burgess used the flat to satisfy both his espionage and sexual needs: 'It sometimes looked like a disorderly house [brothel] in every sense of the term. For Guy brought men along with whom he was conducting unnatural [sic] love affairs ...'[12]

Nor was this merely salacious tabloid journalism. As a subsequent internal Downing Street report noted, stories abounded of 'the Bentinck Street flat as the scene of drunken orgies (during one of which Maclean was homosexually compromised) and of Communist and sympathetic intellectuals'.[13]

MI5 had turned a blind eye towards this activity – possibly because its own head of counter-espionage, Guy Liddell, was a frequent (if seemingly chaste) visitor. But as the months of Blunt's interrogations ground on, the flat's locus of illicit sex and known spies demanded an urgent re-examination of all the 'Bentinck Street Associates': Wright returned to MI5's old files and carried out new interviews with those who had made previous disclosures.

Goronwy Rees was among the first to be summoned. He had been one of Blunt's earliest recruits, and if he was keen to downplay the importance of what he might have accomplished on Moscow's behalf, he was very willing to identify fellow intellectuals who had also been approached. The names were politically incendiary.

Sir Stuart Hampshire had graduated from Balliol College, Oxford, in 1936 with a first-class degree in 'Greats'[14] and had been elevated to the position of Fellow, teaching philosophy to the university's pre-war students. He had earned a reputation for left-wing views and had travelled throughout Europe with Burgess. In 1940 he had been commissioned as a military intelligence officer and had joined the elite team who broke German codes, laying the foundations for MI5's counter-espionage Double Cross System; after work he had been a frequent visitor to Blunt and Burgess's Bentinck Street flat. At the end of the war he joined the Foreign Office, before returning to academia and a distinguished career at Oxford and Princeton.

In his new interview, Rees was adamant that Burgess had once made an attempt to recruit Hampshire as an agent for Soviet intelligence. If that snippet of pre-war history was troubling enough, Harold Wilson's new Labour government had recently asked Hampshire to carry out a top-secret inquiry into the future of GCHQ and American demands that it should pay some of the costs of satellite-based espionage. The analysis was planned to last a full year and would involve access to highly sensitive British and US signals espionage techniques.

Wright was appalled to discover that despite their acknowledged association, after Burgess's defection no one had troubled to speak with Hampshire about his former friend – much less subject him to any form of security vetting. Nor was the Security Service management willing to remedy the oversight: MI5's spycatcher was told that for as long as he led Downing Street's inquiry into GCHQ, Hampshire was strictly off-limits.

Frustrated, Wright contented himself with interviewing both men's old university colleagues; according to a file note in 1965, one of Burgess's contacts – his name has been deleted – said that 'it would not surprise [Redacted] if it was discovered that Hampshire had been recruited by Burgess pre-war'.[15]

It was a flimsy scrap of unverified suspicion, but when Wright was finally permitted to interview Hampshire, the academic admitted that Burgess had, indeed, made an approach, suggesting during a drink-fuelled supper that he should sign up and 'work for world peace'. If, by his own account, nothing had come of this, the fact that Hampshire had never reported the attempted recruitment – even after Burgess's defection – was disturbing.

When Wright confronted Blunt with this evidence, Blunt was anxious to downplay its significance, blandly asserting: 'I shouldn't have thought that Stuart [Hampshire] was interested – he's politically conscious ... but I shouldn't have thought that he was involved in the game of politics in any way that would have been useful to Guy at all.'[16]

MI5 seemed as anxious as Blunt not to disturb the old skeletons. When he reported his concerns to his masters at Leconfield House, Wright was told to drop any further investigations. The Director General was, as Wright later wrote, 'desperately embarrassed' and fearful of the potential for yet more scandal to reach the ears of US intelligence: 'the Hampshire case was carefully buried forever'.[17]

This was not an isolated interment. In his interviews with the Security Service, Michael Straight had named Patricia Rawdon-Smith as one of Blunt's likely recruits. According to a later memo in Downing Street's files he identified her as someone 'who might have been [a] mole'.[18] She had lived in the flat until 1943, when she married Richard Llewelyn-Davies, a former member of the Apostles at Cambridge.

The couple had both gone on to glittering political careers: in January 1964, Richard had been ennobled as Baron Llewelyn-Davies; Pat would join him in the House of Lords three years later, and serve as the Labour government's chief whip there until 1979. Yet there is no record of any investigation into Straight's allegation in any prime-ministerial or MI5 file: as with Stuart Hampshire, Wright's inquiries were blocked.

Nor did he fare much better with the next name on the list of Blunt and Burgess's suspicious visitors at Bentinck Street. David Footman was a distinguished veteran of the First World War – he was awarded the Military Cross for 'exemplary gallantry' – a published novelist and a well-regarded expert on Soviet communism.

In the interwar years he studied at Oxford University, where he was remembered as notably 'pro-Communist'. Despite this, in 1935 he was recruited to MI6 and quickly became head of its section seeking out political intelligence across Europe; a year later he recruited Burgess to ferret out communist activity in the media – an unfortunate instance of handing a fox the keys to the hen house.

During the Second World War, Footman became SIS's chief of counter-intelligence for southwest Europe and earned a reputation supporting the communist Yugoslavian resistance leader – and later Marxist president – Josip Broz Tito. After the war, he returned to academia at St Anthony's College, Oxford; here, in addition to his association with Burgess, he maintained a close friendship with Kim Philby.

Wright sought out two of Footman's closest friends – Goronwy Rees and his wife, Margaret – and pumped them for information. Their advice was unequivocal. 'Guy used to praise [him] as the most extraordinary and remarkable man,' Rees told Wright in March 1965. 'And all these people whom Guy referred to in those terms, I would have regarded as being worth investigating – David especially because ... he was a member of the Security Service [sic] and continued to be a great friend of Guy's – and was part of this extraordinary little group that used to meet [at Bentinck Street] every Monday night ...'[19]

Wright's account of this interview, entered in MI5's registry, recorded Rees stressing 'that he had always considered David Footman to be a much more important spy than Philby'; for her part, Margaret described Footman as 'probably their closest friend' but insisted both she and her husband were convinced that he had been very deeply involved [in spying for Moscow] and might still be.'[20]

The Reeses were not alone in their suspicions. In the early autumn, Wright interviewed another (unidentified) former intelligence officer, who said that 'Footman's Yugoslav record, together with his close association with Burgess and Philby, plus his Marxist views must surely ditch him. He said he felt that Footman must have been involved.'[21]

Unsurprisingly, Wright applied for a Home Office warrant to tap Footman's home telephone. The heading on the resulting report is revealing: 'David Footman, Suspected former R.I.S. [Russian Intelligence Service] agent'.[22] Yet, as the transcript of his interview with MI5 shows, Footman was treated with the softest of kid gloves.[23] Shortly afterwards, the investigation into Footman, like Stuart Hampshire's and Pat Llewelyn-Davies' before him, was discreetly abandoned.

Wearily, Wright returned to the Courtauld Institute. He was by now convinced that Blunt and Burgess were the centre of an extensive series of 'concentric rings, each pledged to silence, each anxious to protect its secrets from outsiders ... Each ring supported the others, and made the task of identifying the inner core that much more difficult'.[24]

Under the terms of his immunity deal, Blunt was required to disclose everything he knew about every member of these circles, but as a subsequent report for the Prime Minister noted, the languid old spy was now extremely reluctant to live up to his side of the bargain.

The conduct of his dealings with interviewing officers has throughout been one of apparently trying to assist the Security Service in tracing unidentified Soviet agents while avoiding any statement which might lead to proceedings against others which might involve him.[25]

Two of Blunt's old comrades particularly excited Peter Wright's interest. The first, Alister Watson, was a well-regarded mathematician and scientist. In 1965 he was a senior member of the Admiralty's highly sensitive Research Laboratory and was due to visit the United States for a briefing on its latest submarine detection techniques. Yet combing through MI5's long-neglected dossiers, Wright discovered that Watson had been an ardent Marxist at Cambridge University, a member of the Apostles and a close associate of Blunt and Burgess. Worse, despite a recommendation that he be investigated, entered in his personal file in 1951, Watson had never been questioned about his friends or his politics, and had failed to disclose either during three internal security vetting interviews.

Blunt tried to dissuade Wright from investigating Watson, murmuring that he was 'not relevant' and, when pressed, complaining that the inquiries he had signed up for were 'so McCarthyite, naming names, informing, witch-hunts'.[26] If that obstruction was by now par for the course, Wright was rather more disturbed by the opposition he encountered from MI5's management.

His lengthy report, requesting the Director General's permission to summon Watson for questioning, was ignored for five months; finally, in late 1965 Hollis grudgingly sanctioned a lengthy series of interviews – on condition that Wright could not play the role of inquisitor. He was relegated to listening to the sessions on headphones in a back room in Whitehall.

Despite this, the interrogations produced startling admissions. Watson acknowledged that he had regularly visited the Bentinck Street flat for meetings with Blunt and Burgess, and that they had introduced him to a 'central European' man there. He then described numerous meetings with this mysterious figure – whose name he said he never knew – in parks, under lampposts and on underground trains. As the interviews dragged on over six long weeks, Watson confessed to further suspicious appointments; after being confronted with photographs, he identified his contacts as three known Soviet intelligence officers – the handlers for Kim Philby and convicted spies George Blake and John Vassall. Each rendezvous – and they were frequent – had taken place close to the Admiralty Research Laboratory in Teddington, but Watson repeatedly denied ever giving the Russians its secrets.[27]

It was, to say the least, a highly improbable story, and Wright was convinced that Alister Watson was 'one of the most damaging of all Russia's spies in Britain'.[28] Yet Hollis blocked requests for his prosecution; instead, Watson's security clearance was revoked and he was quietly transferred away from the Admiralty to a comfortable job at the National Institute of Oceanography. He worked there until he retired, on a full government pension.

If Wright had solid grounds for his conviction that Watson had been a spy – and for his suspicion that Hollis was protecting him – the case against the second name in Blunt's circle was rather more tenuous. Sir Dennis Proctor had enjoyed a long and illustrious career in Whitehall. He joined the Civil Service in 1929 and, identified as 'a high flier', he became assistant private secretary to Lord President of the Council (and former Prime Minister) Stanley Baldwin, and then enjoyed a spell in the Treasury. He left government service in 1950 for a career in shipping, but returned three years later for senior roles in the Department of Transport and the Ministry of Power; in 1965 he retired on full pension to a pleasantly rustic French farmhouse near Avignon.

Three elements in this otherwise impeccable biography excited Wright's interest. Proctor had been at King's College, Cambridge, in the 1930s, where he held left-wing – but not communist – views; he was also a member of the Apostles and a good friend of both Burgess and Blunt.

A search of Burgess's flat after he defected had unearthed an amiable letter from Proctor in which he bemoaned the state of the nation and Whitehall's bureaucracy. The discovery led to an evidently inconclusive interview with MI5's Graham Mitchell; this was followed in 1959 by an equally anodyne attempt at security vetting, during which Proctor played indoor cricket with his inquisitor. Wright was puzzled to find that the Registry files contained no trace of either meeting.

By his subsequent account, Wright prodded Blunt into naming Proctor as 'the best source Guy [Burgess] ever had',[29] and in February 1966 Wright travelled to Avignon to confront his quarry. Over a lengthy and drink-fuelled supper, the two men skirted around the issue until finally, somewhat less than sober, Proctor seemed to make a partial confession; he had greatly admired Burgess and had freely discussed government business – 'no matter how secret' – with his friend. 'Guy had no need to recruit me. He could get anything he wanted. All he had to do was ask.'[30]

Dennis Proctor's wife gave a substantially different version of this 'confession'. It was Wright, not her husband, who had been drunk, and the couple had been distinctly irritated by MI5's molehunter. '[Dennis] was a loyal friend of Anthony Blunt and Guy Burgess,' she told journalist Simon

Freeman in 1985. 'And in some people's minds that means he is tantamount to being a traitor.'[31]

This neatly summarised both the problem and the difficulty in substantiating Peter Wright's growing conviction that Britain's Establishment had been infiltrated by cadres of determined moles, all working for Burgess, Blunt and ultimately Moscow. If nothing came of Proctor's alleged confession – he died in 1983 with his reputation intact – a less happy fate awaited others on Wright's growing list of names.

During one of his lengthy interrogations, Blunt let slip that Burgess's recruitment activities had not, as Wright presumed, been confined to Cambridge University, but had extended to the colleges of its equally illustrious rival at Oxford.

'There was a very close ... Foreign Office [link],' he said. 'It was as an extension of political life in London.' When Wright asked whether he thought 'any of these Oxford contacts were significant' for Burgess, Blunt was unequivocal: 'Yes. He certainly used it to collect information, there's not a shadow of doubt.'[32]

Blunt also volunteered the name of one of his own espionage helpers who could put flesh on the bones of this 'Oxford Ring'. In 1931 Phoebe Pool had won a scholarship to study history at Somerville College and had gravitated to a radical political set revolving around Goronwy Rees. Then, two years later, she joined the Communist Party as an open member; she had not, however, completed her studies at Oxford.

A lifelong sufferer from depression, Pool dropped out before sitting her finals and, after a wartime career in which she wrote magazine articles and worked as an Air Raid Precautions officer, took an external degree in art history at London University. By the 1960s she had joined Blunt at the Courtauld Institute, and the pair wrote a book together on Pablo Picasso's early years.

According to Blunt, before the war Pool had performed a vital role in the complex concentric circles of his agents at England's leading universities. She had, he said, been his courier, shuttling back and forth between Cambridge and Oxford with instructions for those he had talent-spotted. Wright was keen to interview her, but Blunt warned that her mental health was so fragile that a direct approach was out of the question. Instead, they hatched an elaborate plan to use another senior Courtauld employee as an intermediary; Anita Brookner relayed MI5's questions and brought back Pool's responses. These yielded two names who had been key figures in the Oxford Ring: both were politically sensitive, and their exposure would have fatal consequences.

Bernard Floud was then Labour MP for Acton in west London and a rising star in the party. The son of the British High Commissioner to Canada, he had been an undergraduate at Oxford in the 1930s before entering the army as a wartime Field Security officer – a role which gave him access to sensitive military intelligence.

Other posts in government departments followed, and at the war's end he joined the Civil Service. He left in the 1950s to pursue a career first in farming and then in the emerging commercial television sector, becoming a personnel officer at Granada Television before later joining the board of Independent Television News.

But when Floud was adopted as a parliamentary candidate he had neglected to mention his lengthy involvement with communist organisations and their leaders. The second name provided by Phoebe Pool filled out the missing parts of his background.

Jenifer Fischer Williams was upper-middle class, privileged and academically bright. At a time when relatively few women went to university, in the early 1930s, she gained at place at Oxford to read history. She fell in with a group of communist students; one of them was Bernard Floud, who soon became her mentor.

By the time MI5 interviewed Ms Fischer Williams in 1966 she had enjoyed an illustrious wartime career in the Civil Service, including an appointment as Private Secretary to the Permanent Under Secretary at the Home Office, Sir Alexander Maxwell – the most senior mandarin in the department. In 1941 she married Herbert Hart, then an MI5 officer, and eventually returned to Oxford and academia.

The story Mrs Hart told Peter Wright about Bernard Floud was clear evidence of his central role in the Oxford Ring. Throughout her undergraduate years, she said, he had 'nurtured [her] development' and after graduation had 'advised her to join a department of the Civil Service from which information of value could be made available to the CPGB'.[33]

According to Hart, during her time in the Home Office, Floud 'put her in touch with a Communist Party link, firstly with an unidentified Central European contact … secondly with a trade unionist … who replaced the central European and whom she met about once a month'.[34] Phoebe Pool corroborated this story, confirming that she had acted as the courier between Hart and Floud during the same period.

Jenifer Hart claimed never to have betrayed sensitive intelligence during her years as Floud's 'undercover Communist in the Civil Service' – a statement which MI5 did 'not necessarily accept'.[35] Nonetheless, her true value was as a witness against the fast-rising MP for Acton: Wright burrowed back into Bernard Floud's voluminous files – and did not like what he read.

The first uncomfortable discovery was that in 1942 Floud had been removed from wartime intelligence work because of his open support for Communism. Three years later the Security Service opposed his application to join the Civil Service on the belief that he was 'an undercover member of the Communist Party'.[36] The warning was not heeded: Floud had become a very active member of the First Division Association – effectively the trade union for senior Whitehall officials – and had been appointed as Private Secretary to the then President of the Board of Trade, Harold Wilson.

Throughout the 1950s MI5 monitored letters and phone calls to Floud's farm and his family;[37] they showed him to be in regular contact with leading figures in the CPGB. His jobs at Granada Television and ITN, and his election as an MP in 1964, fed Wright's instinctive paranoia about the wholesale penetration of British commercial and political life by Soviet intelligence.

'It may be postulated,' he wrote in an MI5 briefing note, 'that as a member of Parliament, although as yet only a back-bencher, Floud has a potential as an agent of influence. His value to the Russians as an executive of Granada Television and a director of Independent Television News is more immediately apparent.'[38]

There was precious little to support this beyond the limited testimony of Jenifer Hart and Phoebe Pool. But convinced that he had broken a major case, between 1966 and the summer of 1967 Wright summoned Floud for five successive interrogations at an MI5 flat in Mayfair's South Audley Street. The interviews – codenamed ROAST POTATO – proved disastrous.

MI5 found him 'uneasy, evasive and less than frank'; at first he did not remember Jenifer Hart (or Fischer Williams), then vaguely recalled her before eventually agreeing that much of her account was true. But he refused to 'admit to any control or direction of his activities by Communist or RIS masters'.[39]

The Security Service had very little in the way of leverage over its obdurate interviewee. 'He is a shrewd man and is therefore unlikely to tell us anything which he thinks would damage his career, let alone land him in legal difficulties,' Wright wrote in a file note for the Director General in September 1966. The obvious solution was to promise Floud the same immunity deal given to Blunt, Cairncross and Long.

'He is unlikely to tell us the RIS part of his story unless he is provided with an incentive. I would therefore like to put to LA [Legal Advisor] and

DG [Director General] that we can enter the next interview with clearance to offer him such assurance, should we feel that necessary.'[40]

The recommendation fell on deaf ears: no offer was to be dangled, on the curious grounds that MI5 'did not know what offences, if any, [Floud] had committed'.[41] Since the same dilemma had surrounded each of the three earlier immunity deals, the decision made little logical sense. Instead, Floud was to be told once again that unless he came clean at a final interview, the Prime Minister would be informed that MI5 considered him 'a full security risk' – and that his promising political career would be over.[42]

By the time of that final meeting, Floud was suffering from severe depression. His wife had died in January 1967, and he had been prescribed powerful barbiturate sleeping tablets by his doctor; he was – plainly – in no fit state to endure another hostile interview, and Wright was unable to wring a full confession from him. That, however, did not stop MI5 from reaching a damning – if largely unproven – verdict.

'I now have serious doubts about ... the possibility that he may have steered other secret Communists into the Civil Service,' Wright's fellow interviewer from F Branch advised the Director General, '[and] also whether he is not still a secret Communist himself and even possibly a current worker for the RIS.'[43]

By June, the decision was made. On Security Service advice, Home Secretary Roy Jenkins decided there was enough evidence to justify 'excluding Floud from ministerial appointments'.[44]

Four months later Bernard Floud locked himself in the basement office at his home near Regent's Park; he washed down a handful of barbiturates with a substantial slug of whisky and turned on the gas. His son found his body the next morning.[45] Within days, Phoebe Pool – the woman who had first outed Floud as a communist recruiter – threw herself under a train on the London Underground.

The twin deaths brought MI5's investigation of the Oxford Ring to an abrupt end. 'All these suicides,' the Director General told Peter Wright. 'They'll ruin our image. We're just not that sort of Service.'[46]

The interviews with Blunt limped on for several years, but they produced no further revelations. The spider at the heart of the university spy rings refused to divulge any more names of those he had recruited. 'Blunt only provided information against his former colleagues in espionage who were safe, i.e. out of the country or at least no longer in sensitive jobs,' Wright later testified in secret session. The effete old traitor was weighed down by 'the obligation placed on him by those friends, accomplices, and lovers whose secrets he knew, and which he felt himself bound to keep'.[47]

But despite Blunt's determination to protect his friends, Wright deemed the interrogations at least a partial success. They had, he would tell the court in Sydney behind closed doors, identified '35 eminent persons … [who] were formally listed in MI5 files as Soviet agents. These people worked in the highest levels of British government, industry, academia. Many were interviewed by me and a number of them either committed suicide or died mysteriously shortly after they became aware of my interest in them.' This led, in Wright's mind, to a single, inescapable, conclusion: 'There was good reason to suspect that the Establishment was rotten to the core with Russian agents.'[48]

But two troubling questions remained: why had MI5's senior management tried so hard – and so often – to impede the molehunts? And why, given his evident importance, had Soviet intelligence allowed Anthony Blunt to leave MI5 at the end of the war? As the 1960s wore on, Wright became convinced there was a single answer to both. Moscow had another spy inside the Security Service, one who had occupied the Director General's office in Leconfield House.

7. DRAT

> 'Until the end of 1965 when Hollis retired, every case ... was tainted by Russian interference.'
> PETER WRIGHT AFFIDAVIT:
> CONFIDENTIAL MATERIAL,
> NOVEMBER 1986

Every Thursday evening, as MI5's junior staff left to catch trains to their homes in the suburbs and its senior officers retired for convivial drinks at Pall Mall's private clubs, six men and one woman discreetly convened in a conference room on the fifth floor of Leconfield House. Codenamed the FLUENCY Committee, two of its number were employed by MI6, with the rest drawn from the Security Service; all were experienced counterintelligence specialists, and Peter Wright was its chairman.

From its inception at the start of 1965, FLUENCY had a single task: 'to examine all available evidence of penetration of both services'.[1] This mission was both fundamentally important and – on the evidence of the previous twenty years – long overdue. As Wright later explained, 'All the operations against the Russians whether they were double agent or technical operations [had] failed ... fairly soon after they started.'[2]

Yet FLUENCY had no formal status, let alone any actual powers. Instead it was merely a 'working party' set up to 'examine' the apparent problems; nor did MI5, whose remit was defending the realm and its institutions from hostile penetration, even have a dedicated department tasked with protecting the Security Service itself from traitors within its ranks.

It was a symptom of the lingering incoherence surrounding Britain's unaccountable intelligence services and the lack of clear direction provided by their political masters – an omission which was conveniently reciprocal. Although news of the Committee's investigations spread like an unwelcome virus through Leconfield House, its existence – let alone its recommendations – would be hidden from Downing Street for the next twelve years.

Wright's team began by assembling all the evidence of penetration provided by Soviets who had defected. The list turned out to be sizeable: 200 individual leads, many of which had lain for years, unexamined and undisturbed, in Registry files. Most led to the depressing roll call of known spies – Blunt, Burgess, Blake and Philby; they were extracted and set to one side.

But, as a subsequent report for Prime Minister Harold Wilson noted, 'there remained a number of leads where either their origin was not certain or indeed where it seemed possible that the culprit was someone else'. The same memo also noted 'the possibility that people like Philby might have recruited other members [of the intelligence services] before they were themselves detected'.[3]

There were 28 of these solid cases – 'true bills' in MI5 jargon – and each clearly suggested that Moscow had a mole, or moles, inside either MI5 or MI6, or both. This alarming conclusion was supported by one of the best-kept secrets in Western intelligence: VENONA – decryptions of Russian cypher traffic which had been intercepted during the Second World War. Although frustratingly incomplete, to Wright these messages were 'irrefutable evidence [because] if you read somebody's ciphers [that] they didn't intend you to read ... therefore you can believe it'.[4]

VENONA suggested that each KGB handler in London ran at least eight agents; since, as Wright later testified in secret session, 'there were 250 RIS officers in London and if half of them, as we believed, were involved in running agents and if, as we assumed, there were nine spies per intelligence officer, there were at least 1,000 spies in England'.[5]

More specifically, several decrypts gave the codenames of eight Soviet spies inside British intelligence: Blunt, Burgess and Philby were clearly three of them, but as FLUENCY concluded, any one of the other five 'could be the spy inside MI5'.[6]

If this was all sound counterintelligence analysis, the Committee was simultaneously less happily influenced by the CIA's prize defector, Anatoliy Golitsyn. After a brief sojourn in London, during which he had held forth to Wright and Arthur Martin about the urgent need to 'clean house', Golitsyn had returned to Washington DC, where he was given unprecedented access to the Agency's most sensitive intelligence files. With support of its head of counterintelligence, James Jesus Angleton, he began to construct an elaborate – if distinctly questionable – theory of almost unlimited Soviet espionage in both the United States and Britain.

Although Golitsyn admitted that 'details of penetration of intelligence were particularly tightly held in the KGB' – and therefore he had not actually seen the hard evidence – he pronounced that his 'intensive reading' of the CIA's Soviet files made it 'certain that British intelligence had been continually and widely penetrated'.[7] In time, what the Agency later regretfully termed his 'Monster Plot' would cause turmoil in both London and Washington. For the moment, as FLUENCY pored over the collection of Rorschach-like counterintelligence fragments in its own folders, Golitsyn's theories were added to the suspicion that an undetected traitor lurked inside Leconfield House.

By May, senior management at MI5 and MI6 accepted that FLUENCY had established 'not merely that both services had been penetrated by Soviet intelligence, but that the penetration continued'. Two months later, the heads of both Services, Sir Roger Hollis and Sir Dick White, authorised the Committee to pursue further inquiries.[8] It proved to be a fateful decision. Among themselves, Wright and his team had reached a preliminary verdict on the most likely candidate for Moscow's mole: Hollis himself. For the first time in its history, the Security Service was now investigating its own Director General as a possible Soviet spy.

Inevitably, news of this unprecedented development quickly reached Washington, and it inflamed MI5's already-troubled relationship with the CIA and FBI. Both organisations nurtured a deep-seated distrust of their British counterparts: the succession of defections and the scandals of Blake, Philby and Blunt pointed to either gross incompetence or repeated betrayal from within.

Within weeks, the simmering row boiled over. President Lyndon Johnson dispatched two members of his Foreign Intelligence Advisory Board to London; Gordon Gray and Patrick Coyne were ordered to conduct an urgent inquiry into the Anglo–American intelligence-sharing agreements in general, and the efficiency – or otherwise – of MI5's efforts to stamp out Soviet espionage in particular.

The mission was carried out with remarkable subterfuge and – considering the Security Service was supposed to be ever alert to any form of foreign incursion – embarrassing ease. Although Gray and Coyne were given access to Leconfield House and its staff, MI5 was not told the reason for their visits; the CIA's London liaison officer, Cleveland Cram, simply introduced the men as his colleagues to whom the Director General and his officers were expected to afford customary courtesies.

The resulting Gray–Coyne report was coruscating. It denounced the 'inadequate size' of British counter-espionage branches, the 'poor organisation and lack of resources' which hobbled the efforts of 'individually talented officers' and – above all – savaged Hollis for losing the confidence of both his staff and MI5's notional masters in Downing Street.[9]

The verdict was a gift to the CIA's increasingly troublesome head of counterintelligence. James Angleton already thought the Security Service hopelessly archaic and unfit for the challenges of the Cold War; now he privately warned Wright that he intended to use the Gray–Coyne report as justification for a wholesale American take-over of MI5. Wright alerted his bosses and the scheme was swiftly killed: Hollis – humiliated in the eyes of US and British intelligence – persuaded the Foreign Office to make a formal complaint to Washington, and threatened to have Cram expelled if the Agency continued to meddle in his business. For the moment, Angleton backed down.

Yet in truth the United States had genuine cause for concern. FLUENCY had established the clear evidence that Soviet penetration after the Second World War could not be written off as the treachery of already-discovered spies – and that Roger Hollis was the prime suspect. But Wright and his colleagues were working against a deadline which threatened to sabotage their best efforts: in December 1965, Hollis would celebrate his sixtieth birthday and retire to his pleasant cottage in the verdant Somerset village of Calcott. As the abortive inquiry into Graham Mitchell had shown, once the Director General left the building, the molehunters would have little leverage over their target.

Wright pressed for permission to deploy all the counterintelligence weapons in MI5's armoury – full-scale covert surveillance and feeding Hollis barium meals of tempting but bogus data. 'The only way we could have trapped him was to have fed him, and him alone, information of a kind he would have felt obliged to pass on to his controller which may have resulted in a change of conduct on the part of the Russians,' he testified in secret two decades later. But his pleas fell on deaf ears: 'We were denied the use of any surveillance on Hollis … [and] the refusal … was fatal to any prospect of obtaining positive proof.'[10]

Wright did make one, inevitably fruitless, effort at confrontation. Shortly before his scheduled departure, the DG summoned his spycatcher to his office; after a little inconsequential chat, Hollis asked directly why he was under suspicion.

For the next hour, Wright painfully laid out the key evidence – the 'serials' and 'true bills' deriving from the Tisler, Gouzenko, Volkov and Goleniewski allegations: all pointed to the existence of a highly placed mole inside Leconfield House and, since Mitchell had been largely ruled out, the Director General was the only other suspect who matched their descriptions. Yet Hollis seemed cheerfully unworried, joking, 'You have got the manacles on me, haven't you?', before insisting, 'All I can say is that I am not a spy.'[11]

One month later, in January 1966, FLUENCY begged to differ. It produced an updated report for the new Director General, Martin Furnival Jones, which concluded that either Hollis – now assigned the codename DRAT – or Goleniewski's still-unidentified 'middle grade spy' was the mole, and was clear in its advice about which was more probable. 'Not one member was of the view that Hollis was innocent,' Wright later claimed in confidential testimony. 'His full investigation was recommended unanimously by all of the Fluency Committee.'[12]

This suggestion was greeted with horror by the new DG. FJ – as he was universally known – was the first Cambridge graduate and lawyer to ascend to the DG's office; a shy man, whose quiet passions were bird-watching and amateur theatricals, he had been with MI5 since 1941, but was now struggling to keep the peace between two stridently hostile factions inside Leconfield House.

The FLUENCY Committee and its supporters occupied one of the trenches; on the opposite side, old-school officers – often alumni of colonial police and security forces – viewed Wright and his colleagues as incompetent adventurers, pursuing a possibly mythical quarry with the zeal of seventeenth-century Satanism inquisitors.

'There was a witch-hunt going on,' Alec MacDonald – notionally Wright's line manager – later complained. 'Peter, like so many people, wanted to cut a dash in the counter-espionage world and produce something that was really sensational ... he could be very irrational at times ... Once you get bitten by this kind of bug, then you're on a crusade ... [and] anything that doesn't suit your thesis is pushed into the background and ignored.'[13]

It was a view echoed by others in MacDonald's camp. A subsequent internal review by an unidentified Security Service officer accused Wright of 'dishonesty' and of having 'led his witnesses most unscrupulously ... [he] did not scruple to invent evidence where none existed'.[14]

The row reflected MI5's historic divide between 'gentlemen officers' like MacDonald and those like Wright and Arthur Martin who were perceived – and denigrated – as 'mere "NCOs"'.[15] For the amiable, if traditional, FJ, their Hollis recommendation was a Rubicon he had neither the stomach nor inclination to cross.

He summoned the FLUENCY team to an out of hours summit in his office. With a bottle of whisky and pipes of tobacco for sustenance, he denounced their nascent case against his predecessor as 'grotesque' and berated them for the havoc caused by their investigations – 'damage [that] will take a decade to recover from'.[16]

Wright remained unmoved. 'Those of us intimately involved in the Hollis investigation believed that [he] had been a long-term Soviet penetration agent,' he later recalled. '[But] the Security Service [was] anxious that there shouldn't be a high level independent inquiry that might drag skeletons out of the cupboard that they would not want revealed.'[17]

At the end of the meeting FJ pronounced his decision. FLUENCY was to halt its DRAT analysis and focus instead on identifying Goleniewski's 'middle grade' mole. It was a managerial fudge, awarding spoils to both sides while protecting the Service and its cherished (if increasingly tarnished) reputation. The consequence, however, was a disastrous three-year hiatus.

Between 1966 and 1968 the investigators first targeted an entirely innocent (and never named) MI5 officer. Then, when that proved to be a dry hole, returned to drill down again into the abandoned PETERS investigation. Graham Mitchell was summoned for interrogation and eventually – at least to FJ's satisfaction – cleared of suspicion.

As a subsequent report for Prime Minister Harold Wilson belatedly – and ruefully – noted, 'it was 1969 before the case against DRAT began to be assembled'.[18] Fifty of Hollis' former colleagues were quietly questioned, but even this renewed effort was unaccountably hobbled by FJ; he refused once again to sanction physical surveillance of his predecessor, and nor was the retired Director General's home phone tapped – ostensibly due to 'special local difficulties' in Calcott.[19]

At least in part this reflected the uncomfortable reality that MI5's internal warfare had not abated in the previous three years. Opponents of the FLUENCY team accused it of behaving like the Gestapo and shunned its members inside Leconfield House's staff canteen. As the end of the decade approached, Wright discovered, for the first time, how it felt to be viewed with suspicion and hostility: the hunters now increasingly perceived themselves as the hunted.

To defuse this, and to bring some measure of Cold War counter-espionage reality to the creaking Security Service organisation, Wright proposed that a new directorate – codenamed K7 – should take over investigations into internal penetration, and that the Hollis interrogations should be conducted by one of its staff, John Day, a forthright ex-Marine.

By 1970, Day – initially an unbeliever – had reluctantly come to the conclusion that Hollis might very well be what FLUENCY claimed: the most likely candidate for Moscow's mole inside MI5. In June 1970 he wrote a lengthy and seemingly solid report – 'The Case Against DRAT' – which was to be the basis for a series of a long-overdue interviews with the former Director General.[20] A year later Hollis was summoned to MI5's South Audley Street building. The room was wired for sound, and Wright monitored the sessions on headphones from another office.

Hollis initially seemed calm and unruffled – a confidence derived from having been provided with the questions in advance. These set out the key evidence against him: the information provided by Volkov, Gouzenko and Goleniewski, as well as the likelihood that someone had tipped off Philby prior to his defection. Much of this was familiar territory to Hollis: he had, after all, been in office while the leads were developed. But in the years since Hollis' retirement Wright had produced new analyses of the first two cases. For the first, he had ordered a new translation of what Volkov said prior to his failed defection.

MI5's original account recorded his allegation that there was a spy 'who was fulfilling the duties of head of a department of British counterintelligence'; the new version was rather more precise and very much more damning.

Volkov had actually said: 'I know for instance that one of the spies in London is acting head of a section of the British counterintelligence directorate.' The only such 'directorate' was F Branch in the Security Service – and, unlike any of the other possible candidates, Hollis was its 'acting head' during the Second World War.

Wright had also been busy with the Gouzenko files – and in particular his warning about the mysterious British mole ELLI. GCHQ's specialist codebreakers had decrypted a top-priority cable, sent from Moscow to the Soviet Embassy in London within days of Gouzenko's defection in Canada. It showed that urgent high-level consultations about the loss were taking place in the Kremlin; Philby was providing Moscow with inside information about the case, and the final line of the cable showed that his description of the defector's disclosures was accurate. Since Philby had no authorised access to the material, to Wright this was proof 'that Gouzenko's information was correct, that there was a spy in MI5 called ELLI. This is what we call ... "a true bill" ... a real spy.'

Yet despite this, the record showed that Hollis had tried to discredit Gouzenko, submitting a dismissive report of what the defector had told him. Worse, when Wright and his colleagues later re-interviewed Gouzenko and showed him a copy of Hollis' account, 'he denied that he ever said any of that ... and his reaction was that Hollis must be a spy, actually probably ELLI'.[21]

And then there was Philby's defection. MI5's files clearly indicated that 'he had received warning from someone in the Security Service that he was again under investigation and that he would probably be interviewed'. Of the five officers who knew about this plan, only Graham Mitchell and Hollis 'had long enough service and good enough access to information' to have provided the tip-off.[22]

In the next stage of the interrogation, Day took Hollis back through his personal life and pre-MI5 career. He freely admitted having been friendly with notable figures in left-wing circles at Oxford University, and to having travelled extensively in China and Russia during the 1930s. None of this was remotely suspicious and the questions were batted back with ease.

But on the final day of his interrogation, Hollis was curiously evasive about his return to Britain in 1939 and his early days in MI5. He could not remember where he lived or who he associated with, nor could he recall why he had not disclosed his friendship with Claud Cockburn, a pro-communist journalist and suspected Soviet spy who allegedly headed the Comintern for Western Europe – a man on whom MI5 held voluminous files.[23] Security Service rules required that its officers disclose any such relationships; Hollis had not done so – a 'mistake', he now admitted, but an honest one.

To FLUENCY, this dissembling was profoundly suspicious – particularly since as a former intelligence officer Hollis would have known how important details were to successfully navigating a hostile interview. 'We were of the opinion that he was hiding something,' Wright later recalled. 'He seemed unprepared to tell us what went on. He avoided telling us exactly who he was meeting at that time, what he was doing.

'He was given a second opportunity in a subsequent short interrogation to clear this up and failed to do it. We can only conclude that something happened during that period which he was anxious that we should not be able to investigate. We considered that it could well have been either that he was recruited in that period, or that he was re-activated as a spy. Under the circumstances of the interrogation when his whole life was at stake, his career, [that he] did not tell us frankly the truth of what went on was quite incredible.'[24]

At the end of the interviews Hollis remained cool and unshaken: he knew that none of Day's blows had landed sufficiently hard to cause any real damage. To the final two questions – 'Have you ever at any stage communicated official information to any unauthorised person?' and, 'Have you ever been approached by anyone clandestinely to pass

DRAT

information?' – he gave curt, single-word responses: 'no' and 'never'. With that he pushed back his chair and left the building for the train home to Somerset.[25]

Over the following weeks MI5 reached two similar – but tellingly different – verdicts on the case against DRAT. Officially, though 'there remained some reason to doubt that Hollis had been entirely frank during the years 1937–39';[26] it decided that the investigation had been 'inconclusive'. Less formally, Director General Furnival Jones 'was of the opinion that DRAT was not a spy'.[27]

For his part, Wright conceded that the evidence against Hollis was circumstantial but that 'intelligence-wise it is 99% certain that he was a spy'. He also, and with some justification, argued that the inability to prove a case fully was a known – if depressing – fact of life for the Security Service's spycatchers.

'Until we got confessions out of Philby and Blunt and other people we were always in that position, we had to make an assessment as to whether the person was a spy. The evidence against Hollis was far, far greater than any of the other people … It was circumstantial, but it always will be … I think in an issue like this the country should be given the benefit of the doubt, not the individual.'

He also saw the fundamental logical flaw in writing off the investigation with a desultory 'not proven' verdict. 'It is no good clearing Hollis if you accept there was high level penetration without providing another candidate. I think the circumstantial evidence that has been set out for the high level penetration is irrefutable, and Hollis is the best candidate. If it wasn't Hollis, who else was it?'[28]

But one detail above all pointed – at least in Wright's mind – to Hollis having been the post-war mole inside MI5. 'The fact is that from 1951 to 1958 MI5 had no success against the Russians,' he later testified in secret session. 'Until the end of 1965 when Hollis retired, every case, although apparently successful was tainted by Russian interference. After 1965 there was no evidence of such a taint.'[29]

Roger Hollis died in October 1973, his knighthood and pension intact and, since the DRAT investigation remained a closely guarded secret, his reputation officially unsullied.

Despite this inconclusive investigation, and notwithstanding FJ's own rather firmer positive opinion, MI5 kept FLUENCY in business. Its remit remained 'to assess and review any fresh intelligence that may arise affecting PETERS or DRAT or any other case of suspected penetration of the two Services [MI5 and MI6]', and in the summer of 1974 it produced a new report which, according to a memo for Prime Minister Harold Wilson a year later, provided very little comfort for its critics.

> Although there was no direct evidence of current penetration, the evidence from the past of undetected penetration was sufficiently strong to require both Services to commit significant resources to continued study in this field. The weight of evidence of undetected penetration pointed more at the Security Service than MI6 [and] priority should be given to further work on evidence relating to the period from the mid-50s until the early 60s.[30]

That memo – from Cabinet Secretary Sir John Hunt – was the first anyone in Downing Street had heard of the decade-long molehunt and the allegations of Soviet spies inside Britain's twin intelligence bodies – much less the evidence that MI5's late Director General had been considered the most likely traitor.

Nor was this an unfortunate oversight. Throughout the DRAT investigation, Hunt and his counterpart at the Home Office had urged Furnival Jones to brief the Prime Minister and the Home Secretary: FJ had refused point blank.[31] For more than a decade MI5 deliberately kept the most damaging scandal in its history from the politicians to whom it was notionally answerable – the clearest of evidence that it remained as lawless and unaccountable as ever.

Hunt was an experienced and careful mandarin. A less scrupulous Cabinet Secretary – one who placed loyalty to his career over the integrity of public service – might have discreetly swept the penetration problem under a Whitehall carpet. To his credit, Hunt saw his duty was to support FLUENCY's recommendation for further research. But he also realised that it was no longer viable for MI5 to investigate itself: instead, and for the first time, he brought in 'an independent person' – in fact his predecessor as Cabinet Secretary, Lord Burke Trend – to handle all future inquiries.

But before Trend had the chance to get his elegantly tailored knees under this new desk, an unwelcome and distinctly unseemly commotion brought the old rows to the prime-ministerial door. Stephen de Mowbray, one of the SIS officers on Wright's original FLUENCY working party and a man with 'an air of fanaticism about him', arrived at Number 10 and noisily demanded an audience.[32] He told a ruffled Hunt that the PETERS and DRAT investigations had been 'pursued with insufficient vigour and … might be thought at best to fall short of complete impartiality and at worst to constitute a kind of "cover-up" operation'.

To mollify the irate MI6 man, the Cabinet Secretary asked Trend to conduct yet another study of the case against Mitchell and Hollis.[33] That inquiry lasted twelve months; Trend made twenty-two visits to Leconfield House, interviewed most – though not all – of the FLUENCY Committee and ploughed through its extensive files of evidence. But his eventual report reached no new conclusions: Mitchell 'was probably rightly cleared', and although he criticised the three-year delay before Hollis was investigated, he concluded that the inquiry had not been deficient or lacking in impartiality. Ultimately, Trend 'found no reason to dissent from the 1971 judgment that the case against DRAT was at least "not proven" and was not capable of being further pursued unless fresh evidence became available'.[34]

The verdict pleased neither side in the Security Service's internal wars. Those who believed their former Director General was the victim of a vicious witchhunt were frustrated by yet another failure to clear him, while the spycatchers criticised Trend's inexperience in their highly specialised field. '[He] was a very eminent civil servant and not an intelligence officer,' Wright recalled nine years later. 'I don't think he realised that in intelligence cases you very rarely got smoking gun evidence. All I can say is that I did not agree with [his] decision and I know that John Day, the leader of K7 investigation team, did not agree with it either.'[35]

If the sorry saga of MI5's molehunts ended with this inconclusive whimper, it did yield two important advances. By the summer of 1975 the Cabinet Secretary had been persuaded of the need for a wholesale review of the mission and activities of the Security Service, as well as the thorny question of who should exercise political control over it. That August, when, for the first time since the investigations began twelve years earlier, Downing Street was let in on the secret of the Hollis debacle, Hunt sent a lengthy memo on the fiasco, together with a copy of Trend's report,[36] to the Prime Minister.

Harold Wilson was profoundly shocked by its contents. 'This is very disturbing stuff even if concluding in "not proven" verdict,' he wrote in green ink at the top of the document.[37] It was a reaction which should have bolstered the case for the much-needed formal review of Britain's domestic intelligence service; but by then the Prime Minister was embroiled in the tendrils of an unprecedented and wholly illegal plot by a cabal of rogue MI5 officers to force him from office. At its heart was Peter Wright.

8. 'NORMAN JOHN WORTHINGTON'

> *'I considered him to be a traitor. A snake in the grass. An untrustworthy bastard. We discussed how we could fix him, get rid of him.'*
> PETER WRIGHT INTERVIEW: BBC TELEVISION, OCTOBER 1988

The conspiracy began in 1964 with a single document, codenamed OATSHEAF. It ended more than a decade later with four fat files and a plot in which Wright and dozens of intelligence officers crossed the line from habitual law-breaking on behalf of the government to a treasonous plot to overthrow it.

Yet MI5's malign interest in Harold Wilson had deeper and older roots, reaching back to 1947, when, as a 31-year-old rising star in the Labour Party, he was brought into the post-war government as President of the Board of Trade by Prime Minister Clement Attlee.

Wilson had tried to volunteer for the forces in 1939, but his genuine intellect – he had been appointed a don at Oxford at the remarkably young age of 21 and was a widely recognised authority on economics – saw him drafted instead into the Civil Service. It was the friendships he made with suspected communists in Whitehall, before winning a parliamentary seat in the 1945 general election, which led to the Security Service opening its first file on the youthful political tyro.

'The security interest attaching to Wilson,' one of MI5's subversion specialists noted at the time, 'justifying the opening of a PF [Personal File] for him, derives from comments made about him by certain Communist members of the Civil Service which suggested an identity or similarity of political outlook.'

In reality, these suspicions were based on very thin gruel indeed: a fragmentary and barely coherent telephone intercept of one communist civil servant which might – or might not – have indicated some form of joint scheming.[1]

Nonetheless, a new dossier, codenamed 'Norman John Worthington', was entered in the Security Service Registry. Very soon, a flurry of pages would be added to its contents.

In 1947, Wilson was tasked with negotiating the sale of Britain's most advanced jet-fighter engines to the Soviet Union. Attlee and Trade Minister Stafford Cripps saw the deal as a way to ease the crippling economic devastation wreaked by six years of war – a financial crisis exacerbated by America's demands for repayment of debts incurred under the Lend-Lease programme.

The engines, manufactured by Rolls-Royce, were at the cutting edge of jet design, but they were not on the official 'Secret List' and – subject to the granting of a government export licence – could legally be sold for civilian use.

But MI5, more attuned to the threat of the coming Cold War than Downing Street, argued that the proposed agreement was a potential Trojan Horse, which could give Russian intelligence personnel access to highly sensitive military facilities. In a memo in September it warned 'it would be possible for foreign engineers to contact in off duty periods, factory personnel engaged on secret work'.[2]

Attlee and Cripps overruled the Security Service objection, and over the next two years 55 Rolls-Royce Nene and Derwent engines were transferred to the Soviet Union; the sole proviso – which Moscow promptly ignored – was that no military use was to be made of the technology. Although, as a House of Commons committee later recorded, 'there were no losses of technical secrets by the sale of these engines'[3] and Wilson was not responsible for the prime-ministerial decision, the Security Service added his role in the trade to its file.

By the time he resigned from the government in April 1951, in a row over the imposition of charges for National Health Service dentures and glasses, Wilson was perceived to be on the Labour Party's left wing, and after Attlee stepped down as leader, MI5 bugs inside the CPGB headquarters picked up a discussion in which the party's leaders favoured Wilson to succeed him. If this was little more than wishful thinking – their choice didn't put himself up for election – the information was faithfully recorded in the Worthington dossier.

In truth, whatever the Security Service suspected, Wilson was a moderate, firmly rooted in the social democratic centre. In the leadership contest he backed the right-wing Hugh Gaitskell against the left's torchbearer Nye Bevan, and spent the next nine years in Gaitskell's shadow cabinet.

But if his domestic politics were largely unremarkable, Wilson's business dealings and friendships during the 1950s excited a great deal of interest inside Leconfield House. Surveillance on the Soviet Union's London embassy revealed that two Russian intelligence officers working under diplomatic cover had frequent meetings with him, and had garnered the thoughts of Her Majesty's Shadow Chancellor of the Exchequer. This 'political gossip' was fed back to Moscow, where the KGB opened an 'agent development file' for Wilson under the codename OLDING.[4]

Of rather more concern were his commercial relationships behind the Iron Curtain. From 1952 to 1959, Wilson was a consultant to a timber company which imported raw materials from countries throughout the Soviet Bloc. He made twelve separate visits to Moscow during the period, ostensibly drumming up supplies for the firm, but largely to meet Politburo chiefs and thereby burnish his growing reputation as the Labour Party's expert on the USSR. Each of these visits was carefully noted in his growing MI5 file.

This file might have gathered dust among thousands of others in the Registry had Gaitskell not died – in apparently mysterious circumstances – in January 1963. He had recently returned from talks with Soviet leader Nikita Krushchev in Moscow when he collapsed following a viral infection; two weeks later, aged just 56, he died in Middlesex Hospital. An autopsy revealed that an uncommon auto-immune disease, *lupus erythematosus*, had attacked and shut down his heart and kidneys.

The death was widely mourned as 'a personal, political and national tragedy',[5] but for the next six months neither Westminster, Fleet Street nor the Security Service suspected foul play. Even as the Profumo and Philby scandals unravelled the ailing Conservative government and Labour seemed guaranteed to win the next general election, no red flags were hoisted inside Leconfield House when Wilson stepped into the leader's shoes – and became Prime Minister in Waiting.

The arrival of Anatoliy Golitsyn changed that forever. In spring 1963 he left Washington following a row with the CIA, and was hired by MI5 as a consultant. During one of his first meetings, the volatile defector told Peter Wright and Arthur Martin that the KGB had poisoned Gaitskell, and that he knew from reading its files that the Soviet intelligence service would only assassinate a political leader if they had already recruited his successor. This, in turn, meant that Harold Wilson must be a Russian agent.

Golitsyn delivered this startling pronouncement with complete certainty but without a shred of proof. The best he could muster was an assertion, derived from 'personal contacts', that the KGB's 'Department of Wet Affairs' had been planning a 'high-level political assassination in Europe to get their man into the top place'.[6]

Unsurprisingly, MI5's senior management swiftly dismissed this somewhat threadbare theory, but Peter Wright swallowed it completely: from that day on, he was passionately convinced that Wilson was a spy.

True to past form, Golitsyn quickly fell out with MI5 and flounced back to Washington DC six months later. The CIA took responsibility for his case away from his previous handlers and assigned it to the head of counterintelligence, James Jesus Angleton. It was a match made in hell and would come to haunt intelligence services on both sides of the Atlantic for a decade.

In September, Golitsyn was granted a meeting with CIA chief John McCone; he used it to insist that Wilson – now increasingly certain to become prime minister of America's most important Cold War ally – was a Soviet agent. McCone flashed an urgent 'Eyes Only' cable to London, demanding to know if there was any truth in the allegation: the answer was a very firm 'no', and 'with those assurances the DCI [McCone] did not follow up on Golitsyn's claims'.[7]

Angleton, however, was unwilling to abandon Golitsyn's tempting theory. In November, Tennent 'Pete' Bagley, one of his coterie of disciples in the Agency's senior ranks, sought support from a contact inside MI5: he was not disappointed with the response.

'I discovered from Arthur Martin ... that one of Harold Wilson's principal scientific advisors is Captain Ian [sic] Maxwell,[8] who has a long Soviet intelligence background. This may shed new light on [Golitsyn's] report.'[9] Bagley's note set the pattern of what was to follow: in what amounted to an intelligence echo chamber, cables and messages shuttled back and forth between London and Washington, each amplifying the supposed credibility of Golitsyn's allegation that the KGB had assassinated Gaitskell to manoeuvre its agent closer to power.

'Once you assume that it is true that there was a murder, then the next "if" is "was it Gaitskell?"' Bagley later argued. 'If the answers to all of this is [sic] "yes", then of course you would look [at] Harold Wilson ... I think that [in] all of the get-togethers it was understood what we were doing and what we were saying was simply communicating, thinking about it, but strictly between us.'[10]

'Between us' turned out to be rather less than a rigorously applied rule. By the end of the year, eleven months before Britain was due to go to the polls and with Wilson tipped to win, rumour and innuendo about Wilson as a KGB spy swirled through the corridors of Leconfield House, and soon found their way to America's domestic intelligence agency.

'I remember talking to them on my usual daily trip to MI5,' Charles Bates, FBI Liaison in London, recalled. 'And it was comments like, "we're in trouble", "the Empire's going down the drain with this Labourite coming in", "he's gonna sell [out] the country". It's the conversations you would expect from a group of conservatives from the old school, talking about an upstart from the Labour Party who was going to be Prime Minister.'[11]

The talk also reached the ears of the Director of Central Intelligence – and the White House. Walter Elder, Executive Assistant to the DCI, recalled hearing 'through normal liaison contacts that there were people in MI5 who were uneasy at the prospect of Wilson becoming Prime Minister. There was a general concern about his relationships, particularly with the international Labour and Socialists movements, with ties leading back behind the Iron Curtain.'

This was duly relayed to the leader of the free world in his regular intelligence briefings. 'He didn't hear it in terms of the CIA saying "this is what MI5 thinks". He heard more generally that there were people in the Agency who entertained these reservations. And President Kennedy's attitude was: "if there are such allegations, bring me proof".'[12]

'Proof' was no more in MI5's lexicon than 'between us'. Its currency was suspicion, amplified by innuendo, and as the general election approached – and with opinion polls predicting a decent majority for Labour – Wright and other Security Service officers began drip-feeding hints about Wilson's allegedly murky past to sympathetic Fleet Street journalists. William Massie of the *Sunday Express* was discreetly advised that MI5's 'interest in Harold Wilson was not merely a matter of routine security', while Auberon Waugh, then a feature writer for the Mirror Group, was briefed that 'Wilson, by virtue of various indiscretions, was open to blackmail from Soviet sources'.[13]

When Britain voted in October, Labour fared much worse than expected. Wilson won a narrow parliamentary majority of just four seats – and the result could very easily have gone the other way: just 900 votes in eight key constituencies handed him the keys to Downing Street.

By the time he entered Number 10, MI5 had installed covert microphones in his study, a waiting room and in the Cabinet Office – at the request of Harold Macmillan at the height of the Profumo scandal. For the next fourteen years, the Security Service was able to listen to all decisions taken by prime ministers, their senior ministers and staff.[14]

Within a month of Wilson taking office, Angleton arrived, unannounced, in London. He demanded a meeting with Hollis and his senior officers and offered them 'some very secret information from a source he would not name ... that Wilson was a Soviet agent'. There was, the CIA's head of counterintelligence promised, 'more detailed evidence' to support the claim, but he would only provide it if the Security Service guaranteed to keep it 'out of political circles'. Even to a Director General habitually reluctant to keep Downing Street informed, this was a restriction too far: Hollis, then still in power, demurred, and Angleton departed as abruptly as he had arrived, his intelligence undisclosed. The best MI5 could manage was to write a brief account of the meeting; it was filed under the codename OATSHEAF.[15]

James Angleton was 'a spooky character in every sense ... convinced there were Reds under numerous British beds';[16] he was genuinely convinced of the accuracy of the Wilson allegations and – at least to those willing to accommodate his habitual cloak and dagger demeanour – very persuasive. 'He believed it,' Wright recalled in a television interview 25 years later. 'He believed that Wilson was a Russian agent. He really did.'[17]

Nor was Angleton willing to abandon his campaign to 'prove' that Gaitskell had been murdered. His new theory was that the tea and biscuits served to the Labour leader during his talks in the Kremlin were laced with a toxin which brought on lupus; he sent MI5 an academic paper on the disease, published several years earlier in a Russian scientific journal, which reported experiments showing that the disease could be induced in rats by administering a synthetically engineered compound.

Armed with this somewhat flimsy evidence, Wright motored from London to the MOD's Chemical Defence Experimental Establishment at Porton Down in Wiltshire. Its most senior scientist brusquely dismissed the notion that Gaitskell could have been positioned with coffee and biscuits; nor was this an isolated conclusion. Wright and a fellow officer next visited the Harley Street consulting rooms of Gaitskell's cardiologist, Dr Walter Somerville. Was it possible, they asked, that the patient had been administered a pill – possibly dissolved in his tea – which brought on lupus?

'I told them that under no circumstances could this be so,' Dr Somerville insisted. 'They would have to have a literally enormous dose; so many pills, given so often, that it would be impossible for any conscious individual to be unaware of the fact that he was taking this stuff.'

The MI5 officers recorded this diagnosis with a noticeable lack of enthusiasm. 'They seemed to be reluctant to accept this information, and by repeated questions which were couched in slightly different words, they attempted to hold out some hope that the medication could produce these sinister signs and symptoms.'[18]

Nor, much to Wright's frustration, were there any further reported cases of refreshment-induced lupus – an absence he chose to rationalise

'Norman John Worthington'

by speculating that Moscow's mole inside Leconfield House had alerted his KGB masters to MI5's interest in the subject.[19] Undeterred, he turned his attention to Wilson's circle of friends and business acquaintances: since several of these were East European émigrés of distinctly questionable honesty, their relationship with the Prime Minister seemed fertile ground for investigation.

In truth, there was some justification for MI5's unease. For many years Wilson had surrounded himself with a small cadre of very rich but sometimes crooked businessmen, bestowing prime ministerial honours on many of them – a lapse of judgement which his official biographer attributed to a weakness for 'the company of flamboyant self-made men ... a swashbuckling adventurer, especially if Jewish, appealed to him'.[20]

Four of these entrepreneurs excited particular Security Service interest. Robert Maxwell, MP and publisher of hagiographies of communist leaders; Rudy Sternberg, a German-born Jewish refugee from Nazi persecution who had become a plastics-producing plutocrat and owed much of his sizeable fortune to trade with Warsaw Pact countries; Harry Kissin, the son of a Russian grain merchant who helped finance Wilson's private office with the profits of his own Soviet Bloc trading; and Joseph Kagan, a Lithuanian-born industrialist who had fled to Britain after the Nazis invaded his homeland and founded an eponymous textile empire which manufactured one of Wilson's signature clothing items, the Gannex raincoat. MI5 opened files on each of them and began covertly briefing conservative journalists about their contents, as well as the Prime Minister's refusal to heed its concerns. 'We were very suspicious about these people,' Wright later wrote to a journalist, 'and warned Wilson repeatedly about the risks.'[21]

By any reasonable metric, the Labour government achieved remarkable results throughout the 1960s. Its legislative successes included the almost complete abolition of capital punishment, the legalisation of homosexuality and abortion, and the introduction of Britain's first laws against racial discrimination. Yet these liberal advances were viewed with horror by the nation's reactionary conservatives and their instinctive bedfellows in the Security Service. They were similarly outraged by Wilson's determination to reframe the economy and its tax structure.

The country's finances were, admittedly, in some trouble. Labour inherited an £800 million trade deficit; it was a structural black hole which put the pound under unsustainable pressure and would dog Wilson's administration. Finally, in 1967, he took the sensible but politically damaging decision to devalue the currency by 14 per cent. The move was an economic success, restoring a more manageable trade balance, but coupled with tax increases and stubbornly rising unemployment, it strengthened the allegations that his economic stewardship could not be trusted.

Internationally, the picture was no more cheerful. The government came under intense US pressure over Wilson's refusal to support the war in Vietnam. And the 'retreat from Empire' – the granting of independence to colonies, which had begun during Macmillan's 1950s Conservative government – fuelled traditional angst about Britain's diminishing global status.

In 1965 Southern Rhodesia became the poster child for this conservative backlash. When Wilson's government refused to grant independence over its denial of universal voting rights to the country's black population, Rhodesian Prime Minister Ian Smith unilaterally declared his state free of the Crown. Under other circumstances, this act of defiance in a relatively small African country thousands of miles away would not have caused significant problems. But Rhodesia held a totemic place in the minds of middle- and upper-middle-class white Britain, and major companies based in London were heavily invested in its strategic mineral reserves. When Wilson sent Navy warships to impede their attempts to evade trading sanctions, anger at his presumed betrayal took root inside City boardrooms.

That this coincided with a rash of very public and sometimes violent demonstrations, culminating in anti-war protestors clashing with police outside the US Embassy in Grosvenor Square, only hardened a simmering right-wing belief that the government had lost all control, and in 1968 a small group of men with the self-declared mission to save Britain plotted to restore order.

Cecil King was chairman of the International Publishing Corporation – a holding company which owned, among much else, the *Daily Mirror*. On the afternoon of 8 May 1968, King was summoned to the Belgravia home of Earl Mountbatten; he arrived at the elegant flat in Kinnerton Street, to find 'Dickie' (as Mountbatten was known to his intimates) in conversation with Solly Zuckerman, Number 10's chief scientific advisor and a close friend of the Prime Minister.

According to King's version of events, written later that day in his personal diary, Mountbatten launched into a tirade against the government: 'morale in the armed forces had never been so low' and the Queen – who had apparently been receiving 'an unprecedented number of petitions' – was 'desperately worried over the whole situation'. Mountbatten then asked the publishing magnate what, if anything, he should do.

'My theme,' King recorded, 'was that there might be a stage in the future when the Crown would have to intervene: there might be a stage when the armed forces were important. Dickie should keep himself out of public view so as to have clean hands if either emergency should arise in the future.'[22]

'Norman John Worthington'

King's account of this extraordinary meeting is, however, disputed. According to Mountbatten and his supporters, it was the publisher who sought the meeting and who floated the idea of a military coup d'état – a suggestion which prompted Zuckerman to storm out. 'This is rank treachery,' he raged. 'All this talk of machine guns at street corners is appalling. I am a public servant and will have nothing to do with it.'[23]

The plotters of this coup – a 'looney crew', in the forthright words of a subsequent MI5 Director General, Sir John Jones[24] – numbered among their ranks senior military officers, including one Major-General and 'civil servants' of unspecified departments. According to Jones, they believed 'their country was becoming ungovernable'.[25] But without a suitably royal figurehead, the planned military take-over appears to have quickly subsided.[26]

MI5 was well aware of the plot but was unwilling – for the moment – to use its files on Wilson to aid the cause. When Wright warned the Director General that 'feelings were running high' inside Leconfield House, and that some of the younger officers thought 'it was time the public knew the truth', Martin Furnival Jones issued a stern injunction against leaking classified information.[27] Despite this, the Security Service did not see fit to warn the Prime Minister of what amounted to treason: 'You can't go round to ministers every time there's been loose talk by gin-sodden generals,' Furnival Jones later told journalists by way of explanation.[28]

Wright was, in any event, rather more concerned with the perceived threat posed by Wilson's circle of friends: chief among these was Joseph Kagan, the mackintosh magnate. 'We had been suspicious of Kagan for years because of the way he escaped from the Soviet Zone after the war,' he later recalled. 'It had all the symptoms of an escape arranged by the KGB. We became very concerned when it became very clear that Kagan was courting Wilson's friendship and patronage.

'Wilson was warned by successive Director-Generals of MI5 to beware, but took no notice. (Incidentally, the manufacture of raincoats is a well-known cover for Soviet intelligence operations. "The Excellent Raincoat Company" was one of the main cover set-ups before the war for the Soviet network in Europe.)'[29] *

....

* As absurd as this sounded, it was true: Soviet intelligence had set up 'The Foreign Excellent Raincoat Company' in Brussels in 1938 as a cover for its operations in Europe during the Second World War. When the Nazis discovered it, they rechristened the network as *Rote Kapelle*.

It was also true that Kagan had enjoyed a long and close relationship with Richardas Vaygauskas, a Soviet diplomat based in Moscow's London embassy. In reality, Vaygauskas was a serving KGB officer, tasked with recruiting one of Wilson's most prominent associates as an agent of influence. Kagan, a garrulous and boastful individual, duly passed on political gossip gleaned from his frequent visits to Downing Street, and cheerfully introduced him to his own circle of parliamentary contacts. When Labour lost the 1970 general election, Wilson awarded Kagan a knighthood in his farewell honours list, and the tycoon promptly invited Vaygauskas to his investiture ceremony at Buckingham Palace. A year later, the spy was one of those expelled from Britain on the orders of Ted Heath, Wilson's successor in Number 10.[30]

Rudy Sternberg was next on MI5's target list of Wilson's dubious friends. Like Kagan he had been given a knighthood in the 1970 honours list, despite long-standing concerns over his highly profitable business deals with Warsaw Pact states, and his association with no fewer than thirty-two Soviet intelligence officers based in London; 'With some of these he has been on first name terms and remained in touch after they have left the UK,' a Security Service report noted four years later. Although scuttlebutt inside Downing Street held that Sternberg was either a spy or a double-agent, in January 1975 Wilson added a peerage to his friend's resumé.[31]

Six months earlier, the Prime Minister had bestowed the same honour on another associate of great interest to MI5. Like Sternberg, Harry Kissin had made a fortune from East–West trade and had provided funds to support Wilson's private office. But despite their best efforts, Britain's spycatchers could find nothing to indicate he had contact with the KGB, the GRU or any other Russian intelligence operation; instead, his transgressions, dutifully noted in his file in the Registry, involved frequent visits to brothels and his habit of hiring call girls to entertain business contacts. If this, as the Security Service reported to the Cabinet Secretary in the early 1970s, 'hardly amounts to an adverse [security record]', it did in the Director General's view mean the man was 'obviously not ... to be trusted with confidences'.[32]

Aside from their friendship with Wilson, their East European roots and the fact that they had all made personal fortunes from trade with Iron Curtain countries, Kagan, Sternberg and Kissin shared one other common thread: although MI5 monitored them closely – in Kagan's case, at least, it used 'all the mechanism of investigation ... following, telephone taps, microphones, the lot'[33] – it never found a shred of evidence that they posed any sort of security threat to the UK.[34]

This did not, however, stop Wright and his colleagues from spreading their net ever more widely and targeting liberal-minded business leaders, largely on the basis of their support for Wilson. Sidney Bernstein, the founder of Granada Television – the most commercially and artistically successful franchise in commercial broadcasting – was given a peerage in 1969: Wright viewed him as 'a very suspicious character',[35] and for many years the Security Service maintained 'an extremely interesting file' on Bernstein.[36] MI5's file on Bernstein shows that he had financially supported the Communist Party in the 1930s, and had known a pre-war Soviet spy, Otto Katz. However, he broke with the CPGB after the Nazi–Soviet Pact in 1939 and the Security Service verdict that this was bogus, and that Bernstein remained a 'secret Communist', was based on the 'not verifiable' information of a single secret source.[37]

Its dossier on Solly Zuckerman, the government's chief scientific advisor, pioneering zoologist and peer of the realm, was even more extensive, and apparently included details of surveillance operations at his country home.

'Solly Zuckerman had a cottage in the wilds of Essex,' Wright later wrote. 'It was called "World's End"! He used to hold very off weekend parties there ... There were also suspicious left-wing people there ... Solly had a considerable file in the office and many people were suspicious of him. As you know he is a South African Jew with no fundamental loyalty to the UK. A lot of his defence decisions ... were extremely suspect.

'He was considered to be untrustworthy basically because he was considered to take decisions popular to the Labour Party, particularly to the left wing, and not in the best interests of the UK. We never proved any Sov. Bloc connections, but he was certainly a blackmailable character.'[38]

Quite how Zuckerman might be vulnerable to extortion by Moscow's intelligence services – particularly since he had absolutely no contact with them[39] – was left conveniently unexplained. Wright and his cabal of rogue officers simply presumed him to be dangerous on the grounds that they were close to Wilson – a man whom they believed to be 'an agent of influence' for the KGB.[40]

It was the clearest of evidence that in its obsessive quest for suspected spies, the cabal inside the Security Service was willing to ignore one of its few foundational orders: to remain 'absolutely free from any political bias ... [and to] have no connection with any matters of a party political character'.[41] As Wilson later told BBC reporters Barrie Penrose and Roger Courtiour, some MI5 officers were 'very right-wing. They would naturally be brought up to believe that Socialist leaders were another form of Communist.'[42]

Wright and his colleagues leaked their entirely groundless suspicions to right-wing journalists. Auberon Waugh, then writing a political diary column for the influential hybrid satirical/investigative magazine *Private Eye*, was one of the grateful recipients, and duly published pieces obliquely referring to 'a known Moscow stooge close to the centre of power'. It was, he later gleefully admitted, 'a lovely idea – to have a Prime Minister who was a major security risk and who may be open to influence from the KGB or the Soviet Union. It is a lovely idea to play with and, you know, we played with it like mad.'[43]

The smears soon found a receptive audience in British boardrooms. As the 1974 general election loomed, Wright was invited to meet a clandestine syndicate of former intelligence officers and prominent businessmen led by James Goldsmith, a virulently right-wing financier, corporate raider and company asset-stripper.[44]

'We represent a group of people who are worried about the future of the country,' Goldsmith announced over a meal at a London hotel, before explaining that they were determined to prevent Wilson and the Labour Party returning to power. 'It could spell the end of all the freedoms we know and cherish.'

The key to achieving their goal lay, they knew, inside Leconfield House: would Wright agree to hand over 'anything on Wilson' in return for a 'handsome' fee, to be paid after he left the Security Service?[45]

MI5 certainly held the requested material. Its files on 'Norman John Worthington' – now swelled to four volumes, in total around four inches thick – documented Wilson's 'past contacts with Communists, KGB officers and other Russians'. They were locked away in a closely guarded section of the Registry, accessible only by permission of the Director General. As Wilson prepared to re-enter Number 10, the latest DG, Sir Michael Hanley, took unusual precautions 'to conceal its existence within the Security Service ... [He] instructed that the card referring to the file should be removed from the Registry Central Index, with the result that "a look-up on Harold Wilson would therefore be No Trace".' Only the most senior management – the heads of individual sections, ranked as Directors or Assistant Directors – and the Legal Advisor, Bernard Sheldon, knew of its presence. The Service's notional political masters – the Home Secretary and PM – were, as usual, kept in the dark.[46]

Wright ultimately decided that leaking such sensitive information to a rag-tag group of political adventurers was impossibly risky. He reported the meeting to Hanley and agreed not to have anything to do with Goldsmith's plot. But the idea of using the files to sabotage Labour's election campaign was too tempting to abandon altogether; instead, he pulled together a hardcore of thirty similarly minded officers to mount their own plot to stop Wilson.

'A lot of people,' he recalled in a later television interview, 'regarded him as a snake in the grass. An untrustworthy bastard ... I considered him to be a traitor. I didn't trust him ... because for ten years he had collected a large group of advisors and friends round him, who were not to be trusted.'

This cabal met in secret once the Director General and his senior staff had left Leconfield House in the evening. 'I was always very careful to have any sort of discussion which you didn't want to go to the management after hours: people like Hanley certainly went home on time ... [and] we discussed how we could fix him [Wilson] so to speak ... get rid of him.' These 'deadly serious' discussions were – by any standard – treasonous, but Wright was unrepentant. 'Well, there were so many times that one was putting oneself, in connection with one's job, beyond the law that this sort of thing did not worry one.'

The scheme to 'fix' the Labour leader – to prevent him winning the election – amounted to outright blackmail: Wright was to copy the Worthington files and then threaten Wilson with leaks of their contents to the press unless he quietly quit the race.

'That idea came from me ... What I wanted to do was to show Wilson that we'd got it and that we wanted him to resign: that there would be no publicity if he just quietly went ... It was a last resort ... I honestly think that Wilson would have folded up. He wasn't a very gutsy man, you know.'[47]

But gradually the illegality of this plan dawned on the plotters. The initial group of thirty dwindled steadily until, by the end, there was only one man left in favour: Peter Wright. Now entirely isolated, he finally realised that he risked both exposure and – as his own retirement approached – the loss of his pension. Reluctantly, he too abandoned the conspiracy.

In March, Wilson re-entered Downing Street at the helm of a fragile minority government; six months later he won a slim three-seat parliamentary majority in the second general election of the year, and rumours of the rogue coup plot reached him the following summer. In August 1975, the Prime Minister lunched with publisher and wealthy philanthropist George Weidenfeld in the House of Commons restaurant. Weidenfeld warned his old friend about stories circulating in 'high society' about 'Communists' in Number 10.

'They came and went,' the publisher recalled later, 'but they were repeated in clubs, in drawing rooms, in country houses – re-told, embroidered, second and third hand, and it did look as if there was an orchestrated effort to denigrate and smear him.'[48] Wilson was profoundly shocked. He returned to Downing Street and summoned Hanley for an urgent confrontation. The Director General admitted that there had been 'a dissident faction' inside MI5 but insisted the problem had been 'solved'.

For the next year, Wright kept a deliberately low profile, working intensely – and often abroad – on the still-incomplete VENONA decryptions of Russian cypher traffic. When he did, briefly, discuss the plot with the Director General, Hanley warned him that 'there will have to be an inquiry'.[49]

The same general thought had already occurred to the Cabinet Secretary – the government's chief liaison with the intelligence services. In July he wrote a formal memo, suggesting a full investigation of MI5 and its actions. 'It is many years since such an enquiry was made,' Sir John Hunt reminded the Prime Minister. 'Without implying any criticism ... some of us feel that the time has come for a further look at the purpose it serves, the way it sets about its tasks and the resources it needs to cope with them.'

The mysteries of the budget provided to the Security Service were particularly anomalous, since it was 'subject to no external audit or control'. If this was to some degree 'inevitable', Hunt believed that it reinforced the need for a wide-ranging review.

If he had stopped there, the Cabinet Secretary might have stood a slim chance of winning MI5's backing. But Hunt argued that the time had come for long-overdue external scrutiny of the Service's entire remit and operations:

> We want an independent review of the Service against the background of its responsibilities for counter-espionage, counter-subversion, counter terrorism and protective security advice; and comments on the way it determines or receives its requirements; how it determines its priorities among those requirements; how it determines its manpower and budgetary needs; and on its general efficiency and morale.[50]

This external investigation never happened. Instead, Hanley conducted his own internal review – with predictable results. 'It would take some imagination to say that things are improving here,' he wrote to Wright the following summer, 'but ... the firm is doing quite well and passed the recent examinations.'⁵¹ Shortly afterwards, Harold Wilson unexpectedly announced his resignation, and in April Foreign Secretary James Callaghan took over the premiership.

The opportunity to resolve the Security Service's ambiguous legal status, and to place its operations on a lawful footing, was lost. It was a failure that would have profound consequences a decade later.

Had MI5 been subjected to a thorough and impartial review, it should have been troubled by the frequent appearance of one of the Service's most celebrated alumni in all its scandals – a man who was the common thread linking the Cambridge Spy Ring, the recruitment of Anthony Blunt, unlawful surveillance and the 1974 Wilson Plot. Very soon he would also play a central role in the *Spycatcher* drama.

9. ROTHSCHILD

'During my investigation of Soviet penetration I used to brief Victor regularly and in considerable detail, meeting with him at least once a month.'
PETER WRIGHT AFFIDAVIT: CONFIDENTIAL
MATERIAL, NOVEMBER 1986

On Friday, 30 January 1976, Peter Wright left MI5's London headquarters[1] for the final time. His last act before walking out into the gloom of a winter's night was to sign a declaration, acknowledging that he was still bound by the Official Secrets Act and banned from disclosing on television, to the press or in a book any of the secrets he had gleaned during his twenty-year career.

'I understand,' he confirmed in a pro-forma statement which would soon prove distinctly troublesome, 'that I am liable to be prosecuted if, in either the United Kingdom or abroad, I communicate either orally or in writing ... any information acquired by me ... which has not already officially been made public ... unless I have previously obtained the official sanction ... of the Department.'[2]

With that, MI5's most experienced counter-espionage and counterintelligence officer left the building.

After 36 continuous years in government service, and approaching the mandatory retirement age of 60, Wright had been looking forward to a comfortable life in the country with his wife, Lois, and their grown-up children. Lois had a smallholding with horses and Wright, as a keen sailor, had every reason to anticipate a pleasant post-work idyll on, or near, the water. But shortly before his retirement, the Security Service brusquely informed him that it would not live up to the promises it had made in 1955.

101

To Catch a Spy

When he joined the Service he had been forced to give up all the pension rights he had accumulated during his previous fourteen years in the Admiralty's Scientific Service. Since MI5 did not officially exist, this sizeable benefit could not be transferred to his new employer – a minor detail it had dismissed with an airy assurance that it would make up the difference with ex-gratia payments. It was not to be.

'In the new, gray MI5,' he later complained, 'a gentleman's agreement was a thing of the past. According to the rules, I had no case for a pension, even though every scientist who joined the Intelligence Services after me was able to transfer his pension ... It was a bitter blow.'[3]

This betrayal, as Wright saw it, left him with a sizeable financial problem. His final pension would now be a few hundred pounds per month, only 60 per cent of what he had been promised – a reduction that was impossible to live on: he began casting about for alternate sources of income.

A part-time security consultancy in the financial industry seemed initially promising, until the Security Service discreetly advised him it would not look kindly on the appointment. With that domestic avenue blocked, and unable to survive in inflation-racked Britain, Wright looked abroad. One of his daughters lived in Tasmania, Australia's sleepiest state, where land was both plentiful and cheap; shortly before his retirement, the tenacious spycatcher purchased a run-down property in the tiny backwater community of Cygnet and embarked on a new career as a horse-breeder.

If this promised to be a good investment in the medium to long term, the immediate problem was how to finance its start-up: Arab stallions were not cheap, and MI5 would not pay the first lump sum of his pension until after his birthday in August. To bridge the gap in cash flow he turned to an old friend and colleague for a loan of £5,000 – equivalent to £31,000 today.[4]

The name of his benefactor was Victor Rothschild. It was the start of a business relationship that would haunt Wright and prove catastrophic to the Security Service for the next thirteen years.

If anyone matched the Security Service's criteria for a long-term Soviet agent it was the Third Baron Rothschild and his second wife, Tess. Both had been at Cambridge in the early 1930s, where Victor had been a leading light in the Apostles; both had moved easily among the circles of student communists, and Tess Mayor (as she was then) had enjoyed a passionate love affair with a prominent CPGB member. For his part, Victor had begun what would become lifelong friendships with no fewer than five known or suspected Russian spies, and recommended three of them for jobs in MI5 or government departments handling sensitive intelligence secrets.

The list of Rothschild's close university chums included most of the canonical Ring of Five – Kim Philby, Guy Burgess and Anthony Blunt – and the names of two of their sources, Alister Watson and Stuart Hampshire. The identity of Tess Mayor's lover was equally troubling: Brian Simon was a leading communist and member of the Party. Not only did they maintain most of these friendships for several decades, but after his graduation Victor hired another foreign intelligence agent as an advisor.

In 1936 Victor inherited his noble title, and with it a £2 million personal fortune (the equivalent of £114 million today). He contemplated joining the Rothschild family's eponymous bank but was drawn instead to scientific research. That, however, left him with the problem of how to manage his newly acquired fortune: he turned to one of his closest Cambridge associates for advice, Guy Burgess.

It was a strange choice: Burgess was a flamboyant drunk, an incorrigible pursuer of (then illegal) homosexual affairs, and had no apparent expertise in the rarified world of high finance. Despite this, at the start of 1937 Rothschild hired him, at the rate of £50 per month, to provide investment advice.[5] With His Lordship's blessing, Burgess roped in a young German-born Argentinian named Rudolph ('Rolf') Katz, who had arrived in London the previous year.

Katz was a mysterious individual, and one who quickly attracted MI5's attention: he was suspected of being an undercover spy for the Nazis, with connections to the Gestapo. If this was hopelessly inaccurate – the Security Service later discovered that the young man was in fact a Soviet agent, and had probably been one of Burgess's early handlers[6] – in 1940 Katz was formally expelled from the United Kingdom on suspicion of espionage.[7]

It was a measure of the chaotic nature of MI5's wartime recruitment that neither this connection, nor his friendship with known communists and CPGB members, was considered when Rothschild was recruited to the Service. A similar myopia afflicted Rothschild's successful recommendation of two of his friends to the Security Service: Tess Mayor and Anthony Blunt.

Nor had they been the only questionable beneficiaries of his backing: in May 1939 Rothschild wrote a hearty letter to the Admiralty, endorsing Alister Watson – 'an exceptionally brilliant person … I hope you will be able to fit him in somewhere' – for a sensitive scientific post.[8]

The distinctly curious wartime Bentinck Street ménage – as MI5 later described it – was another wildly fluttering red flag. Tess and Patricia Rawdon-Smith shared the ground floor, with Burgess and Blunt occupying the upper rooms; all entertained a motley assortment of intelligence officers, communists with Security Service files and one-night-stand sexual partners, often picked up by the men in their trawls for rough trade. If Rothschild himself didn't live in the property, he was certainly aware of its unsavoury reputation: as he later admitted to Wright, local police told him they had mounted an extensive surveillance operation on the house 'because they suspected it was a brothel. This was because of the constant stream of men visiting the establishment.'[9]

Since homosexuality was then a criminal offence – and a known vulnerability for blackmail by hostile intelligence services – and because senior MI5 officers were frequent (if sexually blameless) visitors, Rothschild should have reported the antics to his employers in the Security Service. He chose not to: it would not be the last inexplicable lapse in His Lordship's disclosures.

Victor joined MI5 in May 1940, and, with Tess as his secretary, was quickly assigned to counter-sabotage operations. Throughout the war he earned a reputation for genuine courage in defusing unexploded German bombs, and was awarded the George Medal for 'dangerous work in hazardous circumstances'.[10] In 1944 he was sent to Paris to 'engage in counter-sabotage behind [the] lines',[11] and ran double agents against German stay-behind groups,[12] operations for which the United States rewarded him with the Legion of Merit.

Ostensibly, both Victor and Tess left MI5 at the end of the war. She found new employment as secretary to Philip Noel-Baker, then Minister of State in the Foreign Office and soon to join the Cabinet as head of the Air Ministry; Rothschild returned to science, and combined academic posts with the first of an accumulation of senior roles in government departments. They married in August 1946 and divided their time between a Mayfair town house and Merton Hall, a handsome Elizabethan manor in Cambridge.

In reality, though he was no longer on the Security Service payroll, Rothschild was, at best, only semi-detached from intelligence work. MI5 made frequent use of his consultancy services, and in March 1953, when Britain and the United States instigated a coup d'état in Iran, ousting the reformist and anti-colonial Prime Minister Mohammad Mosadegh, MI6 used him to recruit and handle a spy in Tehran.

'When the Mosadegh crisis was going on in Iran,' Wright later testified in a secret court session, 'Victor used his influence to procure the services of an agent called Shapoor Reporter who was ... then the *eminence grise* behind the Shah and did all the arms buying for the Shah. Victor ran him for MI6 up until the early 1970s.' Five years later, Rothschild developed a 'special grease' to protect equipment both SIS and MI5 needed to bury in the jungles of Borneo.[13]

By then, the first stirrings of unease had finally penetrated the walls of Leconfield House. In the wake of Guy Burgess's defection, a search of his flat uncovered letters documenting his close friendship with Rothschild, the curious contract for investment advice, and the even more peculiar involvement of 'Rolf' Katz – now known to have been a spy. Since His Lordship had disclosed precisely none of this during his service with MI5, Arthur Martin sought 'guidance on whether Lord Rothschild should be questioned concerning the financial advice which Rolf Katz, [gave] through Guy Burgess'.[14] None was forthcoming: it would not be the last time the Security Service turned a conveniently blind eye to Rothschild's failure to report suspicious contacts.

In May 1955 the Kremlin-authorised Society for Cultural Relations with the USSR invited Victor for a three-week tour of Russia's scientific institutions in the autumn of that year. Since he was a former intelligence officer and, at the time, employed by the British government's Agricultural Research Council (in addition to holding several other high-profile posts in major private industries), the visit would have to be reviewed and approved by MI5. He wrote to the Director General, asking for a meeting. But when Sir Dick White agreed, Rothschild unaccountably failed to arrange a date; when the day came – and passed – for the proposed trip, the Director General simply shrugged and 'decided not to pursue the matter'.[15]

Early the following year internal disquiet increased after Goronwy Rees's salacious revelations in the *People* of Burgess's sexual indiscretions in His Lordship's Bentinck Street flat. Rothschild, sensing what was in the wind, wrote to White with what purported to be an honest account of his association with the defected traitor. Describing his letter as 'in the nature of a self-insurance for the future when people such as yourself ... might not be around', he falsely denied hiring his university friend to provide financial advice, insisted he had never known that the man was a communist – much less 'a Communist agent' – but also claimed that during the war he 'had a hunch that there was something fishy about Burgess' and had reported this to MI5.[16]

Like much else His Lordship would have to say on the subject, this was simply untrue: there was 'no record' in any Security Service file of Rothschild passing on any such warning.[17] Nor did it explain why Tess Rothschild continued to correspond affectionately with Burgess's mother after his defection, nor why the couple had kept entirely silent about their friendship with him. By autumn 1957 these successive lapses were causing serious unease inside Leconfield House. In October, the deputy head of its counter-espionage branch lodged a carefully critical note in the files.

> It seems probable that Lord and the second Lady Rothschild could at the time of Burgess and Maclean's disappearance have come forward with quite a lot of background on Burgess, his connections and the Bentinck Street ménage. This they did not do.
> I think that it would be fair to say that on the contrary Lord Rothschild has been plainly anxious to play down the extent of his connection with Burgess and that when he did come forward with this information it was purely to safeguard his position ... I do not think, however, that his reticence is due to any sinister motive but merely springs from self-interest ... It is possibly a fair assumption ... that Lord Rothschild thinks the state has responsibilities towards him rather than he towards the state.[18]

It was a view shared, with some perspicuity, by the Service's head of personnel. 'My own opinion, based on personal knowledge of him,' noted John Marriott, 'is that as a scientist and a wealthy man of assured position and a first rate conceit of himself, he is as likely as anybody I know to take the law into his own hands and arrogate to himself the right to decide to whom and in what circumstances he would be justified in imparting information, without regard to what he would consider to be bureaucratic red tape.'[19] It was a prediction MI5 would have been wise to heed. It did the opposite.

After Blunt's confession in 1964, telephone and mail intercepts showed that Tess was in the habit of holding lengthy, and highly affectionate, conversations with the old traitor, and that he enjoyed frequent weekends at the Rothschilds' country mansion. Despite this, as Wright ramped up investigations into the Apostles, the Ring of Five and the post-war careers of Cambridge communists, MI5 launched a bizarre scheme to use the couple as advisors.

'It would astonish me if there was anything sinister about the Rothschilds,' Wright blithely informed his superiors in November 1965. 'I have heard nothing but good from everybody I have talked to.

'On the other hand, Lord Rothschild did know most of the people we are concerned with before the war in their Cambridge days and later, and Lady Rothschild, as Tess Mayor, was an inhabitant of the now notorious Bentinck Street ménage during most of the war. I feel certain that both of them can help us in our present research.'[20]

For the next six years, Wright dined and enjoyed lengthy drinking sessions with the Rothschilds, revealing to them MI5's most sensitive inquiries. 'During my investigation of Soviet penetration, including the investigation of Hollis, I used to brief Victor regularly and in considerable detail, meeting with him at least once a month,' he later testified in a closed court session. 'This was done with the knowledge of Sir Martin Furnival Jones, Sir Roger Hollis and Sir Michael Hanley. Each of them only instructed me not to brief Rothschild in writing.'[21]

If both Lord and Lady Rothschild continued to lie about their own past communist associations, Victor was perfectly willing to denounce others for failing to disclose their pre-war friendships with the Cambridge spies. Over dinner at his Mayfair *pied-à-terre* in February 1966, Rothschild pronounced it 'totally inexcusable that [Stuart] Hampshire had not reported on Blunt and Burgess at least in 1951 – particularly since he had been "in the business"'.[22]

Since the Rothschilds were equally guilty of the same sin of omission, this criticism demonstrated remarkable chutzpah; nor did it prevent Victor from subsequently sponsoring Hampshire's application for government consultancy work, after he knew MI5 had investigated his old friend as a suspected Soviet agent.[23]

By the time MI5 finally realised the dangers of its arrangement with the couple, Rothschild was inextricably woven into the fabric of Whitehall, industry and academia. 'There are few threads in the seamless robe of the British Establishment which have not passed at some time or other through the eye of the Rothschild needle,' Wright later recalled.[24]

A flurry of internal MI5 memos between April 1969 and January 1970 bemoaned the fact that: 'One consequence of [our] liaison ... is that they are in some measure privy to our interests and, indeed, our secrets.' This was particularly problematic since: 'Tess Rothschild in particular has not been entirely frank with us ... She has volunteered singularly little information about ... her political affiliations at Cambridge, yet she was associated with communists there and it seems doubtful whether subsequently she would have continued to live in the Bentinck Street ménage unless she ... had common interests with the other residents.'[25]

If Tess had been less than forthcoming, at least one of her former communist contemporaries had been unequivocal about her enigmatic 'political affiliations'. That same January, Ian Henderson confirmed that the future Lady Rothschild had enjoyed a passionate undergraduate affair with prominent CPGB member Brian Simon, and that to his certain knowledge 'in relationships of this sort ... it was a case of "love me, love my politics" ...

[so] of course she must have been a Communist ... Oh yes, Tess must have been "in"'.[26]

Two other reports came to similarly uncomfortable conclusions. The first noted that although MI5 had 'no evidence suggesting that Rothschild was a Russian spy', his association with those who were made him 'a bad security risk', and criticised the special treatment afforded to the couple. 'Rothschild seems to have kept odd company and to some extent continue[s] to do so. It also seems to have become almost a legend that he and Tess are above suspicion while others, with "lesser crimes of association" are considered suspect.'[27] The second was rather more pointed: 'As we now know that Blunt was a Soviet agent, Rothschild may be in the same category.'[28]

But all of this came too late to hinder Rothschild's unstoppable rise. At the end of 1970, Prime Minister Ted Heath was minded to appoint him to head up a new and powerful 'Think Tank'. The Central Policy Review Staff was tasked with coordinating policy across all government departments, and since it would have access to a vast range of classified and secret information, Downing Street asked the Security Service to update His Lordship's positive vetting.

Under normal circumstances this would have been little more than routine Whitehall paper-shuffling, but it forced MI5 to confront its previous security failings. For more than a decade, despite knowing about Rothschild's dubious history, successive Director Generals had ordered that whenever an enquiry was received a single – and entirely inaccurate – response was to be issued that 'no record against' him was held in its files. The particular problem now was that in 1968 the Ministry of Technology had conducted its own vetting, during which it had been 'briefed in some way about his association with spies' – a revelation which made MI5's 'NRA' verdict somewhat tricky to explain.[29]

Once again Rothschild's value to both Leconfield House and Downing Street overrode the 'oddities' in his security record.[30] He duly took up his post inside the Cabinet Office at the start of 1971; within weeks he proved his value as a conduit for passing MI5's covertly gathered intelligence to Number 10.

His immediate target was Jack Jones, the democratically elected General Secretary of the Transport and General Workers' Union – then one of the most powerful trades unions in Britain – and the leader of a short-lived national docks strike which had briefly disrupted food supplies soon after Heath took office. In the 1930s and early 1940s Jones had been an open member of CPGB – and had fought with the International Brigade against Franco's fascists in the Spanish Civil War; although he had left the Party in

1942, he remained on good terms with its officers and in 1969 MI5 sought Home Office approval to tap his phone.

Harold Wilson's Labour government had refused, but its Conservative successor was rather more enthusiastic. Although the Director General 'did not think it at all likely that an investigation of Jones would result in him being charged with espionage ... an operation against Jones and his wife would produce intelligence which would be of great value in particular ... to the Government generally in the field of industrial disputes'. Ted Heath promptly approved the interception warrant.[31]

Conducting electronic surveillance of a trade union leader without any evidence of criminal actions – much less anything which threatened the defence of the realm – was strictly outside MI5's notional legal remit. But with no external supervision – the warrant was issued in secret – the Security Service was once again free to ignore the law on behalf of its political masters. Peter Wright was its chosen vector for sharing the proceeds.

Rothschild, inevitably, was at the heart of the scheme. As Wright later testified in a closed court session, 'Victor asked me to find out whether [Jones] was in fact a Soviet agent. He told me that Ted Heath wanted this information. FJ agreed I should do this report and told me to give it to Rothschild.'[32]

Wright's long-suppressed account of what he provided to Rothschild clearly shows that MI5 was 'not investigating Jones in a counter espionage sense', but that he believed only his masters' refusal to sanction the unlawful installation of covert surveillance equipment was preventing him uncovering the truth. 'I went on to say ... that without permission to install technical aids such as [covert] microphones on Jones, it was very unlikely that we could get the evidence we required to establish whether Jones was in any way controlled by the Russian Intelligence Service.'[33]

He was not. The telephone taps ran for a year and revealed no sign that the TGWU leader was communicating with Soviet agents; rather, they showed 'positive evidence of a growing distance between him and the CPGB'.[34]

None of this gave Rothschild pause for reflection. He missed intelligence work with its 'heady brew of intrigue and secrecy',[35] and took to adopting a cover name – 'Simpson' – for 'security purposes'; to support this risible 'disguise' he carried a briefcase engraved with the initial 'S'.[36] More worryingly, throughout his three years at the helm of Heath's Think Tank, he repeatedly meddled in MI5 politics and policy.

Furnival Jones was due to vacate the Director General's chair early in 1972. The Home Office, tired of the Security Service's scandals, wanted

Sir James Waddell, a career civil servant and an outsider, to replace him. Rothschild and Wright were horrified: to their mind, Waddell was 'finicky', with an irritating habit of insisting that applications for phone-tapping warrants were completed to 'the last dot and comma'.[37] In late 1971 Rothschild sent Wright to intercede with Heath's young and ambitious Principal Private Secretary.

Robert Armstrong had already been marked out as a high-flyer and had his eyes on the biggest prize in Whitehall: Cabinet Secretary and Head of the Civil Service. He knew that to secure this top job he would need friends in the intelligence service to back his move when an opening presented itself.

Wright's arrival in Downing Street was, therefore, opportune: if Armstrong was initially cautious about pledging support for Rothschild's favoured candidate, Michael Hanley, MI5's Deputy Director General and very much an inside man, the meeting offered the potential for winning future supporters inside Leconfield House. Within weeks, Waddell was ditched and Hanley became Director General.

Suitably encouraged, and with Rothschild's encouragement, Wright took the opportunity to press on his new friend in Number 10 concerns about the glacial pace of Security Service investigations into Soviet penetration. By 1973 it had whittled down the number of ongoing inquiries to five,[38] but it was still determined to keep its political masters in the dark about the extent of the problem.

'I had written a variety of papers for the Home Office on the Ring of Five, but they were mostly unsatisfactory,' Wright later complained. 'The MI5 Legal Department insisted on removing names like Proctor and Watson on the grounds that we had no proof.' To Wright this was a pernickety and wholly unacceptable restriction: 'If we filter out things we believe to be true just because we can't prove them, we're failing in our duty.'

Rothschild suggested he write a new and unredacted account of the Ring, and place it in Armstrong's hands. Several weeks later, at one of their now-frequent meetings, Heath's Principal Private Secretary thanked the spycatcher in fulsome terms. 'Splendid piece of work,' he beamed, 'real intelligence. Not like the civil servant drafts we normally get from the Security Service.'[39]

Splendid or otherwise, Armstrong did not see fit to pass the new report on to the Prime Minister – a decision he later had cause to regret – nor did it provoke any improvement in the pace of MI5's secretive internal inquiries. By the time Wright left for Australia – a departure he viewed as being forced into 'exile'[40] – he was nursing two substantial grievances: the 'betrayal' over his pension, and a conviction that the penetration scandal had been covered up.

If there was little to be done about the former, he carried with him to Cygnet evidence to expose the latter: the names of '35 eminent persons who were formally listed in MI5's files as having been Russian spies', plus an additional 20 Establishment figures whom Wright believed properly belonged on the list. In November 1976 he wrote to Rothschild with the first hint of what he was planning: '[Blunt] shall have a special place in my memoirs. I've still got my notes of my talks with him. Although I found him a likeable chap to talk to, I find it still incredible to look back on some of his admissions to me. His story is a book in itself. Perhaps I ought to write it.'

Alert as always to the danger of his own role in the Cambridge spy rings being exposed, Rothschild promptly warned MI5 that Wright's letter amounted to 'a veiled threat', and stressed the risk posed by a disgruntled former officer 'living 12,000 miles beyond the reach of the Official Secrets Act'.

After Hanley responded in remarkably 'nonchalant' fashion, and Wright repeated his intention to write 'a paper on the Russian threat', the Rothschilds took it upon themselves to act as both the midwives for the manuscript and its clandestine censor. In summer 1977 Tess wrote a letter on behalf of her husband: 'V. says he hopes you will write something, but don't post it. He'll be in touch.'[41]

Thus were the first seeds of *Spycatcher*, and the four-year international court battles to suppress it, firmly planted in the dusty earth of a Tasmanian backwater. But as Wright's book sent out its first tentative shoots, many of the shabby secrets which MI5 had so long suppressed were about to be unearthed.

10. EXPOSED

'The Prime Minister's statement is false.'
PETER WRIGHT AFFIDAVIT: CONFIDENTIAL
MATERIAL, NOVEMBER 1986

They were all worried.
For almost fifteen years MI5, Downing Street and Buckingham Palace had contrived to keep the Blunt scandal secret. Three Prime Ministers, the Cabinet Office and successive Home Secretaries had all – belatedly – been briefed about his espionage, his confession, the immunity deal and Peter Wright's extended attempts to extract a complete account of his Cambridge spy recruits, but British intelligence's impenetrable insulation from scrutiny had ensured that the public it supposedly served remained entirely unaware of the long-term treachery of the Monarch's favoured art advisor.

Buckingham Palace had been complicit in this extended cover-up. In 1956 it had knighted Blunt, and although his formal employment as Surveyor of the Queen's Pictures ended in 1972, he had been retained as an honorary advisor for her private collection of artworks. Neither his royal patronage, his knighthood nor his government pension had ever been rescinded – decisions which, as an internal government memo admitted, would be 'difficult to defend' should the truth ever be revealed.[1]

The possibility of exposure had been on Whitehall's mind from at least 1974. That summer the Cabinet Secretary sent a gloomy note to the Prime Minister warning that 'a good many people, both in public life and in Fleet Street, already know a certain amount of the story, even if in garbled and inaccurate form'. Sir John Hunt dolefully noted that Blunt was now 66

To Catch a Spy

and had recently been dangerously unwell: 'his illness was a reminder and a warning ... we should not underestimate the situation which may arise when [he] dies'.[2]

Four years later, Blunt remained obdurately healthy (and notably unrepentant), but the dam of official secrecy was about to be breached. On 9 November 1978, *The Times* published a brief story about a forthcoming book bearing the working title *The Fourth and Fifth Men*. Its author, award-winning former BBC journalist Andrew Boyle, had ferreted out the identities of both hitherto unexposed members of the Philby, Burgess and Maclean Ring of Five. If Boyle was unsure whether England's notoriously restrictive libel laws would allow him to name the traitors, his sources were impeccable. 'Key members of the British and American intelligence communities know what I have discovered,' he told the newspaper. 'They have not been unhelpful, to say the least.'[3]

The piece caused immediate disquiet inside Downing Street. Hunt reviewed the previous plan covering exposure: to issue only a terse written notice in the House of Commons, with no follow-up questions permitted. He was now pessimistic about the chances of this succeeding: 'It would not now be possible to get away with ... a brief and uninformative Parliamentary statement,' he advised Prime Minister James Callaghan.[4]

The secret immunity deal was uppermost in the Cabinet Secretary's concern: the revelation that a serving intelligence officer who had betrayed his country to Moscow had been protected from prosecution was guaranteed to cause an outcry. Worse, it now emerged that to secure Blunt's cooperation, the Security Service had exceeded the limited authority granted to it; in late November, Attorney General Sam Silkin told the PM that his predecessor in 1964 'had not in fact sought as wide an immunity as the Security Service had taken upon themselves to give Sir A. Blunt, namely an "absolute assurance" that [he] would not be prosecuted'. The revelation added to Callaghan's existing unease about the lack of effective control over MI5; in the end, he concluded that he had no choice but to shoulder the criticism which would, inevitably, follow. 'It would be better to tell the truth about the decision not to prosecute,' he told Silkin and Hunt.[5] It was an honourable choice by an honourable man – but one which his successor would ignore.

News of his imminent exposure also provoked panic in the elegant occupier of the Courtauld Institute apartment. In the middle of November, Blunt asked his MI5 liaison officer to call on him: he was, as a report on the discussion noted, 'nervous and rather depressed ... [he thought] that Boyle's book would unmask him. He asked if the Security Service could recommend someone to give him legal advice.' When this self-regarding demand was refused, he made a second request: 'whether it would be in order for him to write an apologia and leave it with Lady Rothschild in case of his death'.

This should have rung a loud alarm bell: it suggested that the old spy – who, as the Security Service knew, 'retains some loyalty to the Russians and may even be under a degree of Soviet guidance and control'[6] – was thinking of writing a memoir, which he wanted give to someone who was herself suspected of having been a covert communist agent. Yet MI5 was remarkably untroubled: its (unidentified) officer blandly told Blunt that 'this was a matter for him to decide'[7] – an insouciance which would significantly undermine the government's argument in the *Spycatcher* trials, eight years later.

By the time Andrew Boyle's book was published in the autumn of 1979,[8] a new Conservative government had swept to power. Margaret Thatcher had little ministerial experience – just four years as Education Secretary under Ted Heath – and no previous exposure to the myriad secrets held close by MI5. Nor would she be able to rely on Sir John Hunt for guidance; in October, just before the Blunt scandal finally surfaced, she installed Robert Armstrong as Cabinet Secretary. It would prove to be an unhappy choice, which would lead the new Prime Minister into disastrous intelligence service decisions.

Boyle did not explicitly identify Blunt, referring to him only by the cover name 'Maurice', but in early November, *Private Eye* named the former Surveyor of the Queen's Pictures as the long-sought 'Fourth Man'. As Fleet Street laid siege to the Courtauld Institute flat, Armstrong penned an urgent note to Thatcher, predicting that the story was likely to provoke questions in Parliament to which 'it may be difficult not to give a substantive answer'.

To aid his mistress in this delicate matter, the Cabinet Secretary volunteered to speak with Blunt's lawyer about how the old rogue planned to respond: 'as he happens to be a friend of mine there would be no difficulty about getting in touch with him'.[9]

And, ever solicitous of her inexperience in intelligence issues, Armstrong strongly advised her to trust to his much greater expertise: 'This is a minefield, and if you are not thoroughly familiar with it, it is both easy and dangerous inadvertently to put a foot wrong.'[10]

What followed set a template for the next eight years. The Cabinet Secretary summoned Blunt's solicitor, Michael Rubinstein, to Downing Street and, on the advice of new Attorney General Sir Michael Havers, asked 'to vet any public statements by Blunt to ensure that national security was not affected'.[11] News of this quickly and inevitably leaked, but when the *Guardian* reported the 'stately minuet' of the government's discussions with Rubinstein, Armstrong instructed the Prime Minister's Press Secretary to deny the story. It was 'an absolute travesty of the facts', Sir Robert fumed to Bernard Ingham. 'What is pernicious about this piece is the implication that there is some kind of Security Service censorship on Mr. Blunt's statement and answers. We have not asked Mr. Blunt to submit his statements and answers to us ... The Cabinet Office role in this is a purely passive one; we are only responding to requests made by Mr. Blunt's legal advisor.'[12]

Since this was the polar opposite of the truth, it firmly established the Cabinet Secretary's willingness to lie, safe in the knowledge that the facts would remain locked in governmental filing cabinets for years to come. Nor was he the only powerful figure determined to peddle falsehoods inside Downing Street.

As officials began drafting Thatcher's impending statement about Blunt to the House of Commons, Rothschild reappeared at Number 10. He was, Armstrong recorded in an internal memo, 'surprised to hear that the Prime Minister was disclosing the offer of immunity from prosecution ... [He] said that he himself had had no contact with Sir Anthony Blunt "since this thing broke"; though Blunt had from time to time rung up Lady Rothschild for "solace", she had been very careful in what she said to him'.

He was also happy to report that no journalists had yet contacted the couple, but if they did 'they would both say they knew nothing about Blunt's spying activities until they saw the Prime Minister's statement ... Lord Rothschild had known that Blunt had held Marxist views while at Cambridge, but neither of them had any reason to doubt his loyalty to his country'.[13]

Aside from the potential damage that the truth would inflict on Rothschild's reputation and sizeable ego, he had another reason to attempt a whitewash of his involvement in the scandal. He had recently been granted a personal audience with the Prime Minister, at which he sought to persuade her of the need to create a new intelligence oversight position inside Downing Street.

This powerful individual would be given full access to all MI5's files to identify 'the most dangerous enemies of democracy in this country', and would have to be 'one of those rare people who it is certain is neither a Soviet agent nor sympathetic to Soviet aspirations'. The only suitable candidate for this role, Rothschild advised the Prime Minister, was, of course, himself.[14]

Thatcher was ultimately persuaded that this was a very bad idea – Rothschild was 'obsessed about having access to Security Service files', outgoing Cabinet Secretary Sir John Hunt warned her[15] – but within a year His Lordship would successfully insert himself into the stew of brewing intelligence controversies.

On 21 November the Prime Minister stood at the despatch box to read a lengthy, unprecedented and 'carefully marshalled' statement about Blunt to the House of Commons. She confirmed that 'Professor Blunt had indeed been a Soviet agent', that 'he was recruited for Russian intelligence when he was at Cambridge before the war', and that: 'In 1940 he joined the Security Service.' But from that point onwards, Thatcher's account significantly departed from the truth.

No one knew, she said, 'exactly what information [Blunt] passed ... There is no doubt that British interests were seriously damaged by his activities. But it is unlikely that British military operations or British lives were put at risk. Further, the story that he jeopardised the lives of secret agents in the Netherlands is without foundation; he was never in the Special Operations Executive.' Technically, this was correct, but MI5's own briefings – lodged in Downing Street's files – had clearly stated that Blunt's senior wartime intelligence position had given him access to SOE's secrets. Thatcher's version was, at best, a half truth, designed to mislead.

She was similarly dishonest about the 1964 deal which protected Blunt from prosecution. She declined to identify Michael Straight's confession as the origin of the arrangement, but claimed 'it was not usable as evidence on which to base a prosecution'.

Nor was she any more candid about the decision to authorise immunity. This, she insisted, had been taken by the then Attorney General in his capacity as a law officer, rather than a member of the government;[16] but she omitted any mention of the fact that the blanket assurance which MI5 had given Blunt went far beyond what the Attorney General had actually sanctioned.

As her statement wore on, the Prime Minister's misdirection and outright lying gathered pace. She implied that Blunt had cooperated fully with MI5's inquiries and claimed that the spy rings he had organised involved only 'a very few of that pre-war generation who had Marxist leanings'.

It was now time, she pronounced at the end of her speech, to learn the lessons of this sorry saga. Firstly, it was 'important not to be so obsessed with yesterday's danger that we fail to detect today's ... Our task now is to guard against their counterparts of today.' And what followed from this was an obligation to give full-throated – if democratically unaccountable – backing to Britain's spycatchers.

'The Security Service, by its very nature, has to work in secrecy. It cannot therefore defend itself in public. That task falls to Ministers. The Government's purpose is to do everything possible to improve the morale and effectiveness of the Security Service, and to do nothing to undermine or weaken it.'[17] It was a clear warning that Thatcher would tolerate no external scrutiny of MI5.

The first test of her resolve came swiftly. BBC Television's flagship current affairs programme *Panorama* wanted to question former Attorney General Sir Peter (now Lord) Rawlinson about Blunt's immunity and ask why the self-confessed spy had not been deprived of his knighthood. Armstrong proffered his advice that the government could ride out the controversy by arguing that the decision to spare Blunt from prosecution was 'not unreasonable ... [and] that it would be nonsense to alert other moles by dismissing him and stripping him of his honours'.

Thatcher's response to the interview request was a hostile 'certainly not ... [she] wished all the birdies would stop singing'.[18] Within days she returned to the fray, and showed just how far she was prepared to go to impose her insistence on silence.

Her elevation to Number 10 had coincided with the first tentative steps to drag Britain's antiquated parliamentary democracy into the modern age. For centuries government departments had been able to go about their business untroubled by effective scrutiny from elected members of the House of Commons.

Unlike in the United States, where congressional committees routinely held hearings to investigate Executive Branch policies and decisions, the best that British MPs had been able to manage was individual written or oral questions to ministers. In 1979 a network of formal select committees covering each department was belatedly created; they posed a substantial problem for the Prime Minister and her closest advisors.

A week after Thatcher's statement to the Commons, a senior civil servant picked up rumours that the newly established Home Affairs Select Committee 'might wish to investigate the Blunt case': it was, John Chilcot[19] warned, a thoroughly unwelcome prospect.

'We consider that it would be quite wrong for the Committee to attempt to investigate an individual case in the security field in this way. If they persisted in trying to do so we could quickly reach a position in which the Home Secretary or officials would have to refuse to answer questions on security grounds.'

The ensuing fallout, Chilcot worried, could lead to a minor constitutional crisis. 'This might well provoke a confrontation in which the Home Secretary would be reported by the Committee to the House of Commons for his lack of co-operation. The Government would then have to rely on their majority to support him. Clearly, it would not be in anyone's interest to have such a confrontation, especially in the early days of the Committee's existence.'

Happily, however, a solution offered itself in the shape of the new body's chairman. Graham Page, a former junior minister but otherwise an unremarkable veteran Conservative backwoodsman, had previously been appointed to the Privy Council, Parliament's most exclusive club whose members were bound by a solemn oath of secrecy.[20]

Chilcot suggested that either the Prime Minister or Home Secretary should take advantage of this political freemasonry; they should visit the chairman and 'seek to dissuade him [from allowing the Committee to examine the Blunt case] by drawing attention to the security problem, and indicating that the Government would be obliged to take a restrictive line'.[21]

It was a classic piece of back-room Whitehall chicanery, and very much appealed to the Prime Minister: she promptly volunteered to twist Page's arm in person.[22] But to Robert Armstrong's sinuous mind, the prospect of the Select Committee seeking to 'investigate the Blunt case, or any other individual security case' raised a 'more fundamental question'.

'For the Committee to include the Security Service in its remit,' he wrote to Thatcher, 'would be by implication to concede the argument, which Ministers have never accepted ... that the Security Service should be subject to investigation by a Parliamentary Committee.' Worse, if the Home Affairs Select Committee opened an inquiry into the Blunt case, what was to prevent its counterpart, the Foreign Affairs Select Committee, seeking 'to interest itself in matters of general policy affecting overseas intelligence and communications'.[23]

Dragging MI5's often-soiled linen out into the weak sunlight of parliamentary scrutiny would be bad enough; extending that oversight to the even less accountable MI6 was self-evidently unthinkable.

Ironically, the lack of any formal – let alone legal – basis for the operation of either service proffered a handy escape route. Since neither officially existed and remained 'unacknowledged' by the government departments to which they notionally reported, Armstrong suggested that the relevant committees therefore had no standing to examine what they had been up to. 'I think that one would be on good ground if one were to argue that the Security Service was not "a public body associated" with the Home Office,' he told its Permanent Under Secretary;[24] and what held good for MI5 was equally applicable to its overseas counterpart. With that, the dangerous idea of parliamentary accountability of British intelligence was brushed firmly under the Cabinet Secretary's carpet: it would not be dusted off until after the humiliating debacle of the *Spycatcher* trials.

The Security Service, in particular, had every reason to avoid scrutiny: as its surveillance of Jack Jones demonstrated, by the end of the decade it had abandoned any pretence of political neutrality, and its willingness to bend – sometimes break – the law in pursuit of suspected communists had continued unabated. It frequently inserted undercover agents into trade unions, burgled the homes of their officials to install covert listening devices and tapped their phones.

It also spread its anti-subversion net beyond the unions and into the growing civil rights movement; according to a subsequent MI5 whistleblower, Cathy Massiter, staff and executives of the National Council for Civil Liberties were 'placed on permanent record' as 'communist sympathisers' and police forces were ordered to monitor them.[25]

All of this was carried out covertly, and with no oversight by Britain's elected representatives. While individual MI5 officers believed that 'a little bit more accountability couldn't do any harm', and that this would not 'inhibit the Service from performing its duties',[26] the organisation itself, the Prime Minister and Robert Armstrong, their self-appointed go-between, remained obdurately opposed to any democratic scrutiny. And the occupant of Number 10 had a particular weakness for spies and spying.

'Margaret Thatcher was absolutely fascinated by them: her favourite bedtime reading was espionage novels,' recalled Jonathan Aitken, then a rising Tory MP (and later a minister), who had dated the Prime Minister's daughter, Carol, for several years. 'She loved "the product" delivered to her by the intelligence services. Every evening she retired to the Downing Street flat with a collection of "Red Boxes" [the traditional government briefcases containing scores of urgent documents for review and sign-off]. One of them was bigger than the rest, and since it had a large blue stripe across its lid it was known as "Old Stripey".

'Margaret always opened this box before any of the others because it contained her daily top-secret briefings from MI5 and MI6. She had a really proprietorial attitude about her intelligence services: she was determined that she alone would know what they had been doing.'[27]

This dislike of democratic intrusion was a view once wholeheartedly shared by Peter Wright; he had, after all, exploited its absence to bug and burgle his way across London in the service of the state. But no longer.

The old spycatcher was, in December 1979, more or less happily ensconced in his ramshackle horse stud in Tasmania, and the Prime Minister's statement in the Commons took a little while to reach his rural backwater. When it did, Wright was appalled. Thatcher, in his view, should 'either have said nothing or else made a full and accurate statement about the whole history of Soviet penetration of the British Establishment'. Instead, to his certain knowledge – 'I was the only senior officer of MI5 to serve twenty years in counter-espionage,' he later explained in a secret court session – her account 'was gravely misleading'.[28] He carefully wrote out a list of the most egregious falsehoods.

Her assertion that it was 'unlikely that British military operations or British lives were put at risk' by Blunt's activities was 'absolute poppycock ... Since Blunt was the D-G's assistant for the first half of the war he had access to almost as much information as the D-G did.' In particular, Blunt had 'confessed to having betrayed an agent working in [the Politburo] who was being run by Harold Gibson. This agent was shot following Blunt's betrayal of him.'

The claim that Michael Straight's 1964 confession 'was inadmissible ... is false. The fact was that the law officers felt that in a conflict of testimony a man who was a knight and Surveyor of the Queen's Pictures would be believed.'

It was 'misleading to say that Blunt co-operated with the authorities. In fact our assessment at the time was that he only provided information against his former colleagues in espionage who were safe, i.e. out of the country or at least no longer in sensitive jobs.'

Above all, Wright was outraged by the Prime Minister's insistence that only 'a very few people' had betrayed their country as youthful Marxists. 'By the time I left MI5 in 1976,' he thundered, '35 eminent persons were formally listed in MI5 files as having been Russian spies.' Set against all the facts, he concluded, 'The Prime Minister's statement is false.'[29]

Thoroughly annoyed, Wright now began work in earnest on 'a dossier containing all that I knew about those investigations, including a[n] analysis of the problems of Soviet penetration in the past and how the continuing problem could be met in the future.' Initially, he hoped 'somehow to bring this ... to the Prime Minister's personal attention',[30] but by the end of the year he had come to the conclusion that his evidence needed a wider audience, even if that involved full public disclosure.

'For years the secret services have assumed that their best work is done with minimum reporting and accountability to the government and ultimately the people,' he later told the Sydney court. 'When I was young I readily adopted this philosophy ... I now think this is entirely wrong.'[31]

The question was how to accomplish this radical ambition without putting himself in jeopardy. At the start of the new year he landed on the solution: he would accept permanent exile in Tasmania, and from there covertly feed his dossier into the public domain via an intermediary. In spring 1980 he proposed the scheme to his chosen cut-out: Victor Rothschild.

'It is not the Official Secrets Act that concerns me,' he explained in a letter to His Lordship. 'With all the books written it would be very difficult to make it stick. But I was made to sign a document when I retired, never to disclose anything I knew as a result of my employment, whether classified or not. I can avoid action against me by staying in Australia and never returning to my beloved England.'[32]

It was the start of an extraordinary cloak and dagger scheme which would span three continents and, within five years, lead to the *Spycatcher* affair. But as he began work on his magnum opus, Peter Wright had no way of knowing that half a world away an equally embittered former intelligence ally had also embarked on his own plot to expose MI5's most closely guarded secrets and scandals. Nor could he have guessed the lengths to which the Prime Minister and her Cabinet Secretary would go to hide them.

11. PLOTS

> 'There is certainly a need to know ... I think it might
> be a good idea for you to come over to
> this country for a few days.'
> VICTOR ROTHSCHILD: LETTER TO
> PETER WRIGHT, JUNE 1980

The man with the homburg hat and heavy dark overcoat occupied his usual table. Swathed in clouds of smoke from chain-smoked cigarettes, he downed, as was his habit, an impressively large succession of dry martinis.

James Angleton was, by December 1979, 62 years old and a much-diminished figure. Physically, his tall, always-gaunt frame was now positively wraith-like – a harbinger of the cancer that would eventually kill him. Politically, and in the game of espionage, the CIA's once indomitable head of counterintelligence was already finished: five years earlier he had been forced to resign after the Agency was caught running an illegal domestic surveillance operation.[1]

But neither disgrace nor disease had dimmed his appetites – for food and liquor (in equal and remarkable measures) and above all for interfering in the affairs of Britain's intelligence services and the government they served. His favourite location for extended eating and international politicking was Washington DC's exclusive Army and Navy Club, a stone's throw from the White House at the corner of F and 14th streets.

One lunchtime, shortly before Christmas, his dining companion was a tall, elegant man with the easy bearing of a member of the English upper class. Jonathan Aitken was 37, the son of a Conservative MP and a titled aristocrat, and the great-nephew of newspaper magnate Lord Beaverbrook. After Eton and Oxford University, the youthful Aitken had crammed a great deal of excitement into his early professional life; he saw action as a war correspondent in Vietnam, then worked as a regional television reporter in Yorkshire, before being hailed as a crusading investigative journalist when he beat off an Old Bailey prosecution for breaching the Official Secrets Act.[2]

He used the contacts made on his travels to embark on a lucrative career in international finance and arms exporting – roles he combined from 1974 with a new career as a Tory MP. Handsome, dashing and self-confident, for several years he had also enjoyed a romantic relationship with Carol Thatcher, daughter of the leader of his Party. After that liaison ended he promptly married the glamorous daughter of a wealthy Serbian businessman.

It was during the couple's honeymoon that Aitken was invited to take lunch with Angleton at the Army and Navy Club. The two men knew each other well, and the young MP enjoyed the old spy's carefully cultivated mystique: 'He had this sort of legend,' Aitken recalled in later life. 'I thought he was fascinating, if strange.'[3]

That late December day, Angleton quickly steered the conversation round to the parlous state of Britain's intelligence services. 'The gist of it was that there was still a double-agent in place – or who had been in place until very recently – and that this information had been withheld from the Prime Minister.' Worse, the story had now been discovered by journalists on both sides of the Atlantic, who were planning to publish in the near future. 'Suddenly and out of the blue, Jim asked me if I could get a letter into Margaret Thatcher's hands without her civil servants getting it first.'[4]

To aid Aitken in this endeavour, Angleton provided the names of two retired intelligence officers – one from MI5, the other from MI6 – who would be happy to brief him on his return to London. At the start of the new year, the MP wrote to both on House of Commons notepaper and was mildly astonished to receive a very prompt reply from the former Security Service man. It was Arthur Martin who, it transpired, was now employed as a committee clerk in the House of Commons.

Aitken met the ex-molehunter in a parliamentary dining room and quickly established a firm friendship. 'He was small in stature, an NCO type, but a very good one. He was very cautious, and at first he rather agonized over whether he was going to tell me something or not. But I very much felt he was to be trusted: he was very patriotic.

Plots

'We talked and went round and round the mulberry bush, until he invited me to his home one evening: his wife Joan was there – she was an important MI5 person too.'[5]

The story the Martins wanted to tell concerned the still-secret investigations into Roger Hollis, Graham Mitchell and the lengthy, abortive attempts to unearth the traitor inside Leconfield House. While Aitken thought the couple seemed 'somewhat obsessed by this, they were not scaremongers and didn't have an agenda except the security of the country'. With their guidance, at the end of January he penned a detailed seven-page letter to the Prime Minister, handing it to her personal private secretary to bypass Downing Street's regular Civil Service channels.[6]

> I am writing to you in your capacity as head of the Security Services to ... alert you to possible new disclosures arising out of the Blunt affair. As you are aware, a great deal of information is still circulating among journalists on both sides of the Atlantic. Some of it has already been published, but the most dramatic disclosures of all may yet be forthcoming. My purpose in writing to you is to forewarn you about some of the facts and allegations which could see the light of day.

He then laid out the most serious charges: that British intelligence had been 'penetrated by Soviet agents at a far more senior level than that at which Philby, Burgess, Maclean and Blunt were operating; that the principal Soviet agents were Sir Roger Hollis, the Director General ... and his immediate deputy, Mr. Graham Mitchell'.

Hollis, Aitken alleged, had tipped off Philby, impeded the investigation into Mitchell and 'thwarted' Blunt's interrogation after his 1964 confession. If that wasn't bad enough, 'Hollis and Mitchell between them recruited other unidentified Soviet Agents into the Security Services. It follows from this that our Security Services may still be severely penetrated today.'

He went on to warn that some parts of this story had been discovered by 'one or two expert journalists ... [and] demands are building up for an authoritative and comprehensive statement on events within MI5 ... and these demands would surely explode into a major controversy if further disclosures occurred'. Aitken's solution was for Thatcher to set up 'a major independent inquiry into all these allegations, headed by a High Court Judge ... sitting in secret, supported by his own independent staff drawn from outside the ranks of the Security Services'. In tandem with this external scrutiny, he recommended that Mitchell – then still alive – should be interrogated, and the files 'relating to the alleged treachery of Hollis and Mitchell should be reopened and comprehensively reviewed' with the assistance of the now-retired officers who had conducted the original investigations.

If all of this wasn't incendiary enough, Aitken also proposed that Thatcher should make a new statement to the House of Commons, announcing 'a major reform of the Security Services ... to restore confidence in the Security Services'.[7]

The letter found its way to Sir Robert Armstrong. On 18 February he penned a lengthy memo to Thatcher's office, advising her not to accede to Aitken's recommendations. The MP had, the Cabinet Secretary wrongly claimed, written 'at the prompting' of Barrie Penrose, then working for the *Sunday Times*. 'In my judgment, the Prime Minister would be well advised not to comment in any way on the substance of the letter. Whatever was said would presumably go back to Mr. Penrose and be the object of further investigative treatment.'[8]

Several weeks later Aitken received a 'very terse' response from Number 10. Thatcher ignored his recommendations for an inquiry into MI5, or the issuing of a new statement, and brusquely declared that she was 'aware of the allegations'.

This was true, in letter if not in spirit. Despite Angleton's fears that the scandal had been kept from Thatcher by her officials, within four days of entering Number 10, Thatcher had received a detailed briefing from (then) Cabinet Secretary Sir John Hunt and from MI5 itself; the Security Service's eight-page memo set out the history of the molehunts, the disclosures by defectors which had set them in train and the facts which had pointed at Hollis as the most likely traitor in its ranks. If it also offered equally persuasive exculpatory evidence, unearthed during the years of investigations, the document did not acquit the long-dead Director General entirely. 'No information was discovered to confirm the supposition of espionage; but there remained some reason to doubt that he had been entirely frank about his life during the years 1937–1939,' the Security Service advised, adding that since Hollis's death in 1973 'no evidence has come to light ... to show that he was a spy'.

MI5's report was very carefully modulated to leave the molehunting door open – not least since, as it also noted, there was still 'one lead ... being pursued'.[9] Thatcher, however, blew past the nuance.

'The tenor of her reply was "we don't believe this",' Aitken recalled. 'She decided that Hollis had not been a wrong 'un.' And he knew where this iron-clad certainty originated: 'she would have had Robert Armstrong murmuring in her ear, saying "this stuff is too hot to handle"'.[10]

All of this was, inevitably, conducted in secret. But if the Prime Minister believed the Hollis saga could be kept securely inside a Downing Street and MI5 bubble, she had underestimated both the spycatchers' determination to bring it into the open and the appetite of journalists for espionage scandals.

Arthur Martin continued to divulge details of the DRAT and PETERS investigations to Aitken. That these briefings were unquestionably a breach of the Official Secrets Act never troubled the MP. 'I never really thought about that,' he reflected. 'I felt we were doing the nation's business.'[11] But simultaneously – and without Aitken's knowledge – Martin also began talking to liberal-minded reporters, including Barrie Penrose, one half of the BBC team whose book had revealed Harold Wilson's fears of an MI5 plot to smear him.[12]

By the summer of 1980, news that Penrose was working on a follow-up volume about the molehunts reached the ears of one of his Fleet Street rivals. On 9 June, former Attorney General Sir Peter Rawlinson wrote to Thatcher about a request he had received from Harry 'Chapman' Pincher, the *Daily Express*'s recently departed defence and intelligence correspondent, who had learned of Burke Trend's secret investigation into Sir Roger Hollis. Pincher claimed that he, too, was writing a book about Hollis and wanted government help. 'It was clear that he would like to pre-empt ... Penrose and would present the story more "sympathetically",' Rawlinson told the Prime Minister.[13]

The letter landed on the Cabinet Secretary's desk the next day. To Robert Armstrong's supple mind, it presented an opportunity too good to pass up. He wrote to Thatcher: 'I would usually recommend a very long spoon indeed in dealings with Chapman Pincher. This instance, however, might be the case for an exception to the rule.'[14] The journalist was – in Thatcher's own parlance – 'one of us': right-wing, malleable and dependably supportive of Conservative governments. Carefully briefed, he could be relied on to safely defuse the looming Hollis scandal in an account which would stress that the former Director General had been completely cleared; that this was untrue did not, predictably, pose a problem.

Armstrong knew, however, that Downing Street could not leave its fingerprints on the plan: instead, he proposed using Rawlinson as a deniable cut-out. On 11 June, Thatcher's Principal Private Secretary told Armstrong to go ahead. 'The Prime Minister thinks there would be advantage if you saw Lord Rawlinson on a Privy Council basis,' Clive Whitmore wrote to

Armstrong, 'and put him in the picture, in the knowledge that he would pass on what he was told to Chapman Pincher.'[15] The Cabinet Secretary duly briefed the former Attorney General, who promptly passed on to Pincher the Hollis saga and the government's spin on the story.

It was a grubby scheme: an unprecedented official leak of MI5's most damning secret, which the Security Service had kept from previous prime ministers for almost a decade and hidden entirely from Parliament. Handing it to a journalist via the back-door contrivance of the Privy Council comprehensively undercut Thatcher's proclaimed determination to prevent any scrutiny of Britain's intelligence agencies, and strayed dangerously close to outright illegality.

It was also remarkably naïve. Armstrong grossly underestimated Pincher's willingness to cause mischief and his genuinely extensive contacts among the group of dissident molehunters who fervently believed in Hollis's guilt. Nor did the Cabinet Secretary grasp the determination of men like Arthur Martin and his former FLUENCY colleagues to bring the truth – at least as they saw it – to light.

The leader of that cabal was, in August 1980, languishing in Tasmanian exile, and in some financial difficulty. Peter Wright's stud farm was making little money, and the ramshackle state of his home in dusty Cygnet reflected the hard times on which he had fallen. Now 64 and in poor health, he realised that if he wanted to reveal the depths of Soviet penetration of the Establishment which FLUENCY's inquiries had uncovered, time was of the essence.

He had been hard at work on his thesis, provisionally titled *The Cancer in Our Midst*, and, like Angleton, nursed an unshakeable – if erroneous – conviction 'that Mrs. Thatcher had been misled by MI5 over the extent of those investigations'; but, other than an unrealistic hope that these should form the basis for an official White Paper on the problem, and an equally vague intention to 'somehow bring this dossier to the Prime Minister's attention', he had little idea what to do with his dissertation.[16]

An exchange of letters with his old friend and mentor, Victor Rothschild, provided the catalyst for realising his ambitions. Rothschild was then similarly unwell – a lifelong heavy smoker, that spring he had spent several months in hospital, first for heart surgery and then to recover from a near-fatal bout of bacterial endocarditis – and was facing renewed interest in his association with the Cambridge Ring of Five.

At the press launch of a revised edition of his book about Blunt, Andrew Boyle had told his audience that in the wake of the Burgess and Maclean defections two members of the House of Lords had been questioned by

MI5; mindful of the risk of libel, Boyle named neither – but said that one was a hereditary peer who had served in intelligence during the Second World War. The story quickly appeared, in satirical form, in *Private Eye*.[17]

Despite the fact – then still-suppressed – that MI5 had suspected Rothschild and his wife for almost a decade, His Lordship took umbrage and was only reluctantly dissuaded from suing. 'Things are starting to get rough,' Tess Rothschild wrote plaintively to Wright shortly afterwards.[18]

Rothschild had particular reason for discomfort since he still – ill-health and past communist associations notwithstanding – coveted the Director General's office in either MI5 or MI6, and was shortly planning to plead his case to Thatcher after a private dinner. He decided that a ringing endorsement from a former Assistant Director who had given more than two decades to the Security Service might be a useful prop for his ambitions, and could also help Wright advance his manuscript.

In later years, Rothschild told his biographer that the plan was not of his own making, but had been suggested to him during his stay in hospital 'by a friend of importance and known integrity who had good reason to understand the obligations of confidentiality'. He declined to identify this mysterious visitor and conceded that 'some may think that ... I was being led by the nose'.

If this was characteristically cryptic and inevitably unprovable, it certainly hinted at the growing web of multiple plots to reveal the Hollis scandal. In late June, Rothschild wrote to Wright, sketching out a plan of action.

> I cannot see that it would be a breach of the Official Secrets Act for you to put on a piece of paper, but not to send to anyone, a detailed account of your relationship with me ... and let me have it by a method which I shall let you know in due course.
>
> There is certainly a need to know and you would be only telling someone something that, memory lapses apart, he could put down himself. I think it might be a good idea for you to come over to this country for a few days if you could bear it.[19]

Wright responded eagerly, telling Rothschild he 'would be happy ... to write out a list of his achievements for MI5 which he could publish if necessary'. The only problem was financial: the retired spycatcher regretted that he and his wife were very hard pressed and simply couldn't stump up the funds for a trip to England. He need not have worried: money was the least of Rothschild's concerns, and he was evidently eager to dust off his old tradecraft.

'Shortly after this Victor telephoned me,' Wright later testified. '[He] told me that a courier would shortly be arriving, and could I meet him at Hobart airport. We met the courier and he handed me an envelope with a first class return air ticket to London, open-dated, and nothing else. The courier asked if I had Victor's letter. I said I did and he then asked for it back. I gave it to him.'[20]

The trip was, for a man in precarious health, genuinely daunting. Hobart is more than 10,000 miles from London, and the flights would pass through six time zones and last almost 40 hours. Wright's doctor advised that he should not travel alone, so he exchanged the first-class ticket for two economy fares and, accompanied by his wife, set off for England on 20 August. They landed two days later and drove up to Yorkshire for a week's recuperation with one of their daughters.

On Tuesday 2 September, Wright took the train from York to London and arrived at Rothschild's Mayfair flat in time for a restorative lunch. Over drinks, his host explained that 'he needed a list of his achievements for MI5 because of the rumours circulating about him following the exposure of Blunt'. Wright handed over a three-page testimonial and said he had also brought a rather longer typescript of *The Cancer in Our Midst*. Since this ran to 176 pages and ten chapters, Rothschild suggested that they consider both documents at greater leisure in the country; in late afternoon they motored up to his home in Cambridge.

Over the next two days, Wright refined his statement on Rothschild's Security Service career while His Lordship pored over the manuscript on Soviet penetration in his private study. When both had finished, they reconvened to work out a plan of action.

'I told Victor that the dossier was not complete, but that I wanted him to give it to Thatcher. I explained to him that if it went to MI5 they would simply rubbish it and ignore it,' Wright later explained in court testimony.

But Rothschild's reaction was unexpectedly pessimistic. '[He] said that it was pointless formally giving it to Thatcher, as she would be obliged to give it to MI5,' Wright later testified. 'He said to me: "You know she was sitting on that couch only a few days ago. She doesn't understand intelligence."'

This almost certainly reflected the Prime Minister's refusal, at their recent private dinner, to appoint Rothschild as head of either MI5 or MI6 – a rejection of which Wright was blissfully unaware and about which 'Victor did not elaborate'; but it was the foundation stone for all that would follow in the *Spycatcher* saga. 'I knew him well enough to note the significance of what he had said, and not to question him about it,' Wright later testified.

The main question remained: what was to be done with the unfinished typescript? Happily, Rothschild had the answer.

'He said to me that he thought it was very good [but] it was hopeless putting it through official channels. He said that he thought the dossier should be published. He said that I would need a ghost writer and that if the book made any money I would be helped with my financial problems.' Wright liked the sound of both suggestions, and at 4pm, Rothschild went to make a phone call to a journalist whose 'contacts were so good he could ensure the book was published without official interference'.[21]

It was just seven weeks since Robert Armstrong and Margaret Thatcher had concocted their scheme to leak much of the same story of MI5's internal scandals to Chapman Pincher. By a remarkable coincidence, Rothschild's plan for publishing Peter Wright's dossier involved the same veteran intelligence muckraker.

12. PINCHER

'I concluded that I was being used as part of a deniable operation ... a scheme that was at least tacitly approved'
PETER WRIGHT AFFIDAVIT, NOVEMBER 1986

The conspiracy began with suspicious speed – and with three lies. At 8pm on 4 September 1980 – less than four hours after receiving Rothschild's phone call – Chapman Pincher arrived at the Cambridge mansion. The 120-mile journey from his home in the verdant Berkshire village of Kintbury had been hastened by a chauffer-driven car dispatched by His Lordship; but since Pincher had been kitted out for an afternoon of fly-fishing, it was remarkable that he turned up dressed for dinner and equipped with all he would need for an overnight stay.

The journalist, the old spy and the retired molehunter convened over pre-dinner drinks in the library: each was, from the outset, shamelessly untruthful. Rothschild introduced Wright as 'Philip' and said that Pincher knew nothing of what they were about to discuss; Wright and Pincher pretended not to recognise each other, and the journalist claimed not to know why he had been summoned at such short notice.

The truth was very different. Rothschild had been briefing Pincher about MI5's scandals for the previous four years and knew that the old hack was already working on a book about the Hollis saga. For their part, Wright and Pincher were old acquaintances and had worked together on Security Service business since the 1960s.

Their collective dishonesty that evening set the tone for the next six years. Rothschild and Wright were professional dissemblers, willing and able to lie without remorse in the course of their duties or in pursuit of their individual goals; but of the three conspirators, it was the journalist whose duplicity and ruthless self-interest would cause the greatest trouble.

Harry Chapman Pincher was born, to a resolutely middle-class family, in 1914. At the age of ten, Harry won a prestigious scholarship to the local grammar school, and he progressed to an undergraduate degree in zoology and biology at King's College, London. His first job, as a physics teacher in Liverpool, was interrupted by the outbreak of the Second World War; he joined the Royal Armoured Corps, became a tank gunner and developed a lifelong fascination for military technology.

In 1944, a chance encounter with an old friend, then working for the *Daily Express*, steered him towards a future career in journalism and gave him a taste for leaking official secrets. The reporter wanted information about a powerful new explosive, RDX, which Army scientists were developing: the project was inevitably highly classified, but Pincher was happy to provide the details. The *Express* got its story and marked Pincher out as a post-war prospect.

That the disclosure was unauthorised and, in wartime, unquestionably illegal troubled Pincher not one jot. As he recalled in his memoirs, RDX was an invention which 'would blow thousands to eternity but it propelled me towards prosperity'. Further leaks of intelligence on German V rockets swiftly followed, as did remuneration from his grateful recipient in Fleet Street, and then, after demobilisation, a full-time job with the newspaper.[1]

In the immediate post-war years, the *Express* was the most popular daily newspaper in Britain, with a circulation steadily rising to a peak of more than four million. It was politically on the centre-right – aimed squarely at the ordinary citizen ('the man on top of the Birmingham No.13 bus')[2] – but genuinely dedicated to providing serious stories on issues of public interest: 'a University for the masses', in the words of its celebrated editor, Arthur Christiansen. The paper's team of reporters was 'proud and arrogant and curiously incestuous'.[3] Chapman Pincher, a die-hard Conservative, snobbish and perpetually self-important, was a perfect fit.

From the outset he was convinced that the road to journalistic glory lay in unearthing and publishing more official secrets than any other reporter. He had, especially in the early years of his career, two significant advantages over his rivals: the *Express* was a Tory paper at a time when many civil servants were instinctively opposed to Clement Attlee's Labour government – and he was blessed with a very generous expense account. 'I operated, mainly, by inviting my targets to convivial lunches at restaurants within walking distance of their offices,' he recalled in his autobiography.[4] Within a decade, his proprietor, Lord Beaverbrook, was happily funding lavish meals for Pincher's contacts at West End restaurants and paying for the reporter's Mayfair flat.

Pincher's technique worked deliciously well, and survived successive transitions between Labour and Conservative administrations. He quickly earned a well-justified reputation for scoops based on inside information. If this sometimes caused anxiety inside Downing Street – 'I do not know how the *Express* alone of all the newspapers has got the exact decision that we reached at the Cabinet last Thursday on space [research],' Prime Minister Harold Macmillan complained in May 1959; 'Can nothing be done to suppress or get rid of Mr. Chapman Pincher?[5] – the reporter positively revelled in the notoriety of being the recipient of politically motivated leaks.

When socialist historian E.P. Thompson condemned Pincher as 'a public urinal where ministers and officials queued up to leak', he responded with the proud boast that 'if the information was true, and especially if it was exclusive, I was open for "use" at any time'.[6]

That claim was, at best, half-true. Pincher's *pissoir* was reserved for those with a right-wing agenda, and he was not greatly fastidious about the accuracy of every story offered to him over oysters and Chablis at l'Ecu and other fine-dining establishments. It was precisely these qualities which attracted the attention of MI5.

In 1960 the Security Service recruited Pincher to wine and dine Anatoli Strelnikov, a KGB officer working under official cover as the press attaché at the Soviet Embassy; over generous boozy lunches, and then at a party in his Surrey home, the journalist fed the spy with juicy titbits of bogus intelligence provided by Leconfield House – a mission he subsequently related with characteristic self-regard.[7] The officer who prepared this 'chicken feed' of 'credible but false information' had good cause to remember MI5's enthusiastic intermediary: his name was Peter Wright. 'I was involved in that operation,' he later testified in a secret court session. 'I put the information in the briefcase which [Pincher] took to Strelnikov. [He] would have signed the Official Secrets Act when he started this work as that was the normal procedure for a double agent.'

The Strelnikov mission was but the first of Pincher's efforts on behalf of the Security Service, and throughout the 1960s and 1970s he was frequently used as a reliable vector for feeding 'helpful', if not necessarily true, information to the public via the pages of the *Daily Express* – journalistic favours which were rewarded by regular access to MI5 officers.

'I know from my time in MI5,' Wright recalled, 'that because of Pincher's extremely close links with its legal department which handled controlled leaks of information, Pincher was treated entirely differently from any other journalist. For instance senior intelligence officers would socialize with him, whereas for intelligence officers journalists are normally taboo.'[8]

Some of those officers held very senior ranks inside both MI5 and MI6. Wright's earliest physical encounter with Pincher was – inevitably – over drinks and dinner at a Pall Mall gentlemen's club. 'I first met him with Maurice Oldfield who was then Vice-Chief of MI6. It was in the late 60s. Pincher was eating dinner by himself four or five tables away. Maurice asked if I knew him. I said I hadn't met him and Maurice waved him over and introduced us. Pincher sat down and drank a few glasses of port with us.'[9]

Another of Pincher's sources and dining companions was Victor Rothschild. Shortly after Harold Wilson's resignation in 1976, Rothschild gave the reporter details of the plot by Wright's cabal of MI5 officers to blackmail the Prime Minister with 'evidence' of his Soviet connections – a scandal that was then still unknown outside British intelligence and Downing Street. Pincher duly reported this, heavily larded with a right-wing spin to imply that Wilson had indeed been a spy, in a book two years later. If he coyly referred to his informant as 'a very senior Whitehall personality, whose name I know but whom I will call "Q" to preserve his anonymity',[10] the disguise was paper-thin. 'Q' was the codename of the senior scientific genius in James Bond stories, an 'in-house' reference to Rothschild's own wartime role and one which thoroughly entertained the great man.

Nor was their collaboration confined to the Wilson Plot. By early summer 1980, Pincher was on the trail of the Hollis saga and approached his contact for help. At first Rothschild demurred, advising in July against paying attention to 'a small number of people who have got the subject on the brain to the extent of paranoia … To make a poor pun, I am inclined to think that one should let the dogs lie without comment.'[11]

But two months later Rothschild summoned Pincher, recently retired from the *Daily Express*, to Cambridge to meet – and to work with – the MI5 officer most determined to rouse those dogs from their slumber.

This, then, was the true context to the meeting of the three conspirators that evening in September. Each knew and had worked with the others; each knew the outline of the story Wright wanted to tell – and each knew their own role in the scheme to have it published.

The plan was simple in concept but fraught with legal danger. 'Rothschild,' Wright later testified, 'said that I would provide the information, Pincher would write the book and Rothschild would use his Swiss bank to channel half the royalties to me in Tasmania.'[12]

Paradoxically, of the three men who toasted this agreement over post-prandial nightcaps, Peter Wright was the least exposed: his name would not appear in either the eventual publisher's contract or in the manuscript itself. If providing the journalist with information gleaned during his years inside MI5 unquestionably breached the undertaking he had signed on retirement, the law underpinning this had a fundamental flaw: for all its draconian provisions, the Official Secrets Act could not be used against British citizens living outside the United Kingdom – especially if their unauthorised disclosures also took place abroad.

For that reason, Wright refused to show his ten-chapter manuscript to Pincher in Cambridge; he also refused a suggestion to hand it over in London the following day, insisting he would only do so once he returned to the safety of his Cygnet stud farm. With ill grace, the journalist reluctantly agreed to fly out at the start of October.

Pincher himself, and Victor Rothschild, faced much greater legal risks. Thirteen years earlier Harold Wilson's Labour government had learned that the *Sunday Times* was planning to send a reporter to interview Kim Philby in Moscow, and the Foreign Office asked the Attorney General for advice on whether the newspaper, its reporter or the defector himself could be prosecuted under the Official Secrets Act.

In November 1967, the Attorney General decided that, while Philby could only be brought to book if he returned to the UK, proceedings could be brought against both the *Sunday Times* and its reporter for inciting a former member of the intelligence service to breach the Official Secrets Act and for receiving information prohibited by the Act. The penalty for either offence would be a substantial prison sentence.[13]

Although the government decided not to pursue this oppressive attack on press freedom – that autumn several British papers carried interviews with the unrepentant Soviet spy – the law officer's advice was passed on to Leconfield House and, as the spycatcher leading MI5's investigations into the Ring of Five, to Peter Wright. He, at least, knew the very real dangers of exposing his former employer's confidences, and he was initially puzzled by Rothschild's eagerness to risk prosecution.

'It struck me as particularly odd,' he later testified, 'that Rothschild should suddenly seek to secure the publication of MI5's secrets about the molehunts, since he had always before counselled caution ... [but] Victor was always very secretive and it was not done to ask him questions.' Ultimately, Wright decided that the plan for Pincher to ghost-write his account must have received covert blessing from the Security Service or the Prime Minister.

> [Victor] loved to exert influence behind the scenes. His wealth and position are so great that I could not believe he would risk it for such a scheme if it was not at least tacitly approved ... I concluded in my own mind that I was being used as part of a deniable operation.[14]

This assumption was at least partly correct. Whatever Rothschild's actual role or motive, the plot hatched by Armstrong and Thatcher two months earlier for Pincher to be secretly briefed about Hollis by Peter Rawlinson was precisely the 'deniable operation' which Wright suspected.

Nor was his own motivation entirely altruistic. Desperately short of money, he insisted that the proposed book's advance and royalties should be shared equally – a condition Pincher grudgingly accepted with three crucial caveats. The first was that the reporter was to offset his 'expenses' against the payments; the second was that Wright's 50 per cent would be paid by Rothschild, via a new company, Overbridge International, formed in the British Virgin Islands tax haven specifically for the project.[15] But the third condition preyed upon Wright's inexperience with journalists and publishing deals: Pincher carefully omitted any mention of the lucrative newspaper serialisation rights that would inevitably accompany publication. It was a loophole which, within six months, he would exploit to the full.

Wright flew home to Tasmania a few days later. It would be the last time he saw the country he still loved and to which he had given genuine service: from the night he agreed to betray its secrets, he knew he was irrevocably an outcast who would die in exile.

Pincher followed him at the start of the next month, arriving in Hobart on 12 October. By his own somewhat dubious account, he travelled under a pseudonym – 'Dr. Chapman' – because his own name was 'rare and peculiar ... [and] too easily recognizable'. He was shocked by the dilapidated state of Wright's home – 'a three room shack made, apparently, from two apple-pickers' huts' – but rather more troubled by his own basic accommodation and the paucity of refreshment on offer in the town's sole hotel.

Despite this unwelcome privation, he stayed for a full week; Wright picked him up every morning in an old truck bought on credit – the 'never

never' – an arrangement so alien to Pincher's rather more pampered experience that he presumed it must be 'peculiar to Australia'.

Together, the two men worked through the typescript for *The Cancer in Our Midst*. It was, the reporter pronounced, unpublishable in its extant form, and would need complete reorganisation, followed by wholesale rewriting. Nor was the title to Pincher's liking; instead, he proposed to call the book *Their Trade Is Treachery* – the name of an internal 1946 MI5 training pamphlet. But his overriding concern was the need for a truly sensational revelation around which the rest of the story could be wrapped: the Hollis scandal was just the ticket 'to make the book saleable'.

Wright happily agreed, but for his own security refused to allow his co-author to take away any documents which could be traced back to him or his antiquated typewriter; instead, he insisted that Pincher laboriously write out detailed notes by hand. 'Almost everything he told me that eventually appeared in *Their Trade Is Treachery*,' Pincher later wrote, 'was given to me verbally and had to be noted down and then copied out longhand late at night when I was back at the hotel.'[16]

Wright also insisted on precautions for future collaboration. The ten-hour time difference and the cost of phone calls between London and Tasmania meant – in those pre-email (and even pre-fax) times – that letters were the only viable way to communicate. Drawing on his own exploits and experience, Wright presumed that MI5 would probably take an interest in correspondence regularly shuttling back and forth, and insisted on elaborate precautions to frustrate its interception or understanding: both men would use cover names – he would once again be 'Philip', while Pincher was to be 'Henry' – and a crude horse-breeding code was adopted to obscure the subjects under discussion. For good measure, Wright wanted all letters heavily sealed with Sellotape: it would not stop the Security Service from opening the envelopes, but the tampering would be impossible to conceal.

At the start of December, Pincher completed a two-page proposal for his regular British publisher, Sidgwick & Jackson. The synopsis boasted that the book would 'expose ... the true extent of the Communist conspiracy to undermine the fabric of British life ... the dramatic search for "moles" inside MI5 and the Secret Service ... and the chief suspects'. It also hinted at the source of these dramatic revelations: 'All the information in this book has been gleaned from authorities who are deeply concerned about the Soviet penetration of Whitehall and its offshoots and believe that the public needs to be warned about its full extent and purposes.'[17]

The pitch document found immediate favour: by the end of the month, Pincher signed a contract with the publisher, with a handsome advance on royalties of £30,000 – the equivalent of £120,000 today – to be doled out in three equally staged tranches. The first payment of £10,000 – half of which would be routed to Wright via Rothschild's offshore banking scheme – was due early in the New Year. It did not, however, run entirely smoothly.

Between January and May 1981, Wright repeatedly had to chase his share of the advances. A flurry of letters between Cygnet and Kintbury showed that His Lordship was unexpectedly tardy in making the payments. 'Five [thousand pounds] is on the way by the V-channel,' Pincher promised on 7 January, an assurance that he had to repeat three weeks later: 'Our mutual friend has just confirmed that the deposit for the mares is on its way to you.'

It wasn't, and by the end of March Wright was both desperate and irritated by the unreliability of the process. When Pincher raised the problem with Rothschild, it was clear that his promised support was now no longer a priority. 'I had a session with our "horse-coper" [Rothschild],' the reporter wrote on 31 March. '[He] says he cannot safely change the arrangements in the foreseeable future and ... he rather regards himself as having completed his contribution.'[18]

There was a reason for His Lordship's sudden volte-face. On 23 March the *Daily Mail* began a lengthy serialisation of *Their Trade Is Treachery*, which was published three days later. Both events caused a predictable media stampede; but the public controversy was a minor squall compared to the unseen storm which had roiled Downing Street and MI5 for almost two months.

Pincher had delivered the manuscript to Sidgwick & Jackson in the middle of February. Almost immediately, one of the publisher's directors, the hotel and catering magnate Sir Charles Forte,[19] sent a copy to the Cabinet Office.[20] The text made for uncomfortable reading: Pincher had laid out the results of Wright's investigations into Blunt's communist recruits, the suspicions about Wilson's Eastern European associates, and accused civil servants of 'cold feet' in their reluctance to tackle the problem of Soviet penetration.

But it was his blunt assertion that MI5's former Director General had been a spy for Moscow which caused the greatest alarm inside Number 10. 'The case against Sir Roger Hollis, and the way in which both that and the allegations against Mitchell are treated, are so detailed and accurate that they could only have derived from a person or persons actually involved in the investigation of those cases or from someone with access to the files of those investigations,' Armstrong wrote to Thatcher on 17 February. Worse, despite the Cabinet Secretary's covert plot to have Pincher present a 'sympathetic' account of the internal investigation, 'he gives the impression that Lord Trend concluded that Hollis was probably guilty, whereas of course Lord Trend's conclusion was that, while it was not capable of proof, there was certainly no conclusive evidence that he was guilty'. In reality, as Armstrong's memo noted, Trend had estimated, on 'the balance of probability', that there was a 20 per cent possibility that Hollis was a spy.[21]

Armstrong and Thatcher's gambit to ensure that Pincher exonerated MI5's former Director General had clearly failed miserably. As Nigel Wicks, the Prime Minister's Personal Secretary, noted mournfully: 'I am afraid that this is going to give us nothing but trouble.'[22]

The sole crumb of comfort was that despite this litany of MI5 failings, Pincher professed himself satisfied that there was no need for any external scrutiny. 'In my opinion,' he pronounced with characteristic immodesty, 'any inquiry except by people with personal knowledge of security and Intelligence operations would be of little use.'[23]

On 12 March, two weeks before the *Mail* serialisation was due to begin, MI5 sent Armstrong its verdict on the identity of the former Security Service officers suspected of leaking to the reporter: it had established the names of 'several sources' but was 'a long way from obtaining hard, usable evidence' with which to charge them under the Official Secrets Act.[24]

In truth, prosecution was the very last thing the Cabinet Secretary wanted. A lengthy trial was guaranteed to unearth the government's own deal to use Pincher and would expose both Armstrong and Thatcher to possibly fatal political outrage. But he also knew the names of at least two of the troublesome reporter's informants. 'Pincher is known to be acquainted with Lord Rothschild,' MI5's report had noted,[25] a warning which the Cabinet Secretary followed four days later with an internal letter to the Prime Minister, advising that 'there is some reason to think that Mr. Pincher's main source is Mr. Peter Wright, a former member of the Security Service and of the team that investigated the Hollis case, who is known to have been dissatisfied with the conclusion of the investigation. Mr Wright now lives in Australia, out of reach of the Official Secrets Act.'[26]

The decision not to prosecute Pincher – much less his presumed sources – would cause severe difficulties in the *Spycatcher* trials five years later; but a letter Armstrong sent to Sidgwick & Jackson on 23 March, the day the *Mail* serialisation began, would provide the ammunition which damned the Cabinet Secretary and doomed the government's case.

'I have seen the extracts in the *Daily Mail* today from Mr. Chapman Pincher's forthcoming book *Their Trade Is Treachery*,' he wrote to the publisher's managing director, William Armstrong.[27] 'The Prime Minister is in my judgment likely to come under pressure to make some statement on the matters with which Mr. Pincher is dealing.

'I believe you will agree with me that if she is to make a statement, it is in the public interest that she should be in a position to do so with the least possible delay. Clearly she cannot do so until she has seen not just the extracts published in the *Daily Mail* but the book itself. I should therefore be very grateful if you would be willing to make one or (preferably) two copies available to me as soon as possible today or tomorrow.'

Since he had received a copy of *Their Trade Is Treachery* six weeks earlier, and had prepared a full report on its contents for the Prime Minister, the Cabinet Secretary's request was decidedly disingenuous; but the rest of the letter gave an explicit undertaking that the government would make no attempt to block the book in the courts.

'I can also assure you that the only purpose of this request is to equip the Prime Minister to make a statement, if she should need or be minded to do so, with the least possible delay. The request is not made with a view to seeking to prevent or delay publication, and I can assure you that we shall not do so.'[28]

Three days later, on 26 March, Margaret Thatcher was chauffeured from Downing Street to the Houses of Parliament. Though Pincher's book stopped short of recommending a full inquiry, Thatcher and Armstrong were moved to action. The carefully crafted statement prepared for delivery to the House of Commons was an attempt to put an end to the uproar over the journalist's revelations about MI5 and its scandals. Instead, it would provoke new breaches in the dam of official secrecy – and breathe new life into Peter Wright's smouldering anger.

13. WHO IS TALKING?

'Had Mrs. Thatcher told the truth ...'
PETER WRIGHT AFFIDAVIT: CONFIDENTIAL
MATERIAL, NOVEMBER 1986

'With permission, Mr Speaker, I will make a statement about the security implications of the book published today.'
At 3pm on 26 March 1981, Margaret Thatcher stood up in the House of Commons. It was her second attempt in three months to clear up the festering mess of MI5's historic scandals and it marked a noticeable change in her approach to parliamentary oversight of the intelligence services. In her previous appearance at the despatch box, to confirm Blunt's treachery and immunity deal, she had departed from the traditional governmental position of refusing to make any comment on issues of security; while she had been rather less than frank, her speech reflected an early belief that at least some sunlight should be allowed to penetrate the shadowy world of counter-espionage. Her statement on Pincher's revelations firmly redrew the curtains.

'I think with Blunt that she was lurching towards being an open government Prime Minister,' recalled Jonathan Aitken. 'Thereafter she became a very closed government leader.'

In fairness, Thatcher's grip on power, and especially on her own party, was tenuous in the early months and years of her premiership. She had entered Number 10 with a decent 44-seat majority, but the hard medicine of her economic policies was already being felt across the country, and there were rumblings of discontent among more moderate Conservative

MPs. Aitken saw that 'the ship of state was very leaky and rocky: outwardly the Queen's government was going on well, but we politicians knew the fragility beneath, and that the chances of an internal coup against her were enormous'.[1]

The decision to address publicly Pincher's accusations that Sir Roger Hollis had been a traitor was not easily taken. For a full week, the Prime Minister and the Cabinet Secretary had taken soundings on how to tread the very thin tightrope of protecting MI5 without revealing their own involvement in briefing the reporter, or encouraging yet more unwelcome journalistic scrutiny. They toyed with falling back on the old policy of refusing to comment on security, before concluding that this line stood no chance of holding; reluctantly, they prepared a statement, always mindful of the warnings from their closest advisors that this must avoid direct attacks on Pincher.

None of this meant, however, that she intended to be honest. Armstrong's influence and clever misdirection were to be the defining characteristics of her twelve-minute statement to the House.

She began with an attempt at reassurance: the extent of Soviet penetration of the intelligence services had been 'thoroughly investigated after the defection of Burgess and Maclean' and had 'covered not only those suspected of being guilty but all those who could conceivably fit the often inconclusive leads available ... Many people have had to be investigated simply in order to eliminate them from the inquiry'. Other than Philby and Blunt, she asserted, 'there were good reasons for suspecting a few others, but as it was not possible to secure evidence on which charges could be founded they were required to resign or were moved to work where they had no access to classified information'.

If this stayed – just – within the strict bounds of accuracy, her wholehearted defence of MI5's late Director General was much less scrupulous.

'The case for investigating Sir Roger Hollis was based on certain leads that suggested, but did not prove, that there had been a Russian intelligence service agent at a relatively senior level in British counterintelligence in the last years of the war. None of these leads identified Sir Roger Hollis, or pointed specifically or solely in his direction. Each of them could also be taken as pointing to Philby or Blunt. But Sir Roger Hollis was among those that fitted some of them, and he was therefore investigated.

'The investigation took place after Sir Roger Hollis's retirement from the Security Service. It did not conclusively prove his innocence. Indeed, it is very often impossible to prove innocence ... But no evidence was found that incriminated him, and the conclusion reached at the end of the investigation was that he had not been an agent of the Russian intelligence service.'

This was emphatically not the unanimous verdict of Peter Wight's FLUENCY committee, merely the opinion of Hollis's successor – a distinction Thatcher didn't trouble to make. But she quickly swept on to assert that Lord Trend's subsequent secret inquiry had confirmed the exoneration. Pincher, she insisted, was wrong to claim that Trend had concluded there had been long-term penetration of the Security Service 'by someone other than Blunt and that he named Hollis as the likeliest suspect. Lord Trend said none of those things and nothing resembling them.' Nor, had he warned of 'the possibility that Hollis might have recruited unidentified Soviet agents into MI5'.[2]

All three of these statements made by the Prime Minister were substantially false. MI5's own reports – provided to her predecessors in Downing Street – stated that there had been lengthy historic penetration and that Hollis had been identified as 'the most likely suspect'. If the 1975 memo sent to Harold Wilson by his Cabinet Secretary, which summarised Trend and all the internal molehunts, had not referred to Hollis as the progenitor of unidentified spies, it had specifically noted 'the possibility that people like Philby might have recruited other members [of the intelligence services] before they were themselves detected'[3] – a very narrow distinction indeed. But her account of Trend's verdict was the clearest evidence of her willingness to lie to parliament. Armstrong's memo on 17 February had specifically noted the inquiry's conclusion that there was a significant possibility that Hollis had been a traitor: '[although] there was certainly no conclusive evidence that he was guilty ... the balance of probability was that he was not ... [Lord Trend] subsequently put that balance at 80 to 20)'.[4] [5]

What followed was equally misleading. Thatcher told MPs that the time had come for an 'independent review' of MI5's 'procedures and practices ... for the purposes of safeguarding information and activities involving national security against penetration by hostile intelligence services'. To that end, she announced that the Security Commission would carry out an inquiry in to what she coyly referred to as 'the public services', and she undertook 'to make its findings known to the House in due course, to the extent that it is consistent with national security to do so'.[6]

The Security Commission was a curious body.[7] From its inception in the aftermath of the Profumo affair, its seven members had been drawn from the ranks of reliable judges and senior civil servants; they were unelected and responsible only to the Prime Minister who appointed them.

Since 1971 the Commission had been chaired by Lord Kenneth Diplock, whose chief claim to public fame had been abolishing the historic right to trial by jury during the Troubles in Northern Ireland.

When he reported back to Thatcher in December 1981, Diplock was careful to record that his remit had specifically excluded any examination of the allegations of moles within MI5 – a remarkable omission since this was ostensibly the spur for the inquiry. Nonetheless, his additional recommendation – that the existence of MI6 should no longer be a state secret – caused immediate disquiet inside Downing Street. Armstrong advised that this would inevitably 'bring questions about Ministerial control and the Secret Vote and would lead to pressure for some form of Parliamentary scrutiny of the intelligence agencies'. Since this was plainly anathema, he advised the Prime Minister to abandon her promise to report back to the House of Commons. 'I see no need for the Prime Minister to make an immediate announcement,' he counselled.[8]

Nor did she for another fourteen months, and even then her eventual statement was brief and uninformative: 'It would not be in the national interests to publish the report,' she told the House 'with some regret'.[9] It would remain secret until 2014.[10]

As a result, both MI5 and MI6 remained officially 'unavowed' – maintaining an absurd position by which the government refused to acknowledge that two of the most famous, and publicly referenced, intelligence agencies in the West existed outside the world of James Bond or John le Carré. It was a bizarre fiction and one which would cause severe difficulties for the Cabinet Secretary during the coming *Spycatcher* trials.

There was one further peculiar omission from Thatcher's statement about *Their Trade Is Treachery*. Although it was clear that Pincher had interviewed former MI5 officers, who had also plainly broken the Official Secrets Act to give him dramatic details of Soviet penetration and the internal molehunts, there was no mention of an inquiry into how he had come by such closely guarded information.

When a Labour MP raised this in a written Parliamentary Question the following day, the Prime Minister promptly passed the buck. 'An investigation is being made,' she replied to Bob Cryer. 'Any relevant evidence will be submitted to my right honourable and learned Friend the Attorney-General.'[11] Since any such investigation would quickly have revealed the evidence of her own plot to leak the Hollis scandal to Pincher, it was unsurprising that nothing would be heard of it for almost four years.

If Thatcher and Armstrong hoped that her speech would shut down any further leaks and discourage journalists from airing MI5's dirty laundry,

Who Is Talking?

they were naïve in the extreme. Newspapers and television channels took the government's failure either to seek an injunction to block the book or to bring prosecutions under the Official Secrets Act as a green light to look for retired intelligence officers with tales to tell.

'Everyone was looking for these stories,' remembered Paul Greengrass, then a producer with ITV's flagship current affairs series *World in Action*. 'It was open season for MI5 scandals.'[12] For his part, Pincher was sanguine about his protection from prosecution, telling Jonathan Aitken he was 'very confident that he was "away to the races"'[13] and urgently starting work on a follow-up blockbuster. His first phone calls were to Arthur Martin and Peter Wright, but he quickly discovered that a rival author had beaten him to both.

News of Thatcher's speech had already reached Tasmania, and her exoneration of Hollis had infuriated Wright. As 'the only senior officer of MI5 to serve twenty years in counter-espionage' he knew that her statement was 'substantially false ... designed to give the misleading impression that the Hollis evidence could all be conveniently laid at the door of the ancient moles such as Blunt and Philby'. Worse, these 'errors must have been known to those who prepared the brief for the Prime Minister'.

He was particularly incensed by her claim that the evidence of Soviet penetration had been 'thoroughly investigated' and laid to rest without unearthing any post-war treachery inside Leconfield House. 'Had Mrs. Thatcher told the truth,' he later testified in secret session, 'she would have said that there was evidence of Russian penetration throughout the fifties and early sixties, that some of the evidence pointed solely at Hollis, some of it pointed at him and ... Mitchell, some of it was unattributable to any person or a small number of persons and was therefore not pursued by the investigators.'[14] Angry and frustrated, Wright began looking for new ways to expose the truth as he saw it.

Pincher might have been his first port of call, had it not been for two characteristic pieces of double-dealing by the veteran reporter. The first was that he had not discussed one of the central thrusts of the book with Wright – notionally (if not publicly) his co-author. 'Pincher did not at any time show me a synopsis or a complete manuscript,' Wright would tell the court in Sydney five years later. 'I did not see the book until it was published [and] I was very disappointed ... because the last chapter ... concluded there was no need for an inquiry. This conclusion was quite contrary to my views.'[15]

This betrayal – as Wright saw it – was compounded by continuing problems in getting his share of the proceeds. Throughout the spring and summer of 1981, complaints about payment from 'Philip' were a regular feature of the post received by 'Henry' at Kintbury – protests the reporter batted aside with dishonest emollience.

'The Ks you request immediately available,' Pincher wrote in May, before blaming Rothschild for the delay. 'Held up only on advice of our mutual friend.' Two weeks later there was no sign of that 'immediately available' payment, prompting another round of tripartite correspondence and further promises. 'After consultation with your advisor, your Ks for the horses already sold are on the way to you. No more may be expected for three months when your advisor may have organized a new arrangement.'

This was followed six weeks later by yet more handwringing: 'I am appalled to hear that you have not received your stallion proceeds. I set this in motion a month ago and the failure is due to the mechanics at our mutual friend's end. Am doing all I can to expedite.'[16]

Little wonder, then, that Wright sought out a replacement collaborator, complaining that Pincher had 'ripped him off' by withholding, among much else, all of the *Daily Mail* serialisation money.[17]

Rupert Allason was 30 and the son of a lieutenant colonel in the Army who had been Churchill's senior military planner during the Second World War before serving as a Conservative MP for fifteen years. The younger Allason had ambitions to follow his father on to the Tory benches in the House of Commons, but was also forging a career as the author of two richly researched books on British intelligence; he wrote these under the pen name Nigel West.

After the publication of his second book, in 1981, an account of MI5 from its founding to the end of the war,[18] he was approached by Arthur Martin with an unusual proposition. Graham Mitchell, the Security Service's former Deputy Director General and subject of the convoluted PETERS molehunt, was now gravely ill, and Martin – apparently with official blessing – asked West to 'extract a death bed confession' from the man: that he had, after all, been a Soviet spy.

'You don't look a gift-horse in the mouth,' West recalled in an interview 40 years later. 'The Service thought this could be achieved: the question was how, and how well, I should be briefed. Mitchell had an encyclopaedic knowledge going back to 1938 when he joined the Service, and I said unless it could be demonstrated that I knew as much as he did – or at least the background to the case – the whole exercise would be useless.'

Martin agreed, and over several months West was schooled in the arcana of MI5's hunt for traitors in its ranks and how to conduct the

Who Is Talking?

interview. 'I was to give assurances to Mitchell: I was told to promise not to do anything while he was still alive or to embarrass his family: whatever promises needed to be made, I was to make them.'

It was an extraordinary and – given the events of that year – politically risky operation, but West 'assumed that this year-long briefing was official: Arthur was no longer with MI5, but my training sessions included his wife, Joan, so I was reasonably confident that what was going on was above board'.

If the mission ultimately collapsed under the weight of its own improbability – 'I spoke to Mitchell, who refused to see me, so that was the end of that' – West put the experience to good use: 'Every time I went for my briefings, I wrote them up. I didn't say I was going to write them up, but nobody told me not to. And that became the basis of my next book.'[19]

Simultaneously, West was also receiving instruction from Martin's fellow retired molehunter, Peter Wright, to prepare for interviews with Anthony Blunt. Once again, the young journalist believed he was being used in an officially sanctioned operation.

> Blunt only saw me because MI5 had told him to do so ... Anthony had rung them up and asked them whether or not he should talk to me. They wanted to know what Blunt was telling me ... and the only person who knew the story inside out was Wright. And so, literally within half an hour of getting back to my flat in the Fulham Road after talking to Blunt, I would ring Peter and give him a blow-by-blow account of what had taken place. All the names. Everything. I don't know what he was planning to do with that, but [I believed] he was doing this with the consent and approval of the Security Service. That he was doing it on behalf of MI5.[20]

As with Martin's briefings, West made detailed notes of everything Wright told him, and forged all the information into the manuscript for a new book. *MI5 – A Matter of Trust* was to give a far more thorough account of the Security Service's triumphs and scandals than Pincher's bombastic and self-aggrandising *Their Trade Is Treachery*: it named more names, set out the exact structure and varying codenames for each of the Service's branches, and clearly identified its premises.

By any metric, exposing these closely guarded details and unashamedly indicating that they stemmed from interviews with former officers placed West himself squarely in the crosshairs of the Official Secrets Act, but he believed he was 'bullet-proof because I had been authorised to be indoctrinated into all of these cases'.[21]

He was half-right. MI5 did indeed know that Wright and Martin were briefing the journalist, but it had not sanctioned the leaks and was unequivocally unhappy about them. In May 1981, Barry Russell Jones, recently retired as head of agent recruitment for the Service's anti-subversion F Branch, had written to Wright advising him to end the association; two months later, a more formal warning had been issued to both the former molehunters by John Allen, Director of Establishments.

> I am now writing to confirm what Barry said to you on 29 May, that you should not discuss with West any matters arising from your work with the Service. The same of course applies to any other similar approaches.
>
> I am not sure how seriously to take your remark to West that you would 'be writing an accurate history of what happend [sic] but that it would not be published in my lifetime'. But to avoid any uncertainty, I must tell you that your obligation not to make such a record, whether for publication or not, remains unchanged. I have little doubt that the authorities here would respond to a breach of your obligations by invoking any available remedy, under civil as well as criminal law.[22]

In the autumn of 1982 West was about to discover the draconian nature of those 'remedies'. On 27 September he submitted the manuscript for *A Matter of Trust* to the Ministry of Defence for vetting by its D Notice Committee – a peculiarly British body, established just before the First World War, which provides 'advice' to newspapers, the broadcast media and individual authors on whether their proposed publication might endanger national security. Submissions to it are voluntary and the Committee has not a shred of statutory authority, but its recommendations are, by tradition, accepted as the government's own.

Two weeks later, on 13 October, police and a lawyer from the Attorney General's staff hammered on the door of West's flat and served him with an injunction, issued by a judge that morning in an *ex parte* hearing – one which took place without the writer being informed, much less present to defend himself.

This argued that publication of his book 'would cause damage to the Security Service' because it contained 'previously unpublished information classified as "secret"; identifies present members of the Security Service

Who Is Talking?

who have not been previously identified; includes charts which describe in detail the main organisation of the Security Service up [to] 1965', and stressed that these details 'can only have been related to the Defendant by past (or present) members of the Security Service'. Since West had not been given 'authority' to publish any of this, the Attorney General insisted the entire manuscript amounted to a 'breach of a duty of confidentiality owed to the Crown' by those who had briefed him.[23]

Not only had the judge rubber-stamped the demand to injunct the book, but his order came with an unusual and ominous 'penal clause' attached. 'It was a very frightening experience,' West recalled. 'John Bailey, the Treasury Solicitor, was a very threatening individual; he came to my front door, personally, with a police officer, to serve the injunction, and the penal clause said that if I attempted to discuss the injunction with anyone, even a solicitor, I would be arrested and go to prison straight away.'

Shortly afterwards, West was summoned to the Ministry of Defence for a dressing down in the D Notice Secretary's office. 'They went bonkers – they wanted 205 redactions including the removal of an entire chapter.'[24]

Quite why historic details of long-cold molehunts – many of which had already been revealed in *Their Trade Is Treachery* – had to remain secret was never clear to West. But inside Number 10, the Cabinet Secretary was in no doubt that suppressing the book was necessary *pour encourager les autres*.

'Following the publication of Chapman Pincher's book, [West's *A Matter of Trust*] could make it look as if there were some sort of implied licence to former members of the Security Service and the SIS [sic] to be indiscreet', Armstrong advised Thatcher at the start of October.[25] But he was simultaneously aware of the danger of bringing criminal charges, since that might 'raise the questions "who was Chapman Pincher's mole, and why there had been no prosecutions in that case"'.[26]

Instead, the MOD and MI5's legal advisor, Bernard Sheldon, were ordered to negotiate redactions. After two weeks an agreed manuscript was officially sanctioned, but the final version was strangely similar to West's original: only a handful of particularly sensitive names, together with 'a few other limited passages' were removed.[27]

Armstrong, inevitably, put a rather more positive spin on this retreat, telling the Prime Minister that 'the Treasury Solicitor has had greater success than many of us expected', and that 'the agreed amendments would remove virtually all that had not previously become public, they would be embodied in a court order (punishable as contempt of court if breached) and would also apply to the text to be published in the United States'.[28]

But, forced to protect the scheme he and Thatcher had cooked up to help Pincher, the Cabinet Secretary had blundered into a secondary legal problem: the agreement with West established a principle that books drawing on information from MI5 officers could be vetted and redacted, rather than banned outright. 'On balance,' he advised the Prime Minister, 'I consider that ... an agreement with Mr West will represent the least damaging course of action open to us ...'[29] It was a de facto admission which would cause him very real discomfort in the *Spycatcher* trials.

These closed-door negotiations formed the more benign legal element of the government's 'carrot and stick approach'. West was also threatened with a hefty plank of political consequences should he continue to cause trouble – a racing certainty since he had two future books 'in the pipeline'; a memo in the Prime Minster's papers recorded that Conservative Party Chairman Cecil Parkinson was 'commissioned' to warn the young writer 'that his ambitions as a Conservative parliamentary candidate would be better served if he ceased publishing books of this kind'.[30] [31]

In late November, MI5 followed up with a round-robin letter to all its retired staff, pointedly reminding them that they were the beneficiaries of the Service pension scheme. 'Whilst we have no reason to believe that any serving officer of the Security Service has given information to West,' it warned after a newspaper serialisation of *A Matter of Trust*, 'we are aware that some ex-members of the Service have spoken to West without authority ... You may find yourself approached by journalists ... whatever the circumstances you are in no way released from your obligations under the Official Secrets Act or the duty of confidentiality owed by you to the Crown.'[32]

This stern advice was, however, quickly undermined by the government's own chief law officer. On New Year's Day 1983, Attorney General Sir Michael Havers enjoyed a pleasant afternoon shooting party with Chapman Pincher; he was, Pincher wrote to Wright, 'very friendly ... [and] I can assure you that there is no intention whatever of taking action against me, which means you too. Further, I have been functioning for some months as a specialist advisor (paid) to the Parliamentary Defence Committee and have just been appointed chief advisor on an enquiry into positive vetting. I am also elected to a Committee to study censorship problems arising out of the Falklands affair.[33] So I do not think we are unpopular.'[34]

Putting a known journalistic poacher in charge of the government's intelligence-information henhouse hardly suggested a coherent policy on the disclosure of sensitive secrets. But, as Neil Kinnock, shortly to do battle

Who Is Talking?

with Thatcher as Leader of the Opposition, later recalled, Pincher was an 'inside man' with powerful protection.

Because of the extent and nature of his contacts in the security services and in the MOD and the Foreign Office ... he was treated carefully as 'one of us'. He wouldn't be invited to dinner, but any invitations *he* extended would be fulfilled. Whilst they didn't embrace him, they never rebuffed him because he was useful; they believed innately that what he was doing would ultimately come out on their side of the account.[35]

Other journalists were less privileged and felt the full force of Thatcher and Armstrong's determination to clamp down on troublesome reporting. Jonathan Bloch, a South African law graduate and human rights campaigner, had sought refuge in Britain in 1976 following threats from the apartheid-era regime; he arrived on a two-month visa and was given a succession of extensions. Finally, in December the following year, he was granted protected status under the 1951 Refugee Convention due to 'a well-founded fear of persecution if he returned to South Africa'.[36]

In the early 1980s Bloch benefitted from a more generous series of one-year extensions to the visa giving him the right to stay in the UK, but then he applied for indefinite leave to remain. It should have been a routine request, routinely granted, but the young man had committed – in the eyes of the Thatcher government – an unpardonable 'crime': he had co-authored a book about British intelligence.

In March 1983 news of its imminent release reached the ears of Robert Armstrong: he promptly, if incorrectly, advised the Prime Minister that the authors had received 'assistance' – presumably from former Security Service and SIS officers – but, as a handwritten note by a Downing Street official at the top of the memo warned, Bloch's primary publisher was based in the Republic of Ireland, and thus beyond the arm of British law.

'We cannot prevent publication in Eire,' the unnamed civil servant reported, 'and, given that, you may think there is no point in trying to prevent publication in the UK.'[37] It was sound counsel, which both the Cabinet Secretary and the Prime Minister would have been wise to heed.

As with *Their Trade Is Treachery*, the government had surreptitiously obtained a pre-release copy of Bloch's book, *British Intelligence and Covert Action*. All of the information in its 243 pages was drawn from open – and previously published – sources, but an appendix listed, in alphabetical order, the names of MI6, MI5 and GCHQ officers from 1945 onward;[38]

that this, too, was culled from official and published government gazettes of staff in their diplomatic cover departments mattered little to the increasingly intolerant occupant of Number 10. She demanded a review of options to end Bloch's refuge in the UK.

When Armstrong regretfully told her that 'there are no grounds for refusing Bloch's application for permanent residence', she scrawled on top of his memo: 'We must not give in so easily!'[39] She wanted 'a direct approach to the authors and publishers of the book to warn them of the harm done by publication'. This posed a problem, since it would inevitably 'disclose the source of our information about the book'. Instead, the Cabinet Secretary suggested it would be prudent to wait and see before embarking on action – a recommendation to which the Prime Minister responded with a scrawled message in pen, 'maddeningly feeble',[40] then followed up by suggesting 'surely we can change the law to deal with security cases like this?'[41]

There was, in truth, nothing the government could do to block Irish publication, and precious few options for lawful retaliation against the author in Britain. As Home Office officials warned Downing Street, Bloch's status as a refugee meant that if he was summarily deported 'on security grounds' he would easily win an appeal – one which would become yet another public *cause célèbre* – not least since he could show 'that the information ... has already appeared elsewhere, that his activities were not illegal and that all the material obtained by him could readily be obtained by others from published information'.[42] It was a foretaste of battles to come.

Armstrong, meanwhile, busied himself with examining whether Britain could import US legislation which criminalised revealing the names of intelligence staff; he eventually concluded that the American law had never been tested in litigation and that there would be sizeable problems involving the disclosure of evidence should a test case ever reach English courts.[43]

Faced with this insuperable legal hurdle, the government resorted to a grubby back-door solution. As a note from the Foreign Secretary's staff to Number 10 made explicit, Bloch would be granted only a brief six-month extension to his visa – with no promise of any further leeway – in the hope of harassing him into leaving of his own accord: 'Sir Geoffrey Howe thinks that, within the limits of the possible, we should aim to maintain the pressure on Bloch and to leave him uncertain about his long-term future here.'[44, 45]

The Bloch affair was a clear sign of Thatcher's refusal to tolerate any public discussion of MI5 and MI6, and the lengths to which she

Who Is Talking?

was prepared to go to prevent it. Throughout the year she had become increasingly alarmed by the continuing stream of unauthorised disclosure of intelligence secrets, plaintively asking her staff, 'Who is talking and what are the sanctions?'[46]

Within six months, she would know the disquieting answer to the first of those questions, as a succession of former MI5 officers outed themselves, and their often dubious activities on behalf of the state, in very public fashion. Peter Wright was one of them, then preparing for his first television interview to denounce the Prime Minister, the Security Service and the British Establishment. And the government would discover that it had very little power to silence him or his former colleagues.

14. OUT IN THE OPEN

*'The country should be given the benefit of the
doubt, not the individual'*
PETER WRIGHT INTERVIEW: WORLD IN ACTION,
16 JULY 1984

On 23 November 1982 the phone rang unexpectedly in Peter Wright's dilapidated house in Cygnet. The caller introduced himself as Paul Greengrass, a producer with Granada Television's flagship current affairs programme *World in Action*.

Greengrass was then 31. Long-haired, with a drooping Zapata-style moustache, he looked 'like a Trotskyite bomb-thrower';[1] if his politics were, in reality, rather less extreme – 'I've always been mainstream Labour; left of centre but not far left of centre,' he reflected 40 years later – he nonetheless encapsulated many of Wright's most deeply held prejudices. His employers had also long been on the old spycatcher's list of suspected communist helpmeets: Sidney Bernstein – the subject of a 'very interesting' MI5 file – had relinquished control of Granada by now, but the station had a well-earned reputation for challenging governments, the courts and the commercial television regulator.

In the 1970s, the Independent Broadcasting Authority (IBA) had banned three of its programmes, and in 1980 a *World in Action* investigation into alleged malfeasance at the British Steel Corporation provoked a major row which saw two of its producers threatened with prison and the prospect of swingeing fines on the company. Neither of these threats had worked, and the programme defiantly stood its ground.

157

Greengrass had not given Wright any advance notice of his arrival. He had flown to Tasmania with little more than a letter of introduction from Nigel West and the deep pockets of his employers. That evening, he explained he was calling from the Returned Servicemen's League club, just down the street from the horse-stud. Would it be possible, he asked, to meet? Wright paused for a moment before rumbling: 'you'd better come and have a drink'.[2] It was an invitation that would, eventually, land both men in court.

The producer's own motives were straightforwardly journalistic. He hoped to secure a scoop: the first on-camera interview with a former Security Service officer about the Roger Hollis affair. And he believed that the recent history of unattributable briefings by retired intelligence staff meant that the old dam of official secrecy was crumbling.

'As the 80s opened, the code of *omertà* started to break down and suddenly you could see a secret history becoming visible,' Greengrass recalled. 'I was part of a group of people all interested in this area: we were the post-Watergate generation, driven very much by how things were in America and we saw the excessive secrecy in Britain as un-modern and holding the country back. We believed it was healthy to get all these bulging skeletons out in the open. And the reality was also that spy stories were catnip for newspapers and for television.'[3]

He found Wright a frail and much-troubled man, brooding in his exile over the perceived betrayal by his country, but sustained by the support of his family and a passion for nature.

> He was devoted to his wife, Lois, and she to him. They would walk every evening down the little lane – not very far because he couldn't walk very far – hand in hand. She was small but formidable; if you saw her you'd think she was the stable hand – checked shirt, jeans and someone who could throw a bale of hay up six feet high.
>
> Together they were eccentric, very English and they existed in a world of horses and the seasons: Peter had a deep knowledge of plants and animals and a real love of the natural world – it's where he found peace.[4]

Peace, though, was then proving elusive. Despite his chicanery over the proceeds of *Their Trade Is Treachery*, Chapman Pincher was harrying Wright to divulge further revelations to boost the prospects of a new edition. 'Horse sales [the code for book proceeds] have slumped and need stimulation,' he wrote before sending a list of 30 detailed questions.

Out in the Open

'Let me have any comments soonest because even if they are too late for the paperback of my book, they will be helpful in the publicity to boost sales through radio, TV appearances and press articles. There's nothing like news stories for stimulating sales ... The great thing is to have the meat and then we can make and market the rissole.'[5]

Though he did not know it, Greengrass had arrived at a propitious moment. Wright was then pondering how to get his still-unpublished dossier on Soviet penetration into the growing debate about MI5, its scandals and its lack of accountability. He had, Greengrass realised, 'a tremendous chip on his shoulder' and a profound bitterness towards the British Establishment. 'He always felt that he was not accepted as an equal by people he called "the velvet-arsed bastards". That was a favourite phrase of his.'[6]

But he was not yet ready to step out of the shadows and into the sunlight of a personal appearance. He told the young producer he needed time to think about the proposed interview.

Surprisingly, given their fraying relationship, he turned to his former co-author for advice: the response was characteristically self-serving. Pincher cautioned against trusting any other journalist: Nigel West had 'dirtied the nest for everybody', while the *Sunday Times* duo of Barrie Penrose and Simon Freeman were dismissed as 'arch-shits'. Nor was the veteran muckraker impressed by *World in Action*'s promise to defend Wright against government retribution after transmission of the proposed interview. 'I do not wish to be unkind to Granada,' he warned, 'but would you have the resources to sue them if their management reneged on such an agreement?'[7]

In truth, there seemed little likelihood of any official reprisal. In February 1981 one of Wright's old colleagues had given the first television interview by a former MI5 officer. Tony Motion had been a member of Wright's FLUENCY committee, and was happy to tell the BBC's *Panorama* team about his years in the Security Service.

> My first job when I started was really just to learn the way about and the ... way the office worked with all its tremendous paperwork and huge filing systems. [The Registry] is absolutely vital ... if you don't have any records you can't get anywhere. One always imagines that MI5 is tremendously sort of glamorous, chasing people in the streets, that sort of thing. But in fact really 95% of it is based on thorough detailed research of records.

It was an anodyne recollection – and the existence of the Registry was well-known to the Service's opponents in Moscow – but Motion quickly moved on to rather more detailed revelations about MI5's precautions when its officers were engaged in questionable activities.

> I used to carry a little card – we all did ... if we were in the operational side. They were carefully guarded ... and it had a photograph of myself with my name in it, and it had the address of the War Office ... It just said 'this person is on special duties and any help that may be given, we'll be very grateful'.'

He also frankly described surveillance operations and techniques, including a mission targeting Hungarian spies working under diplomatic protection.

> 'Instead of covertly covering members of the Hungarian Embassy who we know to be intelligence officers, we did it quite overtly and we really sat on their tails as close as I am to you. And I actually did this myself.
>
> When [the diplomat] came out ... we literally sat on his tail and we jumped from taxi to taxi with him. We went into restaurants with him, we went into gentlemen's cloakrooms with him. The object really was to see whether it will have any effect on his sort of mentality, his approach, would he get very, very frustrated and would it sort of psychologically disturb him?
>
> And the other [aim] was to see whether ... we'd force him to ... take some risks which we may be able to cover in a covert way. I don't think it worked actually ... but ironically I think it does work when the Russians do it to our diplomats.

The interview also yielded a first-person description of the investigation by MI5's molehunters into suspected Soviet sleeper agents at Oxford University.

> One of the things I was doing was to look at the Communist Movement at Oxford in the thirties. I mean, after all one had seen the same situation in Cambridge ... it was a reasonable assumption that the Russians would have [been] just as successful [at Oxford] as they were at Cambridge ... Anybody who had been through Oxford in the thirties were by then pretty senior people. And if somebody had been recruited at Oxford and we didn't know about it they might be in the Ministry of Defence or Foreign Office or Parliament. It was our job to find out about it.

Out in the Open

Motion's revelations comprehensively shattered the notion that retired Security Service officers could never speak publicly about what they had done on behalf of the state, or what they had learned in the process. *Panorama*'s interview aired on BBC1 in prime time, yet neither MI5 nor its masters in government made any attempt to block the broadcast or to retaliate against the whistleblower. For his part, Motion had, like Wright, come firmly to the conclusion that a little disinfecting sunlight was long overdue.

'I've often asked myself that question,' he mused towards the end of his interview, 'and ... I cannot see it could do a lot of harm to the Service. I can't believe that it would. I can't see, anyway, how it would inhibit the Service from performing its duties, and therefore if that's correct I think it's fair to say that a little bit more accountability couldn't do any harm.'[8]

Yet despite the evident lack of appetite within Downing Street or his former employers to silence retired MI5 officers, at the end of 1982 Wright remained uneasy about breaking cover. Over the next eighteen months he corresponded with Greengrass, but still refused to agree to his own interview.

Two events changed his mind. In September 1983, Michael Bettaney, a heavy-drinking and profoundly unstable MI5 officer serving in the elite counter-espionage K Branch, was charged with six Official Secrets Act offences of passing highly sensitive documents about British intelligence to the KGB's resident head of station at the Soviet Embassy in London. If the mechanics of his betrayal had bordered on ineptitude – he crudely stuffed the first batch of papers through the Russian spy's home letterbox – the Security Service's own conduct had been equally incompetent. Bettaney was openly disaffected with the Service's monitoring of domestic 'subversives' and had recently been convicted of public drunkenness and of fare-dodging by using an expired railway season ticket; neither his criticisms nor the pair of offences prompted anything more serious than a written warning.

In April 1984, after an eight-day trial held entirely *in camera*, Bettancy was sentenced to 23 years in prison. One month later, one of his former K Branch colleagues published a lengthy first-person attack on MI5's failures, its self-regarding 'old boy' culture and its addiction to secrecy.

'The glamour of MI5 in the public eye,' Miranda Ingram wrote in *New Society* magazine, 'largely rests on the work of K, the counter-espionage branch, where both Michael Bettaney and I worked ... In fact, the day-to-day work of intelligence officers is not particularly glamorous. They spend a lot of time merely keeping files up to date and storing information. Only the secrecy of the information, and the elaborate procedures for locking away bits of paper, detract from the routineness of it all. However, the very nature of an intelligence officer's work, whereby he is acting as a judge on his fellow-citizens, does put him in a position above the ordinary man.'

This bogus mystique, Ingram complained, was the prime cause of a toxic in-house complacency.

> Glamour and secrecy combined to make for a very elite club. Some accept membership as a birthright. To those of the new broader intake, who were not born to expect easy superiority, membership is a privilege. To both types, belonging to MI5 offers a private thrill: this is a security which can compensate for many social or personal inadequacies ...
>
> The intake is now broader than the old days, when one simply 'knew a chap'. However, the overall tone is right-wing ... Those who dissent from the overall tone are also faced with a problem ... there is a lack of flexible debate within the service about the interpretation of 'subversion'. In the prevailing right-wing atmosphere, an officer who dissents from the official line does not feel encouraged to voice his concern. He feels that to do so would be futile, or, unfortunately, that it would be detrimental to his career ... So initially he keeps quiet. This is where the situation becomes dangerous.

If Ingram's criticisms were coruscating – an insider attacking the fundamental foundations of the supposedly secret service – her prescription to restore its health was just as unwelcome.

> Public accountability would benefit both the Service and the public ... Once the Service was seen to be openly respectable it could relax its secrecy paranoia ... and concentrate on being an efficient and intelligent body. Whilst the Security Service remains a total independent and unaccountable body, public suspicion will continue to grow, and, in turn, secrecy will become more obsessive.[9]

Curiously, given what was to follow in the *Spycatcher* affair, no action was taken against Miranda Ingram for breaching a duty of confidence, nor against *New Society* for publishing her article. In Tasmania, Peter Wright took note of this, and of the Bettaney case, which showed clear evidence of continuing Soviet penetration of the Security Service; after a full year and a half of dithering, he contacted Greengrass and agreed to a recorded interview.

Out in the Open

The producer and his colleague, veteran journalist John Ware, promptly flew to Tasmania with *World in Action*'s in-house film crew. They set up a makeshift studio in a hotel room in Hobart and prepared for their scoop; but Greengrass had distinctly modest ambitions for the production. 'What John Ware and I wanted to do,' he recalled, '[was to ask ourselves] what was the thing we could contribute? Men like Arthur Martin and Angleton were busy leaking: we were looking at this unfolding story about Hollis with different threads to be followed, and we felt that what we could do was get one of these guys on camera. It's the old thing about the antiseptic quality of daylight. If we could get one of them on camera, you get them on the record; they're no longer talking unattributably.'

He need not have worried. For all his initial hesitancy, from the moment Peter Wright sat down in front of the film crew, Greengrass 'had an overwhelming sense of a man carrying an immense psychological burden ... and I felt strongly that he had a psychological need to unburden himself'.[10]

His instincts proved correct. For more than an hour, as successive magazines of 16-millimetre film cranked through the camera's gate, Peter Wright gave a detailed account of the hunt for a mole in MI5's midst, and calmly parried Ware's sceptical cross-examination. The team flew back to London, well-satisfied with the interview.

But neither of the producers was entirely convinced by Wright's unwavering conviction that Roger Hollis had been a Soviet spy; over the following weeks they approached the late Director General's son and twenty former MI5 and MI6 officers, seeking either to corroborate or undermine the old spycatcher's version of events.[11] Nor were their targets drawn from the lower ranks of British intelligence: one of those who toyed with their request for an interview was Hollis's old boss, Sir Dick White, who held the unique distinction of having headed up both Services.[12] If, ultimately, all declined to appear on camera, knowledge that *World in Action* was preparing an exposé was now an open secret.

In early May, MI5 learned of the planned programme, and that Wright was 'assisting' its production.[13] By 3 July, the Security Service had received 'confidential information' from its own mole in the IBA, Director of Television David Glencross,[14] that 'Granada TV ... intended to show an interview with Peter Wright in which Wright would reopen the Hollis case and in effect present the case against him.'[15] Yet no attempt was made to apply for an injunction, or to request an advance copy for vetting.

Two weeks later, on 16 July, *The Times* reported that the programme would transmit that night; the news provoked a phone call from MI5, asking the government's lawyers to consider demanding 'a preview of the programme and seeking to restrain publication, if necessary by means of an injunction'. Neither option was deemed palatable: according to internal files kept secret for the ensuring 40 years, 'the view of the Security Service conveyed to the Treasury Solicitor's Department was that the interests of the Security Service would be best served by not taking action at that stage'.[16] Behind MI5's surprising change of heart was a realisation that 'if a preview was refused, going for an injunction would undoubtedly be a hard fight and if a preview was agreed the Government could be put in the position of appearing to have approved it whether or not it asked for cuts'.[17] It was prescient advice which Downing Street would have been wise to heed.

At 8pm on Monday 16 July, *World in Action's* dramatic titles – an animation based on the naked figure of William Blake's primeval man, accompanied by thunderous organ chords – announced the latest assault on the fraying reputation of British intelligence.

'Today,' John Ware's narration declared, 'the Hollis case still casts a shadow over the headquarters of MI5 ... a group of senior officers responsible for the case believe that Hollis was guilty and that Mrs. Thatcher was wrongly advised by her security chiefs when she cleared him in Parliament. Now one of those officers has decided to challenge the Prime Minister's statement ...

'Peter Wright was one of MI5's elite molehunters ... [he] has taken the unprecedented step of talking about the Hollis case because he believes MI5 will always be flawed until it learns the lessons of the past.'

Wright's interview amply lived up to this billing. 'Those of us intimately involved in the Hollis investigation believed that [he] had been a long-term Soviet agent in MI5,' he argued. Thatcher had been misled by her intelligence chiefs, 'who were anxious that there shouldn't be a high-level independent inquiry into the Service that might drag skeletons out of the cupboard that they would not want revealed'.

Over the ensuing 50 minutes, the retired spycatcher hit all the highlights of the exhaustive search for a traitor inside Leconfield House: he repeated Anatoliy Golitsyn's claims, tied them to his own research into the previously secret Venona decrypts – 'irrefutable evidence' of '43 [Soviet] spies' operating in Britain – and the failure of all MI5's 'operations against the Russians ... fairly soon after they were started'.

While some elements of Wright's story – PARTY PIECE, Volkov, Gouzenko, ELLI, FLUENCY, the Symonds report and the debacle of the Mitchell investigation – had previously been chronicled by Pincher and West, this filmed interview was the first time the British public heard the

Out in the Open

allegations directly from an intelligence officer at the heart of the scandals. And he put new flesh on the bones of an account of the 'top GRU agent' allegedly sent to Britain to run Hollis in MI5's wartime headquarters at Blenheim Palace.

> She was one of the top spy-runners in Europe. She had been deliberately moved to England and directed to the Oxford area: the V[enona] material proved this. We were convinced she must have been sent there to run a very important spy [and] when one notes that Hollis' department was moved to Blenheim at that time, it suggests it was more than a coincidence.

Wright also laid into Downing Street for blocking his investigations into other suspected spies: he claimed to have identified 'well over forty' of these, but was prevented from digging sufficiently deep to expose them. 'There was first of all the barrier against [investigating] politicians, and secondly people who were in high government departments such as Permanent Under Secretaries of State and people like that. I was not allowed to talk to them until they retired.'

But again and again Wright hammered home his primary charge: that Roger Hollis had been a spy – the traitor responsible for MI5's failed operations – and that the Prime Minister had misled Parliament in her speech which exonerated him. Her statement was, he complained, 'a masterly piece of Whitehall deception because there were ... 28 allegations against him after a year's work, which were considered to be true ... and to say [as Thatcher had] that it could all be explained by Philby and Blunt was rubbish'.

It was a bravura performance, in which Wright willingly acknowledged the fundamental flaw in his case against Hollis. When Ware put to him that the evidence was entirely circumstantial 'and in the absence of conclusive evidence you're really not entitled to say that he was a spy', the old molehunter was ruefully honest.

> Legally, that is absolutely correct; intelligence-wise it is 99 per cent certain that he was a spy ... It was all circumstantial, but it always will be ... [and] I think that in an issue like this the country should be given the benefit of the doubt, not the individual.[18]

For all its openness, Wright's emergence into the sunlight via *World in Action* caused relatively few creases in the fabric of British society.

The country was then being torn apart by the miners' strike. The industrial action led by the National Union of Mineworkers' divisive leader Arthur Scargill, governmental intransigence and allegations of covert MI5 involvement to defeat Thatcher's 'enemy within', and – above all – the shock of pitched battles between police and pickets captured national headlines and the nation's attention. That summer, battle lines were – sometimes literally – being drawn; left and right faced off in the streets, in the courts and in Parliament.

It was an unseen irony that a man whose every political instinct and prejudice matched that of the Iron Lady in Number 10 was now marked out by her advisors as her enemy. Because while Wright's attack on the Prime Minister had not registered with much of the public, it was a source of fury for the Prime Minister's Cabinet Secretary. From July 1984, Sir Robert Armstrong would seek to take revenge.

15. DIRTY TRICKS

> *'Two publishers lost interest in Wright's memoirs after being warned off.'*
> THE OFFICIAL HISTORY OF THE
> SECURITY SERVICE

Her Majesty's Cabinet Secretary was seething. As *World in Action*'s title music and end credits faded out, Armstrong composed two terse notes. The first was to the Prime Minister, advising her that, in the light of Wright's interview, 'We are considering whether there is a case for abating or discontinuing his pension.'[1] That this was not strictly true, and it was he alone who was contemplating financial retribution, was highlighted by his second letter, delivered post-haste to MI5's Director General, Sir John Jones.

> I hope you are reviewing the possibility of discontinuing the payment of Peter Wright's pension. His contribution to the *World in Action* programme ... was self-evidently in flagrant breach of his obligations under the Official Secrets Act ... He is, moreover, in open and defiant breach of [the] trust on which your service depends; we have surely to consider the effects on others if he escapes scot free.[2]

It was unfortunate that the government's most senior civil servant had not troubled to check the statute books before firing off his missives. After taking legal advice, Jones reported that, unless Wright was convicted of a criminal offence, there was no provision to deprive an officer of his retirement benefits. Perhaps, the Director General suggested, Armstrong could explore the possibility of demonstrating official 'displeasure ... by depriving [Wright] of the CBE which he was awarded in the 1972 New Years Honours List'.[3]

That, too, proved to be beyond the reach of Downing Street. Unlike Blunt – the closest comparable case – the old spycatcher had not confessed to betraying his country: in fact, his interview had clearly demonstrated a desire to protect it. Armstrong was left to fume at his own impotence and the law's lacunae.

It was doubly inconvenient that this concluded with the unfavourable outcome of his enquiries into the drafting of a new statute, modelled on America's controversial and untested law, which would make it a criminal offence to reveal the name of anyone working for the 'secret services'. 'Whilst all of those I have consulted would wish to protect intelligence identities,' he told Thatcher four days after the broadcast, 'none of us would wish to argue that the gain would be worth the cost of winning it.'[4] It was sound counsel, and in the coming months the Cabinet Secretary would have been wise to remember his own advice.

For his part, Wright was unwilling to let go of his obsessive belief in Soviet penetration of MI5, Whitehall and the British Establishment. *World in Action* had put fresh wind in his tired sails, and he now asked Greengrass to pass on his dossier of evidence to the Chairman of the House of Commons Foreign Affairs Select Committee.

Sir Anthony Kershaw was a decorated Second World War cavalry officer – he had been awarded the Military Cross for bravery during the Tunisian campaign – a former barrister and, after almost twenty years as an MP and junior minister in Ted Heath's government, a Conservative Party grandee. His position as head of the Select Committee bestowed him with the power to open parliamentary hearings which could expose the intelligence services to much-needed scrutiny.

He was already deeply concerned by the Hollis affair: two days after *World in Action* aired, he wrote to Thatcher warning that suspicions about MI5's former Director General were not confined to Wright and his FLUENCY colleagues.

> I have in my constituency a gentleman who until fairly recently was second in command at GCHQ. He tells me that some years ago when the Russian defector Petrov joined our side from his post in Australia the information about this was, unusually, largely obtained by intercepts from Cheltenham.

After the defection Roger Hollis, who at that time was at MI5, asked my friend whether he would tell him how it had been done. My friend said that as it was on a need to know basis he would not do that. Hollis then went to the Chief of GCHQ and insisted with great emphasis that he should be told how it had been done. However, the Chief backed up my friend and Hollis was not told. My friend said that thereafter he always regarded Roger Hollis as suspect.[5]

The Prime Minister did not trouble to reply to Kershaw's letter. It was simply parked in Downing Street's files, where it would languish, undisclosed, for the next four decades.

When Wright's dossier – titled *The Security of the United Kingdom Against the Assault of the Russian Intelligence Service* – landed on Kershaw's desk it ran to 160 closely typed pages, carefully divided into ten chapters, and looked remarkably like the first draft of a book. It arrived at the end of July 1984, with a note asking that he bring it to the attention of the Prime Minister in confidence; instead, the MP handed the papers to Robert Armstrong. They did not find favour: at a meeting on 30 July, the Cabinet Secretary blithely pronounced that all of Wright's allegations 'had been thoroughly and carefully studied … [and that] there was no new evidence in this material'.[6]

Kershaw, however, proved unwilling to be fobbed off with bland reassurances. 'The point about the Hollis affair,' he wrote to Armstrong on 10 August, 'is surely that there was a strong possibility that he was a traitor, and that the only prudent, and indeed reasonable way to react, is to assume that he was a traitor when deciding what steps are necessary to ensure that nothing of the same ever happens again. Those steps must include some sort of monitoring organisation.'[7]

Not for the last time, Downing Street chose not to listen to well-intentioned advice. In early September, a meeting between the Cabinet Secretary and MI5 decided that 'the dossier contained nothing new of significance, was factually inaccurate, ignorant of some material facts, made weak or faulty inferences and was selective'.

If this was – just about – arguable, Armstrong's memo to the Prime Minister the following day was largely fantasy: he advised Thatcher that 'the material was old hat' and its overall thrust 'strengthened Lord Trend's conclusion that Hollis was not a Soviet spy'.[8] Since Wright was consumed by the very opposite belief, the Cabinet Secretary's *précis* was fundamentally untruthful. Nor was it likely to survive the next salvo from Kershaw.

On 25 September, the MP was summoned to a meeting inside the Cabinet Office. Armstrong, with MI5's Director General and his deputy at his side, set out 'to put the record straight'. It proved to be an uphill task.

The two Security Service chiefs told Kershaw that 'there had for many years been a small group of specialists which kept under continuous review all available information concerning threats of penetration ... and that the work of this group was under the regular oversight of someone from outside the [intelligence] agencies'. This, as Armstrong's secret minutes of the encounter made clear, was not strictly honest: the notional 'outsider' was, in fact, Lord Trend – the former mandarin who had acquiesced to Thatcher's misleading parliamentary statement on Hollis in 1981.[9]

Kershaw was a loyal Tory, but he had an independent mind and was uneasy at the Security Service's unacknowledged status, as well as the lack of democratic scrutiny of its operations. He sent the Cabinet Office the draft of a speech he planned to make in the House of Commons after the Queen's Opening of Parliament in early November. This argued that the Soviet Union had for years been 'startlingly successful' in spreading disinformation and, citing the cases of Philby, Blunt and Burgess, that it had placed its spies inside Britain's security and intelligence services. But it was his charges about Hollis, and the inquiry into his alleged treachery, which caused most alarm inside Number 10.

> We also know that allegations have been made by those ... in a position to know, that there was another spy who was never unmasked ... I have been sent a mass of evidence about [this] ... [and] it is plain that if there was a spy he did immense harm to this country.
>
> In 1974 an enquiry by Lord Trend, an immediate past secretary to the Cabinet, came to the conclusion that the case had not been proved. Some of us were surprised. Some of us wondered how one man, not a professional security man, could adequately ferret through 30 years of files and secrets and be sure that he had missed nothing, and had been full informed by those whom he questioned ...

The existing system of secret and reactive inquiries, Kershaw's speech charged, was not working. 'What is needed is a permanent presence within the institutions themselves, a sort of Inspectorate-General, keeping a professionally-informed eye on the practices and personalities.'[10]

The idea alarmed and repelled Armstrong in equal measure. He reported back to his mistress, warning her of the risks of 'opening up an issue on which Parliament could run ahead of where the government wished to be', and advising, 'I think we must reserve judgment on whether a speech by Sir Anthony Kershaw would be useful.' [11]

Thatcher agreed and wrote to head Kershaw off at the pass. 'We have special standing arrangements for reviewing all available information concerning threats of penetration,' she insisted. 'They include an element of regular oversight from outside the services as well as the use of specialist analytical and investigative capacity within them.'[12]

Kershaw was no fool. He saw that this 'outside oversight' amounted to little more than Trend reporting privately to the Prime Minister, and that it excluded scrutiny by any genuinely independent body. According to a memo of their subsequent conversation, the MP brusquely told Armstrong that 'he did not regard the arrangements as sufficient – he wanted something like a standing Security Commission – but if this idea would be rejected by the government then he would pursue the matters outside Parliament and not raise this matter in the Debate'.[13]

This tactical retreat incensed Wright. At the turn of the year he wrote to Kershaw, complaining that his dossier had been disclosed to the Cabinet Secretary – a man he now perceived as an enemy and a mandarin willing to go to extreme lengths to silence him – rather than being raised in the House of Commons. Two weeks later the MP responded emolliently, but cautioned that the government's hostility was very real.

'I am sorry that you are distressed that your document was revealed to Sir Robert Armstrong,' he wrote on 18 January 1985. 'I think that this was right in the public interest. When I said that I would not pass it around of course I meant to the media and to anyone else who happened to be curious about it, but it is a very important public matter and it is only right, I think, to treat it on a strictly confidential basis.

'With regard to what you say about prejudicing your position, this in no way was the result of Sir Robert Armstrong seeing the dossier. The Attorney General personally spoke to me before the document was shown to Sir Robert and he then told me that on the basis of the interview you had already given to the television services he would be inclined to prosecute you under the Official Secrets Act if you were to come to the UK.'

It was a clear warning that Thatcher and Armstrong would brook no opposition, either from inside Parliament or from troublesome former intelligence officers on the other side of the world. 'I am still seeking ways in which I can achieve what you wish,' Kershaw promised, 'without arousing such public hostility that our purposes would be frustrated.'

There was a curious coda to the Tory grandee's letter, and one which seemed to undermine the government's claims to be protecting the Security

Service from a dangerous renegade. 'You might like to know,' he told Wright, 'that those of your old colleagues in this country whom I have seen pay the highest tributes to you and I am sure they are richly deserved.'[14]

Inside Downing Street, the Prime Minister was becoming increasingly autocratic and unwilling to tolerate dissent. 'She was insecurely regal,' recalled Neil Kinnock, who had faced her across the despatch box for more than a year. 'She used to do regal things in order to prove to herself that she had the power, and she generally enjoyed the opportunities provided by what could broadly be called security tensions.'

The proximate cause of this growing intransigence had been the attempt on her life during the Conservative Party Conference the previous autumn. In October 1984 the Provisional IRA planted a bomb in the Grand Hotel in Brighton: the explosion killed five people and maimed many more, but Thatcher narrowly escaped injury. The experience hardened her belief that no one outside her close circle of Conservative friends and advisors was to be trusted.

'Her instincts about those issues were partisan rather than patriotic,' Kinnock, now a Labour life peer, remembered 40 years later. 'She would try to exploit evidence of security problems, or threats to the overall security of the country, to try and demonstrate a kind of latter-day Churchillianism. But I don't think her interest in these things went much further than that.'[15]

She remained the dominant figure in British politics, but in the early winter of 1985 the Prime Minister was given a stark warning that her bunker mentality on the need for official secrecy was not entirely shared by the public. From January to February, a senior official in the Ministry of Defence was put on trial at the Old Bailey: Clive Ponting was charged with breaking the Official Secrets Act by providing a Labour MP with two confidential documents about the sinking of an Argentinian cruiser, with the loss of several hundred lives, during the Falklands War. At the time, Thatcher had told the House of Commons that the warship *General Belgrano* posed a threat to British forces inside the government's self-declared 'total exclusion zone'; the internal documents showed that in reality it was outside the zone and sailing away from the Royal Navy when it was destroyed.

The Ponting prosecution was the first trial of a civil servant for providing secret documents to Parliament. He admitted giving them to Tam Dalyell, a veteran opposition firebrand, but claimed he had done so in the public interest.

Legally, this was no defence: the Official Secrets Act contained no provision allowing unauthorised disclosure, however well-intentioned, unless it was 'in the interests of the State', and on 8 February the judge, Mr Justice

McCowan, issued a 'directed verdict', ordering the jury to find the defendant guilty. But three days later, the jury defied him: the twelve men and women unanimously acquitted Ponting.

It was – or should have been – a clear sign that the popular mood was turning against official secrecy. The only consolation for Downing Street came in McCowan's summing up, which enshrined in law that 'the interests of the State' were whatever the government of the day pronounced them to be.

'I direct you,' he told the jury, 'that those words mean the policies of the State as they were in July 1984 ... not the policies of the State as Mr. Ponting, Mr. Dalyell, you or I think they ought to have been. "The policies of the State" mean the policies laid down for it by its recognized organs of government and authority ... the policies of the State in July 1984 were the policies of the Government then in power.'[16]

But this small crumb of legal comfort was the last Thatcher and Armstrong would receive in 1985. Two weeks after the Ponting debacle, the Cabinet Secretary learned that Channel 4 was preparing to transmit a one-hour television documentary exposing the latest MI5 scandal: titled *MI5's Official Secrets*, at its heart was a whistleblower from inside the Security Service.

Cathy Massiter joined MI5 in 1970, and from 1981 to 1984 had worked in F Branch, monitoring domestic 'subversion'. What she saw there prompted both her resignation and her decision to speak publicly about the Security Service's surveillance of supposedly dangerous left-wing groups.

Before her interview was broadcast, the IBA stepped in to ban the film. It did so on the advice of its lawyers that, whistleblower or not, she was clearly in breach of the Official Secrets Act, and that 'until it became clear whether or not the government intended to prosecute', Channel 4 and the IBA itself ran a substantial risk of ending up in the dock with Massiter.

While the Attorney General pondered this latest headache, *samizdat* copies of the programme were shown to MPs inside the House of Commons and to journalists at an impromptu screening at a London hotel. Entrepreneur Richard Branson added fuel to the fire by selling copies of the video, stamped with the logo of his Virgin Records label and bearing the dramatic subtitle 'The Programme That Couldn't Be Shown'. Faced with this comprehensive defiance, and with the Ponting acquittal fresh in his mind, the Attorney General backed away from authorising any prosecution under the Official Secrets Act.[17] On 6 March the IBA reversed course, and two days later Channel 4 transmitted the film.

Massiter's extended interview in *MI5's Official Secrets* demonstrated how little had changed in the use of dirty tricks by Britain's domestic intelligence agency since Peter Wright's 'bugging and burgling' heydays. 'We were violating our own rules,' she alleged. 'It seemed to be getting out of control.' To her certain knowledge, the Security Service had tapped the phones of trade union officials, as well as entirely legal organisations, including the Campaign for Nuclear Disarmament and the National Council for Civil Liberties (NCCL).

> Anyone who was on the National Executive of NCCL, who worked for NCCL or who was an active member to the degree of being ... a branch secretary would be placed on permanent records. Enquiries would be instituted to identify such people and ... the police were asked to report on the activities of NCCL in their area.

From the 1970s to 1981 those targeted officials included the NCCL's former general secretary, Patricia Hewitt, and its legal officer, Harriet Harman. Both were now closely involved in Westminster politics: Hewitt was Neil Kinnock's closest aide in the office of the Leader of the Opposition, while Harman had been elected as a Labour MP. According to Massiter, MI5 had opened files on them despite knowing neither had done anything remotely illegal; instead, on the authority of an Assistant Director, the Security Service had placed both of them in its crosshairs for the 'offence' of defending the public's freedoms. 'What seems to have been the deciding factor was his own view that NCCL's attacks on certain institutions such as the police were deliberate attempts to undermine these institutions.'

Nor were civil rights groups alone in attracting MI5 surveillance. Based on her own experience, Massiter revealed that it had infiltrated undercover agents – moles – into trades unions: 'These people are working within ... legitimate organisations ... and yet have this sort of dual role of reporting back to the Security Service on ... what goes on within the union.'

Car plants, the fire brigade and – perhaps less surprisingly – the National Union of Mineworkers were singled out for telephone tapping, surveillance and infiltrations; all of this was undertaken not for the defence of the realm, but in the political interests of the government of the day. It amounted to a wholesale breach of the Maxwell Fife directive under which MI5 notionally operated and, in Massiter's view, 'highlights very clearly this extreme ambivalence between what the Security Service is there to do ... and what actually happens in practice, which is in effect to [go] quite a long way beyond those guidelines'. [18]

The government's response to the allegations followed a familiar Whitehall tactic. The Prime Minister asked the Chairman of the Security

Commission 'to investigate whether the Service had obtained the necessary warrants for telechecks and whether the criteria for phone tapping were being complied with'.

Lord Bridge was 68 years old, but evidently worked at remarkable speed on these instructions. From 28 February to 6 March, he examined all the Home Office warrants for phone intercepts over the previous fifteen years. Since there were 6,129 of these, and His Lordship's seven-day schedule was interrupted by both a weekend and two days in which he sat as judge in the House of Lords, he arrived at his verdict surprisingly quickly: 'all was well and there had been no wrongdoing by either government or [the] Security Service'.

Predictably, Thatcher did not publish the Security Commission's findings, instead verbally relaying his reassurance to the Commons: it provoked widespread incredulity and ridicule. Former Home Secretary Roy Jenkins charged that Bridge 'had been made to appear a poodle of the Executive', while the *Daily Telegraph* – usually a bastion of Tory values and unwavering support for the Prime Minister – denounced the report as 'hasty and bland ... the Bench's answer to fast food, a juridical Big Mac'.[19] It was a public relations disaster – and one which would come to haunt the Cabinet Secretary in the *Spycatcher* trials.

Thatcher's prime concern, however, was the risk of further disclosures by disgruntled former officers. On 4 March, at a valedictory meeting with Sir John Jones prior to his impending retirement, she asked the Director General 'if he thought there were any more Massiters in the Service: "She said that she was very concerned about the morale of the Security and Intelligence Services"'. He was, apparently, happy to reassure her on both fronts.[20]

Unfortunately for the government, Jones's faith was misplaced and short-lived: at the same time as the respective dramas of *World in Action*, Ponting and *MI5's Official Secrets* were causing headaches inside Downing Street, the issue of memoirs by former MI5 officers once again forced its way to the top of Robert Armstrong's inbox. His responses during the early months of 1985 were extraordinarily contradictory, but betrayed his deep-seated animus towards Peter Wright, and his willingness to use backroom arm-twisting to silence him.

In the six years since his exposure and public disgrace, Anthony Blunt had turned his fragrant hand to an account of his life, his career in MI5 and his efforts on behalf of Soviet intelligence. In January, Armstrong learned that after Blunt's death in 1983 this document had been lodged at the British Library, covered by an embargo which would keep it secret for

25 years. Given the government's self-proclaimed belief that all Security Service officers – traitors or otherwise – were bound by a lifelong duty of silence, what transpired displayed a remarkable lack of concern.

Blunt's brother, Wilfred, had read the memoirs and advised MI5 'that he did not think they contained much of interest to them'. On the basis of this distinctly flimsy assurance, Armstrong, Lord Trend and a representative from the Service held an informal meeting with the Chairman of the British Library Board and agreed that since 'it would not be possible to read the papers without the Keeper of Manuscripts at the Library becoming aware that the embargo had been broken … it was decided not to seek access unless there were some definite reason to believe the papers included important and relevant material'.[21]

By the government's own metric Blunt's manuscript unquestionably broke the much-vaunted duty of silence, but it would be another two years before Armstrong troubled to examine it – an insouciance in stark contrast to his reaction to whispers that Peter Wright's memoirs were being touted to London publishers.

Wright had been brooding on Pincher's betrayal and the failure of Kershaw to gain any traction for his dossier on Soviet penetration: he wrote to Paul Greengrass asking the producer if he would be interested in ghost-writing a book.

'What Peter had done with Pincher left him feeling more self-hatred and less peace,' Greengrass recalled four decades later. 'He had told it all to Pincher, who had written it up in *Their Trade Is Treachery*, but with a classic Pincher-esque spin … he had tried to ride two horses at the same time: he wanted the intelligence services to be both excellent, but simultaneously scandalously terrible. My impression was that Peter deeply needed something that would allow him to put it all away.'

The answer, as Wright saw it, was a book written and published under his own name, the contents of which he would control. Initially Greengrass was unconvinced; *Their Trade Is Treachery* had so comprehensively exposed the tawdry saga of MI5's past scandals that there was little new to say. But he quickly saw that a much more personal account of the old spycatcher's remarkable career could be more rewarding.

> I told Peter that the only book which I could see as being interesting would be one which recorded his whole life. By then I'd spent a fair amount of time with him and I was very interested in his early life. I was interested in the fact that Peter overcame an horrendous childhood: he was a very damaged boy – he had a terrible, crippling

stammer and a terrible lack of self-esteem – so how had he become the man who genuinely performed very real service for the State? I wanted to describe the whole journey, from his work with his father, the Admiralty, his early successes in MI5, and then his descent into conspiratorial thinking and ultimately becoming a sort of pariah. And from there, taking the step from the secret world to becoming a leaker and coming into the daylight. Making sense of how that happened could be, I thought, an interesting book. And Peter agreed.[22]

With the support of a literary agent, Greengrass began pitching the idea to London publishers: inevitably news of the proposal leaked. Bernard Sheldon, MI5's legal advisor – its only semi-acknowledged representative – turned to the tried and tested tactics of backroom arm-twisting; as the Security Service's authorised history admits, he 'initially hoped to prevent publication by warning off potential publishers. Wright's literary agent was successfully identified and two publishers lost interest in [the] memoirs after being warned off.'[23] But Sheldon's writ – so often law for Fleet Street and Grub Street – did not run to publishing houses outside the United Kingdom.

William Heinemann Ltd boasted a roster of illustrious authors – works by H.G. Wells, Rudyard Kipling and Graham Greene formed the backbone of its fiction list – and had been in business for almost a century when the proposal for Wright's book landed on the desk of Managing Director Brian Perman. His initial reaction was that it was 'an inspired leak', covertly authorised by MI5 or Downing Street.

'The fact that the government had remained quiet since the *World in Action* programme made me feel that possibly they knew what Wright was doing and they were quietly letting him get on with it,' he told the BBC in 2015. Nor did the publisher foresee huge profits to be made: 'I didn't immediately think "my heavens – this is an incredible revelation" ... There was never really any idea that this was going to make a great deal of money.' The advance Perman offered reflected this modest prediction: £18,000, the equivalent of around £53,000 today, was little more than half what Pincher had been paid for *Their Trade Is Treachery*.[24]

If the London-based publisher saw little danger of incurring governmental wrath, it still thought it prudent to farm Wright's book out to one of its overseas sister companies. In March 1985, Heinemann Australia signed a contract with 'Project Tasmania Associates' – the cover name Greengrass and Wright chose for their partnership; as an extra precaution, its address was shown as care of a literary agency in New York.[25]

But neither of the newly signed authors anticipated any trouble from the British government. 'At that stage I had absolutely no worries that there would be any attempt to stop us. Our *World in Action* programme had gone out without interference, so it never occurred to me that it would object,' Greengrass remembered.[26] 'I don't think either of us had any sense that this was going to be some great *cause célèbre*.'[27]

Their optimism would prove short-lived. Word of the Australian publishing deal soon reached Downing Street, and Armstrong sent a warning letter to the Prime Minister's private office. The memo poked the smouldering fires of Thatcher's stubborn insistence on the need for secrecy. 'She felt particularly outraged by Peter Wright's activities because a member of the Security Service who had signed the Official Secrets Act, and sworn to keep everything confidential, was prepared to breach those conventions and rules,' Armstrong subsequently recalled. 'If [he] was allowed to get away with this scot-free, other members of the Security Service who felt very aggrieved and upset by what he was disclosing ... would feel that they had the right to publish to correct it.'[28]

With that, an irreversible decision was taken. From then on, Her Majesty's Government would pursue its recalcitrant former spycatcher to the ends of the earth. Literally.

Portrait of the Spycatcher as a young man: Peter Wright at work as a farm hand in Scotland, circa 1932. *(© Jenny Andrews)*

Peter Wright, Tasmania, 1988. The British government's attempts to ban *Spycatcher* turned the book into a global bestseller. *(Associated Press / Alamy Stock Photo)*

Left: Sir Roger Hollis, MI5 Director General, 1956–65. Peter Wright believed Hollis, codenamed DRAT, was a Soviet mole. *(Keystone Press / Alamy Stock Photo)*

Below: Wright and a cabal of rogue intelligence officers believed Prime Minister Harold Wilson was a Soviet spy and planned to blackmail him into resigning. *(Evening Standard/ Hulton Archive/Getty Images)*

Sir Anthony Blunt, wartime MI5 officer, traitor and Soviet spy recruiter, faces the press, November 1979. *(Keystone Press / Alamy Stock Photo)*

Chapman Pincher, journalist and MI5 agent: the British government used him to leak 'safely' the Hollis scandal. *(Jacob Sutton / Gamma-Rapho / Getty Images)*

Lord Victor Rothschild dodges reporters after his role in *Spycatcher* was revealed, November 1986. *(David O'Neil/ANL/Shutterstock)*

Wright, with lawyer Malcolm Turnbull, holds an angry press conference about his involvement with Rothschild. Sydney, November 1986. *(John Nobley/Fairfax Media via Getty Images)*

The *Spycatcher* defence team: *(l–r)* Paul Greengrass, David Hooper and Malcolm Turnbull.

Above: Cabinet Secretary Sir Robert Armstrong is confronted by a photographer at Heathrow airport en route to the *Spycatcher* trial. Moments later he smashed the man's camera. *(ANL/Shutterstock)*

Left: Sir Michael Havers, the Attorney General in whose name the *Spycatcher* case was mounted. *(Trinity Mirror / Mirrorpix / Alamy Stock Photo)*

Right: Tony Benn MP holds a public reading of Wright's still-banned *Spycatcher* book in Hyde Park, August 1987. *(PA Images / Alamy Stock Photo)*

Below: Margaret Thatcher with her official biographer, Charles Moore. He was given privileged access to her secret *Spycatcher* papers. *(Nick Rogers/ Shutterstock)*

A Spy in Exile: Peter Wright with his wife, Lois, arriving at court in Sydney, November, 1986. *(Paul Matthews/Fairfax Media via Getty Images)*

16. HUBRIS

*'It might be better to have tried and failed than to give
the impression that the government did not care
enough about conduct of this kind'*
ATTORNEY GENERAL'S OFFICE ADVICE,
JUNE 1985

On Sunday, 31 March, news broke of Wright's memoirs and his publisher's determination to evade British censorship. 'In order to forestall any move by the Security Services to stop the book,' the *Observer's* gossipy diary column informed its readers, 'Heinemann has taken the prudent step of asking the Australian Attorney-General for his views on the scheme ... [It] has been cheerfully told it can go ahead without fear of reprisals. And just in case MI5 decides to try and have copies impounded when they come to this country, a large warehouse in Amsterdam has been rented for distribution purposes.' The newspaper ended its story with a prescient warning for the government and its spies, should they try to impose a ban: 'Happily, MI5 is going to lose this one.'[1]

The taunt was calculated to provoke the Security Service, and duly succeeded. New Director General Sir Antony Duff authorised MI5's legal advisor to make a third attempt to pressure Heinemann into backing down. When this proved no more fruitful than the two previous bouts of arm-twisting, he complained to Downing Street, demanding that the Prime Minister order the Attorney General to send a swift and stern letter to the publisher, warning it not to proceed with the book.

Duff was a former Cabinet Office official[2] and found his old colleague, Robert Armstrong, sympathetic to the request. But at the Royal Courts of

Justice, the government's legal experts were rather less convinced by the wisdom of the Director General's argument. In early June, Henry Steel, the Attorney General Sir Michael Havers' legal advisor, cautioned that if Heinemann ignored this thinly veiled intimidation, the Attorney General might then inexorably be forced into issuing legal proceedings: since both the publisher and the author were in Australia, and thus outside UK jurisdiction, he queried whether the government could actually make good on its threat.

Behind this equivocation was a realisation that Downing Street's hubris risked dragging Havers into a losing fight, one for which he would eventually carry the political can. It was the first indication of a sizeable faultline in the notionally united ranks lining up against Peter Wright, and one which would shatter very publicly when the case finally came to court.

But Steel was also aware of the government's evident determination to present itself as making a principled, if probably doomed stand to silence its talkative retired intelligence officer – a calculation he summarised as 'better to have tried and failed than to give the impression that the government did not care enough about conduct of this kind to do anything about it'.[3]

By the middle of the month Armstrong was firmly at the helm of Downing Street's nascent battle formation. He summoned Duff and Bernard Sheldon from MI5, Sir Colin Figures, the head of MI6, and Treasury Solicitor John Bailey, for talks in Number 10. The presence of Bailey, the government's chief legal bruiser who had personally served Nigel West with an injunction three years earlier, was a clear sign that the Cabinet Secretary intended to take no prisoners.

Sure enough, the minutes of the discussions, on 17 and 25 June, recorded a conclusion that 'legal action should be taken both in the UK and in Australia provided that there was a reasonable chance of success'; Bailey, like Armstrong a bullish advocate for official secrecy, advised that in order to steer clear of the minefield of arguing over the actual contents of the book – which none of those assembled had seen – the case would have to 'rest on the general principle of damage from disclosure by former intelligence officers'.[4]

He also offered the opinion that in light of a recent court decision, 'there was some reason to hope an action in Australia might be successful'.[5]

This was magical thinking. The case in question – Commonwealth v. John Fairfax & Sons Ltd – had been decided in December 1980 by the Australian High Court – the country's apex judicial forum, equivalent to the House of Lords in Britain, which has particular jurisdiction over issues affecting the federal constitution. It involved a plea by the government in

Canberra for an injunction against a media conglomerate which planned to publish a book examining Australian defence and foreign policy; the manuscript drew heavily on official documents and cable messages – material which the plaintiff complained was confidential and would cause substantial damage to the national interest.

The court bluntly rejected this argument in terms which should have been a warning to Bailey and Armstrong. Sir Anthony Mason's[6] verdict ruled that first and foremost, a claim of confidentiality could only succeed if the information was genuinely confidential: since much of it had been previously published, the government's case failed to overcome this initial hurdle. But the most telling section of his judgement set out the second, equally insuperable barrier for ministers seeking to protect official secrets – that disclosure would cause genuine harm.

> It is unacceptable in our democratic society that there should be a restraint on the publication of information relating to government when the only vice of that information is that it enables the public to discuss, review and criticize government action. Accordingly, the court will determine the government's claim to confidentiality by reference to the public interest. Unless disclosure is likely to injure the public interest, it will not be protected.[7]

The British government's aim to silence its old spycatcher in an Australian court fell foul of both of those criteria: nonetheless, at the end of June, Armstrong sought the Prime Minister's permission to launch injunction proceedings against Wright and Heinemann, telling her that MI5 together with 'other officials and lawyers ... all consider that the Government should endeavor to prevent Mr. Wright ... from publishing this book'. Did she agree? Thatcher scrawled a brief assent at the top of this memo – 'Yes'. With that single word, the power of Whitehall's purse and the weight of its hostility were irrevocably, and fatefully, set in motion.[8]

Two months later, at the Cabinet Secretary's direction, Stephen Jacques Stone James, an expensive firm of external Sydney-based lawyers, fired off letters to Wright and to Heinemann's offices in London, Melbourne and Sydney, warning that publishing 'information or knowledge gained during the course of his duties ... would be a breach of Wright's duty of confidentiality, owed to the British Government'.

For good measure, the publisher, too, would face action, unless each party agreed within seven days to abandon the book.[9] This was a crude attempt at intimidation. 'The British Government tried to put pressure on the board of Heinemann,' recalled David Hooper, an English lawyer who would shortly be hired to represent the publisher. 'They got at a few of the board members in London ... and Brian Perman was subjected to very great pressure.'[10]

In other circumstances, this tactic might have worked. But that year the global Heinemann empire had been bought by the Octopus Group, a publishing conglomerate led by Paul Hamlyn. A German-born Jewish refugee who had fled to London from Hitler's persecution in 1940, Hamlyn was successful, wealthy and stubbornly resistant to governmental bullying: within the week, each of the three recipients of the warning letters sent back identical polite acknowledgements, but gave no indication that they proposed to heed the threats.[11]

Downing Street now began work in earnest. In theory, the case would be brought in the name of the Attorney General and would carry the imprimatur of his twin roles, as both a senior member of the government and its notionally independent legal advisor.

That, however, posed a substantial problem. Havers harboured very real doubts about the argument he would be expected to make, and was reluctant to take the blame for what he rightly saw would be the eventual outcome: failure and public humiliation. Fortunately – for him, at least – Armstrong and Thatcher made little secret of their contempt for their most senior legal advisor.

'It was amazing he was ever made Attorney General or anything else,' said Jonathan Aitken, then a loyal Tory backbencher. 'He was a sort of genial drunken barrister who somehow got in the House of Commons. But a great legal mind he absolutely was not. They decided to get rid of him quite quickly: they said "we can't have this chap", and he was pushed out very sharply.'[12]

In truth, Aitken's assessment was only half correct. 'Havers wasn't stupid, but he was nobody's fool,' opposition leader Neil Kinnock argued. 'The role of Attorney General is peculiar in that they are expected and duty bound to act as lawyers, but of course they are politicians in the Cabinet.

'It means that attorneys general come in two sizes: those that will tell the Prime Minister, "You must do this", or those who are prepared to say, "You shouldn't do that". Michael Havers was one of the type who said, "Well, this could be edgy but if, politically, the Government believes that we should seek to suppress publication, I can provide you with a legal argument."'[13]

While that argument would officially carry his name, by the end of the summer it was the Cabinet Secretary who led the charge – an outcome with which Havers was perfectly happy. 'It seems to me that he was the natural fall-guy,' the Attorney General later told a television interviewer.[14]

And from the outset, the case was plagued by inexperience. Having sought the lead role, Armstrong was disconcerted to discover that he would be required to put his own head in the noose by swearing the necessary affidavits on behalf of the government. 'I hope it may be possible for someone to [swear] on my behalf,' he pleaded.[15] It was not: he had inveigled himself into the role of chief intelligence advisor to the Prime Minister and as such, as Henry Steel happily reported, 'knows far more about the circumstances of Peter Wright [than the Attorney General's staff] as well as a great deal about the Security Service'.[16]

The next mistake highlighted the incompetence of Armstrong's management: the Australian lawyers he had hired to press the government's case sent notice of its litigation to Heinemann's subsidiary office in New South Wales, rather than to its headquarters in Victoria. The result was that the case would be heard in liberal Sydney rather than the more conservative milieu of Melbourne. It was a schoolboy error and one which would come back to bite the Cabinet Secretary.

On 9 September 1985, Armstrong filed his first affidavit with the Supreme Court of New South Wales. It stressed his seniority as head of the British Civil Service and that in addition to serving Thatcher as Cabinet Secretary, he was 'the Prime Minister's principal official advisor in relation to matters of security and intelligence' – and thus admirably qualified to represent the British government in its request to suppress the memoirs of a former MI5 officer.

Throughout his twenty-year career in MI5, Armstrong asserted, Peter Wright had been 'a servant of the Crown', whose work gave him 'access to highly classified information, a great deal of which was, and still is, of the highest sensitivity'. If this was unarguably true, the next section of the Cabinet Secretary's complaint highlighted the dangerous flaws in his case.

> I submit that it was an implied term of [Wright's] contract with the British Security Service that at all times, both during and after the termination of such employment, he should not communicate, other to a person to whom he was authorised to communicate it, any information which he had obtained or to which he had access. No authority has been given to [Wright] to record, publish or otherwise disclose ... [this] information.
>
> The publication of any narrative ... which is based on information available to him as a senior member of the British Security

Service would be likely to cause unquantifiable damage [to] the work of the British Security Service and thereby the national interest of the United Kingdom.

Nor was this 'damage' confined to Britain alone. Aware of the need to explain why a court in Sydney should insert itself into London's fight, Armstrong argued that Wright's memoirs would adversely affect 'the intelligence and security services of friendly foreign countries with which the British Security Service is in liaison [and who] would be likely to lose confidence in its ability to protect classified information'.[17]

Beneath this tortured prose was both a clear warning that Australia's national interest might also be threatened and an underlying mantra to which the British government would thereafter cling desperately: that every intelligence officer owed a duty of lifelong confidentiality to his or her employers. Unfortunately for the Cabinet Secretary, there was no basis for any of this, either in law or in reality.

The first and fundamental problem was that the only hard evidence of any obligation to keep quiet was the declaration Wright had signed under the Official Secrets Act – a law which could not be enforced outside the United Kingdom. There was certainly no written contract of employment because, since it did not officially exist, MI5 had never issued one. Nor was Armstrong's claim of an 'implied term' likely to succeed unless the government could show that it had assiduously enforced this with other former members of the Security Service.

It could not. Beginning in the year Wright joined MI5, there had been a steady trickle of unauthorised public disclosures by a succession of British intelligence officials. Sir Percy Sillitoe's published memoirs of his time as Director General had gone far beyond the text agreed by Whitehall. A decade later a veteran of Churchill's secret espionage and sabotage 'army', Bickham Sweet-Escott, had encountered no opposition to his account of service with the Special Operations Executive.[18]

There had been a similar lack of effort to ban a book by former MI6 officer Leslie Nicholson about his exploits before, during and after the Second World War. If this was written under a *nom de plume*, the author's true identity was an open secret; like Sweet-Escott he was never served with an injunction, nor punished after publication for his indiscretion.[19]

This pattern of official tolerance of disclosure was repeated in the late 1970s and early 1980s: both the Security Service and successive governments knew that former officers were briefing journalists for books about MI5's history and scandals; they were left entirely free to unburden themselves of these sensitive secrets, even when they gave television interviews or wrote first-person magazine articles. The revelations by Tony Motion, Miranda Ingram, Cathy Massiter and Peter Wright himself were clear evidence of the selectivity of the supposed duty of confidentiality.

Nor was Armstrong's warning of the potential damage from spy memoirs to Australian national security likely to survive thorough scrutiny. ASIO, MI5's sister organisation in Canberra, had cheerfully helped Soviet spy Vladimir Petrov pen his post-defection book, and had even assigned one its most senior directors to ghost-write it.[20]

Nonetheless, the Supreme Court was initially inclined to listen. On 10 September, the day after the Cabinet Secretary filed his affidavit, it granted a temporary injunction, banning Heinemann from publishing the book and Wright from disclosing anything relating to information gained during his years with MI5.

The key word in this order was 'temporary': injunctions are emergency procedures, issued to maintain a legal status quo pending a full hearing on the merits of the case. Mindful of the holes in the government's argument, Armstrong submitted a second affidavit on 27 September, which attempted to shore up his claims about the potential harm Wright's memoirs would wreak.

> The Plaintiff is not ... in a position to particularise the damage that will be caused ... but [it] would be likely to endanger the effective discharge by the Service of its current and future responsibilities and, as a consequence, be of value to a foreign power ...
>
> The dangers ... could arise notwithstanding that the information disclosed was unclassified and is on its face, and in isolation, apparently innocuous. Such information may take on a wider significance if put together with other information in the possession of other persons and thereby ... enable them to check the veracity of their sources ...
>
> Furthermore, information which appears to be innocuous at a particular date or to a particular officer may at a later date become significant.[21]

The only solution, he insisted, was to take the purist approach of banning any and all 'unauthorised' publication by former intelligence officers. It was an argument that appealed greatly to Number 10 and which, had the forthcoming hearing been in an English court, would certainly have found judicial favour.

'The government was so used to winning this sort of action in the UK that it assumed the Australian courts would do the same,' Heinemann's eventual external lawyer, David Hooper, argued. 'It presumed that they would just put up the Cabinet Secretary's affidavits about the untold damage in terms of security that the book would cause, and the case would be over. It never occurred to any of them that they could lose.'[22]

The first indication that this confidence might be misplaced landed in the middle of September. Armstrong had been certain that the New South Wales judiciary would be as accommodating as its London brethren: he was therefore 'shaken' to learn from the Attorney General's advisors that, far from taking his written submission as gospel, the Sydney court would insist that he testify in person at the full hearing.[23] It was not a prospect which pleased the Cabinet Secretary, and he 'optimistically' sought to avoid what promised to be a lengthy and uncomfortable mission. That hope was dashed when the government's Australian lawyers bluntly explained that the rules of the New South Wales bench allowed no exemptions to spare even the most elevated officials from cross-examination.[24]

His unhappiness was not eased by the reappearance of a ghost from MI5's past. At the end of September, Victor Rothschild turned up at the Cabinet Office with a demand for governmental protection. His Lordship told Armstrong that since it was likely he would be named in Wright's book, Downing Street should issue 'a pre-agreed statement' clearing him of any involvement in the still-festering scandals of the Ring of Five, the Cambridge Apostles and his old friend Anthony Blunt.

This was a distinctly odd request. Unlike Number 10, which had yet to set eyes on the manuscript, Rothschild had seen and supported the early draft given to Pincher, and had a very good idea that the final version would flatter him. Ultimately, Armstrong concluded that the visit had been 'an oblique warning to the government that if it tangled with Wright, it risked tangling with him too'.[25]

A less arrogant Prime Minister and a more resolute Cabinet Secretary might have taken this advice to heart and quietly stepped back from the fight. Unfortunately, the reins of Britain's affairs of state were then in rather less humble hands.

'Margaret Thatcher had all kinds of blind spots,' was the rueful opinion of Jonathan Aitken, who had first-hand experience of her character. 'What she needed in the decision to send Armstrong to Australia were strong voices arguing the other way; she needed somebody to tell her that she, as Prime Minister, would be dragged through the mud and that the Cabinet Secretary will be bruised, those Australian lawyers don't give any quarter and there will be bad headlines. But she and Robert did it all on their own. And Robert was not a fighter: he was a "smooth man" not a "hairy man".'[26]

In late November, the mood inside Number 10 darkened further when the latest advice arrived from its Australian lawyers. They had belatedly spotted the largest flaw in the government's case: that although it knew about Pincher's *Their Trade Is Treachery* well in advance – and that Peter Wright had been its prime source – there had been no attempt to block publication. This reeked of double standards, an unpleasant odour which the Sydney court would not fail to detect with displeasure. The only viable way out of the mess was to abandon the claim for blanket secrecy, and take issue with the dangers of specific allegations in the book.

There were two substantial problems with this plan. The first was that Heinemann had not yet provided a copy of the manuscript; the second was that wading into arguments about the nitty-gritty of Wright's individual allegations would irrevocably concede that he was not bound by universal lifelong confidentiality: that was a road which held considerable danger. Any discussion of Pincher's 1981 book would almost certainly expose the fact that the Prime Minister and the Cabinet Secretary had arranged for him to be discretely briefed. That was so politically incendiary as to be unthinkable.

Backed into an uncomfortable corner, Armstrong fell back on his most tried and tested tactics: falsehood and disinformation. He suggested planting an 'arranged' Parliamentary Question which would allow the Prime Minister to 'put clearly on the record that information provided by recent defectors decisively confirms the conclusion that Sir Roger Hollis ... was not ... an agent of the Russian Intelligence Service'. According to the Cabinet Secretary's memo, these defectors – Oleg Gordievsky and Vitaly Yurchenko – had 'amply confirmed' that MI5's former Director General was not a Soviet mole.[27] The truth was rather different.

Gordievsky was, unquestionably, a brave former Soviet intelligence officer who had worked undercover for MI6 for many years. But he had only joined the KGB in 1963 – two years before Hollis left Leconfield House – and his information was largely unprovable. Yurchenko's evidence was even less reliable, since within days of Armstrong's endorsement he had re-defected back to Moscow, where he was honoured with the Order of the Red Star for running a successful disinformation operation against the West.

For once Thatcher saw the inherent peril: she firmly vetoed the planted PQ proposal, ordering her office to advise Armstrong that she was 'not entirely convinced that the new information has "amply confirmed" the conclusion that Sir Roger was not a Soviet agent. She does not believe that the information was quite as decisive as that.'[28]

The only shaft of light in this otherwise gloomy picture was that on the other side of the world Heinemann was drowning in the cost of fighting the injunction. Its strategy was to argue that all the substantive allegations in Wright's manuscript had already appeared in other books. If this amounted to an unusual sales pitch, it was unquestionably true and, given the rules laid down in previous cases, legally sound; but it was also ruinously expensive.

Sandy Grant, an old publishing hand brought in to steady the ship, found that the company's lawyers had spent several weeks 'reading every spy book, at $500 an hour. They had already racked up around $450,000 in bills. I'm sure the British Government had a view that we were financially vulnerable.'[29]

In December 1985, Heinemann sought new and rather less traditional advice. David Hooper was an unusual figure in the staid world of English law: the son of a diplomat, he had been educated at Eton and Oxford, before joining a leading London firm and going on to earn a reputation as a scourge of the Establishment. He was already heading to Australia to spend Christmas with his family. Intrigued by the case, he volunteered to spend a few days visiting Wright in Tasmania and to report back with his view on the prospects for success. He found the old spycatcher in financial trouble and in truculent mood.

> When I met him, Peter was very hard up, and was living in pretty straightened circumstances. The home he and Lois shared was a single storey bungalow with about three of four rooms in it, and he told me that the Australian lawyers were running up astronomical bills; he said that nine of them had all come to quiz him in his tiny little house.
>
> His physical health was not good, either; but mentally he was sharp and he was obsessed with his argument. He was also very unhappy about the way he'd been treated.[30]

Hooper left Cygnet convinced that whatever Heinemann decided, its author was determined to battle on – an assessment re-enforced by a letter Wright sent to the publishers.

> David Hooper appeared to understand what it is all about. It is a battle against the deliberate suppression of facts, which should

be exposed in the national interest. It is a battle against the use of Australian law to achieve a purpose which could not be achieved under British criminal law. It involves a gross denial of justice for myself. It is a *political* case which *must* be fought and *can* be won.[31]

By temperament and by training, the English solicitor was inclined to agree. The questions he pondered, as the new year dawned, were how to win and who would lead the publisher's charge into battle. At the start of January 1986 he found both answers in a newly opened small firm of Sydney solicitors.

It was a propitious encounter: within twelve months the young man Hooper met, who had only just hung his sole-practitioner shingle, would become the most celebrated media lawyer in the world – and the nemesis of Robert Armstrong and the British government.

17. TURNBULL

'Tell Wright he had better seek some medical advice before he comes to Court'
JOHN BAILEY, UK GOVERNMENT LAWYER,
APRIL 1986

Malcolm Bligh Turnbull was 31 but had already packed a great deal into his short career. The son of a prosperous hotel broker and a celebrated actress, academic and feminist, in 1977 he graduated from the University of Sydney with a degree in arts and law. He combined these academic efforts with freelance journalism, covering politics and law for Australian magazines and television, before winning a prestigious Rhodes Scholarship to top up his legal studies at Brasenose College, Oxford.

In 1980 he married Lucy Hughes, the daughter of a leading Australian QC and former Commonwealth Attorney General, and, on their return to Sydney later that year, Turnbull was admitted to the brotherhood of New South Wales barristers. The financial life of a self-employed advocate can be unreliable, but aided by the reputation he had earned as a journalist and his father-in-law's connections, the practice quickly prospered. Turnbull's career as a barrister was to be short-lived, however: in March 1981 he stood as a Liberal Party[1] candidate for election to the House of Representatives, and came within a whisker of winning a seat.

Then, in late 1982, the colourful Australian entrepreneur Kerry Packer hired the ambitious young lawyer as in-house counsel for his media empire. For the next five years Turnbull represented Consolidated Press Holdings Group, and when his employer found himself in the crosshairs of a Royal Commission inquiry, gained first-hand experience of governmental and legal duplicity.

In 1983 the Commission was investigating trade unions and organised crime. In the course of its deliberations, its head, a prominent Melbourne QC, falsely targeted the mogul on suspicion of tax evasion, drug trafficking and murder: Turnbull's forensic lawyering – and his astute use of the media – was the vital factor in debunking each allegation, and led to Packer receiving a public apology from the federal government.[2]

With another young lawyer, Bruce McWilliam, Turnbull established an in-house law firm to support the Packer empire in its myriad legal issues, but by the end of 1985 Turnbull and McWilliam were keen to branch out on their own.

New South Wales' legal profession was, like its English counterpart, divided into two distinct – and sometimes mutually hostile – branches: barristers, who appeared as advocates in court, and solicitors, who did everything else from drafting wills and conveyances to preparing the briefs on which the advocates relied in their courtroom appearances.

But there was a provision in the law allowing for an unusual hybrid creature – a solicitor-advocate who, while not formally a barrister, was permitted to appear in court on behalf of clients, albeit without the traditional wig and gown. Turnbull found that dual role appealing: he enjoyed advocacy, but also the commercial wheeling and dealing he had been doing as Packer's in-house lawyer. He persuaded Packer that he could handle all his corporate work while simultaneously catering to the needs of other clients; at the start of January 1986 the offices of Turnbull McWilliam, Solicitors opened for business in a building next to Packer's HQ, half a mile from the Sydney Opera House.

Within days David Hooper arrived at the Park Street office bearing the brief for defending Heinemann and Peter Wright. He was, however, less than cheerful about the chances of success. 'The starting position looked pretty negative,' Turnbull later recalled. 'The publisher had been advised by a couple of legal law firms, and four of our top "silks", that the case was a loser. These weren't just QCs on the political right; those on the left said the same thing.

'And it wasn't just Australian lawyers. One very prominent left-wing London barrister also thought the case was hopeless, but suggested that I should take the case anyway, make a couple of grand speeches and then lose gallantly. That didn't appeal to me: if I signed on, I was only interested in winning.'[3]

As he examined Sir Robert Armstrong's verbose affidavits, Turnbull found himself agreeing with the sentiment underlying the British government's overarching argument: that Wright owed a lifelong duty of confidentiality to MI5. 'After all,' he wrote later, 'one could hardly run an intelligence service if its former officers could willy-nilly publish books about their activities.'[4]

But the problem for Armstrong and his mistress in Downing Street was that a succession of former intelligence officers had been permitted to do just that; it was the fundamental flaw in the British government's case – a fault-line specifically identified as fatal by Australian law, and one which offered Turnbull a clear path to victory.

In the middle of January, he advised Hooper that Heinemann had three very strong defences: all had their roots in the *Fairfax* case, which set out the test for preventing the publication of confidential material. The first was that the book disclosed clear evidence of illegal activity by MI5 – a revelation no Australian court was likely to suppress. The second was that if, as Wright alleged, Moscow had successfully penetrated the Security Service, the KGB would already know all the secrets he exposed, and therefore the manuscript could do no actual harm. But the third leg of Turnbull's argument would prove to be the most crucial: almost everything in what was now formally titled *Spycatcher* had already been published and, as a result, could not still be considered confidential.

Both the law and the facts seemed so obvious that Turnbull was convinced that, if faced with a robust response, the British government would offer to settle the case by agreeing redactions of the book's most sensitive information. He duly ended his letter to the publisher with an optimistic prediction: 'I would be very surprised if the British Government would want Mr. Armstrong to be cross-examined about the British Security Service in public in Sydney.'[5]

He was both right and wrong. The Cabinet Secretary was certainly increasingly uneasy about the prospect of appearing in the witness box, and told his legal advisors that 'he would not want to give evasive answers at the outset, only to have things wrung out of him in court'.[6] But Turnbull had underestimated Margaret Thatcher's obstinacy: having signed up to Armstrong's calamitous scheme, the Prime Minister was now determined to plough on with litigation, whatever the cost. 'She could be pig-headed like there was no tomorrow,' was Jonathan Aitken's rueful assessment.[7]

There was one further obstacle to Turnbull's hope that the British government would come to its senses and agree redactions to Wright's memoirs: as winter turned to early spring, neither MI5 or Downing Street had actually seen the troublesome manuscript. To Sandy Grant, this made the timing of a break-in at Heinemann's Australian premises more than a little suspicious.

'The government was very anxious to see the manuscript,' he later remembered. 'Then I walked into the office one morning to find we had been done over. The filing cabinets had all been emptied, which isn't a normal theft from a business office, and nothing was stolen: the place had just been broken into and turned upside down.

'Our office was near the centre of Melbourne's business district – a bit like Shoreditch is to London's West End – and it was just a normal 1980s publishing office: it wasn't like we had drugs in there that thieves would be looking for. It seemed very possible that the burglars were looking for the manuscript.'[8]

If so, the thieves left disappointed: Wright and Greengrass were old hands at maintaining security, and the precious draft was under lock and key elsewhere. But by then, Grant, Turnbull and Hooper were also convinced that someone – they assumed it was MI5 – was tapping their phones. 'We thought it was almost certain that they were doing this,' Hooper recalled four decades later. 'Nonetheless, we had to communicate, and fortunately it was just at the time when faxes were starting to come into being, which I believed were difficult to intercept. But I also had this feeling that if these guys can get into government and commercial systems, how were we going to compete against that?'[9]

They had an additional cause to worry about attempts to discover their strategy. Paul Greengrass's involvement as the book's ghost-writer was then unknown; as a London-based UK citizen, he and the defence team feared that when the British government discovered his role it might prosecute him under the Official Secrets Act, and use its draconian powers to impose a substantial prison sentence.

Turnbull pondered the problem and came up with a solution which provided cover for the journalist and brought his expertise on board: with Granada TV's approval, he hired Greengrass as a consultant to the legal team. 'Paul was a mine of information about intelligence affairs,' he later recalled. 'He had read every work ever published about espionage and so I gave him the job of cross-referencing *Spycatcher* against those books to show that it really contained nothing new.'[10] This was a vast yet vital undertaking, and it would, in time, be used by the British government to harass both men.

The first indication that Whitehall intended to fight a dirty campaign came at a brief procedural hearing on 10 February 1986. Its Australian lawyers asked the court to consider barring Turnbull from representing Heinemann and Wright, explaining that due to his previous 'close connections' with the media there was a risk that 'confidential material' might find its way to the press.

Since these same lawyers also held a contract to represent a major chain of Australian newspapers, it was a bid of impressive chutzpah; the presiding judge brusquely dismissed it, decreeing that the publisher and former spy had the right to retain whatever counsel they chose.

In late March, Turnbull handed over the manuscript to the British government, and once again suggested that, just as had happened with Nigel West's book, the Treasury Solicitor should negotiate mutually acceptable excisions to Wright's memoirs. The plea fell on resolutely deaf ears.

When the Cabinet Office finished reading the pages, it pronounced itself appalled by the danger they posed. Internal memos recorded that *Spycatcher* 'revealed techniques, liaison arrangements with other security services and past targets for surveillance that could adversely affect relationships with other countries'.[11] The fact that these details were at least twenty years out of date, and that, as he later testified, Wright had 'taken great care not to disclose anything which in my view as a professional intelligence officer might damage national security'[12] apparently mattered little.

This, added to the fact that Whitehall knew Wright had previously provided all of these secrets to Chapman Pincher for publication in *Their Trade Is Treachery*, made the British government's obduracy inexplicable to Turnbull. As faxes flashed back and forth between Sydney and London, he flew down to Tasmania to meet his client for the first time: he was shocked by the conditions he found at Duloe Arabians Horse Stud.

'I was confronted with a vision of rural poverty rarely seen in Australia,' he wrote after the conclusion of the *Spycatcher* trials. 'The whole place was in disrepair and the house was a two-room hovel ... they were obviously stony-broke.'[13] At the end of their meeting, if he was not entirely convinced by Wright's insistence that MI5's former Director General had been a Soviet mole, Turnbull at least came away profoundly impressed by the old spy's sincerity and determination to fight on.

> Peter's motivation was very genuine. He had written a series of briefs about Hollis over the years and absolutely believed Hollis was a spy. That doesn't of course mean he was necessarily right. There was a wilderness of mirrors in that era. But the way they treated him was just infamous – absolutely terrible. They took the view that he was one of the lower orders and didn't need to be treated respectfully. That was the attitude – totally: he wasn't a 'chap'. He was a player not a gentleman.[14]

On his return to Sydney, Turnbull fired the first shot in Wright's defence. He formally asked the British government to explain precisely which parts of the manuscript it found objectionable. In the third week of March, he followed up this initial salvo when the case made its first appearance in the court of Mr Justice Philip Powell, demanding that Armstrong file a detailed Statement of Claim, setting out the basis for his argument.

In what would soon become a familiar pattern, Whitehall's local lawyers prevaricated, pleading for time to get the government's papers in order. Powell was unimpressed: the case, he ruled, had already dragged on far too long, and he ordered London to produce its reasoning by 28 April. It was a small victory, and one which encouraged Turnbull's confidence. 'I think,' he wrote to Heinemann, 'they may try to settle before the 28th.'[15]

Twelve days before the appointed deadline, the British government proved him unduly optimistic. Its response insisted that Wright, as a former officer of MI5, had an obligation not to communicate any information, however unimportant, gleaned during his service without explicit authorisation.

Somewhat puzzled, Turnbull once again pressed for precise details of which parts of the book broke this duty of confidentiality: eventually, at the end of April, London responded. All of the manuscript – with the possible exception of the chapters describing Wright's childhood and adolescence – were deemed *verboten*.

Discouraged but still intent on brokering a deal, Turnbull flew to London for a meeting with the Treasury Solicitor. But if he and David Hooper hoped to persuade the government's legal bulldog to see reason, the first few minutes of their discussion provided an uncomfortable reality check.

John Bailey was elegantly tailored and neatly coiffed, but from the outset he adopted the role of Whitehall's bare-knuckle street-fighter. Her Majesty's Government, he told Turnbull and Hooper, believed the entire manuscript was pernicious and a danger to national security; the Prime Minister would not agree to resolve the problem with a censor's blue pencil – only unconditional surrender by Wright and Heinemann, and an undertaking to abandon *Spycatcher* permanently, would mollify the Iron Lady in Downing Street.

As tempers frayed, the meeting became rancorous. 'Bailey was pretty hostile and intimidating,' Hooper recalled, 'and he clearly underestimated Turnbull.'[16] Finally, as Heinemann's legal team got up to leave, the Treasury Solicitor grabbed Turnbull's arm and issued a thinly veiled threat: 'Your client [is] a very sick man, isn't he ? You tell him from me that he'd better seek some medical advice before he comes to court.'[17]

The confrontation shocked Turnbull profoundly, and he left London angry but determined not to yield. Back in Sydney, and mindful of Heinemann's mounting costs, he agreed a fixed fee to fight the battle to the bitter end. And he knew exactly how he could win.

Under New South Wales' rules of jurisprudence, before a case comes to trial both sides have the right to issue 'interrogatories' and to demand 'discovery' of relevant documents from their opponents. The former are equivalent to the American system of depositions, and responses to them are sworn under oath. Turnbull's plan was to force the government to explain exactly which parts of Wright's book it objected to, and specifically which sections contained material so secret that by revealing it he put Britain and her allies in danger. Interrogatory number 60A was typical: 'Please nominate the items of information in the manuscript which are not considered by the British Security Service to be already known to the security forces of the Soviet Union.'[18]

The answers – if Whitehall was prepared to provide them – would back Armstrong into an evidential corner from which there would be no escape when the full court hearings began. 'Malcolm's tactic was brilliant and audacious,' Greengrass recalled. 'Essentially, he decided to turn the case round and put the British government on trial rather than Peter Wright. Rather than fight on their territory, he wanted to fight on his.'[19]

At a hearing on 12 June, Mr Justice Powell ordered London to file its answers to the interrogatories by 23 July. The ruling encouraged Heinemann's legal team: despite Bailey's posturing, Turnbull remained convinced that sane counsel would eventually find its way to Downing Street and the case would be quietly settled out of court. 'I could not believe that someone as realistic as Margaret Thatcher would want to embark on such a fruitless exercise,' he wrote later. 'Wright after all was one of her admirers ... [and] held extreme right wing views.'[20] It was a perfectly rational legal assessment, but politically naïve and thus always doomed to founder on the rocks of prime-ministerial intransigence.

On 22 and 23 June, Number 10's mood was hardened further by reports in the *Observer* and *Guardian* respectively. Neither newspaper had seen the manuscript, but their stories – the first to be published in Britain – detailed some of the key revelations in *Spycatcher*, including Wright's claim to have 'bugged and burgled' on behalf of MI5 and the plot by rogue Security Service officers to blackmail Harold Wilson into resigning. The following day, during the hearing in which the government was supposed to file its responses to the interrogatories – but again prevaricated – its Australian counsel accused Turnbull of leaking the information to Fleet Street; after a furious row, the government barrister backed down and apologised, but it was another clear warning that Whitehall was prepared to play hardball.

Four days later the High Court in London granted an *ex parte* injunction to the Attorney General, banning the two newspapers from 'disclosing or publishing ... to any person, all or any of the information obtained by Peter Maurice Wright in his capacity as a member of the British Security Service ... or taking any step to further the publication to or by any other person of a book concerning the British Security Service written by Peter Maurice Wright'.

Mr Justice Macpherson's ruling was unprecedented for its breadth and inflexibility. Not merely were the newspapers silenced, their editors and journalists were included by name in its sweeping prohibitions. All were forbidden to report or publish any 'information provided by [Wright], or any information, copies, extracts, excerpts from the said book or manuscript thereof'.[21]

The papers promptly appealed, arguing that much of the material in Wright's manuscript had previously been published and was therefore no longer confidential; nor had Macpherson taken any account of previous case law which established a defence of public interest and which took a dim view of governmental attempts to impose 'prior restraint' on the press. For their pains, both titles achieved only a minor victory – allowing them to print whatever had been previously published in Chapman Pincher's *Their Trade Is Treachery* or words spoken directly by Wright during his broadcast *World in Action* interview.

The win, however, came with a sizeable sting in its tail: the modified injunction widened the original prohibition on the journalists to include anything which 'they know, or have reasonable grounds to know, to have come or been obtained, whether directly or indirectly, from Peter Maurice Wright'.[22] In practice, this threw a blanket of secrecy over every aspect of the story; unsurprisingly, the papers appealed again.

On 25 July the case came before the Court of Appeal and, more specifically, one of the Conservative Party's favourite right-wing judges. Sir John Donaldson QC was 65, an alumnus (like Blunt, Philby and Burgess) of Trinity College, Cambridge, during its gilded interwar years; he then stood (unsuccessfully) as a Tory parliamentary candidate, before wartime service in the Army and a brief spell as a Lieutenant Colonel in the British military administrations ruling Germany after 1945.

He became a High Court judge in 1966, and five years later was elevated to head Ted Heath's short-lived Industrial Relations Court – earning Whitehall plaudits and public opprobrium in equal measure for a succession of controversial rulings which saw trade unionists sent to prison. For good reason, union leaders christened him 'Black Jack', and almost 200 Labour MPs signed a petition demanding his dismissal.

When she arrived in Downing Street, Thatcher promoted Donaldson to the Court of Appeal, and in 1982 she bestowed on him the ancient title Master of the Rolls – the head of all civil justice in England and Wales. By the time the *Spycatcher* newspaper injunctions reached his desk, Donaldson's previous rulings from the criminal bench had cemented his reputation as a 'hang 'em and flog 'em' judge: in particular, he achieved notoriety during the trial of the Maguire Seven,[23] not least for publicly regretting he could not sentence the innocent defendants to death – a miscarriage of justice for which he would be eventually reprimanded.

This, then, was the man tasked with weighing the interests of a government bent on silencing a troublesome old spy against the freedom of the press to report his allegations about MI5's criminality and incompetence. The newspapers argued that reporting allegations of MI5's habitual law-breaking and its penetration by Soviet intelligence was firmly in the public interest; the Attorney General relied on Robert Armstrong's affidavits in the Australian proceedings to claim that Wright's claims threatened national security, and that British newspapers should be prevented from reproducing any part of them.

From its first words, Donaldson's ruling made clear the contempt with which England's conservative judiciary viewed the liberal-leaning press. 'Prior restraint are two of the most emotive words in the media vocabulary,' he began ominously, before damning the *Guardian* and *Observer* with the faintest of praise. 'It has to be said that they ... are responsible newspapers, which, whether or not restrained by injunction, will no doubt make their own assessment of the public interest before publishing anything relating to the Security Service.'

From there, and for the rest of his 22-page ruling, Donaldson sailed out on the open seas of his own opinions; that few, if any of these were supported by any statute did not appear to trouble England's second most senior judge. It was, he asserted, vital that MI5 should be protected from public scrutiny, and axiomatic that those chosen to serve within it should never reveal anything – however trivial – about their employment or duties.

> The obligation of confidentiality which is implicit in the acceptance of appointment in the Security Service ... is a lifelong obligation, wholly unaffected by retirement ... [and] extends to sensitive

information and material ... However the obligation also extends to mundane matters which, in any other context would have no confidentiality.

By this remarkably extensive standard, everything from the widely publicised location of MI5's headquarters to the daily options on its staff canteen menu were so important to British national security that they should, for ever, remain secret. Nor was the fact that information had been previously published enough to strip away this need for *omertà*, even when the government itself had been the source of the disclosures.

This double standard was at the heart of the Australian litigation, and unsurprisingly the newspapers' barristers pointed to the evidence that Downing Street had either encouraged Chapman Pincher to write *Their Trade Is Treachery* with the assistance of retired MI5 officers, or had turned a conveniently blind eye to both the book and Peter Wright's appearance on *World in Action*. Surely, they pleaded, this meant his revelations in *Spycatcher* were 'now public knowledge and have lost their confidentiality?' The Master of the Rolls casually batted this away on the sole basis of his own presumption over what might have occurred.

> It is undoubtedly the law that no one is entitled to seek the assistance of the courts to maintain a confidence, if he had himself allowed it to become common knowledge ... [but] this argument assumes that publication of Mr. Wright's comments was authorised by the Crown, but of that there is no evidence whatsoever. In the case of Mr. Chapman Pincher's published works, no one with authority to authorise publication may have known of what was intended before it was done.
>
> In the case of the Granada Television programme, there was advance publicity, but the appropriate officers of the Crown may not have appreciated to the full what was intended ... All that can be said is that if the Crown had moved swiftly, it might have been able to obtain injunctions preventing publication. Authorising publication is one thing. Failing to prevent it is quite another and is not sufficient to destroy the essential confidentiality of the material.

In fairness to Donaldson, he had not seen the evidence that the government had deliberately leaked the Hollis scandal to Pincher, or the fact that it had known well in advance about Wright's televised interview: all of the documents relating to both were still locked in Downing Street's basement.

But on the basis of what he said next, it is debatable whether the facts would have made any difference. Moving on to Wright's claims that the Security Service routinely committed criminal offences, Donaldson simply invented an entirely non-existent element of its governing orders.

'That the Service is subject to the law is not in doubt,' he proclaimed, 'and was affirmed by a Direction of the then Home Secretary ... Sir David Maxwell Fife'. Had Donaldson taken the trouble to examine the document in question he would have found that this instruction did not appear anywhere in its six short paragraphs; but even if MI5 had transgressed, the learned judge concluded that this was none of the media's business.

> It by no means follows that, because the public interest in exposure of wrongdoing would justify the communication to the police or some such authority of material which has been unlawfully obtained, it would also justify wholesale publication of that material in a national newspaper ... Given the special nature of the work of the Security Service, such publication could not possibly be justified ...

Ultimately, Donaldson ruled in dismissing the appeals: secrecy was paramount.

> Thus is it the obligation of officers of the Service to keep confidential the very fact that they are so employed, where they are employed and every aspect of their work. In a word, in so far as it lies in their power, their duty of confidentiality extends to making and keeping it 'the Service that never was'.[24]

That ringing diktat was a foretaste of how English judges would repeatedly bend both the law and the facts to accede to the government's wishes. The *Guardian* and *Observer* lodged an appeal to the House of Lords – then the highest court in the land – but they knew it would be months, possibly years before Their Lordships found the time to consider the merits of allowing British citizens to know what the Security Service they paid for had been up to.

Ten thousand miles away, the New South Wales Supreme Court was inching towards a less deferential view. Whitehall had eventually filed its response to Turnbull's tricky interrogatories, but for the most part refused point blank to provide the required information: page after page contained the leaden phrase 'the Plaintiff objects to answering this ... on the grounds that it does not relate to any matter in question between the parties ... and that it is vexatious and oppressive'.[25]

Since all the questions related directly to the British government's bid to ban *Spycatcher*, this was not a stance ever likely to survive scrutiny by an Australian court. Nonetheless, on 11 August, Armstrong doubled down on the government's intransigence, filing yet another affidavit in which he airily declined to describe which of the specific allegations in Wright's manuscript were problematic; this time he put forward the novel explanation that he was 'not able to comment ... without giving rise to the risk of doing the damage which it is the purpose of these proceedings to avoid, namely of disclosing information which is confidential'.[26]

It was an entirely circular argument: Her Majesty's Cabinet Secretary could not identify the dangerous secrets because they were secret and to do so would be dangerous. Unsurprisingly, that day's hearing was quarrelsome, and it was plain to the government's lawyers that Mr Justice Powell's patience was wearing thin.

Downing Street was acutely aware that its case was on very thin legal ice and in need of political support. In early August, Armstrong contacted his counterpart in Melbourne. 'We think,' he wrote to the Australian Cabinet Secretary, 'that we are fighting a battle whose outcome is important to others as well as ourselves.'[27] The Australian government was less convinced: it would give no response to London's plea for several months.

Backed into a corner by Turnbull and facing the judge's evident irritation, Armstrong, Thatcher and their legal advisors took a fateful decision in the second week of August, which turned any faint hope of success into certain defeat. It would also expose the British government to worldwide ridicule and contempt.

18. CHARADES

'The British Government's list of documents was totally inadequate.'
MR JUSTICE PHILIP POWELL, UNITED KINGDOM VS. HEINEMANN AUSTRALIA & PETER WRIGHT

'If you cannot ride two horses at once,' an old political maxim warned, 'you shouldn't be in the circus.'[1] By mid-summer the British government was still relying on twin, conflicting arguments in its bid to ban Wright's memoirs. On one hand, it claimed that he owed an absolute and lifelong duty of silence which trumped any public interest defence of revealing MI5's criminality, but if the court rejected that proposition, it simultaneously demanded the right to challenge the individual allegations in *Spycatcher*.

'Essentially they wanted two bites at the cherry,' Malcolm Turnbull concluded. 'If they didn't win on their absolutist position, they sought a fallback option which would allow them to debate the merits of what Peter had written.'[2] The problem was that to keep this contingency plan alive, London would first have to answer every one of Turnbull's troublesome interrogatories – a concession it had resolutely refused to consider.

Throughout much of the initial skirmishing, the government believed it could get away with straddling these two horses. Accustomed to the deference of English judges, it presumed that Mr Justice Powell would not force it to provide detailed responses to Wright's claims of Security Service scandals, nor the equally tricky issue of why other authors had been allowed previously to expose them.

'They were so used to winning such actions in the UK that they assumed the Australian courts would do the same,' was David Hooper's verdict. 'They expected simply to put forward the Cabinet Secretary's affidavits about the damage the book could cause, and that would be that.'[3]

Unfortunately for Armstrong, Thatcher and the Attorney General, Powell was disinclined to take their word for this sweeping assertion. By mid-summer it was clear that he was likely to reject the first leg of the government's argument on the grounds that there was no legally enforceable obligation of confidentiality in Australia, and then require it to admit or deny each claim of criminality, connivance and semi-official leaking.

On 14 August, Downing Street's Australian lawyers came to the Sydney courthouse and proposed a novel way out of London's dilemma: they filed an admission that 'for the purposes of these proceedings only ... the allegations and matters contained in Mr. Wright's manuscript are true'. In addition, and on the same condition, it agreed that Cathy Massiter's televised statements about MI5 illegally bugging and monitoring trade union officials and civil liberties organisations were similarly accurate.[4]

It was a remarkable – and shamelessly cynical – volte-face. Five years earlier, in response to Wright and Pincher's revelations in *Their Trade Is Treachery*, the Prime Minister had stood up in the House of Commons to deny all their claims; and in March 1985 she and her ministers told Parliament that Lord Bridge's inquiry had disproven Massiter's account of unlawful phone tapping by the Security Service. Now, the government argued that all of these claims remained false in London, while simultaneously being 'true' in the New South Wales Supreme Court.

Fleet Street greeted this descent into Alice in Wonderland absurdity with open contempt – not least since it was very clearly at odds with the injunctions still gagging the *Guardian* and *Observer*. The London *Evening Standard* summed up the reaction with a pithy two-word verdict – 'MI5 Charade'.

For his part, Malcolm Turnbull was convinced that the move signalled a new realism dawning in London. Two weeks later he telephoned Jonathan Aitken, whom he had known at Oxford, asking the MP to 'act as a go-between' and to offer a deal by which, 'in return for a few cuts (not too many) in areas where it could be agreed that the book prejudices UK national security the book would be published, the British Government's face would be saved and Sir Robert would avoid "getting carved up into little pieces under cross examination"'. As internal Cabinet Office files recorded, 'Turnbull simply cannot understand why no-one in the UK seems willing to make a political deal instead of continuing with a lawyer's kamikaze mission.'⁵

'I honestly thought they would come to their senses,' he recalled decades later. 'I couldn't believe they would be mad enough to allow this to develop into an even bigger political scandal.'⁶ Not for the last time, he underestimated the determination of the British Prime Minister and her Cabinet Secretary to silence Peter Wright, whatever the cost.

'[Turnbull] says that he has no desire to bring discredit on the British Government, and that his client (Mr Wright) is a patriotic man and could be persuaded to delete particular passages from the book if he were satisfied that their publication was new and damaging to the national interest,' Armstrong advised Thatcher in early September. 'In other words, it is suggested that we should do the same sort of deal with Mr Wright as we did with Nigel West on his history of MI5. The crucial difference is, of course, that Mr West was not and Mr Wright was a member of the Security Service ...'⁷

Since the government knew – and West had confirmed – that his book was based almost entirely on interviews with retired MI5 officers, the distinction was wholly artificial; but it was the first hint of what would become one of Armstrong's new lines of attack – that as an 'inside man', Wright's first-hand revelations were inherently more dangerous to national security than those same disclosures reported anonymously via the typewriter of an 'outside' journalist.

This intransigence was all the more remarkable in the light of discussions then taking place inside Downing Street. By late September, the government realised its case was in trouble: its Sydney lawyers had advised that unless the Australian government rode to London's rescue with a declaration that publication would be against the country's interests, 'we are likely to lose'.⁸

At the beginning of October the prospect of failure was looming ever larger. 'It may be that we shall not in the end prevent publication,' Armstrong wrote to Thatcher. 'Our Australian counsel has estimated informally that we have a better than 50 per cent chance of winning ... [but] it is quite possible that we shall lose in the court of first instance ...'

Worse, even if the government eventually prevailed in Sydney, it was likely that Wright's memoirs would be published elsewhere.

> If we win the case, there will still be a risk that the same or other publishers will try to bring the book out ... in the United States or some third country ... [and] ... At the end of the day, even if the

book itself were never published, much of the contents ... would be likely to emerge gradually and become widely known.

Nonetheless, the Cabinet Secretary advised the Prime Minister that fighting for a doomed cause was more imperative than winning:

> It is important to do all we can to prevent it, not least in order to deter other members and former members of the intelligence services from seeking to publish books ... If published, Wright's book would attract great publicity and cause damage politically and to the standing of the Security Service ... the book could stimulate renewed pressure for external oversight of the intelligence services ...[9]

As Stella Rimington, then a senior MI5 officer and later to become Director General, saw it, the government had to be seen to silence Peter Wright, whatever the cost: 'it was decided to pursue the book through every possible legal channel, whether there was any hope of success or not', she wrote in her own subsequent memoirs.[10]

That the sizeable bill for this quixotic battle would be paid by British taxpayers does not appear to have troubled the Cabinet Secretary or the Prime Minister. 'We must [continue],' Thatcher scrawled in biro at the top of Armstrong's memo. 'I am utterly shattered by the revelations in the book. The consequences of publication would be enormous.'[11]

On 7 October a terse message was sent to Sydney: 'There is no possibility of a settlement on the basis of Mr. Turnbull's proposals.'[12]

Armstrong once again pleaded with his Australian counterpart to intervene in the trial. 'The British Government has for some time been in touch with Australian officials and intelligence agencies, seeking support in its action,' a background briefing prepared for the Cabinet in Canberra recorded. 'Its legal representatives consider [our] support to be essential if they are to succeed.'

Armstrong's previous appeals had been chiefly concerned with securing political cover, but as the Australian memo noted, there was now an urgent need to shore up the gaping hole which had emerged during the pre-trial proceedings and which threatened the entire basis of London's case.

> The trial judge ... has said that he places great weight on an indication of Australia's public interest in the affair. He has several times said in preliminary hearings that he understands and accepts that Wright's manuscript is of concern to British national security, but

since he is judging in an Australian court under Australian law, he wants the Executive to tell him if and how publication would affect Australia's public interest.

The problem, as this internal report admitted, was 'there is nothing in Wright's manuscript of which the disclosure would directly threaten Australian national security'. The most which could be argued was that 'the indirect effects could well be substantial and damaging'.[13]

Australian Prime Minister Bob Hawke was a popular centre-left former trade union official, with limited sympathy for belligerent Conservative administrations back in the motherland. But, apparently without fully grasping the implications or details of the request, he told his law officers to see what might be done.[14]

The decision delighted Downing Street. One evening in the late autumn Sir Michael Havers was enjoying a convivial boozy session in the bar of the Garrick Club, near Covent Garden. In time, the drinks took their toll and Her Majesty's Attorney General wandered into the gentlemen's toilets to relieve himself; he found Paul Hamlyn, Heinemann's owner, similarly engaged at an adjacent stall.

'Paul told me it was a pretty aggressive encounter,' Sandy Grant, the publisher's MD, remembered. 'Havers had appeared next to him in the *pissoir* and warned him off. He said there was no point in continuing because he had the support of the Australian government to stop the book.

'Paul was a silent sort of man – that was his tactic for dealing with all conversations. He let Havers say his piece, then rang me from the Garrick and said, "You have to do something about the Australian government supporting this trial." I phoned Turnbull that evening and he quickly got in touch with Bob Hawke.'[15]

Turnbull was incensed by the incident. He dashed off an acerbic letter to Hawke's law officers warning that, unlike Wright's memoirs, London's back-door arm-twisting posed a genuine threat to Australian interests.

> In our view, the British Government's only motive for seeking to suppress the book is evidence that the Prime Minister of the United Kingdom, Mrs. Margaret Thatcher, made a false statement to the House of Commons in March 1981 concerning the investigations into Sir Roger Hollis.
>
> In other words, the efforts to suppress this book are essentially political efforts ... to prevent political embarrassment for that Government and its advisors ... Australia should not run to

Mrs. Thatcher's whistle. It should not protect Britain from the consequences of its past crimes.[16]

Turnbull's tactic worked – temporarily. The Australian Cabinet blinked and paused its plans to intercede in the case; it would not do so until the last possible moment, and the affidavit it ultimately supplied was so half-hearted that Australian newspapers dismissively termed it 'the Claytons intervention' – Claytons being the brand of a widely ridiculed non-alcoholic local drink.[17]

With the trial now less than a month away, the British government's case looked remarkably threadbare. Other than Armstrong's affidavits, it had filed no substantive supporting testimony: an absence which explained the sudden and belated arrival of a sworn statement by an 'Anonymous Deponent'. This mysterious individual – neither the court nor the defence lawyers were permitted to know his (or her) identity – claimed to have been an MI5 officer from June 1950 to December 1976, and to have conducted training courses for new recruits; one had been Peter Wright.

But since the slender, three-page document contained nothing more than an assertion that Wright had been 'expressly forbidden to discuss the Service or its work with relatives, friends or strangers ... [or to] disclose anything whatever to do with the Service' it added little of any value.[18]

What weight it might have carried was also promptly undermined. On 23 October, David Leigh, the *Guardian*'s foremost investigative reporter, telephoned the Treasury Solicitor, seeking the government's reaction to a forthcoming book on the Blunt scandal. The authors of *Conspiracy of Silence*, Barrie Penrose and Simon Freeman, had interviewed, formally and on the record, numerous retired British intelligence officers. Not merely were these some of the most senior figures in the espionage business – their cast included the former Director General of both MI5 and MI6, Sir Dick White, and his deputy in SIS, Sir Maurice Oldfield – but all had agreed to be quoted as contributors. Was it not a little odd, Leigh asked John Bailey, that at the same time as Downing Street was spending substantial sums of taxpayers' money to block Wright's memoirs on the grounds of Security Service confidentiality, this new book contained verbatim statements from his colleagues and his old boss?

Bailey swiftly summoned Penrose and Freeman to his office for an extended and hostile meeting. The journalists were forced to endure a long recitation by MI5's legal advisor, highlighting forty of the troublesome quotes from intelligence officers; they left after three hours, convinced that an injunction banning the book would follow shortly.

Curiously, it did not. On 6 November, Bailey wrote to their publisher's lawyer, advising that the government did not intend to block publication. 'I should place on record,' the Treasury Solicitor explained, 'that if former members of the Security Service who have been quoted in *Conspiracy of Silence* did indeed speak to Mr. Penrose and Mr. Freeman as they are said to have done, and have communicated to them material acquired or derived from their employment, they have been guilty of a breach of their duty of confidentiality owed to the Crown of which a serious view is taken.

'Nevertheless, every such case is considered in the light of its particular facts and I am instructed to inform you that, having regard to considerations of public interest and national security, it is not proposed to make application to the court to restrain the publication of the book based on duty of confidentiality.'[19]

Since the basis of the government's case against *Spycatcher* rested entirely on the need to enforce this 'duty' as a way to discourage other officers from going public, the decision made no logical sense – though since *Conspiracy of Silence* contained an entire chapter attacking Wright as a 'Maverick Inquisitor', his lawyers suspected a desire for political advantage might explain the contradiction.

The government's decision not to suppress Penrose and Freeman's unsanctioned interviews with retired intelligence officers also ran counter to Armstrong's fourth and final affidavit, filed with the New South Wales Supreme Court two days earlier. Over sixteen pages, the Cabinet Secretary asserted in excruciatingly cumbersome language that any breaches of the obligation of perpetual silence could put Britain at substantial risk.

> The effective functioning of the British Security Service and the national security of the United Kingdom is likely to be damaged by unauthorised disclosures in respect of the Service. I consider that unauthorised disclosures by a member or former member of the [Security] Service, of investigations by and operations of the Service, whether current or past, are capable of causing such damage …

Nor did it matter that most of the information in *Spycatcher* had previously been published in newspapers, books and on television.

> The mere fact that certain material may have been published by a person to all the world does not mean that a republication to the

world of the same material by some other person cannot cause any damage ... because the second person may add to the credibility of the material.[20]

Armstrong's airy dismissal of the irrelevance of prior publication was a transparent attempt to disguise the substantial Achilles heel in the government's case. But whatever Downing Street, Whitehall or MI5 chose to believe, 'prior publication' was one of the fundamental tests set out in the *Fairfax* case; this had made crystal clear that information already in the public domain could not simultaneously be confidential. If the British government wanted the Australian court to ban Wright's memoirs, it would have to prove that they revealed new and dangerous secrets.

That it was neither willing nor able to do so – for the obvious reason that previous books by Chapman Pincher and Nigel West had already exposed almost all of the scandals set out in *Spycatcher* – was highlighted by the continuing battle over Turnbull's interrogatories and demands for discovery. Since *Their Trade Is Treachery* had gone on sale without any official interference, and the Attorney General had negotiated pre-publication redactions to *A Matter of Trust*, Turnbull repeatedly sought disclosure of all official records relating to both books.

For weeks, the British government obfuscated and delayed. At hearing after hearing Mr Justice Powell instructed London to produce the documents, and for good measure ordered it to pay Wright's legal costs. Each time, the government stalled until, in early October, Turnbull lost patience and formally complained; the judge promptly issued a fifteen-day timetable for delivery of the material.

True to form, the government ignored the deadline for three weeks, before filing a belated response containing none of the requested documents: once again, Turnbull trudged back to Powell's chambers and demanded a hearing. After listening for two days to a litany of excuses, the judge imposed a second order for discovery; that, too, was largely disregarded, and a new raft of documents, disclosed in early November, still contained no papers relating to the Pincher and West books. One week before the trial's scheduled start date, an increasingly frustrated Powell issued a third and final order. Like its predecessors, this did not produce satisfactory results.

On 12 November, the government grudgingly filed a 'Supplementary List' of discovery documents; to the judge's extreme irritation, none related to the matters at hand. 'It is unnecessary for me to record the nature and extent of the documents,' an evidently testy Powell subsequently ruled. 'It is sufficient to say that ... the Supplementary List of Documents was totally inadequate.'[21]

Less arrogant inhabitants of 10 Downing Street would have taken note of the judge's fraying patience. Philip Powell was, after all, hardly a radical: an Army reserve captain and leading QC, he had a reputation as a political conservative. But in their unwavering determination to silence Wright and to suppress *Spycatcher*, both the Prime Minister and her Cabinet Secretary were willing to defy his rulings.

'She had a simple conviction,' Armstrong subsequently told Thatcher's official biographer, 'that a man who behaved like a traitor should be pursued ... [and that] others must be frightened off trying to follow in his footsteps.'[22]

Within Whitehall, senior civil servants were increasingly concerned by Number 10's obduracy and its evident inability to grasp the difference between deferential English judges and the rather more robust attitude of Australian courts.

'I don't think the full implications of the trial were taken on board,' reflected Sir Robin Butler, Thatcher's former Principal Private Secretary and Armstrong's eventual successor as Cabinet Secretary. 'The decision [to pursue the litigation] was taken by Margaret Thatcher, Robert Armstrong and Michael Havers alone; the Cabinet would not have been consulted.'[23]

On instruction from this executive trio, on Friday 14 November – with the trial due to open the following Monday – Downing Street's Australian barrister tried to throw yet more sand in the judicial gears. Theo Simos QC informed Powell that Her Majesty's Government now wanted proceedings put on hold indefinitely, so that it could challenge his discovery order in the Court of Appeal. The application provoked undisguised anger from the bench.

'I thought Powell was going to blow his top,' Turnbull later recalled. 'He had handled all the British government's shenanigans with rare patience, but now he was openly furious at this cynical last-minute attempt to derail the trial.'[24]

The judge gave Simos leave to try his luck in the Court of Appeal, but turned the bid for a postponement down flat. The trial would open on schedule, with procedural motions to be heard on Monday 17 November; the first public hearings would begin the following day with the appearance of the British Cabinet Secretary.

But with the battle over the government's withheld documents continuing to fester, Powell's willingness to tolerate British charades was evaporating rapidly. Sir Robert Armstrong could expect no favours, let alone judicial deference, once he stepped into the witness box.

19. ECONOMICAL WITH THE TRUTH

'Do you understand the difference between a truth and an untruth?'
'I hope so.'
CROSS-EXAMINATION OF SIR ROBERT ARMSTRONG,
18 NOVEMBER 1986
UNITED KINGDOM VS. PETER WRIGHT.

Sir Robert Armstrong was a long way from home.

A product of Eton and Christ Church college, Oxford, Armstrong had spent his entire working life breathing the rarified air of Britain's most elevated bureaucracy. A steady climb through the Treasury – Whitehall's traditional fast-track training ground – then five years as Principal Private Secretary to Prime Ministers Edward Heath and Harold Wilson had been rewarded by shiny Establishment baubles: Companion of the Order of the Bath and Commander of the Royal Victorian Order were appended to his name, followed by a knighthood in the Queen's 1978 Birthday Honours.

By May 1979, when Margaret Thatcher strode through the front door of 10 Downing Street, Armstrong was seen as the coming man. His curriculum vitae was 'embossed in gold leaf' and he had earned a reputation as a 'pugnacious backroom operator [who] enjoyed the exercise of power'. The following October she had appointed him Cabinet Secretary to Her Majesty's Government and Head of the Civil Service – the very summit of the mandarin's mountaintop – and thereafter he had carefully positioned himself as 'the ultimate courtier' in her entourage.[1]

Sir Robert arrived in Sydney on 13 November 1986 as the British government's primary witness in its bid to suppress Peter Wright's memoirs.

He was, however, surprisingly unprepared for the spotlight. As he left London 24 hours earlier, he had attacked a freelance photographer at Heathrow Airport. Dennis Stone approached Armstrong as he arrived at the VIP lounge. 'I asked the guy politely if I could take his photograph,' Stone told the Associated Press. 'He hit me with his briefcase and broke my camera.'[2]

Although Armstrong swiftly apologised – 'I'm sorry about that, but I don't know why you wanted to take my picture' – the incident did little to endear the Cabinet Secretary to reporters awaiting his appearance in the *Spycatcher* trial.

There was also little evidence that he or his phalanx of support staff had yet grasped the bracing contrast between Australian and English jurisprudence. In the Royal Courts of Justice – the gothic confection of grey stone in the Strand, where tradition reigned and the government's emissaries were greeted with hushed deference – his affidavits had been treated as unimpeachable gospel bestowed from on high.

The Supreme Court of New South Wales[3] was rather less congenial. A modernist concrete tower on Queen's Square in Sydney's business district, its brutalist architecture reflected the court's no-nonsense approach to litigation.

Inside, Court 8D was as dreary as the building's exterior. Bunker-like and entirely windowless, its furnishings were distinctly utilitarian and there were just eight seats in the press box – painfully inadequate for the number of journalists sent to cover the proceedings. The public gallery was urgently repurposed to accommodate them.

All court battles are, to a greater or lesser extent, theatre. Turnbull, acutely aware that this case would be fought in the media as much as in law, deliberately repositioned his lectern in front of the makeshift press benches; throughout his cross-examination Armstrong would be facing a wall of nakedly hostile reporters. 'I knew he would find that very unsettling,' Turnbull recalled. 'He could not escape the journalists' glares without avoiding eye contact with me.'[4]

Outside, the queue to enter the court grew by the hour. By 9am on Tuesday 18 November – the first day of the trial itself – all seats for the proceedings had long since been allocated; nonetheless, a long line of would-be spectators braved the growing heat and humidity of Sydney's early summer.

Peter Wright picked his way slowly across Queen's Square. A frail figure, looking all of his 70 years, he was supported on one side by his wife, Lois, and on the other by a wooden cane topped with a distinctive brass handle; by common journalistic consent, this undoubtedly concealed a small glass phial of whisky to sustain the old spycatcher through the coming ordeal.

Economical with the Truth

Wright struggled past the gaggle of TV news crews waiting on the pavement. His dark blue suit was worn and of a style long out of fashion. On his head he sported a large felt khaki hat, tied under his chin with a leather thong; the press had been briefed that this was a bushman's hat, brought up to the big city from his stud farm in the wilds of Tasmania. If this was quite untrue – the headgear was a late public relations addition by his advisors – it created an invaluable image: Wright as an avuncular, simple countryman rather than the Crown's portrayal of a traitorous and bitter old spy.

Wright lapped up the media attention. 'They thought I'd be dead by now,' he told reporters. 'MI5 bullied my first publishers [and] spread all sorts of rumours, the bastards. But I'm not going to give in. Mrs. Thatcher's frightened of me – I know that Parliament was lied to.'[5]

In the courtroom, his defence team played up the appearance of plucky underdogs. The representatives of Her Majesty's Government presented a traditional and uniform front; Simos and his deputy were decked out in black gowns and eighteenth-century wigs, backed by a platoon of expensively suited Whitehall bureaucrats, lawyers, press officers and a member of MI5's legal office. By contrast, Turnbull was wigless and supported only by his wife, Lucy, and the slightly rumpled figures of David Hooper and Paul Greengrass.

'It was visually very striking,' Sandy Grant recalled. 'We had just the four of them, while there were about 30 people at the Plaintiff's table. The Government had their Australian counsel, their counsel assisting, junior counsel, the Australian Solicitor General, the British Treasury Solicitor plus a whole host of advisory staff. It looked like a wall of highly priced lawyers occupying one side, and Malcolm, this 31-year-old sole practitioner, sitting on the other. It seemed very unequal: it was David versus Goliath, and Malcolm was David – the young boy facing the large, menacing enemy.'[6]

Shortly after 10am, Simos called his first and chief witness. Her Majesty's Cabinet Secretary walked calmly from his seat behind his lawyers' table to the witness box at the front left of the courtroom. A vain man, expensively attired in a dark Jermyn Street suit and silk Oxford University tie, his luxuriant head of hair swept directly back from his forehead, Armstrong appeared confident and relaxed.

The government's trial strategy was based on a careful risk calculation. As plaintiff's counsel, Simos would normally have led Armstrong patiently through his evidence, giving him ample opportunity to convince the judge of the need to suppress Wright's memoirs.

But, with Turnbull poised to seize on every nuance and quarry for every implication, the QC realised that the fewer words Armstrong uttered under oath the better; this had the distinct advantage of limiting the ammunition gifted to Turnbull's shot locker, but carried the very real danger that all of Armstrong's testimony would be drawn from him under cross-examination and would therefore appear defensive.

Ultimately, caution was to be the watchword. Simos's examination in chief lasted less than a minute. After asking Armstrong to confirm his name, job title and the fact that he had sworn affidavits setting out the government's case, he sat down and passed the Cabinet Secretary over to Turnbull for interrogation.

Turnbull, too, faced a dilemma. This case could either make or break his nascent career as a solicitor-advocate; he was performing in an Australian local drama, but one which would be assessed on the global stage of public, as well as judicial, opinion. Push too hard, too fast and too aggressively, and he knew that *Spycatcher* would be lost; but tread too lightly and the oily, urbane Armstrong would use all the mandarin's dark arts of obfuscation, circumlocution and prevarication to skip through the minefield of problematic evidence.

The key – his only weapon in what promised to be a lengthy battle of wits – would be the British government's assertions, set out in the affidavits and interlocutory pre-trial questionnaires. Turnbull stepped up to his lectern and began asking the Cabinet Secretary about his own words: was everything in those affidavits true? Armstrong replied with a single word: yes.[7]

> TURNBULL: You say there, Sir Robert, that it is the practice and policy of the United Kingdom not to make public information about the work of the Security Services. You say that this has been the consistent practice and policy of successive governments who have recognised that the work of the Service would be made more difficult if ... public attention would be drawn to it?
>
> ARMSTRONG: Yes ... It has been the consistent practice and policy of the government's not to make public information about the work of the Security Services, but when in the view of the government information may be disclosed without risk of damage, it should be done by way of official publication based on official records with a view to giving a comprehensive and accurate account.
>
> TURNBULL: You say that the practice and policy of the government on disclosure of information can be fully effective only if it is followed consistently ... That is your sincere belief, isn't it?
>
> ARMSTRONG: It is my belief. If I have a belief, it is a sincere belief.

Economical with the Truth

And yet, Turnbull demanded, was it not true that 'over the past six years ... there has been a rush of disclosures by former officers of the Security Service into the public domain?' Armstrong regretfully confirmed that this was an unfortunate fact.

Turnbull moved in a little closer for his first thrust of the knife: did the Cabinet Secretary recall that only a year ago one of those officers, Cathy Massiter, had given a television interview in which she accused MI5 of 'extensive phone tapping' of a union official to obtain information about its 'bottom line' in a pay dispute with Ford, and had then passed this on to the company?

Armstrong immediately sensed danger. Not only was this a very recent unauthorised disclosure – one which the government had made no attempt to block – but it was precisely the sort of illegal behaviour by the Security Services described in Wright's memoirs: the bugging of a British citizen whose activities had nothing to do with national security.

In what would become a familiar pattern, he sought to shift responsibility, only to expose gaping holes in the Crown's arguments: the Prime Minister, Armstrong asserted, had asked Lord Bridge of Harwich to conduct an inquiry, and he had reported that any 'interceptions' had been carried out lawfully, under warrant from the Home Office. Turnbull pounced.

> I put it to you that over the last 15 years 6,129 telephone interception warrants have been issued in the United Kingdom ... [Yet] the investigation was carried out over six days and two of those days Lord Bridge sat in the House of Lords. So he did four days work on over 6,000 interception warrants and concluded that nothing wrong had occurred?

It was palpably absurd and, since the government had already admitted – 'for the purposes of these proceedings' – that Massiter's allegations were all true, Armstrong was trapped. He sought refuge by stressing that the public simply had to have faith in Bridge's 'independence and stature ... it is a matter of trust, to coin a phrase'.

Armstrong prized himself on his phrasemaking abilities. His serene and ever-upward path through Whitehall's labyrinthine corridors was founded on his mastery of the art of disguising slippery statements with clever words. This self-confidence now ran headlong into the buffers of Turnbull's rather more direct approach to language.

Was that phrase, he demanded, not the very title of a book about MI5 by the espionage writer Nigel West? And was it not true that, after initially obtaining an injunction to prevent publication, the government had negotiated redactions with West and then allowed him to publish – even though the book made explicitly clear that its revelations had been provided by former Security Service officers, including Arthur Martin and Peter Wright? Surely these disclosures breached the same duty of confidence the government was trying to enforce in this court?

Armstrong fell back on prevarication. The case had been handled by the Attorney General, not the Cabinet Office, and 'I can say no more than that those responsible believed that previously unpublished information classified as secret and obtained in breach of a duty of confidentiality owed to the Crown would be removed.'

And yet somehow, as Turnbull's analysis of both the pre-redaction proofs and the published book showed, the agreed changes were minimal: *A Matter of Trust* included previously unseen charts of the structure of MI5, the codenames and functions of its departments, the locations of its premises and the identities of individual officers. It was, in short, no different in principle to *Spycatcher*.

Turnbull pressed Armstrong to explain why his offers similarly to redact Wright's manuscript had been rejected: much of its text repeated previously published material, yet the government had refused to identify any sections damaging to Britain's national security so that these could be deleted.

Cornered, Armstrong fell back on the absolutist position that as an officer of the Security Service Wright owed an unbreakable duty of confidentiality to the Crown; every dot and comma of *Spycatcher* was therefore prohibited.

> ARMSTRONG: I would argue that publication by Mr. Wright, even of some information which is already in the public domain, could cause detriment to the national security of the United Kingdom.
>
> TURNBULL: All of it?
>
> ARMSTRONG: All of it could.

This proved rather too much for Mr Justice Powell. 'I must say I find myself straining a little,' he rumbled, before posing a hypothetical question to test the limits of the argument. 'Let's assume that in his book Mr. Wright says that the standard small arms issued to MI5 agents is a Walther PPK or even, if one can borrow from Mr. Ian Fleming, a Beretta; how, I ask, could that conceivably affect in any detrimental way the national security interests of the United Kingdom Government?'

At which point the Cabinet Secretary stepped through the looking glass of the government's already-tenuous claims and entered the realms of pure fantasy.

'I think,' Armstrong blustered, 'the general proposition is that information coming from somebody inside the service, carrying greater authority, could be helpful to a hostile intelligence service.'

This was the first test of the government's 'inside man' thesis. By this metric, statements made directly by a former MI5 officer were automatically more valuable to the country's enemies than the very same information, already in the public domain, if that had been reported by an 'outside man' – a journalist or author like Nigel West. Under this extravagant theory, Armstrong insisted, the information itself might not be 'detrimental to national security' but 'the source from which it came may be'.

The proposition was nonsensical; nor could it explain why other senior MI5 figures – including former Director General Sir Percy Sillitoe, officers Tony Motion, Miranda Ingram, Cathy Massiter and Wright himself – had been allowed variously to publish books and magazine articles or give television interviews. Turnbull moved in to land another blow, accusing the Cabinet Secretary of hiding behind 'weasel words ... words which are devoid of content, just like an egg which has been sucked out by a weasel'.

Under pressure, Armstrong's demeanour changed visibly. He began to stutter and pressed himself back in the witness chair; to Greengrass, it seemed that the Cabinet Secretary was trying to retreat as far as physically possible from Turnbull's onslaught.

'It was a supreme piece of advocacy: Armstrong was a very clever man and very good on his feet, and the government had superb lawyers on their side. And Malcolm was this young Turk putting them to the sword with the sheer intellectual forensics and brilliance of his advocacy. He systematically set about demolishing the Government's case in a way that never happened in English courts.'[8]

Nor was Powell prepared to offer any protection. When Simos attempted to run interference, asking to halt Turnbull's questions on the grounds that they were 'not relevant', the judge slapped him down firmly. 'It seems to me that it is relevant ... to establish if much, or even only some part of this material is already in the public domain, allowed or authorised to be published by the Plaintiff.' It was an early, but unmistakable, warning to the government that its case was in trouble.

Armstrong braced himself for further interrogation on the mystery of why West's book could be published yet Wright's should be banned, but Turnbull's cross-examination technique – closer to dramatic American courtroom tactics than the more genteel practices of the Royal Courts of

Justice – was calculated to unsettle his quarry by rapidly switching between lines of attack. He launched into a direct assault on the Cabinet Secretary's honesty – and deftly laid a trap.

> TURNBULL: Sir Robert, how high in your scale of values is telling the truth?
>
> ARMSTRONG: It reckons very high.
>
> TURNBULL: Is it the highest?
>
> ARMSTRONG: There are a number of things which I would not wish to grade in order of priority.
>
> TURNBULL: Would you tell an untruth to protect what you perceived as national security?
>
> ARMSTRONG: I would not wish to do so.
>
> TURNBULL: You may not wish to do so. But can you tell us whether you would under no circumstances tell an untruth to protect national security as you saw it?
>
> ARMSTRONG: I do not think I can answer a question like that. I have not been faced with such a situation ...
>
> TURNBULL: You have never been put into a position where you have to tell an untruth in order to protect the sources or operations of MI5, for instance?
>
> ARMSTRONG: I cannot remember ever being in such a situation.

Immediately, Turnbull flourished and read into the court record the letter from Armstrong to Chapman Pincher's publisher in March 1981, asking for a copy of *Their Trade Is Treachery*, a few days before it was to be published. The Cabinet Secretary's request explained that 'the Prime Minister is likely to come under pressure to make some statement on the matters with which Mr. Pincher is dealing' but could not do so until she had seen the book; he had therefore sought 'one or (preferably) two copies' as a matter of urgency, promising that no attempt would be made 'to prevent or delay publication'.[9]

Armstrong's immediate problem – others would follow in short order – was that the letter implied he did not already have a copy of Pincher's book, when in fact MI5 had surreptitiously 'obtained' one and delivered it to Downing Street almost two months earlier. Since this admission had been forced out of the government in one of the interrogatories, Turnbull knew he had the Cabinet Secretary on the ropes.

TURNBULL: That [letter] plainly conveys ... that the government did not have a copy of the book, does it not?

ARMSTRONG: It does not say that. The letter takes the form it does because ... I wished to protect the source from which it had been obtained.

TURNBULL: So you misrepresented the truth in order to protect a source of MI5 ...

ARMSTRONG: If you wish to put that interpretation on it. I was bound to do so ...

TURNBULL: You said to His Honour a little while ago that you could not remember an occasion when you had been placed in the unhappy circumstances of having ... to lie in order to protect the sources of MI5 or national security ... This letter is an untruth is it not?

ARMSTRONG: It is what I have said. It was designed to protect the confidentiality of the source and to avoid the disclosure that a copy of the book had been obtained. If that is misrepresenting, yes, it was.

TURNBULL: Do you understand the difference between a truth and an untruth?

ARMSTRONG: I hope so ...

TURNBULL: I put it to you that this letter contains an untruth.

ARMSTRONG: Well, it does not contain the truth ...

Caught in the crosshairs of this unforgiving interrogation, Armstrong dissembled: misrepresentation was, he argued, very different to deception, and very far from being the same as a falsehood. Unfortunately, neither the judge – whose interventions now bordered on the incredulous – nor Turnbull were buying this lexicological abstraction.

TURNBULL: That letter contains a lie, does it not?

ARMSTRONG: It contains a misleading impression ... it does not contain a lie, I don't think.

TURNBULL: What is the difference between a misleading impression and a lie?

ARMSTRONG: A lie is a straight untruth.

TURNBULL: What is a misleading impression?

ARMSTRONG: As one person said, it is perhaps being economical with the truth.

In Whitehall's patrician corridors, Armstrong's phrase – loosely borrowed from the eighteenth-century politician Edmund Burke – would have been greeted as a delicious bon mot: precisely the sort of clever evasion with which he had earned his reputation as the ultimate mandarin. In the rather less elevated atmosphere of Court 8D it provoked laughter and ridicule.

'It caused audible gasps,' Turnbull recalled. 'Here was the representative of Her Majesty's Government – the most senior civil servant in Britain – cynically admitting to playing fast and loose with the truth in the witness box.'[10] From his seat behind the defendant's table, Grant observed the reaction on the press benches: it was immediate and raucous. 'The journalists in the jury box got up and literally ran out to file stories about Armstrong accepting that he'd been lying. They definitely knew it was a moment.'[11]

By now, Armstrong's self-confidence had entirely evaporated. Rattled and on the back foot, his stutter returned as Turnbull twisted the knife.

TURNBULL: So you regard it as worthy of the Cabinet Secretary of the United Kingdom to be economical with the truth for the purpose of conveying a misleading impression? ... What assurance do we have from you that you are not doing so today in court?

ARMSTRONG: I am under oath in this Court.

Who, Turnbull then demanded, had taken the decision not to block *Their Trade Is Treachery*? Since it revealed the extraordinarily damaging secret – 'a bombshell' according to Armstrong – of MI5's investigations into the alleged treachery of its former Director General, why was no action taken? And why, since Pincher made explicitly clear in his first few pages that this information had been given to him by Security Service officers, had the government not rushed down the Strand to obtain an emergency injunction? The Treasury Solicitor had done exactly that with Nigel West's book: why was Pincher treated differently?

The Cabinet Secretary was now on very dangerous ground. He admitted that the book unquestionably contained material provided by former MI5 officers which 'could certainly prejudice national security, including current and future operations'. Yet despite having a copy several weeks in advance, someone in the government had decided that no effort would be made to stop publication. Casting around for a scapegoat, Sir Robert fastened on Sir Michael Havers.

> ARMSTRONG: The Attorney General, in his discretion, did not seek an injunction. What his reasons were for that I'm afraid I cannot speculate, because he does not give reasons … the decision is the decision of the Attorney General … he may consult the Prime Minister… but his decisions are his and do not engage the collective responsibility of the Government … The Attorney General decided or was advised that he had no basis to restrain publication.

Playing to the gallery and to the mass of reporters, Turnbull feigned incredulity.

> TURNBULL: I am putting to you that the Attorney General received no such advice at all.
>
> ARMSTRONG: Why are you putting that to me?
>
> TURNBULL: Because if he received that advice, he received it from somebody who should not have got through first year law.

Throwing Havers under the bus was a mistake which would, before long, come back to haunt the Cabinet Secretary and shred the last fraying fibres of his credibility with Mr Justice Powell. But it was a decision forced by the need to protect the shabbiest secret of the British government's crusade against Peter Wright: that, with Thatcher, Armstrong had been the architect and moving force in the plot to help Pincher publish.

Turnbull then pressed home the advantage and lured Armstrong over his notional line of being 'economical with the truth' into outright perjury. 'When did you first become aware that Pincher was writing a book about the Hollis investigation?' he asked; the Cabinet Secretary regretfully said he could not remember, but thought it might have been in February 1981. Since this was just one month before *Their Trade Is Treachery* went on sale, Turnbull challenged his recollection: surely he must have known earlier? In what was fast becoming a tired routine, Armstrong tried to dissemble: 'It is not within my recollection that I did so, that I knew so.'

In an English trial, with a more respectful lawyer, the ploy might have succeeded; in the less genteel arena of Court 8D, with Turnbull set on pinning his victim down, it was bound to fail. 'Did anyone in the service of the government,' he demanded, 'know in late 1980 that Pincher was writing a book about Hollis?' To which Armstrong replied: 'Not to my knowledge.'

This was a straightforward lie. The Prime Minister's June 1980 memo had explicitly approved Armstrong's suggestion to brief former Attorney General Lord Peter Rawlinson about the Hollis saga 'on Privy Council terms, in the knowledge he would pass on what he was told to Chapman Pincher'.[12]

At the time, Turnbull had no means of knowing this since the government was still refusing to provide the court-ordered discovery of its papers; but his suspicions were aroused and he decided to play a hunch.

TURNBULL: Would you agree that Mr. Pincher is a journalist who is known for his conservative views on political matters?

ARMSTRONG: With a small 'c', yes.

TURNBULL: With your familiarity of [sic] security affairs, you would have been aware, would you not [that] prior to April 1981 there were already circulating in political and journalistic circles rumours concerning the investigations into Hollis?

ARMSTRONG: I believe there were – it was around.

TURNBULL: Now I put this to you, Sir Robert, that you and the Prime Minister and the Security Service agreed to let Pincher write his book about Hollis so that this affair would come out into the open through the pen of a safely conservative writer, rather than some ugly journalist on the left.

ARMSTRONG: It is a very ingenious conspiracy theory, and it is quite untrue.

TURNBULL: Totally untrue?

ARMSTRONG: Totally untrue.

Since this was precisely the motivation for Armstrong's plan, his denial was a second unequivocal lie, on oath, to save his – and Thatcher's – skin. His only comfort came in the knowledge that the files which could prove his perjury were under lock and key in a Downing Street basement. They would remain there for almost 40 years.

Economical with the Truth

By the time the court adjourned at the end of the day, Her Majesty's Cabinet Secretary was a diminished figure. His evasive performance in the witness box — and above all his casual admission of economies with the truth — led to awkward questions in the House of Commons.

Former Home Secretary Roy Jenkins asked the Prime Minister whether 'she now appreciates the increasing ludicrousness of the Government's posture before the Australian courts? As an admirer of Sir Robert Armstrong, who served me in two capacities, I deplore the foolish mission on which the Government have sent Sir Robert. May I ask the Prime Minister whether there is any chance of her recovering a sense of proportion on this issue?'[13]

Thatcher took shelter in what would become a familiar and repeated response that since proceedings were underway in Sydney, the entire matter was *sub judice* and thus off-limits for comment.

Her statement had no more merit — or truthfulness — than Armstrong's testimony. The *sub judice* rule existed to protect those facing trial in English courts, whose fate was to be decided by a jury, from prejudicial information which might sway a verdict: neither situation applied to the government's bid before a single judge — deemed by law to be above the risk of prejudice — to suppress Wright's memoirs in an Australian court.

Armstrong, meanwhile, was racking his brains for something to excuse the day's disasters. As he retired to bed, at the British Consul General's residence in the Sydney suburb of Vaucluse, the Cabinet Secretary seized on a helpful coincidence.

England's cricket team was then in the process of thrashing Australia in the first Ashes test. This, he later told his colleagues, explained everything: 'I think that Malcolm Turnbull and Mr. Justice Powell enjoyed taking their revenge on me in the Supreme Court of New South Wales.'[14]

If entirely spurious, the analogy turned out to be somewhat apt. The 1986–87 Ashes series would sputter on for several weeks with victories, losses and draws for both sides. Meanwhile, Sir Robert Armstrong faced the unwelcome prospect of play resuming the following morning in Court 8D, and a succession of tricky wickets thereafter.

20. THE HAVERS CONUNDRUM

'All it requires is for Sir Michael to come to Court to answer these allegations.'
MALCOLM TURNBULL, 19 NOVEMBER 1986
UNITED KINGDOM VS. PETER WRIGHT.

At 10am a small army of British government lawyers trooped into Sydney's Court of Appeal to apply for leave to challenge Powell's discovery order; Turnbull, who had endured a sleepless night, followed nervously behind them. He had hung a sizeable part of his defence on the argument that the Prime Minister, her Cabinet Secretary and MI5 had conspired with Chapman Pincher and had also been willing to negotiate with Nigel West; the documents he had demanded would reveal the extent of Downing Street's collusion and could make or break his case.

The three traditionally wigged judges on the bench gave him scant comfort. Chief Justice Sir Laurence Street, President of the Court of Appeal Michael Kirby, and their junior colleague Justice Michael McHugh were highly experienced and widely respected, but they were hardly revolutionary jurists.

In this rarified arena, it mattered little that the British government could – and should – have challenged the discovery order long before, nor that it was cynically exploiting both Wright's fragile health and Heinemann's depleted funds; from the outset, Street in particular seemed likely to accede to London's request for a full hearing on the dispute – a prospect which filled Turnbull with dread, since it would shutter the proceedings in Powell's court for months, possibly more than a year. He swallowed hard, gripped the lectern and went on the attack.

'The trial has started,' he told the judges. 'The battle lines have been drawn, my old and sick client is in Sydney at considerable expense to himself. My clients' resources are derisory compared to those of the other side. It is plain that here, if there ever was one, is a client with a long pocket, determined to avoid the continued cross-examination of Sir Robert Armstrong in Court 8D.'

It was stirring advocacy, but since emotion alone might not be enough, Turnbull decided to call London's bluff. 'If Your Honours consider granting leave [for the Government to appeal at a full hearing] ... then I will waive my right to discover these documents. I submit I am entitled to have them, but my clients cannot survive more delay [and] more expense. We have been driven from interlocutory hearing to interlocutory hearing.'[1]

The three judges left the bench to confer. Turnbull expected them to take their time to weigh his pleas against the powerful demands of a friendly government, but within minutes they returned to the courtroom and the Chief Justice brusquely dismissed the British application. It was a major victory for Wright, his publishers and especially their young lawyer; for the first time he could see a clear path to fending off the injunction against *Spycatcher*.

'My attitude now was that I thought we'd probably win at trial, and then probably win again in the Court of Appeal,' he later recalled. 'But I was absolutely certain that if it came to it, we'd win in the High Court of Australia – the final court to which the British Government could appeal.'[2]

If the defendants were celebrating, the ruling was a body blow for the Cabinet Secretary – 'he looked appalled', Turnbull wrote after the trial[3] – and for Downing Street. When the news filtered back to Number 10, Thatcher held an emergency meeting with selected ministers; according to internal Cabinet Office records, 'the Prime Minister said that if the discovery order went ahead there would be very good reasons for abandoning the main action'.[4]

Thatcher had a personal motive for contemplating this drastic option: the papers Turnbull had demanded contained cast-iron proof of the tawdry scheme she and Armstrong had cooked up to feed Chapman Pincher with the secrets of MI5's Hollis scandal. If they were disclosed publicly, the Cabinet Secretary's perjury in the Sydney witness box would be revealed, and the political fall-out could bring down the government. But by the end of the meeting a more pragmatic solution was reached: London would agree to comply with Powell's order, but would thereafter prevaricate, delay and try to run down the judicial clock. It was, in short, to be grubby business as usual.

The Havers Conundrum

At 11am, Armstrong returned to the witness box in Court 8D. Turnbull knew he had his quarry on the ropes; over the next six hours he landed a succession of damaging punches, drawing the Cabinet Secretary into a series of evidence-free and often contradictory statements. He began by playing on Armstrong's wounded vanity.[5]

> TURNBULL: Yesterday you told His Honour that republication [of previously published material] by an insider would give the information a more valid prominence ...
>
> ARMSTRONG: That is so ... a statement made by an insider will carry greater authority by the very virtue of the fact that he is an insider or has been an insider ...
>
> TURNBULL: Sir Robert, are you an insider or an outsider in intelligence matters?
>
> ARMSTRONG: It is a nice question ... I am clearly not part of the intelligence or Security Service. I clearly have some knowledge of those matters ...
>
> TURNBULL: But the Director General of MI5 would know more about those matters than you, would he not?
>
> ARMSTRONG: Certainly some of them.

This was a remarkable assertion – the Cabinet Secretary had never served in uniform, let alone in any intelligence body, yet now proclaimed himself to be more widely knowledgeable than Britain's most senior Security Service official – and in short order Turnbull exposed both the shallowness of Armstrong's self-proclaimed expertise and a sizeable hole in one of the government's arguments for the need to ban Peter Wright's memoirs.

> TURNBULL: Sir Robert. One of the points you raise is that if this book is allowed to be published, other friendly intelligence agencies will have less faith in MI5 ...
>
> ARMSTRONG: That is right ... other friendly services will have less confidence in the ability of MI5 to keep confidences.
>
> TURNBULL: One of those friendly agencies is the Central Intelligence Agency of the United States, is it not?
>
> ARMSTRONG: I believe so.

And yet, Turnbull pointed out, since 1978 the CIA positively helped its former officers to write accounts of their experience: its Intelligence Review Board had 'revised 400 manuscripts by 200 authors, only four of whom were not employed by the Agency' – books which were then published with official blessing and sold in American shops. Given this, why would US intelligence agencies 'think less of you if you applied the same principles that apply to their own to your own former intelligence officers?'

The question caused the British government's representative some difficulty. 'Logically,' he responded after some thought, 'you could be right, but I don't know what they would think.' Since a fundamental premise of his affidavits, let alone his testimony that same day, was that he was certain the CIA would lose confidence in MI5 should Britain be so rash as to adopt America's own rules, this made no sense: Turnbull promptly tightened the screw.

> TURNBULL: Why would the Americans judge you and your Service for standards no different to those they apply to their own?
>
> ARMSTRONG: They might very easily do so ... because we shall not be taking the steps that we should be taking to try and keep confidential information confidential or to enforce the duty of confidentiality which both present and former members of the Service owe to the Crown ...

Having helped his witness twist himself into knots, Turnbull then lured him into criticising the US intelligence community whose fragile goodwill apparently needed the protection of an injunction to silence Peter Wright.

> TURNBULL: Does MI5 think less of the Central Intelligence Agency because of its manuscript clearance policy?
>
> ARMSTRONG: I think that it would be thought that the CIA is apt to be more leaky than some other security intelligence agencies, and this policy would be a part of it.

Given the wretched history of British intelligence scandals – the treachery of Burgess, Maclean, Philby, Blunt and George Blake – and their American counterparts' despair over the UK's failures to prevent Soviet penetration, this was chutzpah indeed. But Armstrong sallied forth on the winds of his conviction. 'Our case,' he proclaimed, 'stands on the duty of confidentiality which Mr. Wright owes and has owed to the Crown as a former member of the Security Service.'

The Havers Conundrum

Unfortunately, this too was undermined by the evidence that a succession of former Security Service and SIS officers had repeatedly been allowed to ignore the supposedly inviolable 'duty of confidence'. Turnbull switched back to the dangerous territory of Pincher and his close contacts with government officials and Britain's intelligence agencies.

> TURNBULL: Is it not a fact that Chapman Pincher has had astoundingly good sources on intelligence matters for over twenty years?
>
> ARMSTRONG: He has had very good sources.
>
> TURNBULL: You have done nothing to silence him, have you?
>
> ARMSTRONG: It is not within my recollection.

It was not the first time the Cabinet Secretary had tried to avoid answering difficult questions by claiming not to remember – nor would it be the last – but Turnbull was not prepared to let him off the hook.

> TURNBULL: You really believe you are doing your best to ensure that the Security Service is leak-proof do you?
>
> ARMSTRONG: Making the Security Service leak-proof is not a matter of suppressing Mr. Chapman Pincher.
>
> TURNBULL: It is a question of suppressing his sources, is it not?
>
> ARMSTRONG: One would like to discourage his sources, certainly.

Since Armstrong himself had provided one of Pincher's primary sources for *Their Trade Is Treachery*, there were ample grounds to question the existence of such 'discouragement'. Why, Turnbull asked next, had the government 'taken no steps' to prevent the 'first hand' information fed to Pincher from being published? Once again, the Cabinet Secretary sought a scapegoat: it was the Attorney General, he insisted, who alone had decided not to block the book – a claim Armstrong knew to be false, and which would in the ensuing days come back to bite him.

But, Turnbull insisted, Pincher was far from an isolated example. As the Cabinet Secretary was well aware, Arthur Martin had briefed Nigel West, and a total of 24 retired intelligence officers, including Sir Dick White, the former head of both MI5 and MI6, were quoted by name in Penrose and

Freeman's book on Blunt: were they, too, not subject to the 'obligation of confidence' the government sought to impose on Peter Wright?

It proved to be a difficult question for Armstrong. Because the Secret Intelligence Service was unacknowledged – the government liked to pretend that it did not exist at all – the Cabinet Secretary would not allow the phrase 'MI6' to cross his lips; the best he could muster was to admit that White had been 'head of that other organisation', and that he and his colleagues had indeed given on the record interviews to the journalists. But he claimed that all the intelligence officers named as sources in *Conspiracy of Silence* had 'been reminded' of their duty not to speak. They were not, however, being subjected to any more substantive sanction.

As Armstrong's cross-examination ground on, Turnbull asked why no action had been taken to stop Wright's television interview about the Hollis scandal. The Cabinet Secretary first claimed – falsely – that the government had not known about the *World in Action* documentary until the morning of transmission, then in the next breath was forced to admit that MI5 had known about the programme 'weeks in advance'.

Yet even though Downing Street and the Security Service were aware that their old spycatcher was to be interviewed, that he had been Pincher's primary source and that he was 'likely' to denounce Hollis as a Soviet spy on national television, neither made any effort to obtain a preview tape of the film. It all suggested that supposed duty of secrecy was a charade.

TURNBULL: The Granada Television programme by Wright was publication by an insider, was it not?

ARMSTRONG: It was.

TURNBULL: Therefore it would have fallen four-square within the four corners of your objectionable sort of publication by insiders, wouldn't it?

ARMSTRONG: It would depend on the contents.

This was completely at odds with the Cabinet Secretary's earlier testimony, on oath, that *any* public statement – whatever it referred to – by a former intelligence officer automatically damaged British security; worse, as Turnbull pointed out, not one of MI5's small army of 'experienced investigators', nor any Whitehall official, had troubled themselves to discover in advance what Wright's interview contained.

The Havers Conundrum

TURNBULL: You believe that the national security interests of the United Kingdom were damaged by the Wright television programme?

ARMSTRONG: I think they probably were ... Perhaps more should have been done to find out [what Wright had said in his interview ... but] we assumed that he was going to propose that there should be a further inquiry ...

Under this remorseless cross-examination, the Cabinet Secretary once again lied under oath. Despite documents locked in Downing Street's files which showed that 'by 3 July 1984 the Security Service had confidential information that Granada TV ... intended to show an interview with Peter Wright in which Wright would reopen the Hollis case and in effect present the case against him',[6] Armstrong told the court that the first indication of the film's supposedly dangerous contents came when he and his fellow civil servants read a preview in *The Times* around 9am on the day of transmission.

Turnbull professed himself puzzled: since that was more than eleven hours before the programme was due to air, surely 'there was plenty of time to ... get an injunction against Granada Television?' For the second time that afternoon, the Cabinet Secretary pinned the blame on Sir Michael Havers: it had been up to the Attorney General to decide whether or not to obtain an emergency court order, and events had moved too fast for the government's chief law officer. 'I suspect,' Armstrong airily – and falsely – testified, 'there simply wasn't time to get the act together ... to get a decision in the time available, which at that stage was very short.'

Turnbull was now incredulous. 'So here we have Mr. Wright revealing information – you now know he was going to reveal information which is damaging to national security – and you cannot get a decision out of the Attorney General quickly enough to get the injunction ... How zealous is the Attorney General in his defence of the nation's secrets, Sir Robert? Even the sleepiest man in [his] office would have read *The Times* by nine o'clock ... so he had eleven and a half hours to swear a one-page affidavit, annex it to a summons, and get an injunction. Do you believe the Attorney General is worthy of criticism for this failure to make a decision quickly?'

Belatedly, Armstrong realised that he had gone too far, and tried to repair the damage. 'I don't know where the responsibility lies,' he stammered, before making the position worse by admitting that there were no government records to back up his assertion that Havers alone had taken the decision not to intervene.

TURNBULL: Sir Robert, I put to you that far from being concerned about this programme ... you were so little concerned about it that you knowingly allowed it to go to air without any thought of seeking a restraint?

ARMSTRONG: I think thought was given to seeking restraint but I do not think the decision was taken in the necessary time scale.

TURNBULL: Were there any communications with the Prime Minister or the Security Service made by you concerning the programme that day?

ARMSTRONG: There were no communications with the Prime Minister, but then the decision was not for her: the decision would be with the Attorney General.

The exchange capped a bad day for Downing Street, and after the court adjourned Turnbull warned the government's barrister, Theo Simos, that he would return to Havers' role in the debacle the following morning. Since the Cabinet Secretary was testifying on the Attorney General's behalf, he suggested that the two men should confer overnight and get their stories straight. It was good and, under the circumstances, generous advice: unfortunately, it fell on deaf ears.

The reason for Turnbull's suggestion became clear the next day. He arrived in court clutching a previously unseen document with which he intended to ambush Armstrong.

It had arrived in his office the previous afternoon in a large box containing correspondence between Wright and Pincher about their collaboration and, in particular, about the financial arrangements for *Their Trade Is Treachery*. They had originally agreed to destroy all these letters, but the old spycatcher had instead filed them away securely, and then forgotten about their existence until the trial began.

Aware, as always, that the case was being reported around the world, Turnbull made no effort to hide the document from the phalanx of reporters in the jury box; but before he sought to introduce it into evidence, he returned to the question of Pincher's notably favoured status. Was it not true, he asked Armstrong, that between 1982 and 1983 the journalist had been appointed to not one, but two official roles. Grudgingly, the Cabinet Secretary confirmed that Pincher had indeed been hired as a specialist advisor to the Parliamentary Defence Committee and to a Ministry of Defence committee examining reporting of the Falklands Conflict.

The Havers Conundrum

Since Pincher had been given both jobs despite using Wright's information in his 1981 book, Turnbull suggested that 'it would be fair to say, would it not, that his career following the publication of *Their Trade Is Treachery* was hardly blighted by any official shunning him?' In journalistic parlance, this was a 'when did you stop beating your wife?' question – one to which there was no safe answer; Armstrong meekly responded, 'Not as far as I know.'

TURNBULL: One of Mr. Pincher's better contacts in the Government is the Attorney General, Sir Michael Havers?

ARMSTRONG: I have no knowledge of that ... I am sure they meet from time to time. I do not know whether it could be described as a close relationship.

Waving the mysterious document in front of his witness, Turnbull reminded Armstrong that he had warned the government's QC that he had evidence to support his allegation, and had recommended that the Cabinet Secretary speak to Havers about his relationship with Pincher: had he done so? He had not – nor had Armstrong even discussed the warning with Simos.

Turnbull's evidence was a letter from Pincher to Wright in January 1983, reporting a convivial conversation the journalist had recently enjoyed with the Attorney General about Nigel West's troublesome book *MI5 – A Matter of Trust*.

On New Year's Day I was shooting with Havers, who is very friendly and told me about West's book. It is an extraordinary story ... For reasons I do not understand [Arthur] Martin agreed to see West. Havers told me they met six times and on each occasion, Martin told West secret information. In addition he showed him secret documents ... West then not only quoted Martin by name but quoted from the documents, saying they were secret! ...

Havers then issued an injunction to have the offending parts removed ... [he] told me he is still considering whether to prosecute Martin, but can't do that without prosecuting West who has been adopted as a Parliamentary candidate! ...

I can assure you that there is no intention whatever of taking action against me [over *Their Trade Is Treachery*], which means you too. I lunched with Dickie Franks recently and he told me they ... would rather I did it than anyone else ...

The letter was a genuine bombshell, guaranteed to excite the press corps: not only did it reveal Havers as one of Pincher's shooting-party chums – a senior government minister and law officer who was perfectly happy to discuss an ongoing official secrets case with him between shotgun blasts – but the identity of the journalist's luncheon companion posed an even greater threat to the case against Wright.

'Dickie' Franks was, more formally, Sir Arthur Temple Franks, chief of MI6 from 1979 to 1982. If 'C' – Britain's most senior spy – was cheerfully briefing Pincher over canapés and cocktails, it would be extremely difficult to maintain the claim that all intelligence officers owed a lifelong duty of silence to the Crown.

Turnbull knew, however, that he would face an uphill struggle to get the document into evidence in open court. He began by paying out a little rope with which the Cabinet Secretary might hang himself and his lawyers.

> TURNBULL: On New Year's Day 1983 Sir Michael Havers was shooting with Mr. Chapman Pincher, was he not?
>
> ARMSTONG: I haven't the faintest idea.
>
> TURNBULL: I put that to Mr. Simos last night, and that was one of the matters he passed on to you, was it not?

The government's QC rose quickly to his feet and spluttered, 'It was not put to me that they were shooting. He put to me that they had a conversation.' Feigning outrage, Turnbull told Mr Justice Powell that he was 'struck dumb' by the objection, before stressing that the meeting took place just six weeks after the injunction on West was lifted. But when he asked Armstrong to confirm that Havers had 'disclosed confidential information about the West case' and that the Attorney General had told Pincher 'that Arthur Martin had provided secret documents concerning Soviet Penetration of MI5 to West', the Cabinet Secretary refused to answer; he sat, tight-lipped, in the witness box until Simos stepped in to protect him, demanding that Powell rule the questions out of order.

'It is not proper,' he argued, 'for my learned friend to go on putting all sorts of conversations between other persons at which this witness was not present ... I submit that it is not proper and not admissible and I object to it, your Honour.'

The problem was the glaring absence of Havers, the one minister who could have explained why it was 'proper' to brief Pincher on such sensitive

The Havers Conundrum

secrets. He had chosen not to come to court, instead dispatching the Cabinet Secretary to plead the government's case for him.

'It is a difficulty we face,' Turnbull tartly pointed out. 'We have the Plaintiff, the Attorney General, about whom we have certain information ... I gave my learned friend notice that I would be asking questions about this ... [and] Sir Robert obviously has had the opportunity to make some enquiries. I am duty bound to put them to him because ... part of our case [is] that *Their Trade Is Treachery* was specifically authorised by the Government. All it requires is for Sir Michael to come to Court to answer these allegations ...'

It was a measure of the arcane niceties of jurisprudence, coupled with his own innate conservatism, that Powell felt duty bound to protect the government from unwelcome media attention. 'I offer no criticism of the press when I say that ... things that happen in Court are not ... recorded accurately in terms of legal theory. I can well appreciate that somewhere in the world's press tomorrow will be a headline which says, "The Attorney General and Chapman Pincher at Secret Hideout on the Moors".'

That this potential story would accurately describe exactly what had occurred appeared to be beside the point. As the judge explained to Turnbull, 'if you had ... Sir Michael in the witness box you could cross-examine him to your heart's delight ... [but] you cannot cross-examine a witness [Armstrong] as to the contents of a document which is not his'.

Finally, a compromise – legally sound, but farcical in the real world – was hammered out. The embarrassing letter from Pincher would be 'placed in the hands of Sir Robert', its contents kept from the court record and well away from the prying eyes of the world's journalists; it would not emerge into the public domain until two years after the trial concluded.

Honours just about even, Turnbull returned to the West case and prised from the Cabinet Secretary a resultant admission that Martin, a former senior intelligence officer, had given the young journalist-turned Tory MP secret MI5 documents – and that the government had known this at the time it agreed redactions to *A Matter of Trust*. The Official Secrets Act specifically made it a criminal offence, punishable by imprisonment, for him to have received 'any secret, official code, word or password, or sketch, plan, model, article, note, document or information, knowing or having reasonable grounds to believe .... that the information is communicated to him in contravention of the Act'. Yet, like Pincher, West was never prosecuted. Once again, Armstrong laid the responsibility for this remarkable lapse on Sir Michael Havers: he, as a mere civil servant, could not possibly be expected to explain the Attorney General's reasoning.

A pattern was emerging: whenever the evidence came close to showing that the British government and its intelligence services had connived or colluded with friendly journalists, the Cabinet Secretary regretfully passed the buck to the absent plaintiff on whose behalf he was being cross-examined, while simultaneously admitting that he had never bothered to seek his notional client's instructions.

If this was absurd, the trial descended into pantomime when Turnbull pursued the Franks luncheon disclosures. Simos leaped to his feet, objecting to any questions about the former head of MI6, since that organisation did not officially exist. 'If there is an answer given [in open court] it will be the first time that the matter will have been officially confirmed by an official of Her Majesty's Government,' the barrister complained. Undeterred, Turnbull challenged Armstrong to come clean and admit that Britain had 'a secret intelligence service known as MI6'; the Cabinet Secretary refused, insisting that the most he could manage was to write down his answer on a small piece of paper, for Powell's eyes alone. The proposal was, as Turnbull observed, 'reducing the Court proceedings here to the level of a fine farce'.

By now Simos was alarmed at the spectacle being played out in full view of the press. He repeatedly requested that the court be closed and Armstrong's testimony be heard *in camera*. But Turnbull, aware of the power of a public platform, had one last troublesome name to dangle before the journalists were removed.

TURNBULL: Do you know Lord Rothschild? He is a friend of yours, is he not? You worked with him closely during the Heath government.

ARMSTRONG: I know him. He has been a colleague of mine ... I was the Prime Minister's principal private secretary; he was the head of the Central Policy Review staff, the 'Think Tank'.

TURNBULL: He has been a trusted confidante of Conservative Governments, both now and in years past, on matters relating to intelligence, has he not?

ARMSTRONG: I think that would be an overstatement ... He has occasionally made views [on intelligence matters] known to the Government.

TURNBULL: He is a man who even today still has access to, and confidence from, senior officials involved in British Intelligence?

The Havers Conundrum

ARMSTRONG: I think that those contacts and that confidence is much diminished [but] I should think that they still exist.

TURNBULL: Have you received any reports from the Security Service concerning Victor Rothschild's role in the publication of *Their Trade Is Treachery*?

ARMSTRONG: I would not wish to answer those questions in open court since any information I have on those matters is confidential.

TURNBULL: Have you learned other than from the Security Service that Victor Rothschild procured the publication of *Their Trade Is Treachery*?

ARMSTRONG: I don't wish to discuss that further in open court.

Since Armstrong knew perfectly well that Rothschild had been the book's impresario and had paid Wright a half share of the proceeds, the Cabinet Secretary's desire to gain the sanctuary of a private hearing was understandable.

Affecting a show of reluctance, Turnbull bowed to Simos' demands to remove the press and spectators. 'I do state,' he told Powell, 'that I am opposed to this cross-examination being in closed court. I do not believe [this information] is of a kind that is properly confidential because it does relate to the publication of a book which is in the public domain.'

But he had done enough. His pointed questions had set two hares running in the press – the role of the government's most senior law officer and one of its most famous former MI5 officers in ushering top-secret intelligence information into the public sphere; he knew both the Attorney General and the noble Baron would come under intense scrutiny and face demands to explain their actions. Neither was likely to make Armstrong's life – or the bid to silence Wright – any easier.

There was one final skirmish before the proceedings were taken *in camera*. Simos insisted that Paul Greengrass should be excluded along with all the other journalists; Turnbull objected – the producer was an essential member of his legal team and would be needed to provide detailed information in real-time. Ultimately, Powell agreed to let him remain – though not before threatening contempt-of-court sanctions should any of the confidential proceedings leak to the media.

It was a small and seemingly unimportant squabble, but it presaged the British government's next tactic: it was about to resort once again to dirty tricks.

21. SMEARS

> 'This information has been placed in the public domain by the British Government in an effort to discredit me.'
> PETER WRIGHT: PRESS STATEMENT,
> 25 NOVEMBER 1986

The ceremonial jousting of Prime Minister's Questions is one of the more celebrated elements of British Parliamentary democracy; it is also symptomatic of its anachronistic and antediluvian nature.

In theory, the leader of Her Majesty's Government is required to present him or herself at the despatch box and respond to inquiries or challenges from MPs on all sides of the House of Commons. The practice is rather different: questions, usually prefaced with a formulaic and repetitious request that premiers list their day's 'engagements', are planted with tame supporters to yield carefully scripted soundbites of government talking points in time for the evening news. If the Leader of the Opposition and less pliable members are also granted the privilege of putting forward questions, there is no obligation on the PM to give them any meaningful answers. It is, in short, little more than pantomime.

On the same afternoon – London time – that Sir Robert Armstrong stepped down from the Sydney witness box, Neil Kinnock rose to his feet to ask Margaret Thatcher about her Cabinet Secretary's evidence and the role of the Attorney General in the *Spycatcher* saga. More specifically, how had the decision been taken to permit Chapman Pincher to publish Peter Wright's revelations in *Their Trade Is Treachery*?

Is she aware that ... Sir Robert Armstrong has testified that officers of the Crown had photocopies of Mr. Chapman Pincher's book several weeks before it was published in 1981? He has said in court that 'of course' the book contains a substantial amount of information from former officers of MI5 which, in Sir Robert's view, 'could certainly prejudice national security, including current and future operations' ...

Sir Robert has further testified that the decision of the Attorney-General in 1981 was that there was 'no basis on which an injunction could be launched' to prevent the publication of Mr. Pincher's book?

Is it not obvious that any Government who had foreknowledge that information prejudicial to national security was to be published would have absolutely no difficulty obtaining an injunction against its publication? Can the Prime Minister tell us precisely why she accepted that decision by the Attorney-General not to seek an injunction to prevent publication of Mr. Chapman Pincher's book, which was obviously prejudicial to national security?

Kinnock's intervention in the *Spycatcher* affair – the first by a front-bench politician – had been prompted by a late-night call from Turnbull. His cross-examination of Armstrong had convinced him the government was attempting to cover up its role in the publication of *Their Trade Is Treachery*, and that the Cabinet Secretary was attempting to hide behind the Attorney General's constitutionally opaque skirts.

'Armstrong's evidence ... meant that the Attorney General was either monumentally incompetent or was prepared to prostitute ... his great office to lend a little legal colour to what was otherwise a ... political decision,' Turnbull wrote in his subsequent account of the trials. 'The Attorney was either a fool or a knave ... [or] Armstrong was not telling the truth.'[1] But with Sir Michael Havers conspicuously absent from Court 8D, the only route to flushing out the truth lay in the House of Commons.

Kinnock was, however, initially sceptical of Turnbull's client and the appetite of his party to come to the aid of Peter Wright. 'I thought it was just additional evidence from an obvious malcontent about the peculiar goings-on in the secret services,' he later recalled.

'Very little was going on inside Westminster about the case at the time, because most of the attention was on the claims that Wright was making about the activities of MI5 in the affairs of the Wilson government. That tended to reinforce feelings among my colleagues about the attitude of the

Security Services. People on our side were intrigued by it, but the attitude was: "pity this bloke is a lunatic, because otherwise what he's saying is quite serious". They instinctively wanted to take the allegations seriously, but Peter Wright didn't seem to be much of a hook to hang it all on.'[2]

Nonetheless, Turnbull persevered and eventually persuaded the Labour leader to raise the case at PMQs.

In the three years they had faced each other across the despatch box, the antipathy between Kinnock and Margaret Thatcher had blossomed into a deep mutual loathing. He saw her as partisan, autocratic and 'insecurely regal'; for her part, the Iron Lady viewed him, along with almost all Labour MPs, as inherently untrustworthy quasi-communists.

Inevitably, his challenge to the Prime Minister received a characteristically evasive response. Since court proceedings were 'ongoing', Thatcher argued, it would be 'inappropriate' for her to answer any questions about what the government had or hadn't done to assist Pincher. Nor would she commit to making a detailed statement once the unpleasantries in Sydney concluded: her sole concessions were a vague undertaking eventually to 'consider carefully any questions that are put to us in the light of the usual customs and conventions', and an assurance that her Attorney General would 'answer in his own way'.[3]

The latter response proved to be as inaccurate as previous statements: over the coming days, weeks and months, Havers would refuse to provide any information to MPs while the court hearings dragged on.

But Kinnock's intervention provoked an immediate hostile reaction: within a week the government mounted an underhand operation to discredit him in Parliament and the press. Thatcher's press officers held unattributable 'Lobby briefings',[4] telling journalists that ministers believed Kinnock had shown he could not be trusted on matters of national security, and were considering excluding him from the intelligence information traditionally provided to opposition leaders. It would not be the only smear campaign that autumn.[5]

The following morning, the hearings in Sydney descended further into farce. Simos submitted yet another updated Statement of Claim on behalf of the British government. Much of it was boilerplate – verbose duplications of the thesis that Wright owed a lifelong duty of *omertà* to the Crown – but one section was particularly absurd. Now London argued that even the passages in *Spycatcher* which repeated information previously published by other former MI5 officers were inimical to British national security because 'detriment will flow from the fact that the same material is again published by an officer of the Service'.[6] In other words, other MI5 officers had been allowed to disclose these secrets but Wright – alone – had to be silenced: it smacked of very personal animus against him.

Additionally, Simos announced that despite having previously agreed to abide by Powell's order to hand over the discovery documents, his clients now wanted to reopen the issue at the start of the following week; worse, he was instructed to advise the court that the government was also contemplating making public interest immunity claims for some of the papers.

PII is an antique blunderbuss of English common law; it has no statutory basis, but relies instead on the accumulated silt of judicial rulings to allow ministers to sign certificates which block the disclosure of evidence that the government claims could affect national security. By 1986, English judges had a sorry history of rubber-stamping PII claims, but extending this privilege to hearings in foreign jurisdictions was, to put it kindly, novel, and Number 10 knew that it had no legal basis for the argument: 'It is not open to us to claim public interest immunity in the courts in Australia,' an internal Downing Street memo had noted on 13 November.[7] Exasperated, Turnbull demanded an end to London's 'twists and turns'.

Powell was also becoming visibly impatient, but he agreed to wait until the next week to consider the arguments in detail. With that, Armstrong was summoned back to the witness box for a further day of cross-examination. It went no better than his previous outings.

Turnbull first forced him to admit he had personally been warned that Arthur Martin had given top-secret MI5 documents to Nigel West; remarkably, the Cabinet Secretary 'did not know' whether these had ever been recovered, and 'could not remember' whether he had advised the Security Service to do so.

He had a similar lapse of memory over magazine articles published by Miranda Ingram and Cathy Massiter about their work for the Service, but grudgingly confirmed that he knew of no action being taken against them; it was, as Turnbull tartly observed, 'hardly consistent with your zealous concern to protect the nation's secrets, was it?'[8]

Next, Turnbull demanded an explanation of the puzzling decision not to block Pincher's *Their Trade Is Treachery* – a book which, as MI5 and Downing Street knew, was primarily based on Wright's revelations.

TURNBULL: In 1981 you knew that it was possible to seek an injunction to restrain the author and the publisher if they had received confidential information in breach of confidence.

ARMSTRONG: I knew that it was possible to apply for an injunction, yes ...

TURNBULL: You were advised that the Attorney General took the view that there was no reason to seek an injunction ... but the Attorney's expressed basis for his decision was inconsistent with what you knew the law to be, was it not?

ARMSTRONG: It is not for me to query the Attorney General's view of what action he should take ... I don't argue with the Attorney General on points of law ...

Curiously, to the best of the Cabinet Secretary's somewhat equivocal recollection, Sir Michael Havers had not troubled to provide the Prime Minister or her senior advisor with any explanation of his decision, nor had he ever committed it to paper. His conclusion had, instead, mysteriously wafted over from his office in the Royal Courts of Justice to Number 10.

This peculiarly nebulous way of conveying a legally inconsistent determination on a matter of national security troubled Mr Justice Powell greatly. 'As I understand it,' the judge mused just before the court broke for lunch, 'the advice was unsound ... I cannot understand why someone did not hotfoot it up the Strand and get an *ex parte* injunction ... I do not see how they could have failed.'

The afternoon's proceedings proved no more comfortable for Armstrong. Turnbull swiftly switched tack to explore the claim that silencing Peter Wright was essential for Britain's national security. Wright's book detailed the plot by rogue MI5 officers to force Harold Wilson – a democratically elected Prime Minister – from office. 'Can you imagine,' he asked, 'a more heinous breach of the lawful obligations that bind this Service?' Surely the public had a right to know about treasonous activities by the intelligence officers it paid for?

Once again, the Cabinet Secretary was caught between the government's admission that – for the purposes of the trial – every word in *Spycatcher* was true, and Australian law, which frowned on attempts to suppress exposure of illegal official actions.

He agreed that the Wilson Plot had been a 'very serious breach' of MI5's directive, but insisted that it was up to the government – and the government alone – to be told about this and to decide what, if anything, should be done. Turnbull promptly turned the screw.

TURNBULL: Do you say, no matter how black, under no circumstances can it be revealed to the public if it concerns MI5?

ARMSTRONG: I don't say anything of the kind. I say there is a balance of consideration ... Whether, in a hypothetical situation, it should be exposed in the public interest would be a matter to be decided on the circumstances of the day ...

TURNBULL: Sir Harold Wilson made this allegation about plotting against his government some years ago ... There has been no public enquiry into that allegation at all, has there?

ARMSTRONG: There has been no public enquiry, no.

TURNBULL: Has there been a private enquiry?

ARMSTRONG: I expect there has been a private enquiry in MI5 [but] I have not seen the results of it.

TURNBULL: Have you asked to see the results of it?

ARMSTRONG: No.

TURNBULL: You are the Prime Minister's principal advisor on security matters and you have not asked to see the results of the enquiry into allegations that MI5 had plotted to overthrow the Government of Harold Wilson?

ARMSTRONG: No. Matters of the management of the Security Service are under the Director General, who answers to the Home Secretary not me.

With that, the Cabinet Secretary threw a second government minister under the bus crash of his sworn testimony. He found himself on equally tricky ground over Cathy Massiter's filmed interview in the Channel 4 documentary *MI5's Official Secrets*. He confirmed that the government had seen an advance copy of the programme, and that he had sent it to the Security Service for a detailed damage analysis of her revelations about phone tapping of trade union officials and civil liberties campaigners; but he was distinctly evasive over what happened next.

TURNBULL: She had only recently retired from MI5 had she not?

ARMSTRONG: Fairly recently, I cannot remember exactly when.

TURNBULL: So her information was current and up to date, was it not?

ARMSTRONG: It was about a year old.

TURNBULL: But it was considerably more up to date than any information Mr. Wright would be able to tell us about?

ARMSTRONG: By definition.

Yet although the Cabinet Secretary confirmed that MI5 'made it clear that the programme was damaging' and that he shared this assessment, Channel 4 was given an official green light to transmit the film; nor had Massiter been prosecuted for her disclosures, even though she was, by Armstrong's own definition, 'an insider'. What, Turnbull demanded, was the difference between her 'comprehensive breach' of the duty of confidentiality and Wright's revelations in *Spycatcher*?

Caught on the horns of the government's absolutist argument, Armstrong tried to square the circle: the issue now, apparently, was a question of degree, not principle.

'The distinction between Wright and Massiter,' he asserted, 'is that this is a full-scale book with a great deal of information in it, a good deal of which has not reached the public domain and which is a comprehensive breach of [the] duty of confidentiality ... I can distinguish between a book which purports to give an account of a full lifetime of service and the kind of material that was in Ms. Massiter's programme.'

Aside from the glaring inconsistency of the Cabinet Secretary's logic, his claim was also fundamentally untruthful. Wright had very deliberately not described broad swathes of his work for the Security Service – notably the many years he had toiled on intelligence relating to the Troubles in Northern Ireland – and almost all of the remaining sensitive information in *Spycatcher* had previously been published by other authors. Surely, Turnbull asked, MI5 had carried out an assessment of his manuscript to work out which material was already in the public domain and which information was so out of date as to render it harmless?

Under pressure, Armstrong admitted that 'a great deal of work has been done on the manuscript' and that 'it was thought that the publication of some of the material would be damaging'.

TURNBULL: But you are not prepared to say which 'some'?

ARMSTRONG: Certainly not in open court, and I doubt even if *in camera*.

TURNBULL: So you come out 10,000 miles ... you have sworn four lengthy affidavits calling for suppression of this book ... and you are not in a position to tell His Honour which parts of the book would prejudice the operations of MI5?

ARMSTRONG: It is very difficult to make a damage assessment of that kind before a book is published.

It was an entirely circular, catch-22 of an argument. The government's Security Service had conducted an assessment which concluded that publishing some of Wright's account would harm national security, but was unable to specify exactly which parts were damaging because the book had not been published.

Turnbull then raised Cathy Massiter's claims that MI5 had tapped the phones of trade union leaders during a pay dispute. This provoked an immediate response: Simos jumped to his feet and asked the judge to rule the questions out of order. Powell was not impressed: whatever discomfort Armstrong might face in responding was 'the result of Her Majesty's Government shooting itself in the foot; because for the purposes of these proceedings it admits the truth of the allegations'.

Cornered, Armstrong attempted to justify the interceptions on the grounds that one of the union leaders was a card-carrying communist, and there was 'a need to know what was the influence of the Communist Party in the conduct of those [pay] negotiations'. As to the equally surveilled and resolutely non-communist officials of the National Council for Civil Liberties, he vaguely 'assumed' that the Director General of MI5 'must have had reasons to believe they were having subversive connections or something'.

By the end of that Friday, what little remained of the Cabinet Secretary's credibility was in tatters. Even the judge was worried about Armstrong's attempts at 'performing intellectual gymnastics: in fairness to Sir Robert,' Powell ruminated, 'I don't want him to do himself a grave injury.'

Over the weekend, the British press mercilessly ridiculed the government's hapless emissary. The *Sunday Times* lambasted the 'Fiasco Down Under', noting that 'even the judge ... regarded as a conservative in Australia, has added to Sir Robert's discomfort, speculating that [he] seemed to have been "put up" to appearing in court and was not qualified to reply to many of Turnbull's points'.

Number 10 was now, the paper reported, feverishly hunting for a scapegoat.

Thatcher was assured that the case against Wright was watertight. The courts in Australia, she was told, would take the same sympathetic attitude as British judges when the catch-all phrase 'national security' was invoked. Yet last week, as Armstrong suffered indignity upon indignity, someone had to be blamed for miscalculating.[9]

Inside either Number 10 or MI5 – both anxious to save their emissary's skin – a decision was taken to place a covert thumb on the scales of Australian justice. It would take less than 24 hours to produce results.

The following Monday, after enduring a torrid day in the Sydney witness box, Armstrong cabled Downing Street with news that Turnbull had made a further offer to settle the case on the basis of agreed redactions to Wright's manuscript. In a lengthy telegram, the Cabinet Secretary advised his mistress that he could see 'advantage in a deal which would establish the precedent of publication by insiders only on agreed terms' – in other words, the same arrangement successfully adopted by the CIA.[10]

He need not have gone to such trouble. Thatcher was resolutely opposed to any compromise, and her officials were pinning their hopes on a smear: while Armstrong testified, someone leaked from the secret court records the previously unpublished financial arrangements surrounding *Their Trade Is Treachery*. That morning – London time – *The Times* splashed a scoop under the banner headline 'Wright was paid for revealing MI5 secrets'.

> An extraordinary secret deal under which Mr. Peter Wright ... was paid 'substantial sums' in royalties for a book on the Security Service by Mr. Chapman Pincher can be disclosed by *The Times* today.
>
> Until now, it was believed that Mr. Wright's sole motive for helping Mr. Pincher ... was that of a crusader exposing alleged traitors inside MI5 in an attempt to clean up British intelligence. However, he had another motive which was money.

In impressive detail, Michael Evans, the paper's Whitehall correspondent, set out the agreement with Pincher and Lord Rothschild that channelled '50% of the royalties from the book to a front company', which duly passed them on to Wright.

That this seismic disclosure emanated from an official briefing rather than old-fashioned investigative journalism was clear from its fourth paragraph: 'The revelation that Mr. Wright was paid "thousands of pounds" for collaborating with Mr. Pincher for his book which was filled with classified information could help the Government's case in Sydney.'[11]

If the intention was to distract from Armstrong's disastrous performance in the witness box, the leaker had cause to celebrate. From the moment *The Times* hit the newsstands, attention shifted from the Supreme Court of New South Wales to the wider global arena of public opinion: the Cabinet Secretary's ordeal would drag on for more than a week, but – with the exception of one notable moment – the drama now played out well away from Court 8D.

For Wright and his family, the implication of the story – that he was motivated by avarice, not patriotism – was profoundly hurtful. His daughter, Jenny Andrews, who lived near her parents and helped run their horse stud, later recalled: 'Even though his pension was not as much as it should have been, money was never his prime motive. His prime motive was serving his country. He loved his work at MI5, knowing this work was helping to keep the country safe.'[12]

For his part, Turnbull recognised the danger posed by *The Times*' story. His strategy for flushing out Havers depended on the goodwill of Kinnock and the British Labour Party; both were already hesitant and would be even less likely to offer support if they believed Wright to be no more than 'a greedy old man'.[13] He told his client that the only way to limit the damage was to hold an urgent press conference, explaining the genesis of his association with Pincher.

Wright was, initially, unenthusiastic. He felt a loyalty to Victor Rothschild and had only reluctantly described the arrangements in his affidavit. But that document was – as yet – not part of the public court records; discussing the financial deal underpinning *Their Trade Is Treachery* at a press conference would expose his old friend and mentor to very difficult questions. Yet, as he watched the legal team ponder the dilemma, Heinemann's Sandy Grant saw Wright's ruthless streak overcome his moral qualms.

> When Malcolm pressed him to give evidence about Victor Rothschild he thumbed his walking stick for a while and in a highly theatrical way said, 'Oh, well ... poor old Victor: throw him to the wolves.' And that's how he decided to allow Rothschild's name to be used. He obviously felt some loyalty to him but was able to be talked round. I don't think there was any real regret there.[14]

The following day, doubts pushed aside, Wright came out swinging. 'I have noted a report in *The Times*,' he told a battery of journalists and television cameras, 'that I received half the royalties in return for my contribution to *Their Trade Is Treachery*. This information has plainly been placed in the public domain by the British Government in an effort to discredit me. Accordingly, I have no choice but to respond ...'

Pausing briefly to stress that he had never denied being paid for giving information to Pincher, he revealed for the first time the curious events which led to their association.

> In the autumn of 1980 I was invited to come back to England by Lord Victor Rothschild. He sent me a first class air ticket. When I arrived I discussed with him, as I had many times before, my concern that the true facts about Hollis, among others, be placed before the Prime Minister. Victor was a man with enormous influence and I felt if anyone could get my view across to the PM, it was he.
>
> Victor said this approach would not work, as Mrs. Thatcher would feel obliged to refer any official approach direct to MI5. He told me the best way to procure a proper investigation of the Hollis affair was to write a book. He told me the book would have to be written by someone else, and he suggested Harry [Chapman] Pincher.
>
> We had dinner with Pincher and discussed it. I was terrified of getting into trouble. Victor assured me it was going to be alright. He told me that he would arrange for his Swiss banking facilities to pay me half of the royalties from the book. He knew I was in financial difficulties and I was grateful for this assistance. It was not the motive behind my helping Pincher, rather [it was] a helpful incidental benefit.
>
> Victor was a very secretive man ... It was not done to ask Victor questions. All I know about Victor leads me to the inescapable conclusion that the powers that be approved of the book. He was so much a part of the establishment, mixing in circles way above my reach, that I could not conceive of him embarking on such a project without knowing it had the sanction, albeit unofficial, of the authorities.
>
> To me, with many years of experience in intelligence matters, and knowing Victor to have had not dissimilar experience, I sensed I was being drawn into an authorised, but deniable operation. I was told only what I needed to know, and the ends I was made to serve were only incidentally my own.[15]

The inevitable ensuing uproar should have taught Downing Street a lesson in the law of unexpected consequences: attempting to smear Wright had set a new hare running in the *Spycatcher* affair. Rothschild immediately complained to Thatcher that he was being slandered and demanded that she provide him with prime-ministerial protection.[16] It was not forthcoming.

The following day, Thatcher and her senior ministers drafted a statement insisting that the government had been 'unaware that Peter Wright had received royalties from Chapman Pincher's book and that they had given no backing to Lord Rothschild in any action he may have taken to act as the book's impresario'.[17] Since this was categorically untrue – Armstrong had told the Prime Minister in July 1981 that it was 'assumed' Wright had received payments from Pincher[18] – it was a measure of the panic engulfing the Cabinet Office. The statement was never issued.

Within 24 hours, backbench Labour MP Tam Dalyell challenged the Attorney General in the House of Commons to explain why Rothschild was not being prosecuted: Havers mumbled a terse response that he was 'considering' the allegations made against the noble lord.[19]

Even the traditionally supportive Tory press now joined the hue and cry. 'Not only is there no end in sight to the Government's embarrassment in the MI5 affair,' the *Daily Telegraph* thundered, 'each day brings more tortuous and bizarre revelations. However well intentioned his motives, Lord Rothschild owes a public explanation of his role in bringing together Mr. Peter Wright and Mr. Chapman Pincher to enable Pincher to write his book *Their Trade Is Treachery* ... The Prime Minister must take a vigorous counter-offensive against her critics, by making the fullest possible statement about the affair. It will simply not do to take refuge indefinitely in claims of national security ... the doctrine of official secrecy, in the Wright case, has damaged the cause of British intelligence, further demoralized its officers and gravely embarrassed the Government.'[20]

Neither Thatcher nor Rothschild rose to this challenge. Over the following days the PM repeatedly refused to give any answers to the House of Commons, claiming – incorrectly – that the ongoing court proceedings in Sydney precluded her from comment, and attacking Kinnock for asking 'unworthy' questions.[21] For his part, Rothschild stayed mum in public, but privately pestered Downing Street with repeated demands for support.

'He became a bloody nuisance,' Robin Butler, the Prime Minister's former Principal Private Secretary, recalled. 'His very devious efforts impinged on the government: they were an extra dimension of annoyance, an additional headache.'[22]

The crisis atmosphere mounted day by day, as political and press demands for an explanation grew ever stronger. Thatcher wanted Simos to make a statement in court denying any governmental knowledge of Rothschild's role in the Pincher book, but since her own diary showed she had taken tea with His Lordship and discussed intelligence matters shortly before the troublesome deal was done, officials warned that 'in the light of further reflection, our counsel should not say ... that the Prime Minister had not discussed Mr. Peter Wright or his book with Lord Rothschild'.[23]

Abandoned – as he saw it – by Number 10, Rothschild turned the screws. In a bizarre letter to the *Daily Telegraph* he now complained that he was being smeared as 'a Soviet agent' and demanded that the Security Service exonerate him: 'The Director General of MI5 should state publicly that it has unequivocal, repeat unequivocal, evidence that I am not, and never have been a Soviet agent.'[24]

Since numerous files, locked securely in the Service's Registry, contained ample evidence that it had suspected him, or his wife, for a decade of spying for Moscow, Thatcher was in dangerous territory; the best she could – reluctantly – manage was a brief and somewhat disingenuous statement that she was 'advised we have no evidence that he ever was a Soviet agent'.[25]

This growing turmoil prompted a panicky late-night phone call from Heinemann's London MD to Turnbull. 'It's all getting terribly political,' Brian Perman complained. 'You're going to bring down the Government.' Turnbull was unmoved: Downing Street had brought the latest debacles on itself – and in the meantime he had its case on the ropes in Court 8D.[26]

In this he was absolutely correct. At the start of proceedings on 27 November, Simos apologetically told the judge that his client had once again reversed course on the never-ending saga of the discovery documents. Although London had previously undertaken to abide by the order to produce this material, it had now decided that if Powell insisted on personally reviewing them, it would launch an immediate challenge in the Court of Appeal.

His Honour was predictably furious. Beneath the QC's respectful language was a clear implication that the British government didn't believe the judge could be trusted with its secret papers.

'I regret to say,' he chided Simos, 'that I am quite unable to predict from one day to the next what is the attitude of the Plaintiff in this case ... The situation I am placed in is, I believe, quite intolerable.'

Duly warned and judicially chastised, the barrister returned to court the next morning and promised that London would hand over the documents the same day. If this felt like a victory, it would prove to be only a temporary respite in Whitehall's extensive smear campaign.

Once again, Armstrong returned to the pillory. He had already spent more than a week in the witness box and now flinched whenever Turnbull prodded him with new questions. That morning he was about to endure further humiliation: having repeatedly insisted that the Attorney General alone had decided not to seek an injunction banning *Their Trade Is Treachery*, the Cabinet Secretary was now forced to admit that this sworn testimony was untrue.

'I am afraid I did mislead the Court in this matter,' he admitted. 'The conclusion that there was no legal basis for restraint was reached after consultation among all the legal advisers concerned ... I'm afraid that I assumed ... that it had been referred to the Attorney General personally. I now understand that it was not.'

Turnbull was incredulous. Who, he demanded, were these legal advisors? Sadly, the Cabinet Secretary was unable to say: 'I have not yet found out who they all were. I am afraid there are no papers in regard to the decision and it may be impossible to find out who were the people concerned.'

> TURNBULL: Sir Robert, what assurance do we now have that any of your evidence can be trusted, given this extraordinary inconsistency that has now emerged?
>
> ARMSTRONG: Well, I'm very sorry that I unwittingly mislead the Court on this matter, but I assure you that I have made every endeavour to answer your questions truthfully and as fully as I can ... I thought I was saying the truth as I know it.

Eventually, Armstrong was forced into a further admission. Although the government's lawyers had known for days that the Cabinet Secretary had lied by blaming the Attorney General, it was only the political tumult in London which had flushed him out. Havers had warned Downing Street that he was 'unhappy' and had threatened to speak out publicly unless the record was corrected. 'Sir Michael Havers has refused to carry the can for this, hasn't he?' Turnbull asked rhetorically just before the court adjourned.

By the start of the following week the government knew it was in deep trouble. Having fought off successive demands from backbench MPs for a debate on the *Spycatcher* affair, on Wednesday 3 December it faced an opposition day motion – a procedural manoeuvre it could not outflank – calling for parliamentary oversight of the Security Service. The roster of MPs lining up to speak promised a very uncomfortable afternoon for Thatcher and her ministers.

By a remarkable coincidence, shortly before the debate began the London *Evening Standard* splashed a front-page story, emanating from one of the government's backbenchers. Richard Saladin Hickmet had been an MP for three largely anonymous years and had made little mark on the House or its business.[27] But, as the paper breathlessly reported, that morning he had tabled an emergency motion alleging that Neil Kinnock 'has a resident mole in the closed court hearings of the Peter Wright spy book case'.

Hickmet named the supposed 'mole' as Paul Greengrass, whom he claimed had been 'privy to the most sensitive areas of the Crown's case'. That this intervention had emanated in Downing Street was confirmed by a subsequent paragraph in the *Standard*'s account: 'Senior ministers are suggesting that the "mole" is leaking information from the closed sessions of the court, including security evidence from Cabinet Secretary Sir Robert Armstrong.'[28]

Turnbull was predictably enraged by the transparent attempt to discredit his legal team – not least since Greengrass had signed a binding agreement never to reveal what he heard in the closed sessions. 'This past week has seen a despicable smear campaign against Mr. Wright, myself and now Mr. Greengrass,' he complained. 'Those responsible for this campaign are plainly endeavouring to pervert the course of justice. They are cowardly and despicable people, whose conduct disentitles them to any respect.'[29]

Nor did Hickmet's effort save the government from a parliamentary savaging. MPs, several of them ministers in previous administrations, queued up to heap scorn on what SDP leader David Owen called 'the rolling farce' of proceedings in Sydney. More pertinently, he proposed a joint House of Commons and Lords Select Committee to oversee MI5 and to ensure it acted legally: 'The Prime Minister must be told by the few members of the Conservative Party to whom she is prepared to listen that she must allow Parliament its proper function of scrutinizing the Security Services.'

Thatcher was not present to hear this suggestion; instead, the Home Secretary, Douglas Hurd, attempted to head off insurrection on her behalf. His performance encapsulated Downing Street's Alice in Wonderland reasoning: although he accepted that discussion of the *Spycatcher* proceedings was not *sub judice* under the rules of the House, nonetheless the government believed itself to be *sub judice* and that any 'observations' it might make 'could be seen by the Australian court as an attempt to influence it or to interfere with the judicial process there'. Since the *Evening Standard* story had been planted with precisely that intention, Hurd's excuse was risible.

'The Government's tactics,' Jonathan Aitken told him, 'remind me of an old strip cartoon in *Punch*. It begins with a rather unpleasant wasp invading a family picnic. The next picture shows the father seizing an umbrella and striking out in all directions. With a hail of inaccurate blows, he breaks the china, tramples the food, smashes the bottles and injures his children.

As the wasp buzzes away, he stands among the destruction he has created saying, "at least that will teach the wasp a lesson".'[30]

Ultimately, despite a succession of impassioned pleas, the government marched its own majority of drones through the MPs' division lobby and defeated the attempt to bring MI5 under democratic control.

But the Supreme Court in New South Wales posed a sterner threat to the Prime Minster's will than the House of Commons – a problem which explained the next instalment of Number 10's winter smear campaign.

The government had finally provided Mr Justice Powell with the discovery documents Turnbull had demanded. As he studied them, Downing Street's briefers fed a new scare story to a friendly newspaper: on 7 December the *Mail on Sunday* reported that 'intelligence chiefs fear that highly secret documents now in the hands of the Australian judge ... could eventually be leaked' and that MI5 had reassigned 'at least 25 staff' in a 'damage limitation' operation to protect them from 'unwanted publicity' should this happen.[31]

Unsurprisingly, this pre-emptive swipe at Powell's integrity swiftly backfired. The following day, the judge arrived in Court 8D seething with anger. 'I wish to make it quite clear,' he lectured the government's lawyers and the assembled press, 'that if the [*Mail on Sunday*] item is ... suggesting that the documents in question have been, or are likely to be, leaked, I make it abundantly clear that ... this will not be as a result of any action on the part of my staff or myself.'

In Whitehall, senior officials realised that the cause was now lost. None of the smears against Kinnock, Turnbull, Greengrass or Powell had succeeded, nor had they protected Sir Robert Armstrong from perjuring himself and incriminating the Prime Minister he served. 'I think we knew that we were going to lose the case,' was Robin Butler's rueful assessment.[32]

As the Cabinet Secretary finally escaped from the witness box, the government's case was all but over. Now it was Turnbull's turn as the circus ringmaster, and his star turn would be the old spycatcher himself, Peter Wright.

22. THE SPYCATCHER

'I have loved Justice and hated Iniquity.
Therefore I die in exile.'
PETER WRIGHT TESTIMONY, 9 DECEMBER 1986

Court 8D was packed to overflowing.
Turnbull had signalled that on Monday 8 December, the defence would call its chief witness to testify in his own cause. Journalists from across the world jostled with spectators for the few available public seats; lawyers crowded the tables on either side of Powell's raised dais. After almost three weeks of sometimes ill-tempered hearings, all were drawn by the prospect of a dramatic denouement to the case of *The United Kingdom vs. Heinemann and Peter Maurice Wright*. They were to be somewhat disappointed.

For much of the morning, proceedings were put on hold, as Theo Simos erected an endless succession of obstacles, behind closed doors, to what could be heard in open court. Wright was anxious about giving evidence – old age and ill health had left him prone to forgetfulness and hesitancy – so Turnbull had decided to walk him slowly through his 31-page sworn statement. That proved unpalatable for the government's QC.

He objected to any public airing of 'all parts of the affidavit which are not relevant to any issue arising on the pleadings ... all parts which are hearsay ... conclusions or inferences of fact ... all parts of the affidavit which constitute evidence in relation to the truth of the content of the Wright manuscript ... [and] all parts which purport to be expert opinions of Mr. Wright [and] his expressions of opinion as to what is in the public interest. We [also] object to all parts of the affidavit which are argumentative [and] all parts which relate to matters admitted in the pleadings.'[1]

Since this list of exclusions covered almost everything to do with MI5's illegal activities, the truth – or otherwise – of Thatcher's statements in Parliament and the curious role of Lord Rothschild in bringing Wright and Pincher together, it was plain that Simos' instructions were to staunch the flow of damaging evidence in front of the press. It was to be the government's last attempt to rescue a case which, in the preceding days, had fallen apart.

Sir Robert Armstrong had flown back to London with his reputation in shreds. The Prime Minister had offered some small comfort, gifting him a brace of whisky bottles for his troubles, and her press team had been hard at work, persuading two national newspapers to run remarkably positive reviews of his disastrous performance in the witness box.

'He is a kind, sensible, intelligent and moderate man,' William Rees-Mogg, formerly editor of *The Times*, wrote in an opinion piece for the *Independent*. 'To give evidence in ockerish Australia is as certain to invite farcical retribution as for a Victorian missionary to try and impose trousers on a cannibal island ... The atmosphere of the court seems to be seething with class resentment as though Powell and Turnbull were citizen *sans-culottes* relishing sending M. le Comte d'Armstrong to the guillotine.'[2]

The *Mail on Sunday* managed to outdo even this sycophancy by summoning the jingoistic ghost of Britain's Victorian and Edwardian glory days. 'Sir Robert is ... the stuff upon which the Empire was made – Gordon of Khartoum, Clive of India, Lawrence of Arabia – what mighty names and mighty deeds they commemorate. Welcome to this pantheon of heroes, Armstrong of Sydney.'[3]

But all the soft soap in Fleet Street's Tory-friendly press could not disguise the fact that the government's case had somehow contrived to plumb new depths after the Cabinet Secretary escaped from court. The federal government in Canberra had been reluctantly prodded into supporting Britain's attempt to silence Wright,[4] but Simos' final witness, Australian Cabinet Secretary Michael Codd, had proved even more hapless than his counterpart in London.

Codd confirmed that he had read the *Spycatcher* manuscript, but refused to say which passages in it the Australian government found objectionable. That, he insisted, was exclusively a matter for the administration in London: instead, it was the mere fact that a former member of the Security Service had written the book which made it 'a class of document' which should not be published. Why then, Turnbull asked, had several Australian intelligence officers been permitted to pen their own insider accounts? Even the retired head of ASIO – Australia's equivalent of MI5 – was then busily engaged in penning his own memoirs. Codd accepted that this was all true, but had managed to persuade himself that these publications were not 'close parallels to the present case'.

He was no more convincing on questions about ASIO's primary partner in the intelligence field: the Australian Cabinet Secretary professed himself unaware of the CIA's policy of positively assisting former officers to write books about their experiences in the Agency.

Next, when Turnbull drew his attention to the Australian Royal Commission on Intelligence and Security, Codd's threadbare arguments frayed completely. Under the chairmanship of Justice Robert Hope, a senior judge in the New South Wales Court of Appeal, from 1974 the Commission had delved into ASIO's twenty-year history of scandals. The organisation had been set up with the guidance of MI5's Roger Hollis and, like its sister service in London, was initially governed by few rules; unsurprisingly, it had viewed operating within the law as strictly optional.

Hope's reports lacerated ASIO's opacity and incompetence, and set out a series of guidelines for its activities. The first, and most fundamental, was that it 'must always comply with the law ... even though the matter with which ASIO is dealing relates to security'. Additionally, Hope ruled, 'ASIO should be careful to ensure that its relationship with any foreign intelligence service is in harmony with the principles of legality and propriety.'[5] That instruction was about to lead the Australian Cabinet Secretary on to difficult terrain.

> TURNBULL: Mr. Codd, you knew that part of the defence case in these proceedings was that MI5 had acted improperly and criminally ... that it had broken the law of England and international law and infringed civil liberties. You knew that, did you not?
>
> CODD: I knew accusations of that kind existed but I have no basis for assuming they were correct.

Mr Justice Powell could not let that pass. 'Forgive me if I interrupt,' the judge rumbled. 'Were you not aware that it had been admitted ... that Mr. Wright's book contains evidence, which for the purposes of this case was to be treated as accepted, of criminal activities on the part of members of MI5?'

Since *Spycatcher* laid out a litany of burglaries, unauthorised telephone taps and surveillance – not to mention the plot to blackmail a sitting Prime Minister – Codd's response plumbed new depths of absurdity: 'I don't recall Mr. Wright in his manuscript saying the activities were criminal.'

Surely, Turnbull demanded, the Australian people were entitled to know that MI5 had acted illegally? Not necessarily, Codd maintained: it was up to the country's intelligence agencies to weigh this against the Hope Commission's instructions.

Ultimately, the Australian Cabinet Secretary stuck unshakably to his British-provided brief, maintaining that if the court allowed the publication of *Spycatcher*, Australian intelligence would, in some indefinable way, blame MI5 and thus the country's national security would be impaired.[6]

By the time he left the stand, Codd's evidence – the last for the plaintiff – had turned out to be less a damp squib than a banger which had exploded in London's hands: visibly unimpressed, Powell dismissed his thesis as 'complete and utter moonshine'.

Despite this, the British government continued to fight a last-ditch effort to limit the damage. 'There were always all these conferences going on, with Simos getting instructions from London,' David Hooper remembered. 'The whole thing was being run from Downing Street. The local lawyers would get an adjournment and go off for hours on end to get their orders.'[7]

Chief among this torrent of instructions was the still-unresolved argument over the discovery documents. A flurry of cables from Downing Street had warned the legal team in Sydney that the official papers relating to *Their Trade Is Treachery*, Nigel West, Cathy Massiter and to Peter Wright's *World in Action* interview 'cannot be discovered'.[8]

Number 10 now instructed its QC in Sydney to tell Powell that the Attorney General was filing an immediate plea in the New South Wales Court of Appeal for a hearing on the issue. The request was granted and, as London had intended, posed a dilemma for Turnbull. If he fought on, the appeal would not take place for several months and the trial itself would be suspended; alternatively, he could try to negotiate a compromise which would keep the main business on track. Reluctantly, he opted for the lesser of two evils: in return for limited admissions by the government, including that it had known of Pincher's book very much earlier than previously admitted, he abandoned his demand to see all the evidence.

It was a legally sensible decision, but it had a lasting and unfortunate effect: the documents which proved unequivocally that Robert Armstrong had committed perjury would be kept secret for almost 40 years.

By the time the defence opened its case, Mr Justice Powell had grown weary of the government's repeated attempts to interrupt proceedings, and so was less than sympathetic when Simos tried to block Turnbull's first witness from testifying.

Gough Whitlam had served as Labor Prime Minister of Australia from 1972 to 1975, when the Governor-General Sir John Kerr – the Queen's representative in her former colony – sacked him and plunged the country into a constitutional crisis. During his three-year tenure, Whitlam's socially liberal government had enacted a raft of progressive reforms: the most notable, for the hearings in Court 8D, was the appointment of Justice Robert Hope's inquiry, which had brought order and legality to Australia's intelligence services.

Despite – or more likely because of – this extensive hinterland, London had ordered its QC to prevent him taking the witness stand. 'Mr. Whitlam will be expressing his personal opinions as to what the Australian public interest requires in relation to the matters at issue in this case,' Simos complained. 'It would be our submission that [this] is not an issue of fact in respect of which experts are entitled to give evidence ... it is not appropriate to call witnesses who would ... be debating issues which are for the court and the court alone to decide.'

Powell dismissed the argument in short order. 'One can take judicial notice of the fact that Mr. Whitlam was for a period of some years the Prime Minister of this country, and one can, I believe, assume that particularly in his role as Prime Minister, Mr. Whitlam was concerned with matters of national security.'

He followed this with a brusque rebuke to the government's barrister. The plaintiff had brought the distinctly underwhelming Michael Codd to give evidence: why, then, should the court 'be deprived of the assistance and opinions of those who are far better qualified?' It was, he ruled, 'a submission which I am totally incapable of accepting'.

When Whitlam settled his six-foot, five-inch frame in the witness box, the reason for London's disquiet quickly emerged: his evidence offered a savage critique of the attempt to muzzle Wright, and of the British government's evident willingness to allow its Security Service to ignore the law – both domestic and international.

'Before [1972] ASIO operated in exactly the same way as MI5,' he testified. 'It would operate in breach of the law. It burgled premises adjacent to diplomatic premises; if it could, it would burgle ... and bug diplomatic premises ... it would watch certain writers; it would infiltrate some political parties.'

With one eye on the British government's refusal to answer questions about MI5 in the House of Commons, and on Thatcher's personal veto of any form of parliamentary oversight, Turnbull then nudged his witness into condemning Britain's lack of democratic scrutiny of what its intelligence services got up to.

'The fact that an organization is secret can never make it unaccountable,' Whitlam pronounced. 'It might be said that the fact that makes it secret makes it all the more necessary for it to be accountable.'

He was equally critical when asked about Cathy Massiter's revelations – claims which, as Turnbull was at pains to remind the court, London had accepted as fact – about telephone taps on trade union leaders, political opponents and campaigning organisations. 'Those allegations would not be tolerated in this country ... MI5 may be free to break the law. ASIO is not,' Whitlam insisted. And he roundly condemned the surveillance of Patricia Hewitt, former General Secretary of the National Council for Civil Liberties: 'I think it is monstrous that persons should be paid for monitoring her activities.'

Finally, Turnbull wound up his examination with a series of questions designed to do maximum damage to the government's case.

> TURNBULL: Mr. Whitlam, based on your experience in intelligence matters, do you consider that there is anything in this book which would, if published, be of assistance to hostile intelligence agencies?
>
> WHITLAM: None whatever ... I think it is very much to Australia's advantage that [Wright's allegations] should be published ... It has a great interest in seeing that all countries conform with international law. We are not only interested in those countries which do. We are also interested in countries which do not – including the UK ...
>
> TURNBULL: Do you consider Australia should suppress a book of this kind [because] a foreign Security Service wants it to be suppressed to protect its interests?
>
> WHITLAM: I believe Australia has to reject such a claim by a foreign Security Service ... It is essential ... that we be seen to act in accordance with international law ... I do not comprehend that the Soviet Union would get very far if it took proceedings in the Supreme Court of New South Wales to prevent a defector publishing a book in Australia which indicated that the Soviet Union had been breaching international law.'[9]

It was a measure of the strength of the former Prime Minister's evidence that Simos barely troubled to cross-examine him. He made even less effort with the next witness.

The Spycatcher

Bill Schaap was a lawyer who had successfully helped numerous American intelligence officers to issue their memoirs via the CIA's Publications Review Board scheme. His testimony was taut and pointed: the British argument that allowing Wright to release *Spycatcher* would damage relations with US agencies was 'untenable ... the information [in it] is virtually all ten to twenty years old. I cannot see how, under the standards applied in the United States, such a book would be suppressed in part or in whole.'[10]

When Turnbull turned Schaap over for cross-examination, Simos sat on his hands and declined to challenge evidence which was so obviously factual: he would – or so the assembled press pack assumed – reserve his fire for Turnbull's final witness – the old spycatcher himself.

At 2.20pm on 8 December, Peter Wright slowly made his way from the defence table to the front of the court. Looking anxious and leaning on his stick with the brass fox-head handle, he climbed the steps into the raised witness box, then gazed back at his small band of supporters and the rather more populated government ranks.

'It was a bizarre sight,' recalled his daughter, Jenny Andrews. 'On one side [there were] rows of gowned and wigged barristers and suited solicitors, on the other side just one man in a suit with a couple of offsiders – one being Paul Greengrass, with his usual longish haircut, dressed in jeans, sneakers and a baseball jacket – sitting at a small table with piles of papers and files at the ready.'

Jenny Andrews was acutely aware of the effect of the hearings on both of her parents. 'Prior to the hearing my mother kept her sanity through the daily management of the stud and the physical work that entailed. I think she found [the trial] hardest. She was out of her comfort zone, whereas my father saw interesting legal arguments and wanted to make sure things weren't missed. But it was stressful for both of them.'[11]

Powell, too, recognised the toll. 'If at any time you feel a little fatigued,' he told the witness, 'let us know and we will take a short break.' It was a considerate offer – one he had previously extended to Armstrong – but it proved unnecessary: in a light baritone, and carefully enunciating his words, Wright began reading from his affidavit.

The testimony itself had a curious and fragmented air – the result of Simos' insistence on removing large swathes of what the old man wanted to say from the public record. But it was nonetheless dramatic: never before had a former intelligence officer testified in open court, and in his quiet, precise diction Wright gave the world's media its first insight into the sheer breadth of his secret work on behalf of his country – both legal and illegal.

He began by explaining the characteristically amateurish way he had been recruited in 1950, and the five years he had spent working for MI5 without pay and in his spare time. The Service was, he testified, in very poor technical shape: 'There was no application or understanding of science ... It was almost a schoolboy operation.'

After a swift, and lightly censored, account of his success in uncovering the mysteries of 'The Thing' – the Soviet microphone which had been unearthed from the walls of the American Embassy in Moscow – Wright then turned to the promises he had been made when the Security Service persuaded him to leave the safe harbour of his position with the Royal Naval Scientific Service to join its ranks full-time.

> MI5 initially offered a job at about £1,000 less than I was being paid at RNSS. One of the matters discussed was pension. Since I had been a civil servant for fourteen years, I had accrued certain entitlements ... The Government contributed double the contribution of the scientist [but] if you left before it matured, you lost the entitlement to the Government's contribution.
>
> The MI5 people were adamant that these entitlements could not be transferred over to MI5 where they said pensions were ... discretionary. They said that I would not be disadvantaged, however, because they would make up any difference themselves. They said that under the 'Secret Vote' they were not vetted on how they paid people ... Relying on these assurances, I left the RNSS.

That gentleman's agreement proved to be illusory: 'The Service failed to honour the undertaking,' he told the court, 'and my pension ... is therefore about 60 per cent of what it ought to be.' Nor was there any possibility of challenging the broken promise: because MI5 did not officially exist, Wright was warned against attempting to enforce any notional employment rights.

> I was told by the MI5 people ... 'you can be instantly sacked, without any reasons ... No staff association or trade union is allowed and any attempt to establish such a body will result in dismissal for all those concerned'.

The Spycatcher

This statement was an accurate description of the relationship between an officer of MI5 and the Crown ... I have seen a senior and distinguished officer of the Service dismissed without notice, without reasons and without pension.

He was just getting into his stride when his testimony ran into the buffers of the first substantial redaction demanded by Simos. Although Wright insisted that he had 'taken great care ... not to disclose anything which in my judgment as a professional intelligence officer might damage national security', the three pages of his affidavit describing the innovations he had brought to MI5 – the SATYR and RAFTER technology which revolutionised its ability to eavesdrop on Soviet transmissions – were deemed too sensitive to be revealed in open court.

Since they had long-since been superseded by 'satellites, microcircuitry and main frame computers', the excision was testament only to the British government's obsession with secrecy, and Wright dismissed Armstrong's contention that enemy intelligence services could 'infer the existence of modern technology from older technology' as 'nonsense ... this is like saying that you can detect the secrets of an advanced fighter plane by studying a Spitfire'.

But the largest, and most telling, censoring of Wright's evidence concerned the counter-espionage investigations in which he had been involved – the hunt for moles within MI5's ranks. All of this had previously been 'extensively publicized' in other books, but he argued that it was vital to discuss it again 'since it goes to the very heart of Britain (and the rest of the Free World's) problem in this field: lack of public awareness of the dangers of penetration'.

That 'public awareness' was exactly what the government sought to prevent, and was the reason it insisted on removing all four pages of Wright's affidavit which addressed the Hollis and Blunt scandals, and the Prime Minister's statements to Parliament about both.

The transcript of his censored testimony – which has never previously been published – showed why the government was so keen to silence its former spycatcher. 'I observe in commencing this part of my evidence,' he began, 'that I was the only senior officer of MI5 to serve twenty years in counter-espionage. I therefore had more experience in that field than any of my colleagues.'

Blunt, he revealed, 'confessed to passing to the Russians everything he saw ... Since [he] was the D-G's assistant for the first half of the war he had access to almost as much information as the D-G did. One specific item he did confess to handing over was the Special Facility microphone which enabled one to turn an ordinary telephone into a microphone thus bugging the room it was used in. He told me that he blew it the first day it was used.'

Wright was particularly incensed by Thatcher's claim in the House of Commons that the information which led to Blunt's confession was 'not usable as evidence on which to base a prosecution'. 'The PM's statement is false,' he charged, 'the simple fact was that the law officers felt that in a conflict of testimony a man who was a knight and Surveyor of the Queen's Pictures would be believed.'

But this was small beer compared to the outright lies which, he claimed, Thatcher had told when reporting to Parliament about the Hollis Affair in March 1981.

[Her] statement is substantially false and its errors must have been known to those in MI5 who prepared the brief for the Prime Minister. I shall deal with the statement a paragraph at a time.

Mrs. Thatcher said: 'The extent of penetration was thoroughly investigated after the defection of Burgess and Maclean' ... but it is simply not correct to say that the extent of penetration was thoroughly investigated. Indeed the contention of my book and my dossier was that there was insufficient investigation.

Following Philby's defection in 1963 effort was stepped up, but senior management were always determined to limit the scope of any inquiries. From 1963 until I left the Service, there were specific instructions from the DG of the day that we were not to take any action that might make the person being investigated defect or cause any other form of political scandal. I had to get the DG's permission before taking any such action and in Hollis' day such permission was nearly always refused.

Mrs. Thatcher said: 'The case for investigating Sir Roger Hollis was based on certain leads that suggested, but did not prove, that there had been a Russian intelligence service agent at a relatively senior level in British counterintelligence in the last years of the war. None of these leads identified Sir Roger Hollis, or pointed specifically or solely in his direction. Each of them could also be taken as pointing to Philby or Blunt ...'

There were a great many leads investigated in relation to Hollis and it is true that most of them did not point specifically or solely at him. However it is quite false to say that none did so and even more inaccurate to say that leads suggested there was a Russian mole in

MI5 'during the last years of the war' and that those leads could be taken as pointing to Philby or Blunt.

The Fluency Committee, of which I was the chairman for seven years, specifically looked at allegations with a view to listing only those which could not be attributed to known spies such as Philby or Blunt. The Fluency Report which exists in MI5's files and was signed unanimously by its members listed 28 instances of undoubted Soviet penetration which could not be attributed to any known spy. Practically all of these were post-war.

The theme of much of my book is the extraordinary failure of MI5's work against the Russians from the end of the war until Hollis retired in 1965 ... The evidence that there had been a mole inside MI5 during the 50s and early 60s was overwhelming and was really made up of the enormous number of operations that went wrong.

The fact is that from 1951 to 1958 MI5 had no success against the Russians and after that until the end of 1965 when Hollis retired, every case, although apparently successful was tainted by Russian interference ... [Yet] after 1965 there was no evidence of such a taint at least until 1976 when I left the Service.

Had Mrs. Thatcher told the truth she would have said that there was evidence of Russian penetration throughout the fifties and early sixties, that some of the evidence pointed solely at Hollis, some of it pointed at him and Mitchell, some of it was unattributable to any person or a small number of persons and was therefore not pursued by the investigators.

Her statement was designed to give the misleading impression that the Hollis evidence could all be conveniently laid at the door of the ancient moles such as Blunt and Philby.

As with her Blunt statement, Mrs. Thatcher, or those who briefed her, pointedly referred to only a 'few others'. In fact ... MI5 files listed 35 eminent persons as Soviet agents. These people worked in the highest levels of British government, industry, academia and so on. Many were interviewed by me and a number of them either committed suicide or died mysteriously shortly after they became aware of my interest in them. In other words there was good reason to suspect that the Establishment was rotten to the core with Russian agents ... I know this because of my investigations into the rings of influence spreading out from the Ring of Five. I was stopped in this because my investigations were embarrassing.

Wright's secret testimony was not limited to generalised complaints about the failure to tackle Soviet penetration at all levels of British society and government. He also submitted a separate – and even more closely guarded – 'annex', revealing the identities of the 35 'eminent persons' who were suspected of being 'agents' for Moscow, and giving a telling insight into the sorry history of further proven cases of treachery.

> In my dossier I list all of the spies discovered between 1927 and 1982 which were publicly revealed. There have been 15 spies overtly discovered and prosecuted ... 13 of those 15 were in departments of British intelligence.

The rest of his redacted evidence was equally startling. Victor Rothschild had continued to work for MI5 and MI6 long after his notional retirement from intelligence work, and had run an agent in the heart of the Shah of Iran's administration on behalf of SIS 'until the early 1970s'. That he occupied this extremely sensitive position at the same time as the Security Service was investigating his links to Blunt, Philby and the Ring of Five was bad enough, but it was remarkable that, as Wright testified, 'during my investigation of Soviet penetration, including the investigation of Hollis, I used to brief Victor regularly and in considerable detail, meeting with him at least once a month ... This was done with the knowledge of [Directors General] Sir Martin Furnival Jones, Sir Roger Hollis and Sir Michael Hanley'.

Chapman Pincher also featured heavily in the suppressed testimony. The journalist whom Rothschild had selected to turn Wright's first manuscript into a book – the much-discussed *The Trade Is Treachery* – was revealed in Wright's secret account to be an agent of long standing for the Security Service and MI6.

> It was well known within MI5 that Pincher was an agent and ... a conduit for misinformation ... Pincher would have signed the Official Secrets Act when he started this work ... I know from my time in MI5 that because of Pincher's extremely close links with MI5, and particularly its legal department which handled controlled leaks of information, Pincher was treated entirely differently from any other journalist.
>
> For instance senior intelligence officers would socialize with him, whereas for intelligence officers journalists are normally taboo.[12]

Given the breadth and the damning nature of these revelations, it was little surprise that the government was determined to silence Wright. If the tradecraft and technology he had described was obsolete and outdated, he remained a fount of very dangerous knowledge about MI5's dirty tricks and political intrigues; worse, as the unredacted latter portion of his testimony made emphatically clear, he had been belatedly converted to the merits of whistleblowing.

> For years the secret services have assumed that their work is best done with minimum reporting and accountability to the government and ultimately the people. When I was young I readily adopted this philosophy ... I now think this is entirely wrong. The work of protecting our society against subversion is too important to leave to the spies ...
>
> The British Establishment has never accepted that it was, *en masse*, penetrated by the Russians. It may be that the Establishment fears that public debate of this problem will cause the people of Britain to have less faith in its leadership than the Establishment would like it to have ... In my life I have seen too many people in power turning a blind eye ... and now I see Mrs. Thatcher misleading Parliament ...
>
> The time has come for there to be openness about the secret world ... There should be a complete change of attitude on the part of the Government and the Security Service and MI6 ...

As Wright reached the end of his evidence, he was visibly exhausted and there were tears in his eyes. He summoned up the last of his failing energy to issue a final, defiant rebuke to those in MI5, Parliament and the press who had denounced him for speaking out.

> I want to stress that my patriotism is undiminished. I worked for my country for more than 30 years and shouldered many heavy responsibilities ... As Pope Gregory VII observed: 'I have loved Justice and hated Iniquity. Therefore I die in exile.'

With that, the old spycatcher stepped wearily out of the witness box. He knew that the next day he faced cross-examination by Simos, and he was nervous. 'Mrs. Thatcher will want him to tear me to pieces,' he told Turnbull.[13]

It was a view widely shared by the pack of assembled journalists and by some of the government's own ministers. At a meeting in the Cabinet Office that morning, the Home Secretary, Foreign Secretary and

MI5 Director General were told that: 'The Treasury Solicitor had already made clear to Mr Simos the political need not to allow Mr Wright to escape cross-examination. Mr Simos should now be instructed that ... Mr Wright should be comprehensively and rigorously but courteously cross-examined.'[14]

And yet, when court resumed the following morning the expected mauling did not materialise: Simos asked only a few perfunctory questions, disputing the reliability of the old man's memory and his ability to predict what historic information might prove helpful to a hostile contemporary intelligence service: none made any great impression. Then, after a bland pro-forma challenge – 'I want to put it to you that Mrs. Thatcher's statements to the House concerning Blunt and Hollis were accurate', followed by Wright's forceful rebuttal – the QC abruptly sat down.

This sudden and limp conclusion confused both reporters and the civil servants dispatched from London to wrangle them. 'It was bizarre that we should make such little attempt to break down Wright's defence,' the government's press whisperer, Sir Ivor Roberts, later told the BBC. 'After all, we were claiming that he was giving away privileged information; but there was no real attempt to nail him on that, and when the journalists asked me afterwards, "what game are your team up to?", I didn't have an answer: I had no idea.'

The reason for this capitulation, Roberts later learned, was a decision taken by Sir Michael Havers: 'I discovered that the Attorney General had heard that Peter Wright was not in the most robust of health and was terrified that he was going to break down and have a heart attack or something if he was being rigorously cross-examined; [he] gave instructions to our team that they must go very easy on him.'[15]

Whether this unexpected consideration for Wright's survival resulted from Havers's own ill health – he endured two heart bypass operations in the 1980s and resigned as Attorney General the following summer – or reflected his known distaste for the litigation and a determination not to shoulder the blame for any further debacles, the decision brought a muted end to the evidence in the *Spycatcher* trials. All that remained were the final speeches from both sides' lawyers.

Closing statements tend to follow one of two formats. Simos' summation conformed to the tradition of English civil proceedings: a dry rehearsal of the key points in his client's case. By contrast, Turnbull's approach was closer to the drama of American trials: on 17 December, he launched a full-throated condemnation of the government's duplicity and ruthlessly attacked the credibility of its chief witness.

> Sir Robert [Armstrong's] evidence and demeanour showed him to be a man with no regard for the truth, rather a man determined to say whatever he felt would advance the Government's cause, regardless of its truth or falsity. His evidence is worthless ... he is an ambassador for Britain, sent abroad to lie for his country.
>
> It is not possible to shield Sir Robert from the consequences of his mendacity, but it would be unfair not to say that the real responsibility for his disgraceful conduct lies with those in London who sent him here to lie and dissemble to this court.

Methodically and forensically, Turnbull dismantled the government's arguments for silencing Wright, insisting that it had conspired with Rothschild to leak the Hollis scandal safely via Pincher, and then sought to cover up its part in midwifing *Their Trade Is Treachery* – the 'prequel' to *Spycatcher* – via the Cabinet Secretary's economies with the truth and his attempts to pin the blame on Havers.

'The Court should take the gravest view of the evidence concerning the Attorney's role,' he thundered, before issuing a succession of rapid-fire challenges. 'Why did Sir Robert lie? Why did the British Government, its Prime Minister and its Attorney General [allow] the lies to be told for so long? Why would Lord Rothschild, with all his connections, wealth and respectability suggest such an unlawful enterprise to Wright, and then procure the writer and act as a channel for the royalties?' It all suggested, as his client had testified, a covert and deniable authorised operation.

Nor, he stressed, were there any major revelations in Wright's own manuscript which had not been previously published in the Pincher book – or indeed those in *MI5 – A Matter of Trust*. Nigel West – by now an elected Conservative MP under his real name, Rupert Allason – had been allowed to negotiate redactions to that manuscript: what made *Spycatcher* so different? Once again, Turnbull repeated his offer to remove any passages in the book which threatened national security.

Fundamentally, he told the court, the case was a test of the right to freedom of speech. 'The public interest in free speech is not just in truthful speech, in correct speech, in fair speech ... the interest is in the debate ... because ultimately these ideas are tested in debate.'[16]

Two days before this stirring call to democratic arms in Sydney, the British government had made clear its antipathy to open discussion of intelligence issues in the House of Commons. On 15 December veteran Labour back-bencher Dale Campbell-Savours lodged a parliamentary motion calling for a judicial inquiry into Wright's claims of an MI5 plot against Harold

Wilson, and with it a new statutory framework for democratic oversight of the Security Service. Despite his impassioned – and lengthy – speech, neither of Campbell-Savours's proposals found favour. The Home Office's irascible junior minister David Waddington dismissed the need for both, and asserted that there was 'general agreement that the responsibilities of the Security Service should not be carried out in a blaze of publicity'.

Both motions were soundly defeated, and once again the curtains of official secrecy were drawn around MI5.[17] Hopes for allowing a little cleansing sunlight to penetrate its corridors now rested entirely with Mr Justice Powell and the New South Wales Supreme Court. On Friday 19 December he formally closed the *Spycatcher* trial, promising to deliver his judgment the following spring.

23. JUDGMENTS

*'Disclosure to the public is called for and
ought to be permitted.'*
MR JUSTICE PHILIP POWELL: 13 MARCH 1987

The British government already knew it would lose.
On 2 December, the Irish High Court threw out an attempt by Sir Michael Havers to ban a small Dublin publisher from releasing the wartime memoirs of a junior MI5 officer. Joan Miller had joined the Security Service in 1939 as a secretary before becoming an agent for its chief spy runner, Maxwell Knight. Her thin volume recounted – posthumously, since she had died two years earlier – her adventures as an undercover operative inside pro-Nazi organisations in London, and her unconsummated romantic relationship with her boss, a closeted homosexual. All of this, as her would-be publisher noted, had previously been described in newspapers and books, although *One Girl's War* also briefly mentioned Knight's belief that Soviet intelligence had penetrated the Service.

London publisher Weidenfeld & Nicolson had originally been offered the book, but its interest in the manuscript was swiftly extinguished after pressure from the Treasury Solicitor. Brandon Books, a small independent imprint based in County Kerry, stepped in and distributed a modest print run to shops throughout the Republic. But before it could go on sale, lawyers acting for the Attorney General disturbed a local judge at his supper and secured a late-night interim *ex parte* injunction on the grounds that 'any [unauthorised] publication of memoirs by a former member of the Security Service impaired the effective functioning of the Service'.[1] Simultaneously,

To Catch a Spy

Havers' staff obtained an injunction in London, blocking any attempt to issue the book in Britain.

But when the Irish High Court considered the application for a permanent injunction, the British government's arguments swiftly ran into judicial opposition. Miss Justice Mella Carroll ruled that the Republic's constitution gave Brandon Books the right to publish the book. Her judgment recorded that the case was a confidentiality dispute between a domestic defendant and a foreign government, and that there was 'no question of the public interest of this State being affected': London, she concluded, had no business asking Dublin to fight its battles.[2]

More pertinently, Carroll cited *Commonwealth of Australia v. John Fairfax & Co.* as the basis for her decision.[3] Since this case lay at the heart of the proceedings in Sydney, it was a clear indication that judges outside the United Kingdom took a dim view of the British government's attempts to ban books on the grounds of claimed confidentiality.

The Attorney General had better luck with his brethren at the Royal Courts of Justice; they granted him a full injunction preventing publication of Miller's memoirs in Britain. But given the notoriously porous border between Ireland and the UK, this would prove to be something of a pyrrhic victory.[4] It was also the last good news the government would receive that winter.

The troublesome issue of Victor Rothschild and his role in helping Chapman Pincher ghost-write Peter Wright's revelations in *Their Trade Is Treachery* refused to subside. Just before Parliament broke up for Christmas, Labour backbenchers harried Havers into ordering an inquiry into 'allegations that Lord Rothschild and Mr. Chapman Pincher had committed offences under the Official Secrets Act'.[5] It prompted His Lordship to give Number 10 a thinly veiled warning that he could cause severe problems for the government should the investigation continue. At a meeting on 8 December he told her officials that 'he would tell the police that he had discussed security matters with the Prime Minister though [he] … had no wish to embarrass the Government and therefore could not reveal his discussions with the Prime Minister about counter subversion; that could lead to dramatic stories about microphones in Mr. Kinnock's office or his home'.[6] Since this implied that Rothschild and Thatcher had contemplated illegally bugging the Leader of the Opposition, his assertion amounted to a barely concealed threat.

In January, the Metropolitan Police Serious Crime Squad duly arrived at Rothschild's London residence. Curiously, given the gravity of the alleged offences, the officers chose not to conduct the interview under caution;

nonetheless, according to the account he gave to his sympathetic biographer, it did not progress smoothly.

The detectives clashed repeatedly with their noble suspect, pointedly asking why he had paid to bring Wright back to England and implying that he had used his considerable wealth as 'part of a devious design'. They were particularly unimpressed with Rothschild's claim that he had merely wanted Wright to provide a testimonial to his work on behalf of British intelligence, and to refute rumours that he had ever been a Soviet agent. Even if true, that hardly explained why he had brokered the publishing deal with Pincher.

'Your cautiousness in respect of government secrecy is well known,' Rothschild's notes of the officers' questioning recorded. 'Yet now you throw caution to the winds and suggest to Wright that [his] dossier should be turned into a book ... Who suggested that the book should be written?' To this tricky question His Lordship responded with a straightforward lie. 'I don't know,' he told the officers. 'It must have been Pincher or Wright or conceivably Pincher's publisher.'[7]

Days later, stewing over the very real possibility of facing prosecution, Rothschild arrived at Downing Street. In a tense meeting with Armstrong, he issued a further warning that if his ermine collar were to be felt, he would name other even more newsworthy figures as his co-conspirators: chief among these was Sir Maurice Oldfield, GCMC, CBE and, from 1973 to 1978, chief of MI6.

According to this latest version of his story, it was the former 'C' who had urged Rothschild to bring Wright and Pincher together, because the spy chief believed the journalist's friendly relations with the intelligence services would ensure the resulting manuscript 'contained nothing new or worth publishing and would not make a book'.

If the police were to discover this, His Lordship now regretfully advised, it would 'support the theory that the Government, sought, promoted or connived at the publication' of *Their Trade Is Treachery* – an outcome which would be 'immensely unwise'. Armstrong saw this for what it was: a warning that prosecuting Rothschild would expose the entire charade which Thatcher and her Cabinet Secretary had asked the court in Australia to accept. He scribbled an urgent note to the Attorney General, suggesting the whole business should be discretely dropped.[8] The advice was heeded; five months later Havers's successor, Sir Patrick Mayhew, told Parliament that the police investigation 'has not disclosed evidence justifying the bringing of proceedings against either Lord Rothschild or Mr. Chapman Pincher'.[9] Since there had never been any doubt that both had broken the Official Secrets Act, the decision not to charge them was a transparent whitewash.

To Catch a Spy

On the other side of the world, Philip Powell had been spending Sydney's sticky summer months labouring on his judgment in the *Spycatcher* case – a task made more onerous by being rostered as duty judge throughout January, coupled with the need to read 33 espionage books and dozens of press articles, as well as viewing numerous documentary films. The workload was demanding, and it was three full months before he was ready to deliver his verdict.

On Friday 13 March, Turnbull, Simos and their supporting lawyers returned to Court 8D. If Her Majesty's Cabinet Secretary and Peter Wright were absent – the old spycatcher was confined to a hospital bed in Hobart, being treated for stress and diabetes, while Armstrong was otherwise occupied in Downing Street – the courtroom was nonetheless crammed. Fleet Street's finest jostled with representatives from newspapers and television channels across the world for seats in the jury box; unlucky latecomers leaned against the walls or squatted uncomfortably on the floor. That they faced a long and tiring day was clear from the impressive size of Powell's judgment, copies of which – each many inches thick – were stacked in precarious towers beside his raised dais.

As he struggled into court through a blitz of cameras and popping flashbulbs, Turnbull was profoundly apprehensive: for the first time in months he contemplated the prospect of losing the case on which his reputation – and his client's future – depended. His fears were groundless: when Powell began reading out his 286-page ruling, it was quickly clear that the British government's bid to silence Wright was to be brutally dismissed.

The judgment took the form of a narrative account, rehearsing the entire chronology of Wright's MI5 career, the long, convoluted story of his molehunts, the investigation into Roger Hollis and the curious saga of Rothschild, Pincher and *Their Trade Is Treachery*. It reproduced documents presented during the trial, which contrasted the British government's lengthy history of sanctioning books, articles and TV interviews by former intelligence officers with its claim that all were bound by an inviolable, lifelong duty of confidentiality; and it cited the verdicts in dozens of previously decided cases as support for his conclusions.

All told, the 85,000-word document had been written with a keen awareness of its place in legal history, and though Powell gently castigated Wright and Greengrass for producing an excitable manuscript 'which seems more appropriate to the *Boy's Own Paper* or *Biggles' Flying Omnibus*[10] rather than to an arid scholarly work', almost every sentence of his ruling lacerated London's arguments and, above all, the integrity of its chief witness.

'Although, after much consideration I find myself unable to accept Mr. Turnbull's submission that Sir Robert Armstrong deliberately set out to mislead the Court,' Powell intoned gravely, 'I have, nonetheless, come to the conclusion that much of his evidence on matters of importance must be treated with considerable reserve.'[11]

This, however, was only the start of Powell's judicial character assassination. The Cabinet Secretary, he pronounced, was little more than a willing mouthpiece for MI5 and his mistress in Number 10.

> Sir Robert Armstrong described himself as 'the Prime Minister's principal advisor in relation to matters of security and intelligence in the United Kingdom' ... upon examination, however it would seem ... that he has no personal knowledge or expertise in matters of security or intelligence – and in particular as to operational matters ... and that any information he might give, or opinions which he might offer, is, or are, derived from others ... [his] knowledge of operational matters and ... the technology of intelligence gathering appears to be virtually non-existent.
>
> While these two facts would be enough to cast more than a shadow of doubt over the assertions as to national security which Sir Robert has made on behalf of the British Government, that shadow is made the more deep by the revelation of the – at least – inconsistent observance by the British Government, if not its total failure to observe, what was put forward as the 'consistent practice and policy of successive governments' in relation to security and intelligence matters, which ... had been adhered to in order to preserve the secrecy or confidentiality of information relating to security and intelligence matters, [and] which was essential if the security and intelligence services were able to fulfil their respective functions.
>
> While I am prepared to accept that the publication of some of the information contained in Mr. Wright's manuscript may provide a source of some embarrassment to the British Government, when one observes all the information – much of it derived from, and some of it directly attributed to, 'insiders' – which because of the British Government's acquiescence or inaction, has already been made available, the claim now that the republication of such information at the hands of an 'insider', will cause detriment sounds decidedly hollow ...

Powell's painstaking perusal of all the books, articles and documentaries – which Simos had insisted he study – was now turned against the British government. 'It would seem,' he announced solemnly, 'that over the last five years or so, former officers including at least one former Director-General [Sir Dick White] have felt free to disclose confidential information received by them while in the Service, and have done so without any action being taken against them; and further, far from appearing to be, even if not being, leakproof ... as a result of the acquiescence or inaction of the British Government, the Service has, for years, leaked like a sieve.'

He then cited the long line of previous books, press stories and television programmes in which former intelligence officers had been evidently permitted to speak on the record without any subsequent sanction; the chief exhibits in this litany of breaches of the supposed duty of confidentiality were the book on which Wright and Pincher had collaborated, and the government's refusal to take any action to stop them.

Although both the Security Service and Armstrong obtained a copy of the manuscript well ahead of publication, and identified Wright as its prime source, 'it would seem that neither Mr. Pincher or any of his suspected sources was approached or questioned ... an omission which, given the view which had been formed that it was preferable that the book not be published ... I can but describe as incredible'.

Worse, Powell recorded, 'incredible though the failure of the security and intelligence services to interview Mr. Pincher or his suspected sources may have been, the failure of the British Government to take any steps to obtain an injunction to prevent publication of *Their Trade Is Treachery* is even more incredible'. Nor was this an isolated lapse.

> It seems to me that the British Government, having had ample notice – in some cases of the ultimate detail – of confidential information intended to be published or televised ... and believing that it was undesirable in the interests of national security that the information be published ... its failure to act to restrain *Their Trade Is Treachery,* [Granada Television's] *The Spy Who Never Was,* [Channel 4's] *MI5's Official Secrets* and [Penrose and Freeman's] *Conspiracy of Silence* cannot be categorized as other than an acquiescence ... and thus as a surrender of any claim to the confidentiality of that information.

All of this pushed Powell towards the inevitable conclusion that 'such an approach appears to make a mockery of what Sir Robert Armstrong has asserted'.

Judgments

Having disposed of this fundamental plank of the government's argument, the judge moved on to the way London had conducted itself in his courtroom, castigating it for the 'serpentine weavings' of its repeated attempts to block witnesses, and its refusal to hand over the documents Turnbull had demanded in discovery.

> The British Government's apparent unwillingness to abide by the decision(s) of the Court ... and [its] wish to perpetually change its ground in search of some obscure tactical advantage which only it could perceive ... do not reflect the type of attitude, or the approach to the conduct of proceedings which one is accustomed to ... expect from governments which have been, or are, litigants in this court.

If this judicial reprimand was unprecedented, there was worse to follow when Powell addressed the contents of Wright's manuscript. He was careful to avoid expressing an opinion on the vexed question of whether Sir Roger Hollis was a Soviet spy, but he was very clear that the implications of MI5's investigation into its Director General for 'acts of treason' were so serious that both British and Australian citizens should be free to hear and discuss them.

> There is much to be said for the view that the public interest in national security calls for further disclosure so that the correctness or otherwise of that information ... may finally be determined ... I would [also] think it in the public interest of Australia that the improprieties of the Service, with which ASIO and ASIS[12] liaise, should be exposed, and the evidence as to Soviet penetration be exposed so that it might be analysed and its effect on the operations of ASIO and ASIS determined.

From molehunts, Powell pivoted to Wright's revelations of wholesale illegality by MI5, and the conveniently blind eye turned by Downing Street to bugging, burgling and unlawful surveillance. This, he found, was of paramount public interest.

> The failure of a government to ensure that its own officers observe the law seems to me to strike at the very root of a democratic society ... if the executive, having been informed of crimes and breaches of international law committed by its servants were to

take no action to discipline those servants and to secure their compliance with the law in future ... disclosure to the public is called for and ought to be permitted.

The same principle applied even more strongly to Wright's claim that a cabal of rogue MI5 officers conspired to blackmail a democratically elected Prime Minister. Thanks to Simos' vehement objections on behalf of the government, all of the evidence about this scheme had been taken *in camera*: Powell's references to the plot and to Harold Wilson's belief that he was bugged by the Security Service were the first glimpses of what had been revealed behind closed doors, and they would quickly set a hare running in the House of Commons.

'One or more officers of the Service,' the judge recorded, 'plotted to destabilize that Government by leaking to the press ... details of a security scandal which had occurred some years previously during Mr. Wilson's first term as Prime Minister, as well as information which suggested that the Prime Minister himself was a possible security risk and was under investigation ... Whether or not there was any private inquiry into these allegations ... it appears clear enough that there was no public inquiry; nor does the evidence disclose whether any disciplinary action was taken against the officers of the Service.'

Next, the judge addressed himself to the legal arcana of restrictions on unauthorised disclosures of confidential information – and more specifically to the substantial differences between Australian and English laws.

While acknowledging Sir John Donaldson's scorched-earth approach in the Royal Courts of Justice, Powell noted that he would be guided instead by the *Fairfax* case ruling; this required him to assess whether the material at issue was genuinely confidential, and whether its disclosure would cause real damage. On both counts, he found London's argument wanting.

> First, as is not really disputed by the British Government ... much of the information contained in Mr. Wright's manuscript has already been made available to the public ... in the United Kingdom and elsewhere, in the books and other materials which have been published over the years.

On that basis alone the bid to ban *Spycatcher* was holed below the water line, but the second *Fairfax* test sank the government's case completely. 'A governmental plaintiff will be unable to establish the necessary element

Judgments

of "detriment" unless it can demonstrate that publication of the information will be likely to be detrimental to the public interest,' he explained for the benefit of the press.

It is difficult for me to see in what respects it can reasonably be said that the publication now of information – even if not previously made available to the public – relating to technological matters which are at least twenty years old, and which have long since been made obsolete ... will, in all probability, detrimentally affect the national security of the United Kingdom.

As the day wore on, it was clear that the British government was receiving a historic judicial spanking. Even the sole crumb of comfort Powell offered – he found that although there was 'no statute governing the establishment and operations' of MI5, the Crown had a legal right to expect its officers to stay silent – was swiftly snatched away.

'Although I have held that Mr. Wright was, and remains, subject to an obligation of confidentiality to it,' he concluded, 'the British Government has failed to make out its claim to the relief which it seeks in these proceedings, as much of the information in Mr. Wright's manuscript no longer retains the quality of confidentiality, and the publication of such of the information in the manuscript as might be regarded as still being confidential will not, in my view, cause any detriment to the British Government or the Service.'

With that, the judge dismissed the entire case, ordered London to pay all of Turnbull's costs and recorded that both Wright and Heinemann were to be released from their undertakings not to publish *Spycatcher*, unless the government lodged an appeal within 28 days.

As journalists raced from the court to alert their news desks, one enterprising reporter tracked Peter Wright down in his bed on the fifth floor of the St John of God Hospital in Hobart. When told of the verdict, the old spycatcher simply 'laughed and laughed and laughed'.[13]

Fleet Street's initial coverage of the British government's defeat was largely focused on reaction from inside Downing Street, where the Prime Minister's press advisors sought to spin the judgment as only a temporary setback. 'Thatcher is still determined to stop [the] book's publication,' *The Times* informed its readers. 'Senior ministers believe [Powell's] conduct of the case was bizarre and unreasonable and brought the Australian judicial system into disrepute. They are confident they can win the case before another judge in the New South Wales Court of Appeal.'[14]

The news also came too late for any immediate parliamentary response. MPs traditionally leave Westminster on Friday morning to spend the weekend in their constituencies, so it was not until 3.30pm the following Monday that the matter was raised in the House of Commons. After the Attorney General announced that, on the advice of its Australian counsel, the government intended to lodge an appeal 'as soon as practicable', Sir Michael Havers came under sustained hostile fire.

From the Conservative benches, Jonathan Aitken asked him to consider whether he was 'pursuing a good principle, but by the wrong method? Instead of spending the best part of £1 million of taxpayers' money on what I fear will be a vain attempt to persuade the Australian courts to uphold Britain's narrow view of the Official Secrets Act, will my Right Honourable and Learned Friend and his advisers concentrate on the higher priority, which is to ensure that all present and future members of the security services are given binding and enforceable contracts of employment, the breach of which makes them clearly liable to damages and loss of their pension rights if they dishonour their obligations of confidentiality?'

No, Havers growled. The appeal would not be in vain: 'I would not agree to any appeal unless I felt confident that there was a proper chance of success' – an assurance that rang somewhat hollow given the evidence from the *Spycatcher* trial that Downing Street paid little heed to his advice.

Labour MPs proved equally unimpressed by the Attorney General's announcement. 'Is [he] aware that many people believe that it is simply a further waste of taxpayers' money to pursue the appeal in Australia?' veteran backbencher David Winnick complained. 'Is he aware also that the Opposition are concerned not about the tittle tattle of the memoirs – we all know that Wright is a very embittered individual – but about the need to ensure that there is adequate parliamentary scrutiny of the security services? In view of the allegations that a Labour Government was destabilized ... by the Security Service, will there be a clear promise that there will be a full judicial inquiry into those allegations?'

Havers batted this salvo away with a disingenuous disclaimer that in his particular role as the government's law officer he had 'no power to give any such undertaking'. But he faced a more dangerous attack from Merlyn Rees, who had been Home Secretary when the allegations of a Security Service plot against Wilson first surfaced in 1977. Although there had been a limited internal inquiry into claims that the Prime Minister had been bugged, Rees was furious that Wright's allegations had not been considered, and he demanded a new official investigation. Once again, Havers passed the buck, this time to the current Home Secretary[15] – a referral which was swiftly quashed by Thatcher, who sent her spin doctors to brief the Lobby that she had no intention of allowing any inquiry into MI5.[16]

Predictably, the government waited until the last moment – almost four weeks after Powell issued his judgment – to lodge its appeal. It calculated that the crowded Australian judicial calendar meant that proceedings would not begin until the summer; but if Number 10 hoped this would keep the stubbornly growing controversy off the front pages of Britain's newspapers until after the looming general election – and that Wright's manuscript would remain securely under lock and key for many months – it was to be sorely disappointed.

24. CONTEMPT

> *'The Attorney General is seeking to widen the law of criminal contempt ... this offends the basic principles of natural justice'*
> VICE-CHANCELLOR SIR NICHOLAS BROWNE-WILKINSON; COURT JUDGMENT, 2 JUNE 1987

On Monday 27 April 1987, Britain's newest heavyweight newspaper boasted an international exclusive.

Under the banner headline 'How MI5 plotted Wilson's fall', and across the rest of its broadsheet-format front page, the *Independent* revealed the most seismic allegations in the still-secret *Spycatcher* manuscript: 'Wright book alleges treason, cover-up, assassination plans and incompetence ... Rules on telephone tapping were broken ... Chronicle of Security Service action against friend and foe.'

Founded six months earlier by three veteran journalists in the wake of the Wapping dispute – a bitterly fought conflict between Rupert Murdoch's newspaper empire, backed by Mrs Thatcher's government, and print unions determined to maintain their stranglehold on Fleet Street's technology – the *Independent* positioned itself squarely in the political centre, halfway between the liberal *Guardian* and the generally conservative *Times*. Billboards across London featured its clever marketing slogan – 'It is – Are you?' – and the paper quickly attracted both respected reporters and a growing readership.

Its scoop that morning would, under normal circumstances, have enhanced the reputation of the former and increased the size of the latter.

Instead, it plunged the paper into a prolonged battle with the government and divided the hitherto-unified ranks of England's judges.

In the weeks after Powell's ruling, someone – the *Independent* professed not to know the name of its benefactor – had sent it a copy of the *Spycatcher* manuscript. This unsolicited gift posed a genuine editorial dilemma. Pending the forthcoming appeal, the book remained officially banned in Australia, and the injunctions preventing the *Guardian* and *Observer* from reporting its contents remained in place in the UK; the issue which taxed the paper's lawyers was whether these also applied to all other media outlets – and whether the seriousness of Wright's allegations outweighed the risk of incurring the courts' wrath. Ultimately, the *Independent* decided that news values trumped caution.

'The decision to publish material from the manuscript of Peter Wright's thus far unpublished book was not taken lightly,' editor Andreas Whittam Smith wrote in a solemn editorial. 'Our justification is simple. It is in the public interest that facts about the operation of MI5 become known in order that the debate about the proper oversight and supervision of the security and intelligence services can be better informed.'[1]

The book's revelation of an MI5 cabal plotting to force Harold Wilson from Number 10, the paper's lead story argued, 'underlines the need for some form of oversight of the intelligence services ... the Prime Minister and the Home Secretary have firmly resisted any question of independent monitoring ... yet *Spycatcher* exposes details of a conspiracy against a Prime Minister, which has successfully been covered up ever since'.[2]

Unknown to the *Independent's* journalists, Powell's reference to this plot in his judgment had already led to a sizeable row behind Westminster's closed doors. On 31 March, Wilson's successor as Prime Minister, James Callaghan, held a frosty meeting with MI5 Director General Sir Antony Duff. The DG's note of their conversation revealed the depth of the former Labour leader's anger: 'Callaghan fixed me with a fairly penetrating, not to say hostile glance, and said that even if only a tenth of what Wright had said about destabilizing the Wilson government was true, it was still "a bloody disgrace" that it had happened.'

Duff protested that he had ordered a 'stringent internal inquiry ... which examined all relevant files and interviewed all relevant Security Service officers' – Wright, the scheme's originator and driving force was curiously not contacted – that had concluded 'unequivocally' there had been no 'attempt to destabilize [Wilson's] government'.[3]

Since he had never served in intelligence prior to being made Director General, and had no personal knowledge of MI5's turbulent post-war history, this assurance failed to quell disquiet in Parliament's corridors. But the Director General's commitment to defending his Service – right or wrong – was underlined by a note he sent to Robert Armstrong two days later, demanding an aggressive Cabinet Office clampdown on officials who were beginning quietly to accept the need for democratic oversight of MI5; in somewhat tangled prose, he denounced the timidity of those whose 'style ... does not seek to raise the temperature'.[4]

The Cabinet Secretary himself was by now one of those senior figures contemplating change. In the months since his humiliation in Sydney, Armstrong had turned his mandarin mind to the matter and reluctantly come to the conclusion that, for its own protection, the Security Service should be formally re-established on a statutory basis; this, he advised Thatcher, would 'ease' many of the problems which the Wright case had exposed.[5] His view was supported by the Home Secretary: on 7 April, Douglas Hurd sent Thatcher a note warning her that the *Spycatcher* case had 'hardened Parliamentary opinion' about the need for reform.[6] But neither man's advice made any impact on a Prime Minister resolutely committed to retaining sole power over intelligence issues – an intransigence duly demonstrated in the government's response to the *Independent* scoop.

The *Independent*'s exclusive was quickly picked up and recycled by two other London papers, the *Evening Standard* and the *Daily News*.[7] By the end of the day all three had been served with an emergency injunction, obtained by the Attorney General in an *ex parte* hearing to which they were not invited. That, unfortunately, was not to be the end of their legal problems.

The same afternoon, Duff returned to the fray, venting his ire at Downing Street and demanding a forceful public rebuttal of Wright's allegations. 'I am not skilled in these matters,' he informed Armstrong, 'but my gut feeling is that ... the sort of impact we will be hoping for is more likely to be achieved by a colourful choice of words than by a carefully balanced statement in which every word is judged by reference to its precise bureaucratic meaning.'[8] He followed this with a second memo to the Cabinet Secretary, warning that 'after the battering of the last few months ... I now fear that real damage will be caused to the standing of the Service'.[9]

Loyal, as always, to the intelligence services he had courted throughout his Whitehall career, Armstrong advised Thatcher to make a 'brief but trenchant' statement, 'attacking irresponsible investigative journalism and the Opposition MPs who aided and abetted it'.[10] No such declaration immediately materialised, but the Prime Minister was very much disposed to quash any suggestion of an official investigation into what MI5 had done to her predecessor.

In good part this was informed by a characteristically aggressive memo from her powerful Press Secretary. 'Any inquiry,' Bernard Ingham growled, 'is doomed before it begins to eventual dismissal as a whitewash. Current thinking is riddled with self-delusion. I consider that a far more effective remedy would be for the secret services (who have, after all, largely got themselves into this mess) publicly to shut up and secretly to grit their teeth, pull themselves together and get on with it.'[11]

His advice was heeded: at a meeting in Downing Street, Thatcher rejected the idea of an examination of the Wilson Plot, declaring that 'there was practically nothing to inquire into'[12] – an assertion rather undermined by a warning from her own staff prior to the meeting that a 'disadvantage of an inquiry is that ... we cannot be sure that it will not turn up something awkward'.[13]

Having set its face against scrutiny of MI5's allegedly treasonous activity, the government moved to make an example of the troublesome newspapers which had exposed it. On 29 April, lawyers for the Attorney General trooped back to the Royal Courts of Justice and secured – once again *ex parte* – an order charging the *Independent*, the *Evening Standard* and *London Daily News* with criminal contempt of court on the grounds that the earlier injunctions against the *Guardian* and the *Observer* remained in force. It was a draconian move, and – at best – legally dubious.

The common law of contempt stretched back to the thirteenth century and for more than 700 years was not considered by Parliament. In 1981 a new Contempt of Court Act entered the statute books as a measure to protect the integrity of active proceedings. Most frequently, contempt cases were brought against newspapers or broadcast media whose reporting threatened a defendant's right to a fair trial by prejudicing the jury, and breaches were generally dealt with by way of a stiff fine. But the Act also provided for a rather more alarming penalty – a prison sentence of up to two years.

The problem for the government's attempt to punish the *Independent* was that neither this paper, nor the *Evening Standard* and the *London Daily* News, had been party to the proceedings against the *Guardian* and *Observer*, and a small mountain of case law held that only those named in the original injunctions could be guilty of a contemptuous disregard for them. Facing the prospect of two years behind bars, the editors of the *Independent*, *Evening Standard* and *London Daily News* applied to have the charges struck out, and a full hearing was set down for later that spring.

While they waited, the MI5 scandal began spinning further out of the government's control. On 3 May, safely beyond the reach of English courts, the *Washington Post* alerted American readers to the most dramatic allegations in *Spycatcher*: for the first time the scandal of the Wilson Plot was exposed in the United States, and the story swiftly attracted interest in the manuscript from New York publishers.

It also added to the growing pressure on Downing Street. Two days later Duff demanded a public rebuttal of Wright's revelations: 'the allegations of plotting against a Prime Minister are so uniquely awful that, in my view, they call for open and categorical denial,' he wrote to the Prime Minister.[14] Simultaneously, after Callaghan made it known that he planned to call for an independent inquiry, Thatcher urgently dispatched Armstrong to dissuade the political grandee from speaking out[15] – a fool's errand which backfired almost immediately.

Twenty-four hours later, Callaghan issued an acerbic press release calling for a judge-led investigation into the Wilson plot – a demand amplified that afternoon in the Commons by his successor as Labour leader. Neil Kinnock drew the Prime Minister's attention to the statement, and invited her to order an investigation 'to gain an independent verdict on the past and to safeguard the future'.

Thatcher had no interest in disturbing the dust of recent MI5 history and fell back on her familiar tactic of dissembling. The events in question had, if they happened at all, taken place under previous governments. 'It would not be appropriate for me or other members of this Administration to see papers relating to that time, and we have not asked to do so,' she told MPs, before assuring them of her own complete confidence in MI5's integrity.

> I can tell the House that the Director General of the Security Service has reported to me that, over the last four months, he has conducted a thorough investigation into all these stories, taking account of the earlier allegations and of the other material given recent currency. There has been a comprehensive examination of all the papers relevant to that time. There have been interviews with officers in post in the relevant parts of the Security Service at that time, including officers whose names have been made public.
>
> The Director General has advised me that he has found no evidence of any truth in the allegations. He has given me his personal assurance that the stories are false. In particular, he has advised me that all the Security Service officers who have been interviewed have categorically denied that they were involved in, or were aware of, any activities or plans to undermine or discredit Lord Wilson and his Government when he was Prime Minister … No evidence

or indication has been found of any plot or conspiracy against Lord Wilson by or within the Security Service.

Further, the Director General has also advised me that Lord Wilson has never been the subject of a Security Service investigation or of any form of electronic or other surveillance by the Security Service.

Whatever Duff might have told his mistress in Number 10, Thatcher's statement was flatly contradicted by on-the-record published interviews with numerous former intelligence officers, the 'Norman John Worthington' file locked in MI5's Registry, and the government's acceptance in the *Spycatcher* trial that all Wright's allegations were true. Unsurprisingly, Callaghan was not impressed.

'It is all very well for her to be convinced about these matters and for me to be convinced about them, but it is important also that the public should have confidence in the service,' he insisted. 'In my judgment, it would be much better to clear the matter out of the way [with] an independent inquiry from outside the Security Service ... I beg the Right Honourable Lady not to close her mind to that even now. If she does not do so, these allegations, and in some cases inventions, about the Security Service will carry on and the contents of the book will continue to be dribbled out in one country or another. Every time that happens there will be a fresh spate of allegations and charges. The Security Service and everybody else will still rest under those allegations.'

In was a measure of Thatcher's disdain for both Parliament and the electorate that she refused to be swayed. 'Some people would never be satisfied and would go on raising matters again and again,' she told the House. 'Some people ... wish to undermine the Security Services. This is their way of doing it. I have made it clear that I do not intend to institute a further inquiry. It is not necessary; it is not justified.'[16]

Within a week, the accuracy of Callaghan's prediction became clear to Number 10. Prompted by the *Washington Post* story, Penguin Books' American subsidiary signed a deal for the US rights to *Spycatcher* and announced plans to publish the manuscript almost immediately. Thatcher panicked, and dispatched her most trusted fixer, William, First Viscount Whitelaw, to strong-arm the chairman of Penguin's London-based owners, Michael Hare, Viscount Blakenham.

Whitelaw had previously discussed the troublesome publication with his fellow peer, assuring Number 10 that he was 'on the closest terms with Lord Blakenham', that he was 'certain that [Blakenham] would not want his company's US subsidiary to be the first to publish the Wright book, and that he will use every effort to ensure that this does not happen'.[17]

By May, it was clear that this agreement between gentlemen would not hold. The best Blakenham could offer was to delay the book's release until July – helpfully after the coming general election[18] – but his company refused to cancel the contract itself.

The Prime Minister was not used to such rude rebuffs of her wishes, and instructed her staff to seek an injunction, blocking publication in the United States. 'If we can't other books will be published,' she scribbled on the top of a memo to her Principal Private Secretary, who then had the unenviable task of explaining that the US Constitution explicitly protected freedom of speech, and legal attempts to interfere with this would be 'unsustainable'.[19]

On 20 May, the *Independent's* bid to overturn the Contempt of Court order came before the High Court in London. After three days of submissions from the paper's lawyers and from barristers acting for the Attorney General, the de facto head of the Chancery Division, Vice-Chancellor Sir Nicolas Browne-Wilkinson, promised to pronounce judgment at the beginning of June.

In the interim, Armstrong tried to talk Thatcher into a tactical retreat. He had belatedly grasped the strength of the gathering storm, and suggested she seek shelter by establishing a new committee of Privy Counsellors to oversee the Security Service – albeit one which would report only to her. This, he advised, would appease most MPs, and was likely to be forced on the government anyway should it be sued in the European Court of Human Rights. The Lady, as ever, was not for turning: her opponents, she scrawled on the Cabinet Secretary's memo, 'wished ill to the Security Services … [and] are out to destroy the system at all costs'.[20]

Nothing previously in the career of His Honour, Sir Nicolas Browne-Wilkinson had marked him out as having potential to be one of the Prime Minister's feared cabal of revolutionaries,[21] but on 2 June he dealt a major blow to the government's hopes of suppressing troublesome newspapers and their reporting of Wright's allegations.

The judge had spent the previous fortnight considering the Attorney General's application to hold the *Independent*, the *Evening Standard* and the *London Daily News* liable for criminal contempt of court, and began his ruling with a fierce condemnation of the press's presumed freedom to disclose sensitive intelligence information.

'There ought to be some sanction against the publication of matters which prejudice national security,' he asserted, 'and the decision as to what does prejudice national security should not be left to the individual judgment of the editors of individual newspapers.'

That, however, was as good as it got for the government. The remainder of his judgment took a very traditional approach to the constitutional division of legal responsibility between the legislative and judicial branches.

> I had assumed that the Official Secrets Act provided the necessary sanction. If it does not, then it is for Parliament, if it thinks fit, to provide ... a public law remedy linked directly to the protection of public rights. Private rights should not be bolstered by a distortion of the law of contempt in an attempt to produce judge-made law protecting official secrets.

The fundamental problem, as the Vice-Chancellor saw it, was that none of the papers had been named in the injunction banning the *Guardian* and *Observer* from reproducing Wright's claims in *Spycatcher*; and since they had not been parties to that ruling, they could not be in breach of it.

> The law has never hitherto extended to cover a case such as this where the three newspapers have not aided or abetted the *Guardian* and the *Observer* to breach the 1986 injunctions; there has been no breach of the 1986 injunctions, since the only parties, *The Guardian* and the *Observer*, have done nothing ...
>
> It is almost incontrovertible that ... there ought to be a legal sanction against publishing. The question I have to decide is whether due to the ... existence [of] an order of the court preventing the *Guardian* and the *Observer* from publishing, the appropriate sanction is contempt of court.
>
> I have reached the conclusion that it is not. So to hold would be to subvert the basic principles of our civil law ... It seems to me that the Attorney General is seeking to widen the application of the law of criminal contempt ... the principle contended for by the Attorney General cannot be right ... [it would] make enforceable against third parties an order made in their absence. Such a result offends the basic principles of natural justice.

With that, Browne-Wilkinson dismissed the case against the *Independent* and its two co-accused newspapers, and opened the door to any other journalistic outlet minded to report on Wright's allegations.[22] Before they could so, the Attorney General lodged an appeal, and the ban on revealing *Spycatcher's* revelations was re-imposed.

But the wall of silence was now perilously close to collapsing, and the Prime Minister's refusal to contemplate any democratic authorisation for the Security Services was causing friction with MI5. On 18 June, a week after Thatcher had won her third general election, Duff arrived at Number 10 with bad news, telling the PM: 'the Security Service's ability to undertake operations and the readiness of members of the Security Service to carry them out was being inhibited by the lack of legislative cover, where otherwise illegal activities might be involved'.[23]

In reality, this bland account significantly understates the strength of the warning he issued that morning: Stella Rimington, then a senior counterintelligence officer and later the Director General herself, recorded a more forthright version of the exchange.

> [Duff] took the view that the ambivalent position under which MI5 conducted operations, which were accepted as necessary for the protection of the state and were tacitly approved by its political masters, but which were not covered by statute, was totally unsatisfactory.
>
> Once the position had been highlighted in Peter Wright's book, he was unwilling to continue to carry out such operations, and those which required entry to property were suspended.[24]

Since, as Wright had made clear, MI5 officers had neither the right to complain about their work nor any job security should they attempt to do so, this was by any standard an unprecedented mutiny, and one which made Thatcher's obduracy untenable. Shortly afterwards, the Home Office weighed in, warning that unless the Security Service was put on a statutory footing, Parliament was likely to reject her planned upgrade to the Official Secrets Act;[25] since this included new restrictions on publishing intelligence information, the Prime Minister was effectively shooting herself in the foot.

Not for the first time, or the last, Thatcher resolutely refused to be swayed: as she made clear in a meeting with Jonathan Aitken, a prominent supporter of parliamentary oversight, there was to be no compromise with those who wanted to dilute her personal control over the intelligence services.

> I ran through a list of recent failings and fiascos at MI5, and suggested that a Westminster version of the U.S. Select Committee on

Intelligence might have helped to prevent some of them. 'What rot!,' she retorted. 'That would mean people like you poking their noses into security matters they know nothing about.'

I said that she could select the parliamentary overseers, but without them there would be no external oversight. 'Absolutely wrong. There is perfectly good oversight now. I do it,' she pronounced with ringing certainty.[26]

Nor was Thatcher willing to tolerate any unauthorised disclosures by former MI5 officers. 'She thought the intelligence services would only be effective if their secrecy was preserved, and that people in them had a lifelong duty of confidentiality,' recalled Sir Robin Butler, soon to become her Cabinet Secretary. 'She felt strongly that a member of the Security Service spilling the beans could affect confidence of our allies, especially the United States.'[27]

All of which made a three-page memo from Armstrong on 23 June somewhat odd. He had, belatedly, got round to examining Anthony Blunt's memoirs, held at the British Library with an embargo against their release until the next century; after persuading its chairman to allow the government a private preview, the Cabinet Secretary carefully examined the typescript.

Its opening paragraphs made crystal clear that Blunt intended his book eventually to be widely read. 'It is written for my friends who have stood by me with unbelievable affection and loyalty,' the unrepentant old traitor noted in his preface, 'and for the members of the public who are I believe more numerous than might be supposed, who want to know the truth about my life and actions, as opposed to the versions which have been served up to them by the press – I do not say "the gutter press" because that would imply that some parts of the press were not of the gutter.'[28]

Scattered throughout its 75 pages were the names of MI5 and MI6 officers – several never previously identified – and the locations of Security Service buildings across London. In short, the Blunt memoirs contained precisely the same supposedly dangerous information as *Spycatcher*; yet Armstrong's report assured Thatcher that it was 'concerned more with the development of art history than security matters' and that there were 'no new revelations' about his career in intelligence.[29]

Since this was unequivocally false, it was yet more evidence that the government's insistence on a lifelong duty of confidentiality from all its retired spies was, in reality, focused exclusively on Peter Wright.

On Tuesday 7 July, a tubby and florid man boarded a transatlantic flight on a mission to test the government's claims to destruction. Andrew Neil was 38 and had been editor of the *Sunday Times* since 1983. His appointment by Rupert Murdoch had been controversial: on the political right by instinct, Neil viewed the liberal-leaning journalism championed by his predecessors as outdated[30] and set about repositioning the paper as a champion of Thatcherite, market-led values – property sections and celebrations of consumerism soon overshadowed long-form investigations. But he also recognised the sales potential of an old-fashioned scoop, and, backed by the power of the Murdoch chequebook, had paid $150,000 to secure one.

His tactics that summer were a classic demonstration of Fleet Street's appetite for cloak-and-dagger machinations. Heinemann Australia owned the worldwide copyright to *Spycatcher* and had contracted with Viking Penguin Inc. for publication in America. The *Sunday Times* bought serialisation rights from the Australian company, but with the appeal still pending in Sydney, it could not legally provide the paper with a copy of the manuscript.

The American publisher, however, was under no such prohibition, and had announced that the book would go on sale on 13 July. On arrival in New York, Neil was handed a pre-publication copy, and he promptly caught the next flight back to London. He and a small team of senior journalists spent the next few days frantically filleting the juiciest morsels for a major feature in the forthcoming issue.

All of this was done in strict secrecy: Neil knew that if the Attorney General discovered the plan, he would obtain an emergency injunction, immediately banning publication. Neil worked out an end run – dramatically named 'Operation Eagle' – to avoid this unwelcome prospect. The first edition of the paper, which usually arrived at Downing Street late on Saturday night, made no mention of Peter Wright or his troublesome memoirs; only the subsequent editions carried the serialisation – by which time it was too late for an alert government lawyer to wake up a judge and secure a restraining order. By a happy coincidence, this had a commercial, as well as legal, benefit: the first print run was small – generally no more than 76,000 – whereas 1.25 million copies of the subsequent editions were delivered to newsagents.[31]

The following morning, Monday 13 July 1987, the Attorney General duly issued new proceedings for contempt of court against Times Newspapers Ltd and Andrew Neil, an action which also prevented any further serialisation.

But it was all too late: the same day, bookshops across the United States piled copies of *Spycatcher* on tables at the front of their stores and opened their doors to a flood of eager purchasers. Peter Wright's memoirs, which Thatcher, Armstrong and the massed ranks of government lawyers had fought to suppress for almost two years, were now on open sale – and on their way to bestseller status.

25. FARCE

'I was told that I should not read it. I was also told that if my housekeeper wanted to stand by the fire and read it to me, that would be all right.'
FORMER PRIME MINISTER EDWARD HEATH;
HOUSE OF COMMONS, 15 JANUARY 1988

The scene on the pavement outside Parliament encapsulated the fiasco. On 15 July, MPs arriving for the ritual of Prime Minister's Questions were greeted by an enterprising young businessman bearing two large cases filled with the American edition of *Spycatcher*. Michael Mavin had flown to New York the previous day, bought 140 copies for a cool $3,000 and, after landing back at Heathrow in the early hours, was now hawking them openly next to the Palace of Westminster for £100 each.[1]

Twenty-four hours earlier, veteran MP John Morris – a Privy Counsellor, former Labour minister and respected QC – had requested an emergency debate on the burgeoning controversy.

'The matter is important because the Government have spent a great deal of taxpayers' money in the courts of Australia, the Republic of Ireland and those within this jurisdiction,' he told the Chamber, before savaging Downing Street's pursuit of an evidently hopeless cause.

> The capacity of the Government and their legal advisers to suffer judicial black eyes seems virtually inexhaustible ... The House, traditionally, has been the holder of the nation's purse strings ... The time has come when we should have the opportunity of saying, 'Enough is enough', and when the world of 'Alice in Wonderland',

where the whole world, except a Briton who does not leave these shores or buy a copy from a traveller from America, can read the book in question is clarified. The time has come to justify this futile, farcical performance.

In any normal democracy, Morris' plea would have been successful: the people's elected representatives would have had the chance to debate an issue which had dominated front pages for weeks, and which had been roundly condemned in editorials as an attempt to obstruct 'the right of the British public to know what is known by everyone else'.[2] Britain's ancient parliamentary processes were, however, unequal to the challenge: the Speaker of the House, Tory MP Sir Bernard Weatherill, refused to allow members even to vote on the application, insisting it was not 'appropriate for discussion' under the Commons' archaic Standing Orders.[3]

Prime Minister's Questions the following day proved equally unenlightening. Thatcher batted away a challenge from Neil Kinnock about the now-shredded duty of confidentiality – 'does [she] seriously think that the best way to uphold it is to take action in appeal courts in Britain and Australia and to engage in action which, with the arrival of every transatlantic airliner, is being turned into high farce?' – before attempting to justify her government's determination to ban the book then being sold openly on the street outside the Chamber.

'Will Customs officials be authorised to take from passengers arriving from the United States copies of Mr. Wright's book?' Labour backbencher David Winnick enquired. 'If not, what possible excuse is there for carrying on with the case in Australia?'

The Prime Minister explained that while it was 'technically possible to introduce a ban by amending the open general import licence, the Secretary of State for Trade and Industry has advised his colleagues against such action, because it is likely to be ineffective'. Nonetheless, she announced that ministers were considering legal action to seize the profits from sales of *Spycatcher* in America.[4]

Since any such bid was guaranteed to fail in US courts, it was yet another demonstration of the government's willingness to squander British taxes on a quixotic and doomed mission; but if nothing else, it provoked an angry response from Peter Wright. Thatcher, he told ITN's *News at One* bulletin, was guilty of 'deliberate sabotage', before complaining that the outstanding Australian injunction prevented him from saying more. 'I know why [she] is being a bitch: I can't tell you, but I do know why.'[5]

Two days later, the government's pursuit of the *Independent*, the *Evening Standard* and the *London Daily News* returned to the Court of Appeal, and exposed the deepening fissures in English judicial ranks. The Master of the Rolls and two Lord Justices had been considering the Attorney General's bid to overturn Nicolas Browne-Wilkinson's ruling that the law of contempt could not be sufficiently stretched to land the newspaper editors in prison; on 17 July, Sir John Donaldson once again rode to Downing Street's rescue.

He came, at first, to praise the Vice-Chancellor for his 'judgment of quite outstanding clarity' – and then to bury him under a miasma of his own opinions. 'All concerned,' he pronounced on precious little evidence, 'know that the real issue is whether, in the circumstances of this case, which are not substantially in dispute, the Defendants *could* be guilty of contempt of court.'

Satisfied that this remarkably low threshold had been met, Donaldson proceeded to conflate the question of contempt with the rather different problem of alleged breaches of confidence by the *Guardian* and *Observer*. It was 'a fact of life' that such cases took time to prepare, and the court's job was 'to preserve the rights of both parties until the trial … In a word, if there is a genuine dispute which cannot be resolved at once, the court must hold the ring until this can be done … If the parties are arguing about the ownership of a horse or a car, it may not matter who keeps the horse or car pending the trial. If, as things turn out, the court has given it to the wrong party, it can get it back and give it to the right party after the trial …'

Confidential information was, however, very different to bloodstock or motor vehicles, since 'if, pending the trial, the court allows publication, there is no point in having a trial since the cloak of confidentiality can never be restored'. A useful metaphor, the Master of the Rolls felt, was an ice cube. Kept in a refrigerator, it remained an ice cube, but should it be handed to someone without a fridge, it would rapidly become no more than a pool of water. The *Independent* and its fellow publications were, in Sir John's view, clearly parties lacking adequate refrigeration.

If this was, as he suggested, no more than obvious, it entirely missed the point of the hearing. Had the government wanted merely to stop the papers from publishing Wright's revelations, it could simply have relied on the injunction; instead, it sought to threaten their editors with contempt and a lengthy spell behind bars.

The Attorney General's submission had argued that although the existing injunctions named only the *Guardian* and the *Observer*, he could not have anticipated that their rivals would also be interested in the story:

'how,' Donaldson summarised on the Attorney General's behalf, 'could he be expected to seek an injunction against every newspaper, every radio and television station and every publisher of books and magazines who might obtain this information and take it into their heads to publish it?'

Unfortunately, the statutes required him to do precisely that – at which point, the Master of the Rolls decided it needed to be corrected by a dose of judicial common sense; what followed bore no relation to either the law or the evidence.

'I should like to re-emphasise that this case is not primarily about national security or official secrets,' he asserted in the face of all the facts. 'The national security issue is peripheral.' Instead, the question Donaldson decided he must answer was whether the *Independent*'s publication of part of Wright's manuscript 'would be calculated to obstruct or impede the administration of justice'. Despite admitting that 'there is no reported decision which provides any direct guidance', his answer was affirmative.

'The law of contempt,' he decided, 'is based on the broadest of principles, namely that the courts cannot and will not permit interference with the due administration of justice.' The *Independent*'s story had done just that, so he quashed Browne-Wilkinson's order and sent the case back to the High Court for a new hearing, to be arranged for some time in the distant future.[6]

This delay suited the government well. It was facing a raft of court proceedings in London, as well as the imminent hearing against Mr Justice Powell's verdict, in the New South Wales Appeal Court; kicking the can down the road in London preserved its chances of securing victory in Australia – which might, in turn, shore up its case in the eventual English proceedings. Unfortunately, time was not on the government's side.

Spycatcher was an instant sensation. Within days of publication, it topped the US bestseller charts (and would remain there for the next eleven weeks); Viking Penguin ordered a second print run, and then a third and a fourth. Sales were particularly brisk at New York's Kennedy Airport – the main hub for flights to and from the UK. 'People order ten and twelve copies at a time,' its bookstore manager, Mike Darcy, told journalists. 'We have a sign saying "Banned in Britain" – and that brings them in.'[7] To meet this demand, the publisher set up a dedicated production line, printing 10,000 copies for onward shipping to London.[8]

With the book now freely available on the streets and in bookshops across the country, on 20 July the *Guardian* and *Observer* applied to overturn the temporary injunctions banning them from reporting Wright's allegations. They argued that the American publication had materially changed the situation: the information was now in the public domain and no longer had 'the quality of confidence'. Since that was the sole basis for the Attorney General's case, there was clearly nothing left to argue at any eventual full trial.

The judge hearing this application was once again Vice-Chancellor Nicolas Browne-Wilkinson, and he wasted little time in expressing his unhappiness. 'There seems to have been a temptation to treat this case as an unreasonable pursuit by the Government of unreasonable ends,' he grumbled. 'This is not a view I share. The revelation of secrets of a security agent, it seems to me, is highly important and highly undesirable.'

But neither could he ignore reality. *Spycatcher*'s widespread availability had ensured that the information it contained was in the public domain and therefore no longer belonged to the government, as the Attorney General continued to insist. His claim, Browne-Wilkinson decided, was untenable since it could lead to an absurd conclusion: a British wife, he noted, could purchase a copy of the American edition perfectly legally, but should she tell her husband what the book contained, she would be breaking the law.

> Once the news is out by publication in the United States, and importation of the book into this country, the law could, I think, be justifiably said to be an ass and brought into disrepute, if it closed its eyes to that reality and sought by injunction to prevent the press or anyone else repeating information which is now freely available to all … If the press is precluded from saying things that other people are not precluded from, that seems to be not a freedom of the press but an additional fetter on it.

He duly ruled that the whole point of the injunction had been rendered moot – and freed the two newspapers from their shackles.[9] That freedom evaporated before the ink on his order had dried.

The Attorney General lodged an immediate appeal, and four days later the Master of the Rolls overruled his more junior colleague – his second humiliation of the Vice-Chancellor in less than a week. Donaldson's ruling once again advanced novel legal theories to protect the government's cause. Although *Spycatcher* was freely on sale in Britain, the Master of the Rolls decided the Attorney General still had an arguable case that further publication of Wright's allegations by the newspapers could damage the Security Service, and thereby endanger national security. It was a repeat of Robert Armstrong's similar – and much-ridiculed – claim in the Sydney hearings, and one which relied on the intellectual gymnastics which Mr Justice Powell had denounced.

There was, Donaldson decided, a distinction between information that was public knowledge and information in the public domain. The contents of *Spycatcher* were unquestionably public knowledge, but because the book was tainted by Wright's breach of his alleged duty of confidence, it was somehow not in the public domain: therefore the information still belonged to the government.

The Master of the Rolls did, however, recognise that much of the harm the Attorney General sought to prevent had now occurred, which raised the question of whether maintaining the injunction amounted to an empty gesture. The answer, apparently, was both yes and no: retaining its full draconian force was self-evidently futile, but the need to protect the Security Service from general 'damage' required the court to prevent the newspapers from providing their readers with excerpts from the book. The only small bone Donaldson tossed to the *Guardian* and *Observer* was permission to publish 'a summary in very general terms of the allegations made by Mr. Wright'. This marginal attempt at compromise satisfied neither side, and both promptly appealed once again.[10]

It also provoked savage criticism from even the most government-friendly Fleet Street titles. *The Times* editorial likened the law to a donkey,[11] and *The Economist* magazine agreed, treating its UK readership to an almost blank page in place of coverage of the Wright memoirs.

'*The Economist* has 1.5 million readers in 170 countries,' a small text box explained. 'In all but one country, our readers have on this page a review of *Spycatcher* ... The exception is Britain, where the book, and comment on it, have been banned. For our 420,000 readers there, this page is blank – and the law is an ass.'[12] But despite these trenchant protests, the cloak of official secrecy was draped back over media reporting.

Unfortunately for the government, the court's fiat did not extend beyond the nation's borders. On Sunday 26 July, two days after Donaldson re-imposed a gag on the British press, the Hong Kong-based *South China Morning Post* published a 4,000-word extract from *Spycatcher*, detailing the alleged Wilson Plot and MI5's telephone taps on friendly embassies. The feature was intended to be the first instalment of a three-part serialisation, for which the *South China Morning Post* had paid HK $27,000; that plan was abandoned when barristers acting for the Attorney General obtained an emergency injunction, with a full trial to follow. A week later, the *Dominion*, a conservative morning paper in Wellington, New Zealand, published its own selection of Wright's juiciest revelations; it, too, was swiftly silenced with an *ex parte* injunction.

The government was now racking up legal bills and imminent court hearings on three continents. On 27 July both the New South Wales Court of Appeal and the Judicial Committee of the House of Lords began considering the respective injunctions against Heinemann and Wright in Australia and the *Guardian* and *Observer* in England.

Ten hours ahead of London, the three Sydney judges started first, sitting in the barn-like and intimidating Banco Court. In front of them were twelve volumes of transcripts from the lower court proceedings. Theo Simos, again representing the Attorney General, and a visibly anxious Malcolm Turnbull were present; of Her Majesty's Cabinet Secretary there was no sign. Over the next five days both sides set out their case: Turnbull argued that Powell's ruling should stand, and that London was trying to impose English law on its former colony, while Simos repeated his previous assertion that Wright owed an enforceable lifelong duty of silence to the Crown. A decision was promised in the autumn.

That same day, London time, five Law Lords – more formally titled Lords of Appeal in Ordinary, the most senior court in the land at the time[13] – began an emergency two-day hearing of the case for and against keeping the English injunctions in place pending the full – and still unscheduled – proceedings. Their ruling, issued on 30 July, plumbed new depths of absurdity.

By a split decision of 3–2, Their Lordships reinstated the original injunction, shorn of Donaldson's modest nods towards press freedom, and added an even more draconian – and unprecedented – restriction.

Fearing that excerpts of *Spycatcher* might be read out loud during the proceedings in Australia and then reproduced by the British press, the majority faction of Lords Templeman, Ackner and Brandon imposed a blanket ban on all reporting of Wright's allegations – including any evidence or legal submissions given in the courtroom. Only the final verdict was to be spared this pre-emptive censorship.

It was, if nothing else, a historic decision – never before had British newspapers been prevented from reporting proceedings in open court – and one that seemed to flout Article 10 of the European Convention on Human Rights, which guaranteed freedom of expression. But Templeman insisted it was 'necessary in a democratic society' to ignore the provision 'in the interests of national security' and to protect the Security Service from 'harassment' should Wright's claims be given 'mass circulation'. For good measure, he warned against succumbing to pressure from the media, and turned logic on its head to proclaim that the 'imposition of restraints on the press ... is an expression, and not a negation, of democracy in action'. Truly, Alice was abroad and wandering freely in Their Lordships' Wonderland.

Nor was Templeman a lone critic of Britain's impudent journalists. Lord Justice Ackner savaged their 'hysteria', and warned of 'elements in the press as a whole which lack not only responsibility but integrity'.

Pointing a stern judicial finger at the evidently unfortunate constitutional protection for reporters in America, His Lordship complained that 'the courts [there] by virtue of the First Amendment, are, I understand, powerless to control the press. Fortunately, the press in this country is, as yet, not above the law, although like some other powerful organisations they would like that to be so, that is, until they require the law's protection.'[14]

This provoked a remarkable row in the normally decorous Upper chamber. Lord Bridge, chairman of the Security Commission for the past three years and hardly renowned for radicalism, stepped away from the Woolsack, where the Lords traditionally delivered their judgments, sitting down next to the press table, and his dissenting opinion made clear his contempt for the majority's decision.[15]

> Freedom of speech is always the first casualty under a totalitarian regime. The present attempt to insulate the public in this country from information which is freely available elsewhere is a significant step down that very dangerous road. The maintenance of the ban, as more and more copies of the book *Spycatcher* enter this country and are circulated here, will seem more and more ludicrous.[16]

Political and media reaction to the Lords' ruling was unremittingly hostile. Neil Kinnock denounced it for 'defying all common sense', while his deputy and Labour's Shadow Home Secretary, Roy Hattersley, condemned 'the Government's attempts to stifle the freedom of the press [which] are more akin to the behaviour of an Eastern European communist dictatorship than to a modern western democracy'.[17]

Headlines the following morning were no less acerbic. *The Times* returned to its previous analogy, charging that 'Yesterday morning the law looked simply to be an ass ... By yesterday afternoon the law was still an ass, but as a result of their Lordships' judgment it was no longer a dozy docile domestic creature ... In the hands of Lords Templeman, Ackner and Brandon it had become unpredictable and wild, seemingly responsive only to autocratic whims.'[18] The rather less lofty *Daily Mirror* was more succinct: under an upside-down photo of the three judges, its two-word caption read simply: 'You Fools!'[19]

That weekend the first shoots of civil disobedience emerged. On the morning of Sunday 1 August, Labour MP Tony Benn, a former minister in Harold Wilson's government, arrived at Speakers' Corner in London's Hyde Park – the traditional location for defiant public oratory – determined to flout the Law Lords' ruling.

'The Prime Minister and the law officers ... have betrayed their public trust,' he told a crowd of 500 spectators, journalists and television cameras, flanked by a handful of uniformed police. 'If ministers can arbitrarily ... claim that issues of confidentiality or national security justify a ban on publication, and if the judges issue an injunction, there could be no limit to the suppression of any information which might embarrass the Government.' He then read out ten extracts from *Spycatcher*, including Wright's most serious allegations of MI5 misconduct, before presiding over a raffle of the supposedly proscribed book.[20]

Other public readings swiftly followed across the country; at each, local politicians recited excerpts of the banned text and denounced the government's 'heavy handed' censorship;[21] as in the capital, the police watched, but made no effort to intervene. The BBC, however, was less tolerant when broadcaster (and former barrister) Ned Sherrin read a short passage from *Spycatcher* on Radio 4's gently satirical weekend programme *Loose Ends*, capping this with a sly coda – 'I suppose we have committed some kind of offence'. 'Auntie' was not amused, and the show was re-edited to remove the offending section in time for its subsequent repeat.[22]

Throughout the summer and autumn, thousands of copies of *Spycatcher* arrived in Britain. Bookshops sold them without interference, international retailers took out adverts in British periodicals, offering to ship the book from California or West Germany for the cover price, plus postage and packing,[23] and an enterprising Italian restaurant in Aberdeen gave away free copies with every meal ordered from a special menu.[24]

One of these imported copies was formally placed in the House of Commons library,[25] ensuring – subject to the Speaker's agreement – that MPs could enjoy Wright's dangerous memoirs over restorative drinks in one of the House of Commons' many bars. Less privileged institutions, however, found themselves unable to share the book with their readers. Council lawyers in Northumberland advised the county's elected representatives that they faced prosecution for contempt of court should they allow *Spycatcher* on their library shelves[26] – a warning which proved prescient when a High Court judge banned Derbyshire County Council from stocking the book: in the light of the Law Lords' ruling, Mr Justice Knox pronounced, allowing its ratepayers to borrow the book would be 'the thin end of a very large wedge indeed'.[27]

Their Lordships' ruling was also causing friction between MI5 and Downing Street. At the end of August, Sir Antony Duff complained that

Number 10 'was still not projecting its message on Wright as forcefully as it should'. The Treasury Solicitors had, regretfully, to explain to the Director General that it was impossible to mount their usual back-door briefing campaign because, owing to the court's restrictions, 'the government case could not be made without going into details that could not be revealed'.[28]

The government's lawyers – both in-house and international – were then being kept very busy pursuing the mountains of litigation demanded by the Prime Minister. On 24 August, Hong Kong's High Court lifted its temporary injunction against the *South China Morning Post*: the judge, Mr Justice Barnet, acutely conscious of unforgiving Chinese state censorship across Kowloon Bay, decided that the freedom of the press outweighed the Attorney General's interests in suppressing the book. 'There is a particular sensitivity on the part of the Hong Kong public, to any constraint on or fettering of the free flow of information, comment or news,' he ruled.[29]

Counsel acting for the government lodged an immediate appeal, and two days later – justice moving rather more swiftly in the colony than in the motherland – the Hong Kong Court of Appeal held an emergency hearing. On 8 September, quoting heavily from the Law Lords' ruling in London, its three judges re-imposed the injunction and refused the *South China Morning Post*'s request for review by the Privy Council in London.[30] If Hong Kong's citizens wanted to read *Spycatcher* they would, like the rest of the world, have to purchase imported copies from the United States.

That, however, was the only fillip Downing Street received that autumn. On 17 September, British Labour MEPs read out short extracts from the book during a debate in the European Parliament in Strasbourg: this posed a tricky problem for the government, since the speeches would be reproduced in the *Official Journal of the European Community* – a publication for which Her Majesty's Stationery Office acted as agent in the UK. Under its contract, HMSO was required to deliver the journal to 120 existing domestic subscribers, and to put it on sale in its retail bookshop.

The President of the European Parliament was a Conservative MEP and peer of the Realm. Henry Plumb tried to have the offending passages scrubbed from the official record – a gallant effort on behalf of Number 10, but one which quickly failed.

The implication of this small debacle was not lost on the Prime Minister: 'Her view,' a memo from her private office to the Home Secretary recorded, 'is that we must do everything possible to ensure that one hand of Government does not distribute what the other hand is trying to stop.'[31]

Unfortunately, as Douglas Hurd had to explain while recognising 'the obvious scope for embarrassment if HMSO as a Government Department appeared to be flouting our efforts to prevent distribution of *Spycatcher* ... our freedom for manoeuvre in the matter is very limited'.

It was a measure of Thatcher's obstinacy that the Home Office was then required to work up 'an elaborate stratagem' by which HMSO could be instructed to lie to would-be purchasers, telling them that 'its stock was exhausted' or, if that failed, 'it could procrastinate'. Sadly, this, too, was ultimately deemed impractical since it 'would run the risk of seeming ridiculous'.[32] Her Majesty's Stationery Office duly published and distributed the very material which the Law Lords had banned British newspapers from printing.

Then, on 24 September, the New South Wales Court of Appeal released its verdict on the Australian injunction. It made for grim reading in Number 10: by a 2–1 decision, the judges upheld Philip Powell's decision to allow publication of *Spycatcher*. Speaking for the majority, Mr Justice Michael Kirby first questioned whether 'the courts of this country have any business ... to enforce the duties [of confidentiality] which the [Attorney General] comes here to assert?' He thought not: 'No claim is made that any duty was owed by Mr. Wright or Heinemann to the Crown in Australia.' Instead, the British government was improperly attempting – in the face of every modern precedent (including its own) – to enforce English laws in a foreign country.

But one section of Kirby's judgment should have sounded a clear warning to Downing Street that MI5's opaque status was equally to blame for the loss. Because the Service did not officially exist, there had never been a contract of employment for officers like Peter Wright – and that meant there was no breach of confidence which could be considered by any international court.[33]

Inevitably, the government appealed yet again – this time to the High Court of Australia, the ultimate arbiter of all legal disputes. But it knew that it was chasing a lost cause: a week later, regardless of the outcome of the final hearing, another Australian judge lifted the injunction, and Sandy Grant ordered Heinemann's presses into action.

> We initially printed 20,000 copies, and then within the day we'd committed to another 20,000. Then by the end of the first week it was towards 100,000. We then sold from Australia into Ireland, and from there it was distributed across Europe and sold back illegally into England. In the end we sold 36,000 that way.[34]

Three months later, New Zealand's High Court followed its Australian counterpart, lifting the temporary injunction against the *Dominion* and its owners, Wellington Newspapers Ltd. In denying the British government's claim, Chief Justice Ronald Davison had harsh words for its most senior law officer.

'The attempt by the Attorney General of the United Kingdom to impose upon Mr. Wright the duty of confidentiality, which is pleaded ... as the basis for his action against Wellington Newspapers, is an attempt to enforce indirectly in this country the penal or other public laws of the United Kingdom,' Davison ruled, 'and as such will not be permitted by our Courts.' Adding injury to insult, he then ordered London to pay all the newspaper's costs.[35]

After more than a year of legal battles, the government had precious little to show for the millions it had spent on trying to silence Peter Wright. Courts around the world had dismissed what Turnbull derisively termed 'its absolute tsunami of litigation', and Britain's international reputation had been dragged through the international dirt.

'The principle of a free press hardly seems to concern Thatcher,' *Washington Post* op-ed writer Richard Cohen charged, in a column syndicated to scores of papers across America. 'The so-called Iron Lady maintains that the government has a right to protect its secrets, even though in this case its secrets are no longer secret. She is beating a dead horse to death.'[36]

The Prime Minister's determination to inflict punishment on the equine corpse of its quest was on show again in the Royal Courts of Justice on 21 December, when the latest instalment of the never-ending series of appeal and counter-appeals in the cases against the *Guardian* and *Observer* came before Mr Justice (Sir Richard) Scott. While recording that Peter Wright owed – and had broken – duty to the Crown not to disclose anything he obtained during his employment by MI5, and should the Attorney General choose to sue him in Britain the courts would certainly ban him from publishing his memoirs, he ruled that the case against the two newspapers was completely different.

They had acted independently of Wright, had not aided or enriched him; and furthermore, although the case had long since ceased to be about 'the preservation of the secrecy of certain information' and now concerned 'the promotion of the efficiency and reputation of the Security Service', the papers' stories had been justified because they had disclosed 'iniquity'. He therefore lifted the injunctions – only for them to be re-imposed when the government immediately appealed.[37]

By now these antics had eroded the dwindling patience of Fleet Street's traditional Tory bastions. 'Following the *Spycatcher* case becomes more and more like following the football season ... Long flashes of tedium are lightened by occasional flashes of skill,' *The Times* leader writer informed readers. 'No-one except Britain's enemies can take comfort from the sight of Mr. Peter Wright growing in international respectability ... as his governmental pursuers fall over their own feet in embarrassment and failure.'[38]

It was a view shared by the Security Service. 'In the face of the sustained criticism and vilification of the last year or two, arising chiefly from the ramifications of the Peter Wright case,' Sir Antony Duff wrote to the government, 'the Service has kept up its spirits pretty well. But these unremitting attacks do have their effect and my fear is that in the longer term the Service will be damaged in a number of ways.'[39]

Thatcher was, inevitably, unrepentant. 'The country has to have security and intelligence services,' she told BBC News in an interview on 21 December. 'Our duty as a government is to see that those people who work in those services do not divulge their secrets, because if they did - either for personal notoriety, prestige or for money – there would soon be no secret nor intelligence services and that would undermine the security of the country. That duty is vital. It is vital to your security, it is vital to the security of most people, and I think most people understand the importance of that.'[40]

There was precious little evidence to support this prime-ministerial intransigence. As Christmas 1987 approached, the *Spycatcher* saga had descended into an embarrassing shambles – one exemplified by a brief trial in Ealing Magistrates' Court on 16 December. That Wednesday morning, Michael Mavin, the entrepreneur who had sold copies of the American edition outside Parliament, became the first person to receive a criminal conviction in connection with Wright's memoirs. Mr Mavin was not, however, accused of breaking the Official Secrets Act, or of breaching any duty of confidence; instead, he was convicted of causing an obstruction by hawking his remaining copies on the London suburb's Western Avenue. He was fined £35 and ordered to pay £100 court costs.[41]

By the start of 1988, *Spycatcher* had become a global bestseller: more than a million copies had been sold in the United States, Australia and the Republic of Ireland – and tens of thousands were circulating freely in the United Kingdom. Yet British newspapers, television and radio stations remained banned from reporting a single word of its contents. In January, Thatcher's predecessor as Conservative Party leader stood up in Parliament to denounce her government's obsessive quest to suppress the book.

'Many harsh words have been said about Mr. Wright,' Edward Heath told the House, during a debate on a backbench bill aimed at reforming the Official Secrets Act. 'I must confess that I have not read his book. A friend of mine in America sent me a copy by special messenger as soon as it was published, but I was told that I should not read it. I was also told that if my housekeeper wanted to stand by the fire and read it to me, that would be all right.'[42]

Despite this encapsulation of absurdity, the attempt to loosen the dead hand of official secrecy failed: the government marched its MPs through the Commons' 'No' Lobby and the bill was rejected. Alone among modern Western democracies, Downing Street remained determined to deny its citizens the right to hear what the rest of the world – including hostile intelligence services in Moscow – was free to read.

26. LOSSES

'Everything the British Government was ostensibly trying to do, it achieved the opposite.'
SANDY GRANT, PUBLISHER OF *SPYCATCHER*

The profits – and the losses – kept mounting.

By early spring 1988, a million copies of *Spycatcher* had been sold in the United States, with a further 100,000 in Canada. Another 100,000 were shipped to Europe, and almost 4,000 went on sale across Asia and Africa. The figures vastly exceeded Heinemann's initial modest expectations. 'We originally thought we'd sell around 20,000 copies – at most,' recalled Sandy Grant. 'In the end, including all the American sales, the numbers were in the millions.'[1]

Wright and his publisher also signed deals for the book to be translated into eleven languages: as a result, readers in Japan, China, Germany, Spain, France, Italy, Holland, Portugal, Denmark, Sweden and Finland would have the opportunity to learn about MI5's scandals, at the same time as the British government fought to keep its own citizens from hearing them.

But even in London it was now swimming against an inexorable tide. On 10 February, the Attorney General's bid to re-impose injunctions on the *Guardian* and *Observer* was dismissed by a 2–1 majority in the Court of Appeal.

'For the courts to continue the injunctions further would be futile and just plain silly, now that *Spycatcher* has been so widely circulated, in the English language, throughout the world,' Lord Justice Dillon ruled. 'Everyone anywhere else in the world can read and discuss its contents and the Crown has accepted that it is impracticable to prevent the importation of individual copies into this country, with the result that anyone in this country who wants one can obtain his own copy.'

Of the court's three senior judges, only Sir John Donaldson remained determined, Canute-like, to defy the waves. While accepting that Peter Wright's memoirs had 'underlined a real problem – namely how should any wrongdoing by the Security Service be exposed, and what role can the media properly play in such exposure', in the next breath he denounced the newspapers' decision to publish the allegations: '[This is] as surprising as it is arrogant. Is it really to be said that this is a media democracy rather than a parliamentary democracy?'

Yet even the habitually government-friendly Master of the Rolls was gradually warming to the idea of subjecting MI5 to democratic oversight. 'It may be that the time has come when Parliament should regularize the position of the Service,' he mused – a clear warning that the days of sole prime-ministerial control were waning.[2]

The same thought had occurred to some of the less intransigent ministers in Cabinet. After the court's ruling, Home Secretary Douglas Hurd ordered his staff to prepare a bill putting the Security Service on a legal footing, and by the end of March he brought the first draft to Downing Street. It met with a predictably sniffy response: according to her official biographer, Thatcher 'did not much like the Bill', but in the face of Hurd's 'gentle, reasonable approach', she grudgingly agreed to allow further work on the proposed legislation.[3]

She was not, however, willing to concede defeat in the endless succession of court battles. Once again, the Attorney General lodged an appeal to the House of Lords, hoping to re-impose injunctions on the *Guardian* and *Observer* – and thereby on every other newspaper in the country. That his applications were ostensibly in his role as the government's notionally independent law officer, rather than as a member of the Cabinet, fooled nobody: the motive force behind this fight to the death sat in Number 10, not the Royal Courts of Justice.

At the same time, on the other side of the world, judges in Wellington and Canberra were about to bring to an end London's prolonged international crusade. On 28 April, the New Zealand Court of Appeal dismissed, for good, the case against the *Dominion* newspaper; six weeks later, the three senior judges of the High Court of Australia unanimously rejected the British government's final effort to ban *Spycatcher*, and ordered it to pay all the costs Turnbull had run up on behalf of Heinemann and Wright.

As it turned out, some of those bills were distinctly modest. 'I had a very small team,' Turnbull recalled, 'so the British ended up paying me just under

380,000 Australian dollars' – the equivalent of A$1 million or £550,000 today. The government's own costs – also to be borne by the British taxpayer – were, however, rather more opaque: weeks earlier, the Attorney General told the House of Commons he had frittered away £485,000 on the proceedings in Sydney and Canberra, with a further £110,000 in Wellington and Hong Kong.[4] The resulting total of £595,000 – £1.5 million today – would, as Turnbull correctly predicted, prove to be a gross underestimate.

> Their actual costs would have been many millions. They would have had no change, in terms of actual expenditure on their Australian lawyers, from A$3 million on top of all the costs of flying their people out here. It was a very expensive, and futile, exercise. It was bonkers. Totally bonkers.[5]

It was also remarkably counter-productive. Far from acting as a deterrent to future MI5 whistleblowers, the doomed litigation had shown them how to reveal the Service's secrets with impunity. Future Peter Wrights now knew that they could retire to Australia, and that the courts there would protect their revelations, regardless of the objections of the British government.

Worse, this self-inflicted wound was one which – as David Hooper, one of *Spycatcher's* legal team, observed – had been entirely avoidable: 'There was always a deal to be done; we repeatedly offered to negotiate deletions from the book, if the Government honestly believed they would damage national security. It amazed me that they refused even to consider this.'[6]

His view was shared by the traditional voice of the British Establishment. 'The Government has not emerged with a great deal of dignity from the Australian courts,' *The Times'* leader column thundered on 3 June. 'It has been comprehensively beaten – and in a manner which should have been foreseen. Discretion should now be the better part of valour ...'[7]

Such defeatist sentiments remained, however, anathema to Downing Street. While the world beyond the UK's borders feasted on Wright's memoirs, the government's lawyers were busily preparing for a final battle to suppress them at home.

The Attorney General's attempt to re-impose injunctions on the *Guardian*, *Observer* and *Sunday Times* was due to come before the Law Lords that autumn. Both sides engaged expensive QCs to argue their respective cases vigorously, but behind the scenes their preparations were surprisingly cosy.

The government's chief witness was Sir Robin Butler, the newly installed successor to Sir Robert Armstrong as Cabinet Secretary; one of the senior barristers for the newspapers was both his friend and neighbour, and the pair regularly met for an informal discussion of each other's tactics.

'It was rather funny, really,' Butler remembered. 'We were both living in south London and I used to walk round Brockwell Park with him every morning – we used to walk our dogs together. I was Cabinet Secretary and he was counsel for the newspaper. He would rehearse his arguments for why the book should be published, and I would produce the counter-arguments about why it shouldn't.'[8]

The verdict landed on Thursday 13 October, and hammered the final nail into the coffin of the government's campaign: although the Law Lords unanimously held that MI5 officers were bound by a lifelong duty of confidentiality, and condemned Wright for disclosing its secrets – he had, they charged, been guilty of a 'heinous treachery' and a 'flagrant breach of [his] duty of confidence [which] reeked of moral turpitude' – since the book was freely available to the world and his wife, the Attorney General's demand for a permanent ban on *Spycatcher* was plainly irrational.

'It seems to me to be an absurd state of affairs,' Lord Goff asserted, 'that copies of the book ... should now be widely circulating in this country, and that at the same time other sales should be restrained. This simply does not make sense ... I do not see why anybody in this country who wants to read it should be prevented from doing so.'

Nor did Their Lordships have any patience with the government's claim that to allow British citizens access to the book would adversely impede the Security Service from going about the nation's business. In the opinion of Lord Keith, *Spycatcher's* revelations were now so widely known that 'general publication in this country would not bring about any significant damage to the public interest beyond what has already been done'.

The judgment was also a wholesale and final rejection of Downing Street's tortuous two-year assault on the freedom of the press to report allegations which were plainly in the public interest. Even if Wright had been wrong in speaking out, Their Lordships made clear that the *Guardian* and *Observer* had not collaborated with him, and that their scoops had derived instead from old-fashioned journalism. 'If we are to have a free press in this country,' Lord Griffiths pronounced, 'we have to trust the editors.'

The *Sunday Times*, however, fared less well. The judges viewed its purchase of serial rights to *Spycatcher* as a de facto conspiracy with Wright to boost his bank balance, and they condemned Andrew Neil for employing 'particularly sneaky methods' to dodge the inevitable late-night injunction. Although it, too, was freed from shackles on its reporting and given a green light to publish as much, or as little, of the book's contents as Neil saw fit in the future, Their Lordships ruled that the government was entitled to receive all the profits accruing from the serialisation.

The Law Lords' ruling had one further, ironic outcome – and one which rubbed salt into Number 10's wounds. Their decision explicitly nullified any copyright in the book in the United Kingdom. As Lord Keith made clear, 'Mr. Wright is powerless to prevent anyone who chooses to do so from publishing *Spycatcher* in whole or in part in this country, or to obtain any other remedy against them'. In short, the government's pig-headed insistence on fighting to suppress the memoirs had, in the end, only ensured they would be even more freely available.[9]

Downing Street did its best to spin defeat as a victory, briefing Lobby journalists that the judges' ruling that Security Service officers owed a lifelong obligation of confidentiality 'would serve as a basis for any future *Spycatcher* situations';[10] and the former Cabinet Secretary – recently retired and now ennobled as Lord Armstrong of Ilminster – penned a lengthy opinion piece for *The Times*, arguing that the judgment vindicated his humiliation in the Sydney witness box. 'Perhaps I may be forgiven,' he concluded, 'for thinking that makes all that travelling worthwhile.'[11]

But the claims rang hollow – particularly when the man the government had fought so hard to silence took immediate centre stage in a BBC documentary. On the night the verdict was delivered, *Panorama* broadcast the results of its own investigation into the allegations of MI5's plots to oust Harold Wilson. Former American intelligence officers – all of whom had been briefed on its existence at the time – British journalists and the former Prime Minister's closest associates lined up to support Wright's story. If the old spycatcher now seemed less sure of the exact size of the cabal of rogue officers – 'I think the 30 number is the correct number; if you mean how many people knew something odd was going on, I would say that 8 or 9 knew what we were likely to do' – he remained adamant that the conspiracy had taken place.[12]

Unsurprisingly, the price of the government's obsessive pursuit of Wright – now revealed to be at least £3 million (equivalent to more than £8 million today) – was roundly condemned in editorials.

'The *Spycatcher* affair has brought embarrassment and humiliation for the Crown and its servants – and substantial costs to the taxpayer,' *The Times* informed its readers. 'Logical purity has long been trapped and paralysed inside the *Spycatcher* web. Lord Armstrong's economy with the truth was just the start. There was the continuous curiosity of Mrs. Thatcher being locked in battle with Mr. Wright, one who hated Communists as much as, if not more than, did she. Then began the unedifying spectacle of law lords preventing British newspapers publishing formerly confidential material at a time when it was no more confidential than the contents of any other US bestseller. That particular nonsense, at least, is now at an end.'[13]

Unfortunately for the Prime Minister, there was still a depressing litany of setbacks to endure. The first came less than a month after the Law Lords' ruling: on 22 November, the Queen's Speech – the traditional opening of a new Parliament – included an announcement that for the first time in its history, the Security Service was to be put on a legal footing.

Thatcher had fought long and hard against the plans, but MI5 had finally accepted the inevitable. 'The [Peter Wright] affair did lasting damage to the Service's reputation,' its official history later recorded. 'Never before or since has the Security Service suffered the level of public ridicule provoked by the long drawn-out *Spycatcher* saga.'

More specifically, Director General Sir Antony Duff had warned that the 'threadbare' pretence that MI5 did not exist was 'making it increasingly difficult to recruit and train men and women of quality'.[14] Grudgingly, the Prime Minister gave her assent, and in April 1989 the Security Service Act was signed into law. If it contained no mechanism for parliamentary oversight, it did at least formally recognise that MI5 was accountable to ministers and, crucially, it obliged Britain's domestic spies to seek Home Office approval for 'entry on, or interference with, property'; Peter Wright's successors would no longer enjoy unfettered freedom to 'bug and burgle their way across London'.

More unwelcome changes – at least to Thatcher's mind – followed within twelve months. For years she had set her face against attempts to reform the outdated Official Secrets Act – 'Backbenchers should have nothing to do with national security matters,' she told the proponent of a doomed bill in 1987[15] – but she was forced to relent in the aftermath of *Spycatcher*. The 1989 Official Secrets Act repealed the much-ridiculed 'catch-all' section of its antique predecessor, which had rendered every dot and comma of Whitehall documents secret. It also removed the threat of prosecution for substantial categories of official information and provided a public-interest defence for whistleblowers. Although it exempted the intelligence and security services from this liberalisation, making any unauthorised disclosures by officers an automatic 'absolute' offence, the Act was a clear sign that the Government's iron grip on its records was gradually being loosened.

Nor had the courts finished inflicting defeat. Almost two years after the British media was cleared to publish the contents of *Spycatcher*, the *Independent* and *Sunday Times* were still battling to overcome the contempt of court charges for having done just that. On 27 February 1990, their cases finally reached the Court of Appeal, and ended with a sorry whimper. The judges found both newspapers to have committed contempt, but they ruled that no fines – let alone two years' imprisonment – should be imposed.

The decision raised the question of why the actions had been brought in the first place – a concern which was amplified by the European Court of Human Rights in Strasbourg the following year. The *Guardian*, *Observer* and *Sunday Times* had all lodged complaints against the British government, claiming that its succession of injunctions and contempt charges had violated their freedom of expression – guaranteed by Article 10 of the European Convention on Human Rights. On 26 November 1991, the court ruled in the newspapers' favour, and ordered the government to pay each £100,000 for their troubles.[16]

By the time the verdicts landed in Downing Street, Thatcher was long gone – forced from office the previous autumn by her own party, which had grown weary of her habitual *l'état, c'est moi* hubris[17] and mulish intransigence with friend and foe alike. But to Sandy Grant, Heinemann's Managing Director in Australia, there was a clear lesson to be learned from the five-year *Spycatcher* fiasco.

'Everything the British government was ostensibly trying to do, it achieved the opposite. It made a relatively ordinary story – albeit one which was quite fun – into a global bestseller. In the United States alone, Viking Penguin eventually sold four million copies.'[18]

This unanticipated commercial success also rescued Peter Wright from the parlous financial state caused by MI5's refusal to pay his full pension. Reports in British newspapers that *Spycatcher* had made him a millionaire several times over were somewhat exaggerated – according to Sandy Grant, after deducting sizeable agent costs, Heinemann paid its star author a total of around one million Australian dollars, equivalent to approximately £500,000 – but the proceeds certainly eased living conditions at the stud farm in Tasmania.

'Obviously money was made and money makes a difference, but my parents were always prepared to live frugally to do the things they wanted to do,' the Wrights' daughter, Jenny Andrews, reflected. 'He never expected such public interest, let alone for it to end up on a bestseller list, [but] they were comfortable and made it into a very nice house, crowded with books, desks, filing cabinets, typewriter and horse gear, [using] the money from the book.'[19]

In his co-author's opinion, Wright's earnings were well-deserved compensation for his difficult decades inside MI5.[20] 'He did the State some very real service, but the journey in many ways was a struggle for him,' Paul Greengrass, by now an award-winning Hollywood film director, said decades later. 'He had real talent as a scientist, and when he joined MI5 he was a very popular man; people really valued him. But then he opened the door to counter-espionage, to this wilderness of mirrors. Peter was not psychologically well-equipped for that. It was a tremendous failure of leadership that Peter was led into the places that he was, and was then treated as a pariah. He was handled so badly by these people.'

Those failures, as Greengrass saw them, continued long after the old spycatcher retired to Tasmania. Had MI5 been willing to recognise both his intellect and his determination to unearth long-dead suspected traitors, the book which had caused such trouble might never have been written. 'If someone had said to him: "Peter, we really value your counsel, so when you go to Australia, would you come to the MI5 office in Melbourne and give lectures a couple of times a year, because there are things about the past that only you know" – if they'd done that, nobody would ever have heard of Peter Wright.'[21]

There would be one final vindication for Wright, the unlikely champion of democratic accountability for Britain's spies. Eleven months before his death in April 1995, a much-belated change in the law finally acknowledged the existence of MI6 and brought all three notionally secret services under parliamentary control. The Intelligence Services Act 1994 established a new statutory oversight body of MPs and peers – the Intelligence and Security Committee – tasked with overseeing the policy, operations and budgets of MI5, the Secret Intelligence Service and GCHQ; crucially, it was also obliged to publish an annual report on the operation of the three agencies.

All of this much-needed reform stemmed from *Spycatcher* and Wright's determination to expose the Security Service's past scandals. In the end, the government's hopeless battle to prevent the public from discovering the truth was destroyed by Thatcher's intransigence and Armstrong's duplicitousness, and marked the beginning of the end of Britain's obsessive and stifling official secrecy.

To David Hooper, the old Etonian solicitor who brought Wright to Malcolm Turnbull's door and became an integral element of the victorious legal team, 'the *Spycatcher* affair was really the last throes of the government controlling what could or could not be published. It was the end of the era in which they could tap people up in their London clubs, and offer a deal whereby if you were helpful to them, they would be helpful to you.'[22]

For a time, as new freedom of information legislation eroded the previously impermeable walls of official secrecy, Hooper's optimism appeared justified. But almost four decades after the *Spycatcher* trials, the British government has become adept at finding loopholes in the law; and to protect the secret of Thatcher and Armstrong's shady backroom schemes, it has dusted off the same tawdry techniques which led them to defeat in the Australian courts.

EPILOGUE
Forty Years Later

Deep beneath the warren of offices stretching out from Downing Street across Whitehall, vast collections of files are stored in secure, temperature-controlled basements.

Dating from the early twentieth century to the most recent events in the administration of the United Kingdom, these are Number 10's most secret papers – too sensitive or politically incendiary to be disclosed to the public that paid for their creation. Among them are the Cabinet Office dossiers and the prime-ministerial files on the *Spycatcher* affair, and the story of how and why they remain under lock and key has revealed the depths to which the present government is willing to stoop to evade its statutory obligations, as well as to protect the reputation of Margaret Thatcher and her Machiavellian chief *consigliere*, Sir Robert Armstrong.

Until 2000 the release of government papers was governed by the Public Records Acts of 1958 and 1967, the second of which mandated that official files were to be withheld from the National Archives for three decades after their creation. On 30 November 2000, the Freedom of Information Act (FOIA) came into force, and was – quite literally – revolutionary: it completely reversed the '30 Year Rule', replacing it with a 'presumption' that all official records are automatically open to the public from the day they are written.[1]

Inevitably, this new freedom came with a series of caveats. Given the huge volume of old official papers waiting for release, public bodies were given a grace period to arrange the transfer of their documents to the National Archives in Kew, south-west London; this was set on an annually reducing timescale – currently a maximum of twenty years.

More pertinently, the intelligence services were specifically insulated from FOIA: the new law exempted them from any requirement to hand over their files – however old – to inquisitive citizens. To its credit, MI5 adapted to the spirit of the age, and began voluntarily, albeit at its unfathomable discretion, releasing some of its material to the Archives – but only once these documents had passed their fiftieth 'birthday'. None of its files on *Spycatcher*, Peter Wright, Chapman Pincher, the Wilson Plot or the investigations into Sir Roger Hollis have ever seen the light of day.

Downing Street's own records, however, have no such privileged protection. By law, they must be disclosed, albeit subject to redactions to protect national security. Theoretically, an independent regulator – the Information Commissioner's Office (ICO) – has the power to enforce compliance. There is, unfortunately, a yawning chasm between this theory and practice: the ICO is beholden to the very departments it notionally polices for both funding and its existence, and since 2010 successive administrations have almost halved its budget at the same time as its caseload has more than doubled. The unsurprising result is that several thousand files remain locked in the government's vaults, and the Cabinet Office habitually obstructs lawful requests for their release.

Detailed reports from both the House of Commons Public Administration and Constitutional Affairs Committee[2] and the campaigning group openDemocracy[3] have highlighted the Cabinet Office's routine failure to meet statutory deadlines for responding to FOIA requests and its use of dissembling, delay or outright falsehood to block the disclosure of government records.

The *Spycatcher* files are Exhibit A in this sorry roll call of malfeasance. Between 1979 and 1986, the Cabinet Office created 32 volumes of papers relating to the case and Peter Wright's involvement with Chapman Pincher; the Prime Minister's office produced fifteen more.[4] All should have been sent to the National Archives by December 2019 at the very latest: none were.

Senior government officials have given a succession of contradictory, misleading or plain false explanations for this failure. The first was that COVID had interrupted the transfer of the Cabinet Office files – an impossibility, since the pandemic's effects only began to be fully felt in March 2020 in the UK, a full four months after the deadline. Thereafter, they claimed the files were in the final stages of preparation for release, before contradicting that assertion and insisting they would be withheld until 2029 under an obscure 'Statutory Instrument' for intelligence documents, which trumped the Freedom of Information Act.

Epilogue

Finally, Whitehall pronounced this, too, to be incorrect and that some – but far from all – of the Cabinet Office dossiers might be released a little sooner, subject to redactions to safeguard national security. The ICO – the supposedly independent guardian of the public's right to know – has proved unequal to the task of regulating this delinquency. For three years it wrung its hands, issued timid rebukes for the delays and dissembling, but, when confronted with the government's claim that releasing the documents would be potentially hazardous to Britain's security, ultimately backed away from enforcing compliance with the law.[5] To date, none of the Cabinet Office files have been disclosed.

The tale of Margaret Thatcher's separate prime-ministerial files is even more curious: in September 2023, after the last of many requests to release them for this book, the Cabinet Office sent a resolute formal refusal, once again citing 'national security' reasons.[6] It was surprising, then, that three months later it turned over copies of most of these dossiers to the National Archives. Despite being heavily redacted, no fewer than 3,208 individual pages had been scanned and were made available online – a remarkably speedy volte-face and one for which no explanation was offered.

And yet there is good reason to doubt the honesty of Downing Street's assertion. While insisting its *Spycatcher* files must remain closed to the public, it gave two government-friendly writers access to every page – including all the documents Malcolm Turnbull fought, unsuccessfully, to see during the trial in Sydney.

Ian Beesley holds a PhD in history and is a veteran Whitehall insider. He served in the Cabinet Office, the Treasury and 10 Downing Street under Thatcher's premiership. In 2008 he was contracted to write *The Official History of the Cabinet Secretaries* – a heavyweight 722-page account of the country's most senior servants from 1947 to 2002.

The book was the final volume in a series of official government histories which began in 1919 with detailed accounts of decision-making during the First World War. In 1966 Harold Wilson inaugurated the 'Whitehall Series' – the first peacetime volumes, written by eminent historians who were given 'free access to all relevant material in the official archives', even where these remained closed to every other researcher. The aim was to provide 'a trusted secondary source for historians and researchers while the official records are not in the public domain'.[7]

Throughout the nine years it took him to research and write the book, Beesley was allowed to examine, and subsequently quote from, the still-secret *Spycatcher* documents generated by the Cabinet Office, the Prime Minister's own files and a slew of highly sensitive memos from MI5.

But this privileged access came at a price. 'My text has been vetted against the interests of national security,' he informed his readers – a restriction which raised questions about what had been excised from its version of the saga, particularly in light of its unfailingly favourable portrayal of its subjects. Robert Armstrong was lauded as 'the Ultimate Courtier ... the compleat [sic] civil servant ... a backroom operator of great skill (with a touch of pugnacity) he enjoyed the exercise of power', while his profoundly dishonest performance in the Sydney witness box was sympathetically portrayed as a personal hardship: 'His triumphs were largely private, his failures visible publicly ... No Prime Minister could have asked for a more devoted or skilled bodyguard who would shield them and take the intellectual bullets intended for them'.[8]

Beesley has been unwilling to discuss what he was ordered to leave out of the book, or why he was allowed to view government documents about Wright which were deemed too sensitive to be shown to his lawyer. 'I fear that I am not able to be of any help. I do not have source material or relevant notes,' he wrote in response to a request for an interview.[9]

If the panegyric tone of *The Official History of the Cabinet Secretaries* is largely free of overt political bias, the opposite is true of the second writer to be given free run of the secret files. Charles Moore is a right-wing Tory to the tips of his elegantly crafted brogues. Variously editor of the staunchly conservative *Spectator* magazine, the *Sunday* and then *Daily Telegraph* titles, in 1997 he was hand-picked by Margaret Thatcher to write her authorised biography;[10] work on Volume 3 of this sizeable task began in 2016 and covered the years in which the *Spycatcher* trials played out.

Like Beesley before him, Moore enjoyed remarkably favoured access. 'It was my privilege to see the full range of her papers ... in many cases before the papers were released for public view and in some in which they have not been released at all,' he informed his readers. More tellingly, this occurred inside Downing Street, with the assistance of two senior officials. 'I studied them chiefly, before release, in the Cabinet Office space in H.M. Treasury ... I must thank Roger Smethurst, the Head of Knowledge and Information Management (KIM Unit) at the Cabinet Office for helping me obtain the documents ... [and] David Richardson [who] brought me the papers from basement and strongroom ...'[11]

Among the documents carted up from the bowels of Whitehall were the internal memos revealing the 1980 scheme by Armstrong and Thatcher to help Chapman Pincher publish *Their Trade Is Treachery* by having him briefed on the Hollis scandal. These were the key memos which Downing

Epilogue

Street had refused to disclose to Wright's legal team; withholding them then had allowed the Cabinet Secretary to lie, on oath, during the trial, dismissing Turnbull's claim of complicity as 'a very ingenious conspiracy theory [but] quite untrue ... totally untrue'.

Moore was permitted to read and quote from them – but on the understanding that he would coat them with a friendly spin and thereby defuse their explosive implications. He duly lived up to his side of this bargain, arguing that MI5's 'unavowed' status meant that 'reasons of state sometimes required that information about [it] reach the public domain by surreptitious means'. As to Armstrong's perjury – which could and should have landed the Cabinet Secretary in prison – in Moore's view it was merely 'fortunate that Turnbull had not had sight of his written advice'.[12]

Enabling a friendly writer to release carefully sanitised titbits of damaging records, and thus ensure the story was reported in a manner most helpful to Downing Street, exactly paralleled the original Thatcher–Armstrong plot, and infuriates Malcolm Turnbull: 'The government is repeating exactly what it did with Pincher: it is a classic case of material being made available to a writer regarded as being safely conservative. It's history repeating itself.'

Nor was this merely the outrage of a professional defence attorney wrongly denied vital evidence. In the years after his *Spycatcher* triumph, Turnbull returned to politics, serving first as a federal MP, then a Cabinet Minister and finally, from 2015 to 2018, as Prime Minister of Australia. Well-versed in the rough-house tactics of governing, he was nonetheless profoundly shocked by the underhand deal with Moore. 'I mean, the mendacity of these guys. We're all cynical about politics and Whitehall, but I don't think an official in Australia would be cynical to that level. It's outrageous.'[13]

Neither the government nor Charles Moore – ennobled in 2020 as Baron Moore of Etchingham by then Prime Minister Boris Johnson – have been willing to explain how he was permitted access to files which remained officially secret under national security exemptions to the Freedom of Information Act. The Cabinet Office claimed that to do so would breach Moore's right to privacy,[14] while he refused requests for an interview.

'I do not want to do this,' he wrote in May 2023, 'because it would involve discussing work which I did under confidentiality rules to which I signed up.'[15]

But why, since both Beesley and Moore were allowed to publish parts of the secret *Spycatcher* files – including the revelation that the Cabinet Secretary committed perjury – are so many of these documents still locked in government vaults? Armstrong's successor, Robin Butler, knows what they contain and believes they should be released.

'I can't understand why they are still withheld,' he said in December 2021. 'They've been reviewed [and] I don't see why they should be kept closed ... I can only think that it's just a general presumption that files relating to the intelligence services should remain secret.'[16]

For Neil Kinnock, by contrast, it is a sign of the dishonesty of Thatcher's successors in Downing Street. 'The rational part of me says there's no logical reason not to disclose, especially after the passage of all these decades. In any normal democracy, such decisions would be taken by ministers on advice from their civil servants. But looking at the character of the government, on the basis of all of the record, they are bloody liars – and it's gone right into their bone marrow.

'And so they will just dodge a decision if they can. Liars are evaders, and there are a lot of evaders about.'[17]

But to Jonathan Aitken – who in 1999 was sentenced to eighteen months in prison for perjury during a (unrelated) libel case[18] – the refusal to allow public access to the files may have a more sinister explanation. 'I should think there's some bad-ish stuff on Armstrong and Thatcher in them,' he concluded in late 2021. 'Who else could it be about?'[19]

It is now almost four decades since the Cabinet Secretary was humiliated in court, and public opinion, around the world. Nearly forty years have passed since Thatcher and Armstrong conspired to deceive judges and, despite spending a small fortune of taxpayers' money on court cases throughout the world, ultimately failed to block *Spycatcher*, instead turning it into a global bestseller.

The continuing suppression of its own records about an affair which brought MI5, Whitehall and the British government into international disrepute is the clearest indication that Whitehall remains determined to silence Peter Wright, long after his death – and to conceal the whole truth about the British government's own role in the scandals he sought to expose.

AUTHOR'S NOTE

*'He had softly and suddenly vanished away —
For the Snark was a Boojum, you see'*

Lewis Carroll's *The Hunting of the Snark* was published in March 1876. The fantastical narrative follows a crew of ten wildly disparate individuals, all determined to hunt the Snark, a mythical creature surrounded by a deadly curse: should it turn out not to be a Snark, but the rather more dangerous Boojum, the triumphant finder would 'vanish away' – a fate which duly befell one of the pursuers, the Baker.

The poem, subtitled *An Agony in Eight Fits*, is often described as an example of Carroll's 'nonsense' canon, and he sometimes denied knowing the exact meaning of his work. But there is some evidence that he intended it as a satire on a long-running Victorian legal cause célèbre – the Titchfield Claimant case, in which an Australian butcher pretended to be the heir to a vacant English baronetcy. The fraudster was eventually convicted of perjury and jailed for fourteen years.

The absurdity of the utterly pointless Snark hunt, and the wretched eventual fate of the Baker, struck me as a sharp metaphor for the British government's expensively doomed globe-trotting efforts to silence Peter Wright. But in the *Spycatcher* affair, which was Snark and which the Baker? That, I suspect, depends on which side of the fence you stand.

Certainly, Wright's obsessive molehunting and crusade to uncover Soviet agents – both real and perceived – inside the British Establishment could qualify him as the eccentric Baker. But Margaret Thatcher and Sir Robert Armstrong would be equally strong candidates for the ridiculous hunter – not least since they, unlike Wright, 'softly and silently vanished away' following their encounter with his Boojum. The choice is yours.

To Catch a Spy

Ultimately, like *The Hunting of the Snark*, the long, tangled saga of Peter Wright, Margaret Thatcher and *Spycatcher* is a prime example of something at which this country excels: the unedifying and pointless pursuit of the not-wholly likeable by the very definitely unpalatable – a tragi-comedy, yes, but ultimately a uniquely English farce.

Tim Tate
Wiltshire, January 2024

ACKNOWLEDGEMENTS

I began work on this book in spring 2019.
I had spent the previous two years researching and writing a biography of Michał Goleniewski, one of the most important but least understood Cold War spies; his name was largely absent from most espionage histories of the period, but Peter Wright identified him as an early – and vital – undercover agent for Western intelligence.

Reading that account in *Spycatcher*, and recalling my fascination with the trials at the time, led me to ask what had happened in the aftermath, and to begin the long battle to obtain the British government's files on the affair.

Authors traditionally devote the final pages of their manuscript to a list of those who supported them during its production. My experience of the government's extraordinary efforts to do the opposite leads me to begin with 'dis-acknowledgements': a roll call of those who have exploited every conceivable legal loophole (and some which are almost certainly *not* legal) to keep secret the antics during the Peter Wright saga. So, brickbats rather than plaudits to:

The Cabinet Secretary (at time of writing), Simon Case, who has presided over a department which is at best incompetent and all too frequently shamelessly untruthful.

The Information Commissioner, John Edwards – the statutory regulator charged with ensuring public bodies meet their legal obligations under the Freedom of Information, Public Records and Data Protection Acts. His office is admittedly woefully (and deliberately) underfunded by the government departments he is supposed to police, but rather than fight for the public's right to know, he has instead instituted a process of screening out or abandoning difficult cases.

Members of Parliament from all three main parties also bear the responsibility for failure. There is no all-party group examining Freedom of Information Act problems (though there is a plethora devoted to such vital interests as pubs, polo and philately), and while over the past four years several MPs have made vague promises to challenge the government's obsessive secrecy, all have quickly lost any appetite for the fight.

By contrast, those on the other side of the battle lines have been immensely helpful and supportive. I am particularly indebted to Peter Wright's daughter, Jenny Andrews, and his granddaughter, Holly Wright, for overcoming their initial suspicions to answer my questions. Similarly, Wright's legal team – Malcolm Turnbull, David Hooper and Paul Greengrass – generously gave of their time and offered their insights. So, too, did Sandy Grant, formerly MD of Heinemann Australia.

From differing sides of the political divide, Lord Neil Kinnock and Jonathan Aitken, as well as Nigel West, the espionage author and former Conservative MP, were refreshingly frank about their experiences; and Lord Robin Butler, Armstrong's successor as Cabinet Secretary, was both honest and insightful. I am also deeply grateful to my publishers, Icon Books. It has been a pleasure to work with them again – especially senior commissioning editor Connor Stait, who has been supportive and encouraging from the outset. An appreciative hat tip, too, to desk editor Steve Burdett and designer Anna Morrison.

I also owe a huge debt of thanks to my literary agent, Andrew Lownie. We have worked together since 2015, in which time he has secured numerous publishing deals, both British and international, for six of my books. Andrew is an indefatigable champion for his writers, a bestselling author in his own name and a doughty fighter against official secrecy. I am proud to be one of his authors – and prouder still to call him a friend.

Finally, my family. My children – now all very successful adults – and my remarkable grandchildren are a constant source of delight. Even closer to home, my partner, Mia Pennal, is simply my best friend and my soulmate; her love – as well as her selfless support for my endless burrowing in dusty archives – is at the core of both my continuing ability to work and my happiness.

SELECTED BIBLIOGRAPHY

Aitken, Jonathan. *Margaret Thatcher – Power and* Personality (Bloomsbury, 2013)

Andrew, Christopher. *The Defence of the Realm: The Authorised History of MI5* (Allen Lane, 2009)

Beesley, Ian. *The Official History of the Cabinet Secretaries* (Routledge, 2017)

Hall, Richard. *A Spy's Revenge* (Penguin, 1987)

Hooper, David. *Official Secrets* (Coronet, 1988)

Leigh, David. *The Wilson Plot* (Heinemann London/Pantheon, New York, 1988)

Mangold, Tom. *Cold Warrior – James Angleton, The CIA's Master Spy Hunter* (Simon & Schuster, 1991)

Miller, Joan. *One Girl's War* (Brandon Books, 1986)

Moore, Charles. *Margaret Thatcher – The Authorized Biography, Volume 3* (Allen Lane, 2019)

Neil, Andrew. *Full Disclosure* (Pan, 1997)

Penrose, Barrie, & Courtiour, Roger. *The Pencourt File* (Secker & Warburg, 1978)

Penrose, Barrie, & Freeman, Simon. *Conspiracy of Silence* (Grafton Books, 1986/87)

Pincher, Chapman. *Inside Story* (Sidgwick & Jackson, 1978)

Pincher, Chapman. *Their Trade Is Treachery* (Sidgwick & Jackson, 1981)

Pincher, Chapman. *The Spycatcher Affair – A Web of Deception* (Sidgwick & Jackson, 1987)

Pincher, Chapman. *Dangerous to Know* (Biteback Publishing, 2014)

Rimington, Stella. *Open Secret – The Autobiography of the Former Director-General of MI5* (Hutchinson, 2001)

Rose, Kenneth. *Elusive Rothschild – The Life of Victor, Third Baron* (Weidenfeld & Nicolson, 2003)

Sillitoe, Sir Percy. *Cloak without Dagger* (Cassell, 1955)

Turnbull, Malcolm. *The Spycatcher Trial* (Mandarin, 1988)
West, Nigel. *MI5 1945–1972: A Matter of Trust* (Weidenfeld & Nicolson, 1982/Coronet, 1983)
West, Nigel. *Molehunt: The Full Story of the Soviet Spy in MI5* (Weidenfeld & Nicolson/ Coronet, 1987)
Wright, Peter (with Greengrass, Paul). *Spycatcher – The Candid Autobiography of a Senior Intelligence Officer* (Viking Penguin, 1987/Heinemann Australia, 1988)

ENDNOTES

Chapter 1
1. Christopher Andrew, *Defence of the Realm: The Authorized History of MI5*, p.327. Allen Lane, 2009.
2. Peter Wright, *Spycatcher*, p.29. Heinemann Australia, 1987.
3. Sir David Petrie, 'Director General's Report on the Security Service, February 1941'. National Archives file KV 4/88; declassified April 2000.
4. 'Top Secret. Sir Anthony Blunt: Case History'; report by Sir John Hunt, Cabinet Secretary to Prime Minister James Callaghan, 20 December 1979. National Archives file PREM 16/2230; declassified December 2016.
5. 'Diaries of Guy Liddell [Director B Division, MI5]', 17 December 1945. National Archives file KV4/467; declassified October 2012.
6. In 1924 the Labour government was defeated at the polls after the *Daily Mail* published a letter purporting to be from the head of the Comintern in Moscow to the Communist Party of Great Britain, stating that a Labour government would normalise relations with Moscow and would enable the CPGB to pursue a Bolshevik-style revolution. The document was a forgery and, although never proved, Labour politicians suspected MI5 had played a role in the affair.
7. Christopher Andrew, *Defence of the Realm: The Authorized History of MI5*, p.322. Allen Lane, 2009.
8. Sir Percy Sillitoe, *Cloak without Dagger,* p.xiv & 158. Cassell & Co, 1955.
9. Only six copies were made and distributed to the Prime Minister, the Home and Foreign Secretaries and their Permanent Secretaries. MI5 and MI6 were provided only with a summary of its recommendations. File memo by Sir Edward Bridges, Cabinet Secretary: 28 November 1945. National Archives file CAB 301/30; declassified May 2013.

10. Sir Findlater Stewart, Chairman of the Security Executive: 'Report and Prime Minister's Directive to the Security Service', November 1945. National Archives file CAB 301/31; declassified May 2013.
11. Interview with Jonathan Aitken, Chief Secretary to the Treasury, 1994–95. 13 December 2021.
12. Sir Percy Sillitoe, *Cloak Without Dagger*. p.xiv-xv.
13. Notes of interviews with Dick White by Andrew Boyle, quoted in: Tom Bower, *The Perfect English Spy*, p.138. Heinemann, 1995.
14. 'Publication of Confidential Information': Sir Percy Sillitoe. 'Note for The Record', 23 April 1952. National Archives File CAB 21/3761.
15. Letter from Sir Edward Bridges to Sir Norman Brook, Cabinet Secretary, 13 October 1952. National Archives File CAB 21/3761.
16. Sir Percy Sillitoe to Sir Edward Bridges, 24 September 1952. National Archives file HO287/1415.
17. MI5's files on Marshall and Dewick would remain classified for more than 50 years. National Archives files KV2/1636-1646: William Marshall, declassified March 2004; KV2/3993-3995: Tony Dewick, declassified October 2014.
18. Sir Edward Bridges to Sir Frank Newsham, 10 March 1954. National Archives file HO287/1415.
19. Sir John Hunt, Cabinet Secretary to Prime Minister Harold Wilson, 4 July 1975. National Archives file PREM16/2230; declassified December 2016.
20. Peter Wright, *Spycatcher*, p.10. Heinemann Australia, 1987.
21. Peter Wright, *Spycatcher*, p.16. Heinemann Australia, 1987.
22. Peter Wright, *Spycatcher*, p.12. Heinemann Australia, 1987.
23. Neville Robinson, physicist, quoted by David Leigh, *The Wilson Plot*, p.32. Heinemann, 1988
24. Affidavit of Peter Maurice Wright; United Kingdom vs. Heinemann Australia & Peter Wright, Supreme Court of New South Wales, 8 November 1986.
25. *See*: Tim Tate, *Hitler's British Traitors*; Icon Books, 2018.
26. *See*: Helen Fry: *The Walls Have Ears*; Yale University Press, 2019.
27. Affidavit of Peter Maurice Wright; Ibid.
28. Peter Wright, *Spycatcher*, p.21. Heinemann Australia, 1987.
29. Affidavit of Peter Maurice Wright; Ibid.
30. Sir Percy Sillitoe: *Cloak Without Dagger*. p.v Cassell & Co, 1955.
31. Sir Edward Bridges to Home Office, 18 November 1953. National Archives file HO 287/1415.
32. J.W. Marriott to Peter Wright, 11 July 1955. Exhibits bundle, Supreme Court of New South Wales, Sydney.

Endnotes

33. Declaration (Official Secrets Act) by Peter Wright, 1 September 1955. Exhibits bundle, Supreme Court of New South Wales, Sydney.
34. *The Official Secrets Act and Official Secrets*; House of Commons Briefing Paper CBP07422; May 2017.
35. Affidavit of Peter Maurice Wright; Ibid.
36. John Cuckney joined MI5 in 1947 and spent almost a decade at Leconfield House before becoming a stockbroker, merchant banker and a leading figure in the overlapping 'secret state' circles of defence contractors, industrial espionage and government quangos. In 1995 he was elevated to the peerage as Baron Cuckney.
37. Affidavit of Peter Maurice Wright; Ibid.
38. Peter Wright, *Spycatcher*, p.31. Heinemann Australia, 1987.
39. Ibid.

Chapter 2

1. Christopher Andrew, *Defence of the Realm: The Authorized History of MI5*, p.337. Allen Lane, 2009.
2. Findlater Stewart had joined the India Office in 1903 and spent the next four decades toiling in the foothills of the Empire's bureaucracy. Shortly after the outbreak of war he joined the Security Executive, the overarching body which coordinated Britain's counter-espionage work.
3. Sir Findlater Stewart, Chairman of the Security Executive: 'Report and Prime Minister's Directive to the Security Service', November 1945. National Archives file CAB 301/31; declassified May 2013.
4. 'Directive to the Director General, Security Service; approved by PM' [undated but *circa* April/May 1946]. National Archives file CAB 301/30; declassified May 2013.
5. Sir David Maxwell Fife: 'Directive to the Director General of the Security Service', 24 September 1952. The directive was not publicly disclosed until the publication of the Denning Report on the Profumo Affair in October 1963. Parliamentary Archives.
6. Sir David Glyndwr Tudor Williams QC: Security Service Archives quoted in: Christopher Andrew, *Defence of the Realm: The Authorized History of MI5*, p.323. Allen Lane, 2009.
7. Peter Wright, *Spycatcher*, p.40. Heinemann Australia, 1987.
8. Christopher Andrew, *Defence of the Realm: The Authorized History of MI5*, p.337. Allen Lane, 2009
9. Ibid.
10. Sir Findlater Stewart, Chairman of the Security Executive: 'Report and Prime Minister's Directive to the Security Service', November 1945. Op. cit.

11. Peter Wright, *Spycatcher*, p.55. Heinemann Australia, 1987.
12. Memorandum on MI5's Central Index, undated but *circa* March 1946. National Archives file CAB 301/31; declassified May 2013.
13. It is a measure of the sensitivity of this adventure that all of the files on PARTY PIECE remain locked inside government vaults, and MI5's subsequent authorised 'Official History' devotes just two paragraphs to the operation – and makes no reference to the illegal nature of the operation.
14. Peter Wright, *Spycatcher*, p.70. Heinemann Australia, 1987.
15. The Metropolitan Police Special Branch was Britain's original 'political police' department, and acted for and in conjunction with MI5. Unlike Security Service staff, its officers carried official warrant cards, giving them power of arrest. But the relationship was often fraught and Special Branch resented the untrammelled freedom given to MI5 officers.
16. Affidavit of Peter Maurice Wright – Confidential Material. United Kingdom vs. Heinemann Australia & Peter Wright, Supreme Court of New South Wales, 8 November 1986.
17. Peter Wright, *Spycatcher*, p.110–13. Heinemann Australia, 1987
18. Ibid., p.70; p.54.
19. Peter Wright, *Spycatcher*, p.35. Heinemann Australia, 1987.
20. Christopher Andrew, *Defence of the Realm: The Authorized History of MI5*, p.336. Allen Lane, 2009.
21. Interview with Paul Greengrass, 15 September 2021.
22. Peter Wright, *Spycatcher*, p.93. Heinemann Australia, 1987.
23. Affidavit of Peter Maurice Wright, November 8, 1986: Confidential material. Op cit.

Chapter 3

1. 'Communist Espionage in the United States': Testimony of Frantisek Tisler, May 1960. US Legislative Archives, Washington DC.
2. Prybil's agent was Brian Linney, a 45-year-old engineer working on classified projects for the RAF. When confronted by MI5 he confessed to selling details of Britain's nuclear bombers and air-to-air guided missiles to Czech intelligence – betrayals which 'materially weakened … the defence of the United Kingdom'. He was charged with espionage and, in July 1958, was sentenced to fourteen years in prison. National Archives file CAB 21/4971.
3. Richard J. Heuer: *Nosenko – Five Paths to Judgment. CIA Studies in Intelligence*, Vol.31, No.3, pp.71–101. Originally classified 'Secret', Heuer's analysis was released in 1995. CIA Library.
4. Peter Wright: *Spycatcher*, p.293–95. Op. cit.

Endnotes

5. See: Tim Tate, *The Spy Who Was Left Out In The Cold*, p.312-313. Bantam/Transworld, 2021.
6. The NKGB – 'The People's Commissariat for State Security' – was the successor to the NKVD and the forerunner of the KGB.
7. Diary of Guy Liddell, Head of MI5 B Branch, Counter-Espionage, 5 October 1945. National Archives file KV4/466; declassified October 2012.
8. Diary of Guy Liddell, Head of MI5 B Branch, Counter-Espionage, 20 March 1946. National Archives file KV4/467; declassified October 2012.
9. Report to MI5 by Royal Canadian Mounted Police on the defection of 'CORBY' [Igor Gouzenko], 15 September 1945. National Archives file KV2/1419. Declassified September 2003.
10. MI5 Report: 'The CORBY Case', 25 September 1945. National Archives file KV2/1420. Declassified September 2003.
11. Ibid.
12. Diary of Guy Liddell, Head of MI5 B Branch, Counter-Espionage, 14 September 1945. National Archives file KV4/466; declassified October 2012.
13. Burgess and Maclean were the 'two moles inside the Foreign Office' whom Volkoff had offered to identify.
14. Report by Helenus Patrick 'Buster' Milmo, MI5. July 1951. [In] National Archives file 'Kim Philby (PEACH)' FCO 158/28; declassified October 2015.
15. MI6 Memo: 'PEACH' [Kim Philby], January 10, 1956. National Archives file FCO 158/28; declassified October 2015.
16. Peter Wright: *Spycatcher*, p.44. Op. cit.
17. *Hansard*, House of Commons, 25 October 1955.
18. Telegram CXG.321, 16 September 1945. National Archives – MI5 files on Igor Gouzenko: KV2/1425. Declassified September 2003.
19. 'Soviet Espionage in Canada': RCMP report, November 1945. MI5 files on Igor Gouzenko: KV2/1428. Declassified September 2003.
20. Some of this delay was caused by sometimes difficult tripartite discussions between the British, Canadian and US Government over how to handle the Nunn May revelation.
21. MI5 files on Igor Gouzenko: KV2/1423. Declassified September 2003.
22. Nigel West: *Molehunt*, p.69. Coronet Books, 1986. Hollis' report is missing from MI5's voluminous, but heavily redacted declassified files on Gouzenko. However, much of West's information stemmed from an extensive series of interviews with Wright, who simultaneously

provided the same account to his subsequent co-author, veteran British espionage journalist Chapman Pincher.
23. 'Appendix II', 'Report of the Royal Commission', Ottawa. 27 June 1946. National Archives file KV2/1423. Declassified September 2003.
24. MI5 report: 'Note on the Canadian Case in Retrospect', 15 November 1949 KV 2/1421; declassified September 2003.
25. Peter Wright: *Spycatcher*, p.188. Op. cit.
26. The Ministry of State Security (MVD) was part of the Soviet Union's overlapping internal and external intelligence agencies. In 1954 it was merged into the newly formed KGB.
27. Statement of William Windeyer QC, counsel to the Commission, 18 May 1954. National Archives file (Vladimir Petrov) KV 2/3444; declassified April 2011.
28. The report of Petrov's statement is curiously missing from the 21 heavily redacted volumes of his MI5 file, declassified in April 2011. It is, however, reported in a 1979 report to Prime Minister James Callaghan on the Anthony Blunt affair. National Archives file PREM 19/120; declassified December 2016.
29. Telegram from Graham Mitchell, Head of D1 (MI5 counter-espionage branch) to Security Liaison Officer, Australia, 28 April 1954. KV 2/3441. Declassified April 2011.
30. Christopher Andrew, *Defence of the Realm: The Authorized History of MI5*, p.504.
31. Peter Wright: *Spycatcher*, p.122–23.
32. 'James J. Angleton, Anatoliy Golitsyn and the "Monster Plot"'. CIA Studies In Intelligence, vol.55, no.4. CIA Library; declassified April 2013.
33. Peter Wright: *Spycatcher*, p.170; p.164–66.
34. 'Investigation of Russian Penetration of the Secret Services', MI5 briefing note for Prime Minister, May 1979. National Archives file PREM 19/120; declassified December 2016.
35. Affidavit of Peter Maurice Wright – Confidential Material. United Kingdom vs. Heinemann Australia & Peter Wright, Supreme Court of New South Wales, 8 November 1986.
36. Ibid.
37. Interview with Jonathan Aitken, Chief Secretary to the Treasury, 1994–95. 13 December 2021.

Chapter 4
1. Former Security Service officers, quoted in: 'British Patriot or Soviet Spy? An analysis of Chapman Pincher's Indictment of Sir Roger Hollis'.

Endnotes

John L. Wilhelm (former US Navy Air Intelligence officer) and Paul Monk (former Senior Official, Australian Defence Intelligence Organization). Presented at: Institute of World Politics, Washington DC. 10 April 2015.
2. Peter Wright: *Spycatcher*, p.173. Op. cit.
3. 'Security Service Archive', quoted in: Christopher Andrew, *Defence of the Realm: The Authorized History of MI5*, p.436. Op. cit.
4. Affidavit of Peter Maurice Wright – Confidential Material. United Kingdom vs. Heinemann Australia
5. Peter Wright: *Spycatcher*, p.193. Op. cit.
6. 'Investigation of Russian Penetration of the Secret Services', MI5 briefing note for Prime Minister, May 1979. This report was suppressed for 37 years; the file containing it – PREM 19/120 – was not released to the National Archives until December 2016.
7. Peter Wright: *Spycatcher*, p.176. Op. cit
8. Nigel West: *Molehunt*, p.24. Coronet Books.
9. Peter Wright: *Spycatcher*, p.24. Op. cit.
10. 'Investigation of Russian Penetration of the Secret Services': MI5 report for the Prime Minister, May 1979. [In] National Archives file PREM 19/120; declassified December 2016.
11. Peter Wright: *Spycatcher*, p.316. Op. cit.
12. 'Security Service Archive', quoted in: Christopher Andrew, *Defence of the Realm: The Authorized History of MI5*, p.506. Op. cit.
13. Peter Wright: *Spycatcher*, p.189. Op. cit
14. 'Security Service Archive', quoted in: Christopher Andrew, *Defence of the Realm: The Authorized History of MI5*, p.508. Op. cit.
15. Peter Wright: *Spycatcher*, p.201. Op. cit.
16. Report by Cabinet Secretary, Sir John Hunt, to Prime Minister Harold Wilson, 5 August 1975. National Archives file PREM 16/2230; declassified December 2016.
17. Peter Wright interview: 'The Spy Who Never Was'; *World in Action*, Granada Television, 16 July 1984.
18. 'Security Service Archive', quoted in: Christopher Andrew, *Defence of the Realm: The Authorized History of MI5*, p.509. Op. cit.
19. Peter Wright: *Spycatcher*, p.203. Op. cit.

Chapter 5
1. FBI report on confession by Michael Whitney Straight, 25 June 1963. FBI Vault, Washington DC.
2. Ibid.

3. 'Security Service Archive', quoted in: Christopher Andrew, *Defence of the Realm: The Authorized History of MI5*, p.435. Op. cit.
4. FBI files on Michael Whitney Straight. FBI Vault, Washington DC.
5. MI5 file: 'Klugmann, Norman John [James]'. National Archives file KV2/788; declassified May 2002
6. The international financial firm of J.P. Morgan had, by then, split into two notionally separate branches: commercial banking remained the province of the eponymous outfit, while investments were spun into a new business, Morgan Stanley. In reality, the two organisations remained interlinked.
7. FBI files on Michael Whitney Straight. FBI Vault, Washington DC.
8. 'Investigation of Russian Penetration of the Secret Services': MI5 briefing note for the Prime Minister, May 1979. National Archives file PREM 19/120; declassified December 2016.
9. 'Sir Anthony Blunt: Case History'; report by Cabinet Secretary Sir John Hunt to the Prime Minister, December 1978. National Archives file PREM 16/2230; declassified December 2016.
10. Memo by Sir Robert Armstrong, Cabinet Secretary, 2 February 1983. National Archives file PREM 19/3942; declassified July 2018.
11. 'Sir Anthony Blunt: Case History'; report by Cabinet Secretary Sir John Hunt to the Prime Minister, December 1978. National Archives file PREM 16/2230; declassified December 2016.
12. Arthur Martin, former MI5 officer [quoted in] Barry Penrose and Simon Freeman: *Conspiracy of Silence – The Secret Life of Anthony Blunt*, p.430. Grafton Books, 1986.
13. Transcript of Michael Straight interview with Ann MacMillan, CBC, 24 January 1983. National Archives file PREM 19/3942; declassified July 2018.
14. Hankey's reports were delivered to the Prime Minister at the end of May 1940. National Archives files CAB 63/192 & 193.
15. 'John Cairncross': MI5 memo, 10 January 1980. National Archives file PREM 19/3942; declassified July 2018.
16. 'Security Service Archive', quoted in: Christopher Andrew, *Defence of the Realm: The Authorized History of MI5*, p.435. Op. cit.
17. 'John Cairncross': MI5 memo, 10 January 1980. National Archives file PREM 19/3942; declassified July 2018.
18. 'John Cairncross': MI5 memo, 10 January 1980. National Archives file PREM 19/3942; declassified July 2018.
19. 'John Cairncross': MI5 report, 20 February 1964. National Archives file CAB 201/270; declassified July 2017.

Endnotes

20. Ibid.
21. 'Security Service Archive', quoted in: Christopher Andrew, *Defence of the Realm: The Authorized History of MI5*, p.509. Op. cit.
22. Between 1945 and 1964 MI5's various branches were re-organised five times, often swapping the initial letters which identified them internally.
23. Summary of Peter Wright's career: Annex E to Affidavit of Sir Robert Armstrong, Cabinet Secretary. United Kingdom vs. Heinemann Australia & Peter Wright, Supreme Court of New South Wales, 27 September 1985.
24. Affidavit of Peter Maurice Wright – Confidential Material. United Kingdom vs. Heinemann Australia & Peter Wright, Supreme Court of New South Wales, 8 November 1986.
25. Peter Wright, *Spycatcher*, p.213. Heinemann Australia, 1987.
26. 'Sir Anthony Blunt: Case History'. MI5 briefing note for the Prime Minister, April/May 1979. National Archives file PREM 19/120; declassified December 2016.
27. Ibid.
28. 'Security Service Archive', quoted in: Christopher Andrew, *Defence of the Realm: The Authorized History of MI5*, p.437. Op. cit.
29. Peter Wright interview [quoted in] David Leigh: *The Wilson Plot*, p.75. Pantheon Books, 1988.
30. Leo Long interview: *Panorama*, BBC Television, 2 November 1981.
31. Cabinet Office file CAB 301/855 and Prime Minister's Office file PREM 19/918 are 'closed' as 'sensitive material' under section 3.4 of the Public Records Act.
32. Margaret Thatcher: Prime Minister's Statement on Leo Long, 9 November 1981. *Hansard*.
33. Leo Long interview: 'Panorama', BBC Television, November 2, 1981.
34. Peter Wright, *Spycatcher*, p.230. Heinemann Australia, 1987.

Chapter 6

1. Peter Wright, *Spycatcher*, p.223. Heinemann Australia, 1987.
2. Robert Armstrong, Cabinet Secretary: 'Secret: Background' note for Prime Minister. Undated, but probably November 1979. National Archives file PREM 19/120; declassified December 2016.
3. Blunt Timetable in National Archives file PREM 19/120; declassified December 2016.
4. Peter Wright, *Spycatcher*, p.236. Heinemann Australia, 1987.
5. Ibid., p.224.

6. Affidavit of Peter Maurice Wright – Confidential Material. United Kingdom vs. Heinemann Australia & Peter Wright, Supreme Court of New South Wales, 8 November 1986.
7. The Home Secretary signed a warrant to allow MI5 to tap Blunt's phone and intercept his mail, but there is no record in any official file of authorisation to install a covert microphone.
8. Affidavit of Peter Maurice Wright – Confidential Material. United Kingdom vs. Heinemann Australia & Peter Wright, Supreme Court of New South Wales, 8 November 1986.
9. Ibid.
10. Peter Wright: report of interview with Anthony Blunt, 27 April 1966. MI5 dossier on Goronwy Rees, National Archives file KV 2/4608; declassified October 2022.
11. Anthony Blunt: Memoir. Unpublished manuscript held at the British Library, London. Document reference MS 88902.
12. 'Burgess Stripped Bare': *The People*, 25 March 1956
13. Sir John Hunt, Cabinet Secretary: 'Security of the Secret Services', Report for Prime Minister Margaret Thatcher, May 1979. National Archives file PREM 19/120; declassified December 2016.
14. The study of classical Greek and Roman literature and philosophy.
15. Peter Wright: File note, 29 January 1965. National Archives file KV 2/4607; declassified October 2022.
16. Transcript of Anthony Blunt interview, 5 February 1965. National Archives file KV 2/4607; declassified October 2022.
17. Peter Wright, *Spycatcher*, p.249. Heinemann Australia, 1987.
18. Robert Armstrong, Cabinet Secretary: memo to Robin Butler, Private Secretary to Prime Minister Margaret Thatcher, 23 February 1983. National Archives file PREM 19/3942; declassified July 2018.
19. Transcript of Peter Wright's interview with Goronwy Rees, 19 March 1965. National Archives file KV 2/4607; declassified October 2022.
20. Peter Wright: Note for File, 2 April 1965. National Archives file KV 2/4608; declassified October 2022.
21. Peter Wright: Note for File, 10 October 1965. National Archives file KV 2/4608; declassified October 2022.
22. Extract from telephone intercept, 11 October 1964. National Archives file KV 2/4607; declassified October 2022.
23. Transcript of interview with David Footman, suspected Soviet spy, 20 March 1965. National Archives file KV 2/4607; declassified October 2022.
24. Peter Wright, *Spycatcher*, p.243. Heinemann Australia, 1987.

Endnotes

25. Sir John Hunt, Cabinet Secretary: 'Security of the Secret Services', Report for Prime Minister Margaret Thatcher, May 1979. National Archives file PREM 19/120; declassified December 2016.
26. Peter Wright, *Spycatcher*, p.251-253. Heinemann Australia, 1987.
27. Ibid.
28. Affidavit of Peter Maurice Wright – Confidential Material. United Kingdom vs. Heinemann Australia & Peter Wright, Supreme Court of New South Wales, 8 November 1986.
29. Peter Wright, *Spycatcher*, p.264. Heinemann Australia, 1987
30. Ibid., p.263.
31. Lady Barbara Proctor: interview with Simon Freeman. [In]: Barrie Penrose & Simon Freeman, *Conspiracy of Silence*, p. 468. Grafton Books 1986.
32. Transcript of interview with Anthony Blunt, 5 February 1965. National Archives file KV2/4607; declassified October 2022.
33. Peter Wright: 'Bernard Floud - Security Background Briefing', 2 March 1966. National Archives file KV2/4394; declassified November 2017.
34. Peter Wright: 'The Jenifer Hart Case', 8 March 1966. National Archives file KV2/4396; declassified November 2017.
35. Ibid.
36. MI5 file notes on Bernard Floud, 25 February 1942 & 2 April 1945. National Archives file KV2/4393; declassified November 2017.
37. Floud's wife, Ailsa Craig, and his brother, Peter, were also enthusiastic communists.
38. Peter Wright: 'Bernard Floud – Security Background Briefing', 2 March 1966. National Archives file KV2/4394; declassified November 2017.
39. File note by 'F.4' [MI5's branch monitoring political parties], May 10, 1967. National Archives file KV2/4397; declassified November 2017.
40. Peter Wright: File Note, 19 September 1966. National Archives file KV2/4395; declassified November 2017.
41. File Note by Director General, 14 March 1967. National Archives file KV2/4396; declassified November 2017.
42. Peter Wright: File Note 6 March 1966. National Archives file KV2/4396; declassified November 2017.
43. File note by 'F.4' [MI5's branch monitoring political parties], 10 May 1967. National Archives file KV2/4397; declassified November 2017.
44. File Note by Director General, 6 June 1967. National Archives file KV2/4397; declassified November 2017.

45. Special Branch report of inquest on Bernard Floud, 13 October 1967. National Archives file KV2/4397; declassified November 2017.
46. Peter Wright, *Spycatcher*, p.266. Heinemann Australia, 1987.
47. Ibid., p.225.
48. Affidavit of Peter Maurice Wright – Confidential Material. United Kingdom vs. Heinemann Australia & Peter Wright, Supreme Court of New South Wales, 8 November 1986.

Chapter 7

1. Christopher Andrew, *Defence of the Realm: The Authorized History of MI5*, p.510. Allen Lane, 2009.
2. Peter Wright interview: 'The Spy Who Never Was': *World in Action*, Granada Television, 16 July 1984.
3. Sir John Hunt, Cabinet Secretary. 'Top Secret' Memo for the Prime Minister on the penetration of the Security Service and MI6, 5 August 1975. National Archives file PREM16/2230; declassified December 2016.
4. Peter Wright interview: 'The Spy Who Never Was': *World in Action*, Granada Television, 16 July 1984.
5. Affidavit of Peter Maurice Wright, 8 November 1986: Confidential material. Op cit.
6. Peter Wright, *Spycatcher*, p.184 Heinemann Australia, 1987.
7. 'Security Service Archives' [quoted in]: Christopher Andrew, *Defence of the Realm: The Authorized History of MI5*, p.511. Op. cit.
8. Christopher Andrew, *Defence of the Realm: The Authorized History of MI5*, p.511. Op. cit.
9. Peter Wright, *Spycatcher*, p.273–75. Heinemann Australia, 1987.
10. Affidavit of Peter Maurice Wright, 8 November 1986: Confidential material. Op cit.
11. Peter Wright, *Spycatcher*, p.273–75. Heinemann Australia, 1987.
12. Affidavit of Peter Maurice Wright, 8 November 1986: Confidential material. Op cit.
13. Alec MacDonald, former MI5 officer, [quoted in] David Leigh: *The Wilson Plot*, p. 124. Pantheon Books, 1988.
14. 'Security Service Archives' – analysis by [unidentified] MI5 officer [quoted in] Christopher Andrew, *Defence of the Realm: The Authorized History of MI5*, p.519–20. Op. cit.
15. Interview with Jonathan Aitken, Chief Secretary to the Treasury, 1994–95. 13 December 2021.
16. Peter Wright, *Spycatcher*, p.293. Heinemann Australia, 1987.

Endnotes

17. Peter Wright interview: 'The Spy Who Never Was', *World in Action*, Granada Television, 16 July 1984.
18. Sir John Hunt, Cabinet Secretary: Memo to Prime Minister Harold Wilson, 5 August 1975. National Archives file PREM 16/2230; declassified December 2016.
19. MI5 report: 'Investigation of Russian Penetration of the Secret Services'. April 1979. National Archives file PREM 19/12; declassified December 2016.
20. This document has never been disclosed. It remains locked inside Security Service files. The only account of its contents, in MI5's own 'Official History', unsurprisingly denounces it as 'threadbare' and 'shocking'. Christopher Andrew, *Defence of the Realm: The Authorized History of MI5*, p.517. Op. cit.
21. Peter Wright interview: 'The Spy Who Never Was': *World in Action*, Granada Television, 16 July 1984.
22. MI5 report: 'Investigation of Russian Penetration of the Secret Services'. April 1979. National Archives file PREM 19/120; declassified December 2016.
23. MI5 files on Francis Claud Cockburn. National Archive files KV 2/1543 - 1555; declassified March 2004.
24. Peter Wright interview: 'The Spy Who Never Was': *World in Action*, Granada Television, 16 July 1984.
25. Peter Wright, *Spycatcher*, p.341. Heinemann Australia, 1987.
26. MI5 report: 'Investigation of Russian Penetration of the Secret Services'. April 1979. National Archives file PREM 19/120; declassified December 2016.
27. Sir John Hunt, Cabinet Secretary: Memo to Prime Minister Harold Wilson, 5 August 1975. National Archives file PREM 16/2230; declassified December 2016.
28. Peter Wright interview: 'The Spy Who Never Was': *World in Action*, Granada Television, 16 July 1984.
29. Affidavit of Peter Maurice Wright, 8 November 1986: Confidential material. Op cit.
30. Sir John Hunt, Cabinet Secretary: Memo to Prime Minister Harold Wilson, 5 August 1975. National Archives file PREM 16/2230; declassified December 2016.
31. Christopher Andrew, *Defence of the Realm: The Authorized History of MI5*, p.518. Op. cit.
32. Interview with Jonathan Aitken, Chief Secretary to the Treasury, 1994–95. 13 December 2021.

33. Sir John Hunt, Cabinet Secretary: Memo to Prime Minister Harold Wilson, 5 August 1975. National Archives file PREM 16/2230; declassified December 2016.
34. Ibid.
35. Peter Wright interview: 'The Spy Who Never Was': *World in Action*, Granada Television, 16 July 1984.
36. The report itself remains locked within the closed files of Downing Street and MI5. Hunt's summary of its findings, disclosed more than 30 years later, is the primary official account of what Trend concluded.
37. Sir John Hunt, Cabinet Secretary: Memo to Prime Minister Harold Wilson, 5 August 1975. Op. cit.

Chapter 8

1. 'Security Service Archives' [quoted in]: Christopher Andrew; *Defence of the Realm: The Authorized History of MI5*, p.416. Allen Lane, 2009.
2. 'Sale of Jet Aircraft to Russia': Memo on Security Service Concerns, 16 September 1947. National Archives file BT11/2835.
3. *Hansard*, 23 June 1953.
4. The KGB's apparent hopes of recruiting Wilson proved fruitless – nor did MI5 know of them at the time. The plan only emerged in 1992, when KGB archivist Vasili Mitrokhin defected to London, bringing with him a vast handwritten collection of material copied from its files. Christopher Andrew & Vasili Mitrokhin: *The Mitrokhin Archive*, p.527–29. Penguin, 1999.
5. *Guardian* editorial 'The Death of Hugh Gaitskell': 19 January 1963.
6. Peter Wright, *Spycatcher*, p.362 Heinemann Australia, 1987
7. CIA History Staff: 'John McCone as Director of Central Intelligence 1961–1965, Part Two.' CIA Library; declassified April 2015.
8. In the 1950s and early 1960s, Robert Maxwell, wartime refugee from his Nazi-occupied Czechoslovakian homeland, ambitious global publisher and shortly to become a Labour MP, regularly gave his first name as 'Ian'.
9. Tennent Bagley: internal CIA memo, 23 November 1963. CIA Library.
10. Tennent Bagley interview: 'The Plot Against Harold Wilson'; BBC Drama documentary, 16 March 2006.
11. Charles Bates, FBI Liaison Officer to London, 1958–65, interview: 'Spycatcher – Wright or Wrong'. BBC Panorama, 13 October 1988.
12. Walter Elder, Executive Assistant to CIA Director John McCone, 1961–65, interview: 'Spycatcher – Wright or Wrong'. BBC *Panorama*, 13 October 1988.

Endnotes

13. William Massie & Auberon Waugh, interviews: 'Spycatcher – Wright or Wrong'. BBC *Panorama*, 13 October 1988.
14. 'Revealed: How MI5 bugged 10 Downing Street'. *Mail on Sunday*, 11 April 2010. The story of this unprecedented surveillance operation is remarkable in its own right. It was kept secret from all political leaders until 1978, and never officially disclosed by the Security Service. When MI5 retained historian Professor Christopher Andrew to write its *Authorized History*, he intended to reveal the operation, but was overruled – a decision he criticised as 'hard to justify'. Christopher Andrew, *Defence of the Realm: The Authorized History of MI5*, p.xxi. Allen Lane, 2009.
15. Peter Wright, *Spycatcher*, p.364 Heinemann Australia, 1987.
16. Interview with Jonathan Aitken, Chief Secretary to the Treasury, 1994–95. 13 December 2021.
17. Peter Wright interview: 'Spycatcher – Wright or Wrong'. BBC *Panorama*, 13 October 1988.
18. Dr. Walter Somerville CBE interview: 'Spycatcher – Wright or Wrong'. BBC *Panorama*, 13 October 1988.
19. Peter Wright, *Spycatcher*, p.363 Heinemann Australia, 1987.
20. Philip Zeigler, *Wilson: The Authorised Life*, p.366. Weidenfeld & Nicolson, 1993.
21. 'Peter Wright correspondence' [undated]. Quoted in: David Leigh, *The Wilson Plot*, p.119. Pantheon Books, 1988.
22. Cecil King: Personal diary entry, 8 May 1968. Reproduced in: 'Mountbatten and the coup that wasn't quite': *The Times*, 3 April 1981.
23. Lord Mountbatten of Burma: letter to Hugh Cudlipp, IPC Chairman, 6 November 1975. Ibid.
24. Jones, a former Army officer, joined MI5 in 1955. He was appointed Deputy Director General in 1976, and served as DG from 1981 to 1985.
25. 'Prime Minister faces questions on "coup" attempt'. *Sunday Times*, 5 April 1981.
26. The only official file on the coup – kept secret for 54 years – has been so severely weeded as to remove all Security Service information about the plot. 'Allegations concerning a possible coup in 1968'; National Archives file CAB 301/861; declassified July 2022.
27. Peter Wright, *Spycatcher*, p.369 Heinemann Australia, 1987.
28. Sir Martin Furnival Jones, MI5 Director General 1965–72 interview with Barrie Penrose and Roger Courtiour. *The Pencourt File*, p. 319. Secker & Warburg, 1978.

29. 'Peter Wright correspondence' [undated]. Quoted in: David Leigh, *The Wilson Plot*, p.119. Pantheon Books, 1988.
30. Christopher Andrew, *Defence of the Realm: The Authorized History of MI5*, p.627–28. Allen Lane, 2009.
31. Ibid., p.630–31.
32. Ibid.
33. Peter Wright interview: 'Spycatcher – Wright or Wrong'. *Panorama*, BBC Television, 13 October 1988.
34. Kagan was ennobled in 1976 in Wilson's final honours list. Four years later he was convicted of four counts of tax evasion by theft and jailed. He served ten months in prison, before resuming his seat in the House of Lords.
35. 'Peter Wright correspondence' [undated]. Quoted in: David Leigh, *The Wilson Plot*, p.119. Pantheon Books, 1988.
36. Note in MI5 file on Bernard Floud, 7 November 1961. National Archives file KV 2/4394; declassified November 2017.
37. National Archives files KV2/3221-3222; declassified March 2010.
38. 'Peter Wright correspondence' [undated]. Quoted in: David Leigh, *The Wilson Plot*, p.119. Pantheon Books, 1988.
39. Zuckerman's MI5 files show that while the Security Service monitored him from the 1930s to 1950s it never had any evidence that he was a communist sympathiser, much less an open or even secret party member. They also contain repeated verdicts that he presented 'no threat to security'. National Archives files KV2/3030-3031; declassified September 2009.
40. Ibid.
41. 'Directive to the Director General, Security Service; approved by PM' [undated but *circa* April/May 1946]. National Archives file CAB 301/30; declassified May 2013.
42. Harold Wilson interview with Barrie Penrose and Roger Courtiour. *The Pencourt File*, p. 9. Secker & Warburg, 1978.
43. Auberon Waugh interview: 'Spycatcher – Wright or Wrong'. *Panorama*, BBC Television, October 13, 1988.
44. Goldsmith's role in the early stages of this second coup has never been revealed. Wright's Australian court testimony which named him was censored from the public record. Affidavit of Peter Maurice Wright – Confidential Material. United Kingdom vs. Heinemann Australia & Peter Wright, Supreme Court of New South Wales, 8 November 1986.
45. Peter Wright, *Spycatcher*, p.368 Heinemann Australia, 1987.
46. Christopher Andrew; *Defence of the Realm: The Authorized History of MI5*, p.632. Allen Lane, 2009.

Endnotes

47. Peter Wright interview: 'Spycatcher – Wright or Wrong'. *Panorama*, BBC Television, 13 October 1988.
48. George (later Lord) Weidenfeld interview: 'Spycatcher – Wright or Wrong'. *Panorama*, BBC Television, 13 October 1988.
49. Peter Wright, *Spycatcher*, p.370 Heinemann Australia, 1987
50. Sir John Hunt, Cabinet Secretary: Top Secret memo for the Prime Minister, 4 July 1975. National Archives file PREM 16/2230; declassified December 2016.
51. Michael Hanley, MI5 Director General, letter to Peter Wright, 2 August 1976. Exhibit 27, United Kingdom vs. Heinemann Australia & Peter Wright, Supreme Court of New South Wales, November 1986

Chapter 9

1. The Security Service had recently moved out of Leconfield House to new premises in Gower Street, near Euston Station.
2. Peter Wright: 'Official Secrets Act Declaration on Leaving the Service', January 31, 1976. Exhibit in United Kingdom vs. Heinemann Australia & Peter Wright, Supreme Court of New South Wales, November 1986.
3. Peter Wright, *Spycatcher*, p.367. Heinemann Australia, 1987.
4. Affidavit of Peter Maurice Wright, 8 November 1986. United Kingdom vs. Heinemann Australia & Peter Wright, Supreme Court of New South Wales.
5. Letter from Rothschild to Guy Burgess, 3 February 1937. National Archives file KV2/4531; declassified October 2022.
6. MI5 report on Rudolf Katz, 24 January 1957; National Archives file KV2/4601; declassified October 2022.
7. MI5 letter to the Department of Overseas Trade, 3 October 1940. National Archives file KV2/2179; declassified October 2022.
8. Victor Rothschild: letter to the Admiralty, 16 May 1939. National Archives file KV2/4532; declassified October 2022.
9. Peter Wright: MI5 file note 29 November 1965. National Archives file KV2/4531; declassified October 2022.
10. The London Gazette, 4 April 1944.
11. MI5 report on Victor Rothschild's record of service, 24 May 1946. National Archives file KV2/4531; declassified October 2022.
12. Ludwig Nobel: CIA file. US National Archives RG 263, Box 93, Folder 3.
13. Affidavit of Peter Maurice Wright – Confidential Material. United Kingdom vs. Heinemann Australia & Peter Wright, Supreme Court of New South Wales, 8 November 1986.

14. Arthur Martin: internal MI5 request for guidance, 17 July 1951. National Archives file KV2/4531; declassified October 2022.
15. Sir Dick White, MI5 Director General: file note, 19 September 1955. National Archives file KV2/4531; declassified October 2022.
16. Victor Rothschild: letter to Sir Dick White, MI5 Director General, 26 April 1956. National Archives file KV2/4531; declassified October 2022.
17. MI5 internal report, 19 January 1970. 4 October 1957. National Archives file KV2/4532; declassified October 2022.
18. Courtney Young, D1 (counter-espionage) note for file, 4 October 1957. National Archives file KV2/4531; declassified October 2022.
19. John Marriott, Director B Branch, note for file 30 September 1957. National Archives file KV2/4531; declassified October 2022.
20. Peter Wright, internal MI5 file note, 4 November 1965. National Archives file KV2/4531; declassified October 2022.
21. Affidavit of Peter Maurice Wright – Confidential Material. United Kingdom vs. Heinemann Australia & Peter Wright, Supreme Court of New South Wales, 8 November 1986.
22. Internal MI5 file note of meeting with Lord & Lady Rothschild at 23 St. James' Place, W1, 16 February 1966. National Archives file KV2/4532; declassified October 2022.
23. Rothschild recommended Hampshire to Cabinet Secretary Sir Burke Trend for unspecified consultancy work in January 1971. Trend gave his approval – but only for 'unclassified matters'. Internal MI5 memos, 28 January & 1 February 1971. National Archives file KV2/4533; declassified October 2022.
24. Peter Wright, *Spycatcher*, p.117–18. Heinemann Australia, 1987
25. MI5 internal 'Note for File', 19 January 1970. National Archives file KV2/4533; declassified October 2022.
26. MI5 interview with Ian Henderson, 1 January 1970. National Archives file KV2/4533; declassified October 2022.
27. MI5 internal report 11 June 1969. National Archives file KV2/4533; declassified October 2022.
28. MI5 internal report 18 December 1970. National Archives file KV2/4533; declassified October 2022.
29. Internal MI5 memo on Rothschild's proposed appointment to The Central Policy Review Staff, 3 November 1970. National Archives file KV2/4533; declassified October 2022.
30. File note by Martin Furnival Jones, MI5 Director General, 1 February 1971. National Archives file KV2/4533; declassified October 2022.

Endnotes

31. Internal MI5 file note by Martin Furnival Jones, Director General, October 26, 1970. 'Security Services Archives' quoted in Christopher Andrew, *Defence of the Realm: The Authorized History of MI5*, p.588. Allen Lane, 2009
32. Affidavit of Peter Maurice Wright, 8 November 1986: Confidential material. Op cit.
33. Peter Wright, file note of meeting with Victor Rothschild on 25 August 1971. National Archives file KV2/4534; declassified October 2022.
34. Christopher Andrew, *Defence of the Realm: The Authorized History of MI5*, p.589. Allen Lane, 2009. Andrew claims that after his defection in 1985, former KGB colonel Oleg Gordievsky told MI5 that Soviet intelligence regarded Jones as 'an agent' between 1964 and 1968.
35. Peter Wright, *Spycatcher*, p.349. Heinemann Australia, 1987.
36. Sir Robert Armstrong, Cabinet Secretary 1979–87, interview cited in: Charles Moore, *Margaret Thatcher – The Authorised Biography, Vol.3*, p.234. Allen Lane, 2019.
37. Peter Wright, *Spycatcher*, p.349. Heinemann Australia, 1987.
38. 'Investigation of Russian Penetration of the Security Services': MI5 report, April 1979. National Archives file PREM19/120; declassified December 2016.
39. Peter Wright, *Spycatcher*, p.373. Heinemann Australia, 1987.
40. Affidavit of Peter Maurice Wright, United Kingdom vs. Heinemann Australia & Peter Wright, Supreme Court of New South Wales, 8 November 1986.
41. Victor and Tess Rothschild correspondence, 1976–77, quoted in: Kenneth Rose, *Elusive Rothschild – The Life of Victor, Third Baron Rothschild*, p.246. Weidenfeld & Nicolson, 2003.

Chapter 10

1. 'Blunt and the Palace': memo for the Prime Minister from Sir John Hunt Cabinet Secretary, 8 May 1979. National Archives file PREM 19/120; declassified December 2016.
2. Sir John Hunt: 'Sir Anthony Blunt', memo for the Prime Minister, 3 July 1974. National Archives file PREM16/2230; declassified December 2016.
3. 'Nailed: The Fourth and Fifth Men'. *The Times Diary*, November 9, 1978.
4. 'Sir Anthony Blunt: Top Secret': memo from Sir John Hunt for the Prime Minister, 17 November 1978: National Archives file PREM16/2230; declassified December 2016.

5. 'Sir Anthony Blunt'. Note For the Record of meeting between the Prime Minister, the Attorney General and the Cabinet Secretary, 28 November 1978. National Archives file PREM16/2230; declassified December 2016.
6. 'Sir Anthony Blunt: Case History'. MI5 report, April 1979. National Archives file PREM19/120; declassified December 2016.
7. 'Sir Anthony Blunt: Top Secret': memo from Sir John Hunt for the Prime Minister, 17 November 1978: National Archives file PREM16/2230; declassified December 2016.
8. Andrew Boyle: *Climate of Treason*, Hutchinson, 1979.
9. Sir Robert Armstrong, Cabinet Secretary: memo for Prime Minister, 8 November 1979. National Archives file PREM19/120; declassified December 2016.
10. Sir Robert Armstrong, Cabinet Secretary: memo for Prime Minister, 14 November 1979. National Archives file PREM19/120; declassified December 2016.
11. 'Cabinet Office Paper, 16 November 1979'. Quoted in: Ian Beesley, *The Official History of the Cabinet Secretaries*, p.415. Routledge, 2017.
12. Sir Robert Armstrong, Cabinet Secretary: memo to Bernard Ingham, 5 December 1979. National Archives file 19/3942; declassified July 2018.
13. Sir Robert Armstrong, Cabinet Secretary: confidential memo 14 November 1979. National Archives file 19/120; declassified December 2016.
14. 'Rothschild to Thatcher' [memo], 13 June 1979. Quoted in: Charles Moore, *Margaret Thatcher – The Authorized Biography Vol. 3*, p.234. Allen Lane, 2019.
15. 'Hunt to Thatcher' [memo], June 13, 1979. Quoted in: Charles Moore, *Margaret Thatcher – The Authorized Biography Vol. 3*, p.234. Allen Lane, 2019.
16. The law officers – the attorney general and solicitor general – play an anachronistic role in the United Kingdom's unwritten constitution. They are members of the government, bound by, and to, its collective policies, but are simultaneously 'independent' legal advisors whose decisions are made in a personal capacity. These dual roles frequently conflict; nonetheless they provide very useful political cover to Prime Ministers and their Cabinets.
17. 'Mr. Antony Blunt': Prime Minister's Statement to the House of Commons, 21 November 1979. *Hansard*.
18. Internal Memo from Sir Robert Armstrong to Clive Whitmore, Number 10, 19 November 1979. National Archives file PREM19/120; declassified December 2016.

Endnotes

19. Chilcot was then a senior official in the Home Office; he was knighted in 1990 and became 'staff counsellor' to MI5 and MI6, handling individual complaints about work and conditions, before being appointed to chair the official inquiry into the Iraq War and the accuracy or otherwise of Prime Minister Tony Blair's claims about the threat to Britain posed by Saddam Hussein.
20. The Privy Council was (and largely remains) so devoted to *omertà* that until 1998 even the oath each member swears was, itself, secret.
21. John Chilcot, Private Secretary, Home Office, letter to Nicholas Sanders, the Prime Minister's private secretary, 29 November 1979. National Archives file PREM19/3942; declassified July 2018.
22. Letter from Sanders to Chilcot, 3 December 1979. National Archives file PREM19/3942; declassified July 2018.
23. Sir Robert Armstrong letter to Prime Minister Margaret Thatcher, 3 December 1979. National Archives file PREM19/3942; declassified July 2018.
24. Sir Robert Armstrong, Cabinet Secretary: letter to Sir Brian Cubborn. Permanent Under Secretary of State at the Home Office, 6 December 1979. National Archives file PREM19/3942; declassified July 2018.
25. Cathy Massiter, former MI5 officer interview: *MI5's Official Secrets*; Channel 4, 8 March 1985.
26. Tony Motion, former MI5 officer interview: BBC *Panorama*, 23 February 1981.
27. Interview with Jonathan Aitken, Chief Secretary to the Treasury, 1994–95. 13 December 2021.
28. Affidavit of Peter Maurice Wright – public and confidential material. United Kingdom vs. Heinemann Australia & Peter Wright, Supreme Court of New South Wales, 8 November 1986.
29. Ibid.
30. Ibid.
31. Ibid.
32. Peter Wright, letter to Victor Rothschild, circa May/June 1980. [Quoted in]: Christopher Andrew, *Defence of the Realm: The Authorized History of MI5*, p.760. Allen Lane, 2009.

Chapter 11

1. US Select Committee to Study Government Operations with Respect to Intelligence Activities, 1975–76. Final Report, US Legislative Archives, Washington DC.

2. Aitken had published a copy of the British government's arms deals with Nigeria during the bloody Biafran War. He was charged under the notorious 'catch-all' section 2 of the Act, but acquitted in court.
3. Interview with Jonathan Aitken, Chief Secretary to the Treasury, 1994–95. 13 December 2021
4. Ibid.
5. Joan Martin had formerly been secretary to Guy Liddell when he was MI5's Deputy Director General. She remained with the Service after he retired.
6. Interview with Jonathan Aitken, Chief Secretary to the Treasury, 1994–95. 13 December 2021.
7. Jonathan Aitken MP: letter to Prime Minister Margaret Thatcher, 31 January 1980. Exhibit: United Kingdom vs. Wright & Others, Supreme Court of New South Wales.
8. Memo from Sir Robert Armstrong, Cabinet Secretary, to Clive Whitmore, Principal Private Secretary to the Prime Minster, 18 February 1980. National Archives file PREM19/591; declassified December 2023.
9. 'Investigation of Russian Penetration of the Secret Services': MI5 report, April–May 1979. National Archives file PREM 19/120; declassified December 2016.
10. Interview with Jonathan Aitken, Chief Secretary to the Treasury, 1994–95. Op. Cit.
11. Ibid.
12. Barrie Penrose and Roger Courtiour: *The Pencourt File*. Secker & Warburg, 1978.
13. Confidential letter from Lord Peter Rawlinson to Margaret Thatcher, 9 June 1980. National Archives file PREM19/591; declassified December 2023.
14. Sir Robert Armstrong letter to Clive Whitmore, Prime Minister's PPS, 10 June 1980. National Archives file PREM19/591; declassified December 2023.
15. Clive Whitmore letter to Sir Robert Armstrong, 11 June 1980. National Archives file PREM 19/591; declassified December 2023.
16. Affidavit of Peter Maurice Wright; United Kingdom vs. Heinemann Australia & Peter Wright, Supreme Court of New South Wales, 8 November 1986.
17. Auberon Waugh: 'Lord Rothschild is innocent'. *Private Eye,* 14 June 1980.
18. Kenneth Rose, *Elusive Rothschild,* p.251. Weidenfeld & Nicolson, 2003.

19. Victor Rothschild letter to Peter Wright, 25 June 1980. [quoted in]: Kenneth Rose, *Elusive Rothschild*, p.252. Op. Cit.
20. Affidavit of Peter Maurice Wright; United Kingdom vs. Heinemann Australia & Peter Wright, Supreme Court of New South Wales, 8 November 1986.
21. Ibid.

Chapter 12

1. Chapman Pincher: *Dangerous to Know – A Life*, pp. 23–25. Biteback Publishing, 2014.
2. Tony Gray: *Fleet Street Remembered*, p. 49. Heinemann, 1990.
3. Charles Wintour: The Rise and Fall of Fleet Street, pp. 95–96. Hutchinson, 1989.
4. Chapman Pincher: *Dangerous to Know – A Life*, p.31. Biteback Publishing, 2014.
5. Harold Macmillan, Personal Minute, 4 May 1959. National Archives file PREM 11/2800; declassified April 2006.
6. Chapman Pincher, *Dangerous to Know: A Life*, p.37. Biteback Publishing, 2014.
7. Chapman Pincher: *Inside Story*, pp. 102–07. Sidgwick & Jackson, 1978.
8. Affidavit of Peter Maurice Wright: Confidential Material, 8 November 1986. United Kingdom vs. Heinemann Australia & Peter Wright, Supreme Court of New South Wales.
9. Ibid.
10. Chapman Pincher: *Inside Story*, pp.16–18. Sidgwick & Jackson, 1978.
11. Victor Rothschild letter to Chapman Pincher, July 1980. [Quoted in]: Kenneth Rose, *Elusive Rothschild*, p. 257. Weidenfeld & Nicolson, 2003.
12. Affidavit of Peter Maurice Wright, 8 November 1986. Op. Cit.
13. 'Opinion': Attorney General Elwyn Jones QC, 6 November 1967. National Archives file CAB301/927-2; declassified July 2022.
14. Affidavit of Peter Maurice Wright, 8 November 1986. Op. Cit.
15. Chapman Pincher: *The Spycatcher Affair – A Web of Deception*, p43–44. Sidgwick & Jackson, 1987.
16. Ibid, pp. 26–30.
17. Chapman Pincher: 'Synopsis – Their Trade Is Treachery', 5 December 1980, Exhibit 50, United Kingdom vs. Wright & Others, Supreme Court of New South Wales.
18. Chapman Pincher letters to Peter Wright, January–March 1981. Malcolm Turnbull, *The Spycatcher Trial*, p.100. Heinemann, 1988.

19. He was given a life peerage in February 1982, awarded a year after he gave the government the copy of Pincher's book.
20. Internal Downing Street memo from Deputy Cabinet Secretary Sir Christopher Mallaby to Sir Nigel Wicks, Margaret Thatcher's Private Secretary, 23 September 1987. Prime Minister's file PREM19/2508., declassified December 2023.
21. Sir Robert Armstrong: memo to Margaret Thatcher, 17 February 1981. National Archives file PREM19/591; declassified December 2023.
22. Handwritten note by Nigel Wicks on Sir Robert Armstrong's memo, 17 February 1981. National Archives file PREM19/591; declassified December 2023.
23. Chapman Pincher: *Their Trade Is Treachery*, p.232. Sidgwick & Jackson, 1981.
24. Formal admissions by Theo Simos QC in interlocutory proceedings during the *Spycatcher* trial, 10 December 1986. [Quoted in]: Malcolm Turnbull, *The Spycatcher Trial*, p.185. Heinemann, 1988.
25. MI5 report on *Their Trade Is Treachery*, 12 March 1981. Prime Minister's file PREM19/591. This file was declassified in December 2023 but MI5's memo was removed prior to release. However, the file was provided to, and the memo quoted by, Thatcher's official biographer. Charles Moore, *Margaret Thatcher – The Authorized Biography*, Vol. 3, p. 233. Allen Lane, 2019.
26. Sir Robert Armstrong, letter to Margaret Thatcher, March 16, 1981. Prime Minister's file PREM19/591; declassified December 2023.
27. The two men were not related.
28. Sir Robert Armstrong, Cabinet Secretary, letter to William Armstrong, Managing Director Sidgwick & Jackson, 23 March 1981. Exhibit 3, United Kingdom vs. Wright & Others, Supreme Court of New South Wales.

Chapter 13

1. Interview with Jonathan Aitken, Chief Secretary to the Treasury, 1994–95. 13 December 2021.
2. 'Security': Prime Minister's Statement, 26 March 1981. *Hansard*.
3. Sir John Hunt, Cabinet Secretary. 'Top Secret' Memo for the Prime Minister on the penetration of the Security Service and MI6, 5 August 1975. National Archives file PREM16/2230; declassified December 2016.
4. Sir Robert Armstrong, memo to Thatcher, 17 February 1981. Prime Minister's file PREM19/591; declassified December 2023.

Endnotes

5. Prime ministerial files, kept secret for more than 40 years, show that two days prior to her speech Thatcher held a succession of meetings with Trend in the Cabinet Office, and secured his acquiescence to her untruthful statement. National Archives file PREM19/1952; declassified December 2023.
6. 'Security': Prime Minister's Statement, 26 March 1981. *Hansard*.
7. It was largely mothballed by the early 2000s, and finally abolished by the Public Bodies Act 2011.
8. 'Cabinet Office Papers, 12 & 21 December 1981'. These documents are still withheld from the National Archives, but are quoted in: Ian Beesley, *The Official History of the Cabinet Secretaries*, p.410. Routledge, 2017.
9. 'Public Service Security': Statement by the Prime Minister, 19 May 1982. *Hansard*.
10. 'Security Commission: review of security procedures'. National Archives file PREM 19/1634; declassified December 2014.
11. Prime Minister: reply to written Parliamentary Question from Bob Cryer MP, 27 March 1981. *Hansard*.
12. Interview with Paul Greengrass, 15 September 2021.
13. Interview with Jonathan Aitken, Chief Secretary to the Treasury, 1994–95. 13 December 2021.
14. Affidavit of Peter Maurice Wright – Confidential Material. United Kingdom vs. Heinemann Australia & Peter Wright, Supreme Court of New South Wales, 8 November 1986.
15. Affidavit of Peter Maurice Wright, 8 November 1986. Op. Cit.
16. Chapman Pincher letters to Peter Wright, May–July 1981. Malcolm Turnbull, *The Spycatcher Trial*, p.100. Heinemann, 1988.
17. Interview with Nigel West, 30 November 2021.
18. Nigel West: MI5: British Security Service Operations, 1909–45, Bodley Head, 1981.
19. Interview with Nigel West, 30 November 2021.
20. Ibid.
21. Ibid.
22. Letter from John Allen, MI5 Director of Establishments, to Peter Wright, 20 July 1981. Exhibit, United Kingdom vs. Heinemann Australia & Peter Wright, Supreme Court of New South Wales.
23. Affidavit of John Nursaw, legal secretary to the Attorney General: HM Attorney General v. Rupert Allason, aka Nigel West, 13 October 1982. Exhibit 2, United Kingdom vs. Heinemann Australia & Peter Wright, Supreme Court of New South Wales.
24. Interview with Nigel West, 30 November 2021.

25. Sir Robert Armstrong, memo to Thatcher, 8 October 1982; quoted in Ian Beesley, *The Official History of the Cabinet Secretaries*, p.416. Routledge, 2017.
26. 'Armstrong to Thatcher', 8 October 1982. Prime Minister's file PREM 19/1951. This file was released to the National Archives on 29 December 2023, but it was previously provided to Thatcher's official biographer, Charles Moore. His 2019 book quotes the Armstrong memo, but it is missing from the file released to the National Archives. *Margaret Thatcher – The Authorized Biography, Vol. 3*, p.233. Allen Lane, 2019.
27. Interview with Nigel West, 30 November 2021.
28. 'Armstrong to Thatcher', 18 November 1982. [Quoted in:] Ian Beesley, *The Official History of the Cabinet Secretaries*, p.417. Op. Cit.
29. Sir Robert Armstrong: memo to Thatcher, 18 November 1982. National Archives file PREM19/1951; declassified December 2023.
30. 'Prime Minister's Papers, Security of the Secret Services', 20 June 1983. [Quoted in:] Ian Beesley, *The Official History of the Cabinet Secretaries*, p.417. Op. Cit.
31. The warning had only limited effect. West temporarily shelved his MI6 book, but within two years published two new volumes on British Intelligence, and in 1987 would be elected as Conservative MP for Torbay.
32. 'Dear Pensioner': Letter from John Allen, MI5 Director of Establishments, to retired MI5 staff, 22 November 1982. Exhibit, United Kingdom vs. Heinemann Australia & Peter Wright, Supreme Court of New South Wales.
33. Between April and June 1982, British land and forces fought a ten-week war to reclaim the Falkland Islands and South Georgia from occupying Argentinian troops. The action was successful militarily and politically, and is credited with helping Margaret Thatcher win a landslide victory at the 1983 general election; but the government's heavy-handed control of newspaper and broadcast reporting led to complaints of unwarranted censorship.
34. Chapman Pincher letter to Peter Wright, 27 January 1983. [Quoted in:] Malcolm Turnbull, *The Spycatcher Trial*, p.p. 99–100. Heinemann, 1988.
35. Interview with Lord Neil Kinnock, 1 December 2021.
36. 'Jonathan Bloch': Draft Home Office statement, undated but circa November 1983. Prime Minister's file PREM 19/1621. This file is closed at National Archives by order of the Cabinet Office. It was, however, disclosed to the 'official historian' of the Cabinet Secretaries,

Ian Beesley [Op. Cit.], and to Mr. Bloch; he has provided the author with a copy.
37. Sir Robert Armstrong: memo to the Prime Minister's Parliamentary Private Secretary, 9 March 1983. Prime Minister's file PREM 19/1621; Op. cit.
38. Jonathan Bloch and Patrick Fitzgerald: *British Intelligence and Covert Action*; Brandon Books, Co. Kerry, 1983.
39. Sir Robert Armstrong: memo to the Prime Minister, 11 April 1983. Prime Minister's file PREM 19/1621; Op. Cit.
40. Sir Robert Armstrong: memo to the Prime Minister's Parliamentary Private Secretary, 22 April 1983. Prime Minister's file PREM 19/1621; Op. Cit.
41. Prime Minister's note on Home Office memo, 10 August 1983. Prime Minister's file PREM 19/1621; Op. Cit.
42. 'Bloch': Note by Home Office officials, November 1983. Prime Minister's file PREM 19/1621; Op. Cit.
43. 'Prime Minister's Papers/Publication of *British Intelligence Covert Action*', 19 December 1983. Document withheld from the National Archives, but quoted in: Ian Beesley, *The Authorized History of the Cabinet Secretaries*, p.417. Routledge, 2017.
44. Foreign Office memo to the Prime Minister's Office, 1 September 1983. Prime Minister's file PREM 19/1621; Op. Cit.
45. The tactic did not, in any event, succeed. Forty years on, Jonathan Bloch remains a lawful resident of the United Kingdom.
46. Sir Robert Armstrong to Thatcher's PPS, 20 June 1983. Prime Minister's file PREM19/591 declassified, December 2023. This document was withheld from the file released to the National Archives, but it was provided to, and quoted by, Thatcher's official biographer. Charles Moore, *Margaret Thatcher – The Authorized Biography, Vol. 3*, p. 233. Allen Lane, 2019.

Chapter 14

1. Interview with Malcolm Turnbull, Peter Wright's lawyer: 11 August 2021.
2. Paul Greengrass, *The Reunion*, BBC Radio 4, 10 April 2015.
3. Paul Greengrass interview, 15 September 2021.
4. Ibid.
5. Chapman Pincher: letters to Peter Wright, 1981–83. Provided by David Hooper, Wright's lawyer 1984–87.
6. Paul Greengrass interview, 15 September 2021.
7. Chapman Pincher: letters to Peter Wright, 1981–83. Provided by David Hooper, Wright's lawyer 1984–87.

8. Tony Motion, former MI5 officer: interview in *Panorama*, 23 February 1981. Exhibit 16, United Kingdom vs. Heinemann Australia & Peter Wright, Supreme Court of New South Wales, November 1986
9. Miranda Ingram: 'The Trouble with Security: The background to the Bettaney case by a former colleague who worked with him in MI5'. *New Society*, 31 May 1984. Exhibit 6, United Kingdom vs. Heinemann Australia & Peter Wright, Supreme Court of New South Wales, November 1986.
10. Paul Greengrass interview, 15 September 2021.
11. Interview with David Hooper, lawyer for Peter Wright and Heinemann Australia. 17 February 2022.
12. Paul Greengrass interview, 15 September 2021.
13. Sir Robert Armstrong: memo to the Home Secretary and Attorney General, 8 December 1986. National Archives file PREM19/1953; declassified December 2023.
14. Sir Christopher Mallaby, Deputy Cabinet Secretary, to Nigel Wick, Prime Miniter's Personal Secretary, 21 November 1986. National Archives file PREM19/1952; declassified December 2023.
15. Sir Robert Armstrong: memo to the Home Secretary and Attorney General, 8 December 1986. National Archives file PREM19/1953; declassified December 2023.
16. Ibid.
17. Telex from UK Government office, Sydney, to Sir Robert Armstrong and Sir Christopher Mallaby, 9 December 1986. National Archives file PREM19/1953; declassified December 2023.
18. 'The Spy Who Never Was'; *World in Action*, ITV, 16 July 1984. Exhibit 18, United Kingdom vs. Heinemann Australia & Peter Wright Supreme Court of New South Wales.

Chapter 15

1. 'Prime Minister's Papers, Security of the Secret Services', 16 July 1984. Quoted in: Ian Beesley, *The Official History of the Cabinet Secretaries*, p.457. Routledge, 2017.
2. 'Security Service Archives', [quoted in]:Christopher Andrew, *Defence of the Realm – The Authorized History of MI5*, p.762. Allen Lane, 2009.
3. Ibid.
4. Sir Robert Armstrong: 'Note for Ministerial discussion', 20 July 1984. Quoted in: Ian Beesley, *The Official History of the Cabinet Secretaries*, p.417. Routledge, 2017.
5. Sir Anthony Kershaw: letter to Margaret Thatcher, 18 July 1984. National Archives file PREM19/1951; declassified December 2023.

Endnotes

6. Sir Robert Armstrong: note for file, 31 July 1984. National Archives file PREM19/1951; declassified December 2023.
7. Sir Anthony Kershaw MP; letter to Sir Robert Armstrong, 10 August 1984. National Archives file PREM19/1951; declassified December 2023.
8. 'Cabinet Office Archive, 7 September 1984'. Quoted in: Ian Beesley, *The Official History of the Cabinet Secretaries*, p.457. Routledge, 2017.
9. Sir Robert Armstrong: memo to Thatcher, 28 September 1984. National Archives file PREM19/1951; declassified December 2023.
10. Sir Anthony Kerhsaw MP: draft speech, 2 October 1984. National Archives file PREM19/1951; declassified December 2023.
11. 'Prime Minister's Papers, Security of the Secret Services, 24 September 1984'. Quoted in: Ian Beesley, *The Official History of the Cabinet Secretaries*, p.457. Routledge, 2017.
12. 'Prime Minister's Papers, Security of the Secret Services, 24 October 1984'. Quoted in: Ian Beesley, *The Official History of the Cabinet Secretaries*, p.457. Routledge, 2017.
13. 'Prime Minister's Papers, Security of the Secret Services, 11 November 1984'. Quoted in: Ian Beesley, *The Official History of the Cabinet Secretaries*, p.458. Routledge, 2017.
14. Sir Anthony Kershaw MP: letter to Peter Wright, 18 January 1985. Exhibit, United Kingdom vs. Heinemann Australia & Peter Wright, Supreme Court of New South Wales, November 1986.
15. Interview with Lord Neil Kinnock, 1 December 2021.
16. Mr Justice (Sir Anthony) McCowan: Summing Up, Rv. vs. Ponting, 8 February 1985. Remarkably, this official court document is itself still secret. The government's files on the Ponting prosecution are closed and withheld from the National Archives until 2066. However, a 'contraband' copy of the judgment, provided to the Prime Minister's office on 25 February 1985, was subsequently leaked.
17. Christopher Andrew: *Defence of The Realm – The Authorized History of MI5*, pp.757–58. Allen Lane 2009. No government or Security Service files on the Massiter case have been declassified.
18. *MI5's Official Secrets*, Channel 4 Television, 6 March 1985. Exhibit, United Kingdom vs. Heinemann Australia & Peter Wright, Supreme Court of New South Wales, November 1986.
19. Christopher Andrew: *Defence of the Realm – The Authorized History of MI5*, p.758. Allen Lane 2009.
20. 'Security Service Archives' [quoted in]: Christopher Andrew: *Defence of the Realm – The Authorized History of MI5*, p.559. Allen Lane 2009.

21. 'Blunt Papers: Secret': Internal Downing Street Memo from B.H. Dinwiddy, 14 January 1987. National Archives file PREM19/3942; declassified July 2018.
22. Interview with Paul Greengrass, 15 September 2021.
23. 'Security Service Archives' [quoted in]: Christopher Andrew, *Defence of the Realm: The Authorized History of MI5*, p.762. Op. cit.
24. Brian Perman, former Managing Director, Heinemann (UK), interview on *The Reunion*: BBC Radio 4, 10 April 2015.
25. Contract between Heinemann Australia Ltd and Project Tasmania Associates. Exhibit D, United Kingdom vs. Heinemann Australia & Peter Wright, Supreme Court of New South Wales, November 1986.
26. Interview with Paul Greengrass, 15 September 2021.
27. Paul Greengrass interview on *The Reunion*: BBC Radio 4, 10 April 2015.
28. Sir Robert Armstrong interview on *The Reunion*: BBC Radio 4, 10 April 2015.

Chapter 16

1. 'I Spy': *Observer*, 31 March 1985.
2. Sir Antony Duff commanded a Royal Navy submarine during the Second World War, winning the Distinguished Service Order for a daring escape from German destroyers. In 1945 he joined the diplomatic corps, serving as an ambassador and a high commissioner in Nepal and Kenya, and as the last Deputy Governor of Rhodesia prior to its independence. He moved to the Cabinet Office and, although he had no experience of espionage or agent handling, chaired the Joint Intelligence Committee before being appointed as MI5's Director General.
3. 'Cabinet Office Archive, 4 June 1985', [quoted in]: Ian Beesley, *The Official History of the Cabinet Secretaries*, p.458–59. Routledge, 2017.
4. Ibid.
5. 'Security Service Archives', [quoted in]:Christopher Andrew, *Defence of the Realm – The Authorized History of MI5*, p.762. Allen Lane, 2009.
6. Mason was a former Solicitor-General of Australia who was appointed to the bench of the High Court of Australia in 1972. Fifteen years later he became its Chief Justice.
7. Commonwealth of Australia v. John Fairfax & Sons Ltd. High Court of Australia, 1 December 1980. 147 CLR 39.
8. Sir Robert Armstrong: memo to Margaret Thatcher, 25 June 1985. Prime Minister's file PREM19/1951; declassified December 2023.
9. Index of exhibits: United Kingdom vs. Heinemann Australia & Peter Wright, Supreme Court of New South Wales, November 1986

10. Interview with David Hooper, 17 February 2022.
11. Letters from Peter Wright and Heinemann Australia Ltd to Stephen Jacques Stone James, Solicitors, 26 & 28 August 1985. Exhibits: United Kingdom vs. Heinemann Australia & Peter Wright, Supreme Court of New South Wales, November 1986.
12. Interview with Jonathan Aitken, 13 December 2021.
13. Interview with Lord Neil Kinnock, 1 December 2021.
14. Sir Michael Havers interview: BBC *Newsnight*, 4 January 1988.
15. 'Prime Minister's Papers, Security of the Secret Services, 7 August 1985. [quoted in]: Ian Beesley, *The Official History of the Cabinet Secretaries*, p. 459. Routledge, 2017.
16. 'Cabinet Office Archives, 31 July 1985', [quoted in]: Ian Beesley, *The Official History of the Cabinet Secretaries*, p.459. Op. Cit.
17. Affidavit of Sir Robert Temple Armstrong, Cabinet Secretary, 9 September 1985. United Kingdom vs. Heinemann Australia & Peter Wright, Supreme Court of New South Wales.
18. *Baker Street Irregular*; Bickham Sweet-Escott, Methuen, London, 1965.
19. *Secret Agent*; 'John Whitwell' [Leslie Nicholson]; William Kimber, London, 1966.
20. The ghost-writer was Michael Thwaites, Director of B2. He sent his draft chapters to MI5 for information. Letter from Security Liaison Officer, Office of the High Commissioner for the United Kingdom, to MI5, 28 December 1954. National Archives file KV2/3448; declassified April 2011.
21. Second Affidavit of Sir Robert Temple Armstrong, Cabinet Secretary, 27 September 1985. United Kingdom vs. Heinemann Australia & Peter Wright, Supreme Court of New South Wales.
22. Interview with David Hooper, lawyer for Heinemann Australia and Peter Wright, 17 February 2022.
23. 'Cabinet Office Archive 18 September 1985', [quoted in]: Ian Beesley, *The Official History of the Cabinet Secretaries*, p.459. Routledge, 2017.
24. 'Cabinet Office Archive 4 October 1985', [quoted in]: Ian Beesley, *The Official History of the Cabinet Secretaries*, p.459. op. Cit.
25. Ian Beesley, The Official History of the Cabinet Secretaries, p.459. op. Cit.
26. Interview with Jonathan Aitken, Chief Secretary to the Treasury, 1994–95. 13 December 2021
27. Sir Robert Armstrong; memo to Nigel Wicks, Prime Minister's Private Secretary, 27 November 1985. National Archives file PREM19/1951; declassified December 2023.

28. Nigel Wicks, Prime Minister's Principal Private Secretary, letter to Sir Robert Armstrong, 27 November 1985. National Archives file PREM19/1951; declassified December 2023.
29. Interview with Sandy Grant, former Managing Director of Heinemann Australia, 23 February 2022.
30. Interview with David Hooper, lawyer for Heinemann Australia and Peter Wright, 17 February 2022.
31. Peter Wright: letter to Heinemann Australia; undated, but *circa* January 1986. [Quoted in]: David Hooper, *Official Secrets*, p.321. Coronet, 1988.

Chapter 17

1. The Australian Liberal Party is not, as its name might imply, particularly liberal. Its political orientation is roughly equivalent to that of the Conservative Party in Britain.
2. Royal Commission on the Activities of the Federated Ship Painters and Dockers Union. https://www.parliament.vic.gov.au/papers/govpub/VPARL1982-85No175.pdf
3. Interview with Malcolm Turnbull, 11 August 2021.
4. Malcolm Turnbull: *The Spycatcher Trial*, p.11. Mandarin, 1988.
5. Ibid., p.12.
6. Cabinet Office Archive, 19 September 1986', [quoted in]: Ian Beesley, *The Official History of the Cabinet Secretaries*, p.460. Routledge, 2017.
7. Interview with Jonathan Aitken, Chief Secretary to the Treasury, 1994–95. 13 December 2021
8. Interview with Sandy Grant, former Managing Director, Heinemann Australia, 23 February 2022.
9. Interview with David Hooper, lawyer for Peter Wright and Heinemann Australia, 17 February 2022.
10. Interview with Malcolm Turnbull, 11 August 2021.
11. Ian Beesley, *The Official History of the Cabinet Secretaries*, p.459. Op. Cit.
12. Affidavit of Peter Maurice Wright, 8 November 1986. United Kingdom vs. Heinemann Australia & Peter Wright, Supreme Court of New South Wales.
13. Malcolm Turnbull: *The Spycatcher Trial*, p.17. Mandarin, 1988.
14. Interview with Malcolm Turnbull, August 11, 2021
15. Malcolm Turnbull: *The Spycatcher Trial*, p.26. Mandarin, 1988.
16. Interview with David Hooper, lawyer for Peter Wright and Heinemann Australia. 17 February 2022.

Endnotes

17. Malcolm Turnbull: *The Spycatcher Trial*, p.26. Mandarin, 1988.
18. Interrogatory on behalf of Defendants, 3 July 1986. Exhibit, United Kingdom vs. Heinemann Australia & Peter Wright, Supreme Court of New South Wales, November 1986.
19. Interview with Paul Greengrass, 15 September 2021.
20. Malcolm Turnbull: *The Spycatcher Trial*, p.31–32 . Mandarin, 1988.
21. Mr Justice (Sir William) Macpherson: *ex parte* injunction, H.M. Attorney General vs. The Observer Ltd, Donald Telford, David Leigh and Paul Lashmar; and H.M. Attorney General vs. Guardian Newspapers Ltd, Peter Preston and Richard Norton Taylor. National Archives files J157/65 & J157/66; declassified January 2017.
22. Mr. Justice (later Lord Peter) Millett; H.M. Attorney General vs. The Observer Ltd, Donald Telford, David Leigh and Paul Lashmar; and H.M. Attorney General vs. Guardian Newspapers Ltd, Peter Preston and Richard Norton Taylor; judgment, 11 July 1986. National Archives files J157/65 & J157/66; declassified January 2017.
23. The Maguire Seven – six men and one woman – were convicted of passing nitroglycerin to the IRA in March 1976. They were sentenced to prison terms ranging from five to fourteen years; one died in prison before the convictions were overturned in 1990.
24. Judgment of Sir John Donaldson, Master of the Rolls, 25 July 1986. H.M. Attorney General vs. Guardian Newspapers Ltd & Observer Newspapers Ltd. National Archives file J157/65; declassified January 2017. Donaldson's verdict was supported by the other two judges on the court, Lord Justice Mustill and Lord Justice Nourse.
25. Plaintiff's answers to Defendant's interrogatories, 1 August 1986. Exhibit, United Kingdom vs. Heinemann Australia & Peter Wright, Supreme Court of New South Wales, November 1986.
26. Sir Robert Armstrong, Cabinet Secretary: Affidavit, 11 August 1986. Exhibit, United Kingdom vs. Heinemann Australia & Peter Wright, Supreme Court of New South Wales, November 1986.
27. 'Cabinet Office Archive, 4 August 1986', [quoted in]: Ian Beesley, *The Official History of the Cabinet Secretaries*, p.458–59. Routledge, 2017.

Chapter 18

1. The adage is generally credited to the early twentieth-century Independent Labour MP James Maxton.
2. Interview with Malcolm Turnbull, 11 August 2021.
3. Interview with David Hooper, lawyer for Peter Wright and Heinemann Australia, 17 February 2022.

4. Theo Simos QC: 'Further Amended Reply on behalf of the British Government, 14 August 1986'. United Kingdom vs. Heinemann Australia & Peter Wright, Supreme Court of New South Wales.
5. 'Cabinet Office Archive, 27 August 1986'. [Quoted in]: Ian Beesley, *The Official History of the Cabinet Secretaries*, p.460. Routledge, 2017.
6. Interview with Malcolm Turnbull, 11 August 2021.
7. Sir Robert Armstrong: memo to Nigel Wicks, Thatcher's PPS, 5 September 1986. National Archives file PREM19/1951; declassified December 2023.
8. Ibid.
9. Sir Robert Armstrong: memo to Thatcher, 3 October 1986. National Archives file PREM19/1952; declassified December 2023.
10. Stella Rimington, *Open Secret*, p.188. Arrow, 2002.
11. Sir Robert Armstrong: memo to Thatcher, 3 October 1986. National Archives file PREM19/1952; declassified December 2023.
12. 'Prime Minister's Papers, The Security of the Secret Services', 7 October 1986. [Quoted in]: Ian Beesley, *The Official History of the Cabinet Secretaries*, p.460. Routledge, 2017.
13. 'Proceedings to prevent publication of books about intelligence and security matters: Background': Australian Cabinet Office memo, 31 October 1986. National Archives of Australia; declassified September 2014.
14. Malcolm Turnbull, *The Spycatcher Trial*, p.53. Mandarin, 1988.
15. Interview with Sandy Grant, former Managing Director, Heinemann Australia, 23 February 2022.
16. [Quoted in]: Malcolm Turnbull, *The Spycatcher Trial*, p.54. Mandarin, 1988
17. Affidavit of Michael Henry Codd, Australian Cabinet Secretary, 14 November 1986. Exhibit, United Kingdom vs. Heinemann Australia & Peter Wright, Supreme Court of New South Wales.
18. Affidavit of 'Anonymous Deponent', 20 October 1986. Exhibit, United Kingdom vs. Heinemann Australia & Peter Wright, Supreme Court of New South Wales.
19. Barrie Penrose and Simon Freeman; *Conspiracy of Silence*, p.598–600. Grafton Books, 1987.
20. Sir Robert Armstrong: 4th affidavit, 6 November 1986: United Kingdom vs. Heinemann Australia & Peter Maurice Wright. Supreme Court of New South Wales, Sydney.
21. Powell J: 'Reasons for Judgment', 13 March 1987. United Kingdom vs. Heinemann Australia & Peter Maurice Wright. Supreme Court of New South Wales, Sydney.

Endnotes

22. Charles Moore, *Margaret Thatcher, The Authorized Biography, Vol. 3*, p.240. Allen Lane, 2019.
23. Interview with Sir Robin (now Lord) Butler, PPS to Margaret Thatcher 1982–85 & Cabinet Secretary 1988–98; 20 December 2021.
24. Interview with Malcolm Turnbull, 11 August 2021.

Chapter 19

1. Ian Beesley: The Official History of the Cabinet Secretaries, p.6–7; Routledge, 2017.
2. Cabinet Secretary Hits Photographer with Briefcase: AP, 12 November 1986.
3. The Supreme Court's title is misleading. It is, in fact, the primary tier of New South Wales justice, with both a state Court of Appeal and the federal High Court of Australia above it.
4. Interview with Malcolm Turnbull, 11 August 2021.
5. Peter Wright quoted in: Barrie Penrose and Simon Freeman, *Conspiracy of Silence,* p.603. Grafton Books, 1987.
6. Interview with Sandy Grant, former Managing Director of Heinemann Australia, 23 February 2022.
7. All cross-examination exchanges in this chapter are drawn from the court transcript: United Kingdom vs. Heinemann Australia & Peter Maurice Wright. Supreme Court of New South Wales, Sydney. 18 November 1986.
8. Interview with Paul Greengrass, 15 September 2021.
9. Sir Robert Armstrong, Cabinet Secretary to Sir William Armstrong, Sidgwick & Jackson publishers; 23 March, 191. Exhibit 3; United Kingdom vs. Heinemann Australia & Peter Maurice Wright. Supreme Court of New South Wales, Sydney.
10. Interview with Malcolm Turnbull, 11 August 2021.
11. Interview with Sandy Grant, former Managing Director of Heinemann Australia, 23 February 2022.
12. Clive Whitmore [Thatcher's PPS], to Armstrong; June 11, 1980. National Archives File PREM 19/591; declassified December 2023
13. *Hansard*, 18 November 1986.
14. Ian Beesley, *The Official History of the Cabinet Secretaries*, p.462. Op. cit.

Chapter 20

1. United Kingdom vs. Heinemann Australia & Peter Maurice Wright. New South Wales Court of Appeal, Sydney. 19 November 1986.

2. Interview with Malcolm Turnbull, 11 August 2021.
3. Malcolm Turnbull, *The Spycatcher Trial*, p. 91. Mandarin, 1988.
4. 'Prime Minister's Papers, Security of the Secret Services, 19 November 1986'. [Quoted in:] Ian Beesley, *The Official History of the Cabinet Secretaries*, p.461. Routledge, 2017.
5. All cross-examination exchanges in this chapter are drawn from the court transcript: United Kingdom vs. Heinemann Australia & Peter Maurice Wright. Supreme Court of New South Wales, Sydney. 19 & 20 November 1986.
6. Sir Robert Armstrong: notes on sensitive cases and documents, 8 December 1986. National Archives file PREM19/1953; declassified December 2023.

Chapter 21

1. Malcolm Turnbull, *The Spycatcher Trial*, p.118. Mandarin, 1988.
2. Interview with Lord Neil Kinnock, 1 December 2021.
3. Prime Minister's Questions, *Hansard*, 20 November 1986.
4. The parliamentary Lobby has been an unpleasant feature of British political reporting since the late nineteenth century. The Lobby – a group of journalists approved by the House of Commons authorities – receives off-the-record briefings from government ministers (as well as opposition parties): these are then regurgitated in the press and media as authoritative, but entirely unattributed, statements of fact.
5. Malcolm Turnbull, *The Spycatcher Trial*, p.133. Mandarin, 1988.
6. Plaintiff's Amended Statement of Claim, 21 November 1986. United Kingdom vs. Heinemann Australia & Peter Maurice Wright. Supreme Court of New South Wales, Sydney.
7. Chrstopher Mallaby memo to Sir Nigel Wicks, Prime Minister's PPS, 13 November 1986. National Archives file PREM19/1952; declassified December 2023.
8. All cross-examination and court exchanges in this chapter are drawn from the official transcript: United Kingdom vs. Heinemann Australia & Peter Maurice Wright. Supreme Court of New South Wales, Sydney. 21 November–8 December 1986.
9. Simon Freeman & Barrie Penrose: 'Fiasco Down Under – The Unmaking of Sir Robert'. *Sunday Times*, 23 November 1986.
10. 'Prime Minister's Papers, Security of the Secret Services', 24 November 1986. Quoted in: Ian Beesley, *The Official History of the Cabinet Secretaries*, p.415. Routledge, 2017.
11. 'Wright Was Paid for Revealing MI5 Secrets'; *The Times*, 24 November 1986.

Endnotes

12. Email interview with Jenny Andrews, Peter Wright's daughter, 13 August 2023.
13. Malcolm Turnbull, *The Spycatcher Trial*, p.133. Mandarin, 1988.
14. Interview with Sandy Grant, former Managing Director of Heinemann Australia, 23 February 2022.
15. Peter Wright: Press Statement, 25 November 1986.
16. 'Rothschild [letter] to Nigel Wicks [Thatcher's Private Secretary], 24 November 1986'. Prime Minister's file PREM 19/1952; declassified December 2023
17. 'Wicks to Boys-Smith, 25 November 1986, Prime Minister's file: PREM 19/1952' – Op. Cit.
18. 'Armstrong [memo] to Whitmore 23 July 1981. Prime Minister's file: PREM 19/591; declassified December 2023.
19. *Hansard*, 26 November 1986.
20. 'Secret Motives'. Leader column, *Daily Telegraph*, 27 November 1986.
21. *Hansard*, 27 November 1986.
22. Interview with Sir Robin (now Lord) Butler, PPS to Margaret Thatcher 1982–85 & Cabinet Secretary 1988–98; 20 December 2021.
23. 'Wicks to Boys-Smith, 1 December 1986 Prime Minister's file: PREM 19/1952' – Op. Cit.
24. Victor, Baron Rothschild: open letter, *Daily Telegraph*, 4 December 1986.
25. *Hansard*, 5 December 1986.
26. Malcolm Turnbull, *The Spycatcher Trial*, p.135–36. Mandarin, 1988.
27. Hickmet lost his seat at the 1987 general election and returned to his practice as a family law barrister. He subsequently served as High Sheriff of Somerset from 2017–18.
28. 'Kinnock has mole at MI5 case'; *Evening Standard*, 3 December 1986.
29. Malcolm Turnbull, *The Spycatcher Trial*, p.164–65. Mandarin, 1988.
30. *Hansard*, 3 December 1986.
31. 'MI5 in shake-up to protect agents'; *Mail on Sunday*, 7 December 1986.
32. Interview with Sir Robin (now Lord) Butler, PPS to Margaret Thatcher 1982–85 & Cabinet Secretary 1988–98; 20 December 2021.

Chapter 22

1. All cross-examination and court exchanges in this chapter are drawn from the official transcript: United Kingdom vs. Heinemann Australia & Peter Maurice Wright. Supreme Court of New South Wales, Sydney. 8–9 December 1986.

2. William Rees-Mogg: 'A farce with old friends and a chorus of madmen'. *Independent*, 2 December 1986.
3. 'Brave Sir Robert Fought for Us All': editorial, *Mail on Sunday*, 7 December 1986.
4. 'Cabinet Decision, 10 November 1986', Australian National Archives; declassified September 2014.
5. 'Royal Commission on Intelligence and Security', 1975. Australian National Archives.
6. Cross-examination of Michael Codd, Australian Cabinet Secretary, United Kingdom vs. Heinemann Australia & Peter Maurice Wright. Supreme Court of New South Wales, Sydney. 1 December 1986.
7. Interview with David Hooper, lawyer for Heinemann Australia and Peter Wright, 17 February 2022.
8. Telegram from Christopher Mallaby to Sir Robert Armstrong, 17 November 1986. National Archives file PREm19/1952; declassified December 2023.
9. Testimony of Gough Whitlam, United Kingdom vs. Heinemann Australia & Peter Maurice Wright. Supreme Court of New South Wales, Sydney. 1 December 1986.
10. Testimony of William Schaap, United Kingdom vs. Heinemann Australia & Peter Maurice Wright. Supreme Court of New South Wales, Sydney. 1 December 1986.
11. Email interview with Jenny Andrews, Peter Wright's daughter, 13 August 2023.
12. Peter Wright: Confidential testimony, Testimony of Gough Whitlam, United Kingdom vs. Heinemann Australia & Peter Maurice Wright. Supreme Court of New South Wales, Sydney. 8 December 1986.
13. Malcolm Turnbull: *The Spycatcher Trial*, p.179. Mandarin, 1988.
14. Meeting of Ministerial Group on the Peter Wright Case, 8 December 1986. National Archives file PREM 19/1953; declassified December 2023
15. Sir Ivor Roberts interview: *The Reunion*, BBC Radio 4, 10 April 2015.
16. Malcolm Turnbull: Closing arguments, Testimony of Gough Whitlam, United Kingdom vs. Heinemann Australia & Peter Maurice Wright. Supreme Court of New South Wales, Sydney. 16–17 December 1986.
17. *Hansard*, 15 December 1986.

Chapter 23

1. 'Spy book is stopped'; *Evening Herald*, Dublin, 28 November 1986.
2. Judgment of Miss Justice Melia Caroll, 2 December 1986. National Archives file PREM19/1953; declassified December 2023.

Endnotes

3. Powell J: Judgment in *United Kingdom vs. Peter Wright*, 13 March 1987.
4. Joan Miller, *One Girl's War*, Brandon Books, 1986. Irish copies were quickly shipped to the UK.
5. Sir Patrick Mayhew, Solicitor General, Statement to the House of Commons. *Hansard*, 6 February 1987.
6. Christopher Mallaby: memo to Nigel Wicks, Prime Minister's PPS, 8 December 1986. National Archives file PREM19/1953; declassified December 2023.
7. Kenneth Rose, *Elusive Rothschild – The Life of Victor, Third Baron Rothschild*, p. 278–80. Weidenfeld & Nicolson, 2003.
8. Internal memo: 'Armstrong to Saunders, 4 February 1987'; Prime Minister's file PREM 19/1954. This file was released to the National Archives in December 2023, but the Armstrong correspondence was removed from it. However, the file was previously provided to, and the memo quoted by, Thatcher's official biographer. Charles Moore, *Margaret Thatcher – The Authorized Biography, Vol. 3*, p. 245–46. Allen Lane, 2019.
9. Sir Patrick Mayhew, Attorney General: Written Answer, *Hansard*, 9 July 1987.
10. For readers born after the *Spycatcher* case concluded, *The Boy's Own Paper* featured weekly tales of adventure from 1879 to 1967; *Biggles* – a series of almost 100 novels and stories about a flying ace in both world wars – was a staple of middle-class childhood from 1932 to 1968.
11. All court exchanges in this chapter are drawn from the official transcript: *United Kingdom vs. Heinemann Australia & Peter Maurice Wright*. Supreme Court of New South Wales, Sydney. 13 March 1987.
12. The Australian equivalent of MI6.
13. Richard v. Hall, *A Spy's Revenge*, p.193. Penguin Australia, 1987.
14. 'Thatcher is still determined to stop book's publication'. *The Times*, 13 March 1987.
15. *Hansard*, 16 March 1987.
16. 'Thatcher ignores MI5 inquiry calls', *The Times*, 20 March 1987.

Chapter 24

1. 'When the Security Service turns to treason'; Editorial, *Independent*, 27 April 1987.
2. 'How MI5 plotted Wilson's fall'; *Independent*, 27 April 1987.
3. 'Security Service Archives', [quoted in] Christopher Andrew, *Defence of the Realm – The Authorized History of MI5*, p. 642. Allen Lane, 2009.
4. 'Cabinet Office Archive, 2 April 1987'. Quoted in: Ian Beesley, *The Official History of the Cabinet Secretaries*, p.463. Routledge, 2017.

5. Memo from Sir Robert Armstrong to the Prime Minister, 3 April 1987. Prime Minister's file PREM 19/2500. This file has not been released to the National Archives, but it was provided to, and quoted by, Thatcher's official biographer. Charles Moore, *Margaret Thatcher – The Authorized Biography, Vol. 3*, p. 251. Allen Lane, 2019.
6. 'Prime Minister's papers: reform of the Official Secrets Act, 7 April 1987. Quoted in: Ian Beesley, *The Official History of the Cabinet Secretaries*, p.463. Routledge, 2017.
7. The *London Daily News* was owned by Robert Maxwell and intended to be a '24 hour paper' which challenged the *Standard's* dominance. It lasted precisely five months, closing down in July 1987, just twelve weeks after republishing the *Independent's* scoop.
8. 'Cabinet Office Archive, April 27, 1987'. Quoted in: Ian Beesley, *The Official History of the Cabinet Secretaries*, p.463. Routledge, 2017.
9. Memo from Sir Antony Duff to Sir Robert Armstrong, 28 April 1987. Prime Minister's file PREM 19/2506. This file was declassified in December 2023 but Duff's memo was removed prior to release. However, the file was provided to, and the memo quoted by, Thatcher's official biographer. Charles Moore, *Margaret Thatcher – The Authorized Biography, Vol. 3*, p. 251. Allen Lane, 2019.
10. 'Prime Minister's Papers, Security of the Secret Services, 28 April 1987'. Quoted in: Ian Beesley, *The Official History of the Cabinet Secretaries*, p.463. Routledge, 2017.
11. Memo from Bernard Ingham to Sir Nigel Wicks, Margaret Thatcher's Principal Private Secretary, 30 April 1987. Prime Minister's file PREM19/2506; declassified December 2023.
12. Memo from Wicks to Boys-Smith, 30 April 1987. Prime Minister's file PREM19/2506. This file was declassified in December 2023 but the memo was removed prior to release. However, the file was provided to, and the memo quoted by, Thatcher's official biographer. Charles Moore, *Margaret Thatcher – The Authorized Biography, Vol. 3*, p. 251. Allen Lane, 2019.
13. Memo from Nigel Wicks to Thatcher, 30 April 1987. National Archives file PREM19/2506; declassified December 2023.
14. Memo from Sir Antony Duff to Margaret Thatcher, 5 May 1987. Prime Minister's file PREM19/2506. This file was declassified in December 2023 but Duff's memo was removed prior to release. However, the file was provided to, and the memo quoted by, Thatcher's official biographer. Charles Moore, *Margaret Thatcher – The Authorized Biography, Vol. 3*, p. 251. Allen Lane, 2019.

Endnotes

15. Memo from Sir Robert Armstrong to Sir Nigel Wicks, 5 May 1987. Prime Minister's file PREM19/2506. This file was declassified in December 2023 but Armstrong's memo was removed prior to release. However, the file was provided to, and the memo quoted by, Thatcher's official biographer. Charles Moore, *Margaret Thatcher – The Authorized Biography*, Vol. 3, p. 252. Allen Lane, 2019.
16. *Hansard*, 6 May 1987.
17. Sir Nigel Wicks: memo to Thatcher, 19 March 1987. National Archives file PREM19/2505; declassified December 2023.
18. Memo from Sir Nigel Wicks to Margaret Thatcher, 11 May 1987. Prime Minister's file PREM19/2506. This file was declassified in December 2023 but Wicks's memo was removed prior to release. However, the file was provided to, and the memo quoted by, Thatcher's official biographer. Charles Moore, *Margaret Thatcher – The Authorized Biography*, Vol. 3, p. 251. Allen Lane, 2019.
19. Ibid.
20. Memo from Margaret Thatcher to Sir Robert Armstrong, 26 May 1987. Prime Minister's file PREM19/2506. This file was declassified in December 2023 but Thatcher's memo was removed prior to release. However, the file was provided to, and the memo quoted by, Thatcher's official biographer. Charles Moore, *Margaret Thatcher – The Authorized Biography*, Vol. 3, p. 252. Allen Lane, 2019.
21. The son of a Church of England canon and the grandson of a bishop, Wilkinson was a legal scholar and Queen's Counsel who had been a Lord Justice of Appeal and member of the Privy Council since 1983. His only, subsequent, brush with controversy – he overturned a lower court ruling which opened the door to prosecuting the deposed Chilean dictator Augusto Pinochet – suggested he resided on the judiciary's conservative flanks.
22. Sir Nicolas Browne-Wilkinson, Vice-Chancellor; Court of Appeal, 2 June 1987. Attorney General *v* Newspaper Publishing PLC & Others. National Archives file J157/76; declassified, January 2018.
23. Sir Robert Armstrong: memo to Thatcher, 3 July 1987. National Archives file PREM 19/2507; declassified December 2023.
24. Stella Rimington, *Open Secret – The Autobiography of the Former Director-General of MI5*, p.194–95; Hutchinson/Arrow, 2001.
25. Ian Beesley, *The Official History of the Cabinet Secretaries*, p.464. Routledge, 2017.
26. Jonathan Aitken, *Margaret Thatcher – Power and Personality*, p.518. Bloomsbury, 2013.

27. Interview with Lord Robin Butler, 20 December 2021.
28. Anthony Blunt: *Memoirs*. Typescript held at the British Library and released for public consumption in July 2009.
29. Sir Robert Armstrong; memo to Sir Nigel Wicks, Prime Minister's PPS, 23 June 1987. National Archives file PREM 19/3942; declassified July 2018.
30. Andrew Neil, *Full Disclosure*, p.32. Pan, 1997.
31. 'The Spycatcher – Why Was He Not Caught?' Lord Desmond Ackner, Lord of Appeal in Ordinary, 1986–93; Azlan Shah Law Lecture, 24 September 1989.

Chapter 25

1. 'Banned book on sale outside Parliament': *The Times*, 16 July 1987.
2. *Daily Mirror*, 13 July 1987.
3. *Hansard*, 13 July 1987.
4. *Hansard*, 14 July 1987.
5. Peter Wright interview: ITN, *News at One*, 15 July 1987.
6. Sir John Donaldson, Master of the Rolls; H.M. Attorney General *v* Newspaper Publishing and Others, 17 July 1987. National Archives file J157/76; declassified January 2018.
7. 'Spycatcher sales boom sweeps US'; *Aberdeen Press & Journal*, 4 August 1987.
8. Attorney-General v. Guardian Newspapers Ltd. (No. 2) [1988] 2 W.L.R. 805, 820–21.
9. *Attorney-General v. Guardian Newspapers Ltd.* [1987] 1 W.L.R. 1248, 1306, House of Lords
10. Ibid.
11. 'The Rabbit and the Ass'; *The Times*, editorial, 27 July 1987.
12. *The Economist*, 25 July 1987.
13. The Law Lords – senior judges appointed by the Crown who sat as a panel of the House of Lords – were replaced by the Supreme Court in 2009.
14. *Attorney-General v. Guardian Newspapers Ltd.* [1987] 3 All ER 316.
15. 'Sharp exchange as Lords are split'; *The Times*, 31 July 1987.
16. Attorney-General v. Guardian Newspapers Ltd. [1987] 3 All ER 316.
17. 'Lords ban all reporting of Wright book'; *The Times*, 31 July 1987.
18. 'A very Dangerous Day'; *The Times* editorial, 31 July 1987.
19. *Daily Mirror*, 31 July 1987.
20. 'Benn flouts ruling to read from *Spycatcher*'; *The Times*, 3 August 1987.

21. 'Public readings of banned MI5 Spycatcher book'; *The Sentinel* [daily regional newspaper], 7 August 1987.
22. 'Pssst! Spy book is in the House', *Sunday Mirror*, 16 August 1987.
23. *The Economist;* classified adverts, 22 August 1987.
24. '"Spycatcher" menu attracts the customers'; *Aberdeen Press & Journal*, 18 September 1987.
25. 'Pssst! Spy book is in the House', *Sunday Mirror*, 16 August 1987.
26. 'Warning over Spycatcher'; *Newcastle Evening Chronicle*, 26 August 1987.
27. 'Council slams Spycatcher ban'; *Derby Evening Telegraph*, 17 October 1987.
28. 'Cabinet Office Archive, 28 August 1987'. Quoted in: Ian Beesley, *The Official History of the Cabinet Secretaries*, p.465. Routledge, 2017.
29. Attorney-General v. South China Morning Post Ltd. 8 September 1987. National Archives file FCO 40/2343; declassified April 2017.
30. Attorney-General v. South China Morning Post Ltd. 2 August 1987. National Archives file FCO 40/2343; declassified April 2017.
31. Memo from Prime Minister's Office to the Cabinet Office, 12 October 1987. National Archives file FCO 30/7004; declassified February 2018.
32. Memo from Home Secretary Douglas Hurd to the Prime Minister, 16 October 1987. National Archives file FCO 30/7004; declassified February 2018.
33. Mr Justice Michael Kirby: Judgment, *United Kingdom vs. Heinemann Australia & Peter Wright*, New South Wales Appeal Court, 24 September 1987.
34. Interview with Sandy Grant, former Managing Director of Heinemann Australia, 23 February 2022.
35. 'Judgment of Davison C.J.': H.M. Attorney General v. Wellington Newspaper Ltd, 15 December 1987.
36. 'England's censorship isn't quaint'. Richard Cohen, *Washington Post*, 14 August 1987.
37. Attorney General v. Guardian Newspapers Ltd & The Observer Ltd, 21 December 1987.
38. 'Season without End'; *The Times* editorial, 23 December 1987.
39. 'Home Office Archives', [quoted in] Christopher Andrew, *Defence of the Realm – The Authorized History of MI5*, p. 563. Allen Lane, 2009.
40. Margaret Thatcher: interview on BBC *Nine O'Clock News*, 21 December 1987. Margaret Thatcher Foundation, [documents held at] Churchill College, Cambridge.

41. 'Court fines *Spycatcher* seller'; *Ealing Gazette*, 18 December 1987.
42. 'Protection of Official Information Bill – Second Reading'; *Hansard*, 15 January 1988.

Chapter 26

1. Interview with Sandy Grant, former Managing Director of Heinemann Australia, 23 February 2022.
2. *Attorney General v Observer & The Guardian*. Court of Appeal, 10 February 1988. 3 All ER 545.
3. Charles Moore, *Margaret Thatcher – The Authorized Biography, Vol. 3*, p. 253. Allen Lane 2019.
4. *Hansard*, 10 March 1988.
5. Interview with Malcolm Turnbull, 11 August 2021.
6. Interview with David Hooper, lawyer for Heinemann Australia and Peter Wright, 17 February 2022.
7. 'The Final Chapter?'; *The Times* editorial, 3 June 1988.
8. Interview with Sir Robin (now Lord) Butler, PPS to Margaret Thatcher 1982–85 & Cabinet Secretary 1988–98; 20 December 2021.
9. 'Attorney General v. *The Observer Ltd.* and Others; Attorney General v. *Times Newspapers Ltd*'; Judicial Committee of the House of Lords, 13 October 1988.
10. 'Media freed to publish *Spycatcher*'; *The Times*, 14 October 1988
11. Lord Robert Armstrong: 'In pursuit of *Spycatcher*', *The Times*, 15 October 1988.
12. 'Spycatcher: Wright or Wrong'. BBC *Panorama*, 13 October 1988
13. 'Price and principle'; *The Times* editorial, 14 October 1988.
14. Christopher Andrew, *Defence of the Realm – The Authorized History of MI5*, p.765–66. Allen Lane, 2009.
15. Jonathan Aitken, *Margaret Thatcher – Power and Personality*, p.518. Bloomsbury, 2013.
16. Judgments: 'Case of Observer & Guardian v. The United Kingdom', and 'Case of the Sunday Times v. The United Kingdom'. European Court of Human Rights, Strasbourg, 26 November 1991.
17. Interview with Jonathan Aitken, Chief Secretary to the Treasury, 1994–95. 13 December 2021
18. Interview with Sandy Grant, former Managing Director of Heinemann Australia, 23 February 2022.
19. Email interview with Jenny Andrews, 13 August 2023.
20. In a particularly petty act of spite, the government successfully demanded that Greengrass hand over his own earnings from the book.

Attorney General: memo to Thatcher, 23 November 1988; National Archives file PREM 19/2511; declassified December 2023. Paul Greengrass: email to author, 7 January 2024
21. Interview with Paul Greengrass, 15 September 2021.
22. Interview with David Hooper, lawyer for Peter Wright and Heinemann Australia. 17 February 2022.

Epilogue: Forty Years Later
1. 'Report of the 30 Year Rule Committee,' The Stationery Office [formerly HMSO], 2009.
2. The Cabinet Office Freedom of Information Clearing House: HC 505; published 29 April 2022.
3. 'Access Denied': *openDemocracy*, October 2021.
4. The existence of these files is recorded in the National Archives' catalogue as CAB164/1870-1901; PREM19/1951-1953, PREM19/591, PREM19/2500, PREM19/2505-2510.
5. Author's correspondence with ICO, 2019–23.
6. Author's FOIA requests 2019–23; correspondence with Cabinet Office Minister Baroness Lucy Neville-Rolfe, 12 September 2023.
7. Ian Beesley, *The Official History of the Cabinet Secretaries*, title page folio. Routledge, 2017.
8. Ibid., pp.6–7 & 385–88.
9. Ian Beesley: email to author, 14 March 2022.
10. Thatcher had by then already published two volumes of her own autobiography.
11. Charles Moore, *Margaret Thatcher – The Authorised Biography, Vol.3*, p.xii & xxiv. Allen Lane, 2019.
12. Ibid., p.233 & 241.
13. Interview with Malcolm Turnbull, 11 August 2021.
14. Letter to author from Cabinet Office, 11 May 2023.
15. Email to author from Charles Moore, 13 May 2023.
16. Interview with Sir Robin (now Lord) Butler, PPS to Margaret Thatcher 1982–85 & Cabinet Secretary 1988–98; 20 December 2021.
17. Interview with Lord Neil Kinnock, 1 December 2021.
18. Aitken had sued the *Guardian* for libel over its reports on his dealings with Saudi Arabia.
19. Interview with Jonathan Aitken, 13 December 2021.

INDEX

Ackner, Lord Justice Desmond 303–304
Adeane, Sir Michael 57
Aitken, Jonathan 120, 123–127, 143–144, 182, 186–187, 193, 204–205, 255–256, 282, 293–294, 326, 330, n354, n377
Allen, John 150
Andrew, Prof. Christopher n347
Andrews, Jenny (née Wright) 250, 263, 317, 330
Angleton, James Jesus 74–76, 88–90, 123–124, 126, 128, 163
Apostles Society (Cambridge University) 46–47, 54, 63, 65–66, 102, 106, 186
Armstrong, Sir Robert Temple
  career xi, 110, 213, 324; character xii, 187, 213; attacked photographer at Heathrow airport xii, 214; plot to leak Hollis scandal 4, 127–128, 131, 138, 225, 228, 324–325; first met Wright 110; Blunt exposure 115–116; schemed to circumvent external oversight of MI5 118–120; advised Thatcher to ignore Aitken warning 126; scheme to brief Pincher 127–128, 140–142, 187, 271; *Their Trade Is Treachery* (Chapman Pincher) 139–142, 144–146, 200, 210, 220–224, 231, 244–245, 271, 278, 325; *A Matter of Trust* (Nigel West) 149–152, 210, 217–218, 235, 237, 271; advised Thatcher on Jonathan Bloch 153–154; animus against Wright 166–168, 175; negotiated with Sir Anthony Kershaw 169–171; Blunt's memoirs 175–176, 294; alerted Thatcher to Wright's memoirs 178; led Downing Street's efforts to block *Spycatcher* 179–183; first affidavit 183–184; second affidavit 185; third affidavit 202; fourth affidavit 209–210; suggested planted Parliamentary question 187–188; advised Thatcher against redaction deal with Turnbull 205; assessment of Australian trial prospects 205–206; sought Australian government support 202, 206–207; economical with the truth' xii, 220–222, 271, 315; committed perjury 223–224, 228, 232–233, 256, 260, 325; admitted misleading court 253–254; criticized by Powell 276–278; supported statutory basis for MI5 287, 291; advised Thatcher to attack investigative journalism 287; claimed vindication 315
Armstrong, William 141–142
Attlee, Clement 7, 15–16, 18, 85–86, 134–135
Australian Security & Intelligence Organisation (ASIO) 31–32, 185, 259, 261–262, 279, n363
Australian Royal Commission on Intelligence and Security 259

Bagley, Tennent 'Pete' 88
Bailey, John 151–152, 180–181, 196–197, 208–209
Bates, Charles 89
Baldwin, Stanley 66
Beaverbrook, Lord Max 124, 135
Beesley, Ian 323–326, n358–359
Benn, Tony 304–305
Berger, Ronald and Nancy 19–20
Bernstein, Sidney 95, 157
Bettaney, Michael 161–162,
Blake, George 27, 65, 74, 230
Bloch, Jonathan 153–154, n358–359

379

Blunt, Anthony
  Memoirs 2, 118, 175–176, 294, *n342*;
    recruited Michael Straight for the
    Comintern 48; wartime position and
    work inside MI5 48–49; assignment
    on behalf of the Royal Family 49;
    57–58; appointed Surveyor of the
    Queens Pictures and knighted 49,
    113; recruited John Cairncross 50;
    given immunity 53–54, 113–114;
    recruited Leo Long 54; sexuality 57,
    61–62; education 57; Interrogated
    by Wright 57–71; confessions 57–61,
    64–71, 111; recruited Phoebe Pool
    67–68; central role in *Spycatcher* 99;
    recommended to MI5 by Rothschild
    103; treachery exposed 113–118,
    230; friendship with Rothschilds 102,
    106–107, 115; named in Aitken letter
    125; interviewed by Nigel West 149
Boyle, Andrew 114–115, 128–129
Brandon Books 273–274
Brandon, Lord Justice Henry 303–304
Bridge, Lord Nigel 174–175, 204, 217, 304
Bridges, Sir Edward 9–10, 16
Brookner, Anita 67
Browne-Wilkinson, Sir Nicolas 291–293, 299–301, *n373*
Brundrett, Sir Frederick 12–13
Burke, Edmund 222
Burgess, Guy 9, 29, 31–33, 38, 44, 46–50, 54, 58, 60–67, 74, 103–107, 114, 125, 128, 144, 170, 198, 230, 266, *n337*
Butler, Sir Robin 211, 252, 256, 294, 313–314, 326, 330

Cabinet Office: *Spycatcher* files 321–326
Cairncross, John 50–52, 54, 56, 69
Callaghan, James 99, 114, 286, 289–290
Campaign for Nuclear Disarmament 174
Campbell-Savours, Dale 271–272
Carroll, Lewis
  Alice In Wonderland 3, 204, 255, 297, 303
  Hunting of the Snark vii, 327–328
Carroll, Miss Justice Mella 274
Case, Simon 329
Central Intelligence Agency (CIA) 38, 74–76, 87–90, 123, 229–230, 249, 259, 263
Chemical Defence Establishment (MOD), Porton Down 90
Chilcot, John 118–119, *n353*

Codd, Michael 202, 206–207, 258–260
Comintern [Third International] 36, 48–49, 54, 80
Commonwealth v. John Fairfax & Sons 180–181, 193, 210, 274, 280–281
Communist Party of Great Britain (CPGB) 19–20, 46, 95, 102–103
Contempt of Court 288, 292
Courtiour, Roger 95
Coyne, Patrick 75–76
Cram, Cleveland 75–76
Cripps, Stafford 86
Cryer, Bob 146
Cuban Missile Crisis 35
Cuckney, John 16, *n335*
Cumming, Capt. Mansfield 11

D Notice Committee 150
Daily Express 127, 134–136
Daily Mail 140–142, 148, *n333*
Daily Mirror 304
Dalyell, Tam 172–173, 252
Darcy, Mike 300
Day, John 78–81, 83, *n345*
De Gaulle, Charles 22
Derbyshire County Council 305
Dewick, Tony 9–10, *n334*
Dillon, Lord Justice Brian 311–312
Diplock, Lord Kenneth 146
Dominion, The 302, 308, 312
Donaldson, Sir John 198–201, 280, 299–303, 312
Duff, Sir Anthony 179–180, 286–287, 289–290, 293, 305–306, 316, *n362*

Economist, The 302
Eden, Anthony 17, 21–22
Edwards, John 329
Elder, Walter 89
Elliott, Nicholas 36
European Parliament 3, 306–307
Evans, Michael 249
Evening Standard 204, 254–255, 287–288, 291–293, 299

FBI 9, 14, 25, 36, 42–43, 46–48, 51, 55, 75, 89
Fife, Sir David Maxwell, 18, 174, 201
Figures, Sir Colin 180
Findlater Stewart, Sir Samuel 17–19, *n335*
Floud, Bernard 68–70
Footman, David 63–64

Index

Forte, Sir Charles 140, *n356*
Franks, Sir Arthur Temple 'Dickie' 235–236, 238
Freedom of Information Act (2000) 319, 321–322, 325, 329
Freeman, Simon 66–67, 159, 208–209, 231–232, 278
Fuchs, Klaus 9–10
Furnival Jones, Martin 77–78, 81, 109, 268

Gaitskell, Hugh 37, 87–88, 90
Gilbert & Sullivan 2
Gibson, Col. Harold 60, 121
Glencross, David 163
Goff, Lord Justice Robert 314
Goldsmith, James 96, *n348*
Goleniewski, Lt. Col Michał 26–27, 76–79, 328
Golitsyn, Maj. Anatoliy 32–33, 37, 46–47, 74–75, 87–88, 164
Gordievsky, Oleg 187, *n351*
Gouzenko, Igor: defection 28–31; 'ELLIE' and 'ELLI' spies 28–33, 76, 79, 164, *n337–338*
Granada Television 68–69, 95, 147, 157, 161–165, 232–234, 260, 278
Grant, Sandy 188, 193–194, 207, 215, 222, 250, 307, 311, 317, 330
Gray, Gordon 75–76
Greengrass, Paul
  Assessment of Peter Wright 23, 158–159, 176–177, 195, 318; *World In Action* 147, 157–158, 161–168, 178; sent Wright's dossier to Sir Anthony Kershaw 168; co-author of *Spycatcher* 176–178, 276, 318, *n376–377*; member of Wright's defence team 194, 215, 219, 239, 255–256, 263
Griffiths, Lord Justice Hugh 314
Guardian, The 116, 197–201, 204, 208, 285–286, 288, 292, 299–303, 308, 311–315, 317

Hall, Admiral Reggie 'Blinker' 11
Hampshire, Sir Stuart 62–64, 103, 107 *n350*
Hanley, Sir Michael 96–99; 107; 110–111, 268
Hankey, Sir Maurice 50, *n340*
Hamlyn Paul 182, 207
Hare, Michael, 2nd Viscount Blakenham 290–291
Harman, Harriet 174

Hart, Herbert 68
Hart, Jenifer (*née* Fischer Williams) 68–69
Hattersley, Roy 304
Havers, Sir Michael 115, 152, 180–183, 207, 211, 223, 231, 233–237, 242–243, 245, 250, 252–254, 270–271, 273–275, 282–283
Hawke, Bob 207
Heath, Edward 3, 94, 108–110, 115, 168, 198, 213, 238, 309–310
Heinemann Ltd (publishers) 177–179, 181–183, 188, 193–194, 227, 281, 307, 311–312
Henderson, Ian 107–108
Hewitt, Patricia 174, 262
Hickmet, Richard Saladin 254–255, *n369*
HMSO (Her Majesty's Stationery Office) 306–307
Hollis, Sir Roger
  Investigated as suspected Soviet spy 1, 4, 39, 71, 168–170; tasked Wright with molehunt 26; investigated Gouzenko allegations 30; advised FBI of Philby's treachery 36; fell under suspicion after Philby's defection 38–44; obstructed Wright's molehunts 37–44, 52–53, 56, 65–66, ; closed Straight case 56; hindered Blunt investigation 58–59; chief suspect of FLUENCY committee 75–78, 165, 322, *n345*; humiliated by Gray–Coyne report 76; retired 76; OATSHEAF (Harold Wilson) investigation 89–90; DRAT investigation into him 77, 125–129, 140; interrogated 79–81; inconclusive outcome of DRAT investigation 81–83, 126; death 81; DRAT investigation criticized by De Mowbray 82; case against him 'not proven' 83, *n346*; Aitken warned Thatcher of imminent exposure 125–126; Thatcher statement in Commons 143–147, 266–267; in Powell's judgment 276, 279
Hope, Mr. Justice Robert 259, 261
Hooper, David 181–182, 186, 188–189, 192–194, 196, 204, 215, 260, 313, 318–319, 330
Hoover, J. Edgar 25–26, 36, 43
Heuer, Richards J. 27
Hunt, Sir John 82–83, 98, 113–115, 117, 126
Hurd, Douglas 255, 287, 307, 312

Independent Broadcasting Authority (IBA) 157, 163, 173
Independent Television News (ITN) 68–69, 298
Independent, The 285–288, 291–293, 299–300, 316–317
Industrial Relations Court 198
Information Commissioner's Office (ICO) 322–323, 329
Ingham, Bernard 116, 288
Ingram, Miranda 161–162, 185, 219, 244
Intelligence Services Act (1994) 318

Jagger, Leslie 17–21
Jenkins, Roy 70, 175, 225
Johnson, Lyndon Baines 75–76
Jones, Jack 108–109, 120
Jones, Martin Furnival 40–41, 77, 81–82, 93, 107, 109, 268
Jones, Sir John 93, 167–168, 175, *n347*

Kagan, Joseph 91, 93–94, *n348*
Katz, Otto 95, 103, 105
Keith, Lord Justice Henry 314–315
Kerr, Sir John 261
Kershaw, Sir Anthony 168–172, 176
King, Cecil 92–93
Kinnock, Neil 152–153, 172, 182, 241–243, 250, 252, 255–256, 274, 298, 304, 326, 330
Kirby, Michael 227, 307
Kissin, Harry 91, 94
Klugman, James 47
Knight, Maxwell 273

Lady Chatterley's Lover 3
Lancaster House conferences 22
Leigh, David 208
Liddell, Guy 28–29, 61–62
Linney, Brian *n336*
Llewelyn–Davies, Lady Patricia (*née* Rawdon–Smith) 61, 63
Llewelyn–Davies, Richard (later Baron Llewelyn–Davies) 63–64
London Daily News 287–288, 291–293, 299, *n372*
Long, Leo 54–56, 69
Lonsdale, Gordon (*aka*: Molody, Konon) 27
lupus erythematosus 87, 90

MacDonald, Alec 77
Maclean, Donald 9, 29, 31–33, 36, 38, 44, 46–47, 49–50, 54, 61, 106, 114, 125, 128, 144, 230, 266, *n337*

Macmillan, Harold; 30, 37, 41–42, 52, 56, 89, 92, 135
Macpherson, Mr. Justice William 198
McHugh, Michael 227
'Maguire Seven' 199, *n365*
Mail on Sunday, The 256, 258
Marriott, John 106
Marshall, William 9, *n334*
Martin, Arthur 32–33, 36, 39–44, 46, 48–56, 74, 77, 87–88, 105, 124–128, 147–150, 163, 218, 231, 235–237, 244
Martin, Joan 125, 149, *n354*
Mason, Sir Anthony 181
Massie, William 89
Massiter, Cathy 120, 173–175, 185, 204, 217, 219, 244, 246–248, 260, 262, 278
Mavin, Michael 297, 309
Maxwell, Robert ('Ian') 88, 91, *n346*
May, Alan Nunn 28, 30
Mayhew, Sir Patrick 275
Menzies, Sir Stewart 29
Miller, Joan 273–274
MI5 (The Security Service)
'Unacknowledged' legal status 1, 6, 10, 99, 146, 316; 'habitual law breaking' 2, 17–22, 173–175, 259–260, 261–262, 279–280; damage to morale from *Spycatcher* case 3, 316; external oversight, 3, 98–99, 118–120; Plot to conceal espionage failures 3–4; Leconfield House headquarters 5, 20, *n349;* History of; 6–7; 'defence of the realm' remit 8; 'Secret Vote' budget 8, 14; *'sui generis'* 10; technological limitations of equipment 13; initial approach to Peter Wright 15; 'eleventh commandment' 16; Findlater Stewart report 17–19; 'special facilities' 17–22, 33, 59; operating directives to Director General 18; Operation PARTY PIECE 19–20, 164, *n336;* 'watchers' (A Branch) 20, 26, 42; moved to Oxford area during World War Two 31; 'PETERS' investigation (Graham Mitchell) 38–44, 52, 56, 78, 148; FLUENCY committee 73–83; 128, 145, 159, 164, 168, 267; 'DRAT' investigation (Sir Roger Hollis) 77–83, 276, 279, *n345;* K7 directorate 78–79; Burke Trend brought into to handle internal

Index

inquiries 82–83, *n346*; OATSHEAF (Harold Wilson) files 85–90, 96, *n346*; alleged 1968 coup plans 93; investigated Wilson's associates 93–95; alleged plans for coup against Wilson (1974) 95–99, 245–246, 28, 282–283, 285–290, 315; Blunt exposure 113–11; *Their Trade Is Treachery* 139–142, 143–146, 220–223, 268, 271–272, 324; Source inside IBA 163; Miners' strike 166; criticized by Powell 278

MI6 (Secret Intelligence Service) 29–30, 63, 104–105, 231–232, 238, 268, 318

Mitchell, Graham (*see also*: MI5 – 'PETERS') 32, 38–44, 52, 76–78, 82, 125–127, 147–149

Modin, Yuri 38

Moore, Charles 324–326, *n356, n358, n359, n371, n372, n373*

Morris, John 297–298

Mossadegh, Mohammad 104

Mountbatten, Earl 'Dickie' 92–93

Motion, Tony 159–161, 185, 219

Mowbray, Stephen de 82

Murdoch, Rupert 285, 295

Nasser, Gamal 21

National Council for Civil Liberties (NCCL) 120, 174, 248, 262

National Union of Mineworkers (NUM) 166, 174

Neil, Andrew 294–295, 314–315

Newsham, Sir Frank 10

New Society 161–162

Nicholson, Leslie 184

Noel-Baker, Philip 104

'OATSHEAF' – *see* Wilson, Harold

Observer, The 33, 179, 197–201, 204, 286, 288, 292, 299–303, 308, 311–315, 317

Official Secrets Acts 2, 16, 101, 111, 122, 124, 127, 129, 135, 137, 141, 146–147, 149, 161, 172–173, 178, 184, 194, 268, 274, 282, 292–293, 309–310, 316

Oldfield, Maurice 136, 208, 275

Operation PARTY PIECE – *see MI5*

Owen, David 255

Packer, Kerry 191–192

Page, Graham 119

Panorama (BBC Television) 118, 159, 315

Parkinson, Cecil 152

Penrose, Barrie 95, 126–127, 159, 208–209, 231–232, 278

Perman, Brian 177, 182, 253

Petrov, Vladimir 31–33, 168–169, 185, *n338*

Philby, Eleanor 38

Philby, Harold 'Kim' 1, 28–30, 32–33, 35–38, 44, 46–47, 64–65, 74–75, 79–81, 87, 103, 114, 125, 137, 144–145, 147, 165, 170, 198, 230, 266–268

Pincher, Harry 'Chapman'
Intelligence service asset 4, 135–136, 268; recipient of Hollis leaks; 4, 127–128, 131, 136, 141, 152, 223–224, 227–228, 324; planned book with Rothschild and Wright 133–134, 136–138, 258, 271; early life and career 134–135; accused of being 'urinal' 135; financial arrangements with Rothschild and Wright 138–140, 147–148, 249–252; *Their Trade Is Treachery* 139–142, 143–146, 149, 151, 158–159, 176–177, 186–187, 195, 198, 200, 204, 210, 220–224, 231, 234–235, 237, 239, 241–242, 244–245, 268, 271, 274, 275–276, 278, 324–325; government and intelligence contacts 152–153, 231–232, 234–237; denounced rivals 159

Plumb, Lord Henry 306

Ponting, Clive 172–173, *n361*

Pool, Phoebe 67–68; 70

Post Office Special Investigations Unit 13

Powell, Mr. Justice Philip 196–197, 202–204, 210–211, 218–219, 223, 225, 227–228, 236–239, 244–245, 248, 253, 256–263, 272–273, 276–281, 283, 286, 300–301, 303, 307

Private Eye 96, 115, 129

Proctor, Sir Dennis 66–67

Profumo Affair 37, 87, 89, 145, *n335*

Prybil, Col. Oldrich 26

Public Records Acts (1958 & 1967) 321

Rawlinson, Sir Peter 118, 127, 138, 224

Razin, Lt. Col. Nikolai 31

Rees, Goronwy 49, 61–62, 64, 67, 105

Rees, Merlyn 282–283

Rees-Mogg, William 258

Rimington, Stella 206, 293

Reporter, Shapoor 104

Roberts, Sir Ivor 270
Robinson, Neville 12
Roosevelt, Franklin D. & Eleanor 45
Rothschild, Tess (*née* Mayor)
   Shared Bentinck Street flat with Blunt and Burgess 61; 103–104; communism at Cambridge University 102–103; 107–108; wartime career in MI5 104; married Victor Rothschild 104; corresponded with Burgess' mother 105–106; provided 'solace' to Blunt 106, 116; complained to Wright about Blunt scandal 129
Rothschild, (Lord) Victor
   Joined MI5 7; learned of Philby's treachery 35–36; Bentinck Street ménage 61–62, 103–107; financial relationship with Wright 102; at Cambridge University 102; relationship with Burgess, Philby and Blunt 102–105; wartime career in MI5 104; married Tess Mayor 104; post-war work with MI5 & MI6 104–105, 268; 109–110; MI5 suspicions about 106–108; worked with Wright on Cambridge communist investigations 106–107; appointed head of Think Tank 108, 238; investigated Jack Jones 108–109; introduced Wright to Armstrong 110; involvement with Wright's memoirs 111, 122, 128–131; Blunt exposure 116; sought oversight role with MI5 116–117, 252–253; brought Wright back to England 129–130, 251; planned book with Pincher and Wright 4, 133–134, 239, 136–138, 271; briefed Pincher on 'The Wilson Plot' 136; financial arrangements with Pincher and Wright 137–140, 147–148, 249–251, 271; *Their Trade Is Treachery* 139–142, 252, 271, 274, 276; 278; demanded government 'protection' 186, 251–252 ; named in Australian hearings 238–239; criticised in press 252; threatened Downing Street 274–275; interviewed by Metropolitan Police 274–275
Royal Canadian Mounted Police (RCMP) 28, 30–31

Royal Naval Scientific Service (RNSS) 12–13, 15, 264
Rubinstein, Michael 115–116
Russell Jones, Barry 150

Schaap, Bill 263
Scott, Mr. Justice (Sir) Richard 308
Security Commission 145–146, 171, 174–175
Security Service Act (1989) 316
Sheldon, Bernard 96, 151, 177, 180
Sherrin, Ned 305
Sidgwick & Jackson 139–142
Silkin, Sam 114
Sillitoe, Sir Percy 2, 6–10, 13, 15, 18, 184, 219
Simon, Brian 47, 103, 108–109
Simos, Theo 211, 215–216, 219, 234–239, 243–244, 248, 252–253, 257–258, 260–263, 265, 269–270, 276, 278, 280, 303
Smith, Ian 92
Solomon, Flora 35–36, 38
Somerville, Dr. Walter 90
South China Morning Post 302, 306
Special Branch (Metropolitan Police) 21
Spycatcher US edition 3, 111, 121–122, 289–291, 294–295; 297–298, 300–301, 305, 317
Spycatcher hearings
   Australia 2, 196–197, 201–204, 208–211, 214–239, 243–256, 257–272, 276–281, 283, 303, 307, 312
   Hong Kong 2, 302, 306
   New Zealand 2, 302, 308, 312
   United Kingdom 2, 197–201, 287–288, 291–293, 299–305, 308, 311–312, 313–315
   Strasbourg 2, 317
Spycatcher financial cost 3, 282, 312–313, 315, 326
Steel, Henry 180, 183
Sternberg, Rudy 91, 94
Stone, Dennis 214
Straight, Michael Whitney 45–50, 53, 55, 63, 121
Street, Sir Laurence 227
Strelnikov, Anatoli 135
Sunday Times, The 248–249, 294–295, 313–317
Sweet–Escott, Bickham 184
Symonds, Ronnie 52, 164
Templeman, Lord Justice Sydney 303–304

Index

'The Thing' 14, 264
Thatcher, Margaret
Plot to conceal espionage failures 3–4; appointed Armstrong as Cabinet Secretary xi, 213; plot to leak Hollis scandal 4, 224, 228, 324 ; lobbied by Rothschild 116–117; Parliamentary statement on Blunt 117–118, 266; Parliamentary statement on Hollis 143–146, 266–267; opposition to external oversight of MI5 118–120, 287, 291, 293–294, 312; fascination with espionage 120; brushed off Aitken warning 126–127; discussed intelligence with Rothschild 130; plot to leak Hollis scandal 131, 138, 187, 324; *Their Trade Is Treachery* 143–146, 200, 204, 220, 223, 252, 324; sought to suppress Jonathan Bloch book 153–155; unwilling to tolerate dissent 172, 290; Brighton Bomb 172; agreed to apply for injunction against Wright 181; rejected redactions deal with Turnbull 206, 249; refused to answer *Spycatcher* questions in Parliament 225, 243; considered abandoning *Spycatcher* litigation 228; rejected inquiry into Wilson Plot 288–290; sought to prevent *Spycatcher* US publication 290–291; sought to block European Parliament Journal; 306–307; insistence on 'duty of silence' 309; forced from office 317
Thompson, E.P. 135
Times, The 163–164, 233, 249–250, 281, 285, 302, 304, 309, 313, 315–316
Tisler, Lt. Col. Frantisek 25–26, 32, 76
Tito, Josip Broz 64
Trend, (Lord) Burke 82–83, 127, 141, 145, 170, 176, *n*346, *n*357
Turnbull, Lucy (née Hughes) 191, 215
Turnbull, Malcolm
Early life and career 191–192; assessments of case 192–193, 196, 276, 303; concerned about MI5 surveillance 194; hired Greengrass for defence team 194; offered settlement deal to British government 195–197, 204–205, 249, 271;

shocked at Wright's living conditions 195; assessment of Wright's motives 195; tactics 197, 201–203, 210–211, 214–216, 219–220, 227–229, 260; complained to Australian government 207–208; cost of litigation 312–313; Infuriated by continuing cover–up 325

Vassall, John 65
Vaygauskas, Richardas 94
VENONA (Soviet cypher traffic decryptions) 74, 98, 164
Volkov, Konstantin 27–28, 33, 76, 79

Waddell, Sir James 109–110
Waddington, David 272
Ware, John 162–165
Washington Post, The 288–289, 308
Watson, Alister 65–66, 103
Waugh, Auberon 89, 96
Weatherill, Sir Bernard 298
West, Nigel (*aka* Rupert Allason) 148–152, 180, 195, 205, 210, 217–219, 222, 235, 237, 260, 271, *n*358; *A Matter of Trust* 149–152, 210, 217–218, 235, 237, 271
Weidenfeld, George 97–98
Weidenfeld & Nicolson 273
White, Sir Dick Goldsmith
interviewed Wright 6; dismissive of Sillitoe 9; intervened in 'PETERS' investigation 39; 41; authorised investigation into penetration of MI5 and MI6 75; approached by *World In Action* 163; gave interview to Penrose and Freeman 208, 231–232, 278
Whitelaw, William 290–291
Whitlam, Gough 261–262
Whitmore, Clive 127–128
Whittam Smith, Andreas 286
Willsher, Kay 30
Wilson, Harold – *see also:* 'Norman John Worthington', OATSHEAF; succeeded Gaitskell 37; appointed Bernard Floud as Private Secretary 69; warned that Philby might have recruited more spies 74; receives report on FLUENCY investigations 81–83; shocked by Hollis case 83; MI5 plot to force him from office 83; MI5 interest in 85–87; 'Norman John Worthington' file 86; 290; sale of jet engines to USSR 86;

moderate politics of 86–87; commercial relationships 87; 91; 93–96; OATSHEAF files 85–90, *n346*; devaluation of sterling 91–92; and Rhodesian independence 92; alleged plans for coup against (1968) 92–93; alleged plans for coup against (1974) 95–98, 245–246, 280; 286–287, 289–290, 315 *n348*; resignation 99, 136
Winnick, David 282, 298
'Worthington, Norman John' – *see* Wilson, Harold
Wright, Holly 330
Wright, Lois 101, 130, 158, 188, 214, 263
Wright, Maurice 10–12
Wright, Peter Maurice
Career outline 1–2; belief in widespread communist penetration 1, 20, 71, 110–111, 121–122, 165, 168, 266–269; fed stories to press 2, 96; believed MI5 was out of control 2, 121, 269; Tasmanian horse stud 2, 102, 128, 158, 188, 195, 317; joined MI5 5–6, 16, 264; signed Official Secrets Act 16, 101, 122; early life 10–12, 176–177; employed by Royal Naval Scientific Service (RNSS) 12–13, 15, 264; technological successes 14, 23; 'The Thing' 14, 264; 'SATYR' 14–15, 265; 'CABMAN' 23–24; 'MOP' 23–24; 'RAFTER' 23–24, 265; initial approach by MI5 15; loss of civil service pension 15, 101–102, 110–111, 264, 317; bugging and burglaries by 21–22, 279–280, 316; hunt for mole inside MI5 33, 52–53, 71, 164, 265; Philby investigation 36; encountered opposition within MI5 37, 38–44, 53–54, 56, 58, 62–63, 65–66, 70–71, 76–79; Became head of research, counter espionage branch 52; interrogated Blunt 57–71; FLUENCY committee 73–83; 128, 145, 159, 164, 168, 267; analysed VENONA decrypts 74, 164; confronted Hollis 76–77; perceived as 'NCO' 33, 77; convinced Hollis was a traitor 81, 83, 163–165; on Golitsyn 90; investigated Wilson's associates 93–95; involvement with alleged plans for coup against Wilson (1974) 2, 96–98, 245–246, 280, 315, *n348;* briefed Rothschild on molehunts 107, 268; retired from MI5 101; financial relationship with Rothschild 102; forced into 'exile' 110, 122, 269; planned memoirs 111, 121–122, 128–129; angered by Thatcher statement on Blunt 121, 164, 264–265, 269; support for external oversight of MI5 121; book with Pincher and Rothschild (*Their Trade Is Treachery*) 139–142, 143–147, 149, 151, 158–159, 176–177, 186–187, 195, 198, 200, 204, 210, 220–224, 231, 234–235, 237, 239, 241–242, 244–245, 249–251, 268, 271, 274, 275–276, 278, 324–325; knew Pincher as intelligence asset 136, 268; financial arrangements with Pincher and Rothschild 138–140, 147–148, 249–252; believed he was part of a deniable operation 138, 251; angered by Thatcher statement on Hollis 147, 165, 266–267, 269; interviewed by Nigel West 149–150; attitude towards the Establishment 159; *World In Action* 157–159, 161–168, 200, 232–234; sent dossier to Sir Anthony Kershaw 168–172; political views 197, 315–316; Australian hearings 2, 196–197, 201–204, 208–211, 214–239, 243–256, 257–272, 276–281, 283, 303, 307, 312; court testimony 257–258, 263–270; health 128, 130, 188, 227–228, 275, 281; press conference 250–251;
Attacked Thatcher on television 298

Yurchenko, Vitaly 187

'Zinoviev Letter' 7, *n333*
Zuckerman, Solly 92–93, *n348*